The
Kings of the
Kingdom

The Life of Thomas Rice King and His Family

by

Larry King

Orem, Utah

2008

This book is dedicated to those who read it and can consciously and emotionally prize the worth of the heartbreaking sacrifice, dedication, and vision of the human spirit of those whose lives went before us.

Table of Contents

Introduction

It has been said that recorded history is the memory of a people which gives purpose and meaning to lives that otherwise would run aground in the storms of our own biographies. It is the anchor to which we hold when defining moments create paradigm shifts in direction, focus, or function. To be without memory is to be a ship at sea without a rudder.

Historical memory provides foundational ties which define who we are, what we believe, and what we stand for. Our unique world enlarges to give critical perspective and values when built upon generational experience. Individual lives can only be constructed commensurate with the foundation upon which they are built, and the trials and tribulations of life are more easily overcome by understanding the generations past. Each individual's history is more than the raw data of dates and places, but comprises getting inside the mind and heart, to understand habits, personality, towering strength and gut-wrenching weakness, to find larger-than-life characteristics that define each person as a unique child of God.

Antiquity opens the door to envision more clearly existing opportunities and favors of life. Without history we are blinded by the mountains to be climbed, forests to be explored, and rainbows to be discovered. When this perspective is discarded or blurred by our own careless mistakes or indifference, we sow the seeds of our own destruction as a person, a people, or a nation. Yet, in all historical study it is important for the student and reader to see and to evaluate events and experiences through the eyes and standards of the participant, not their own. What may have been acceptable in one time period may not be in another.

Through an examination of history, the past, the present, and the future become inseparably linked. Through family history our grandfathers and grandmothers are not just faceless people, but they become part of our lives, personalities, and values. We become a living extension of their lives, and from their foundation we have the opportunity to become even greater than they were, and our children greater than we. Is this not the great secret of historical perspective?

The study of Thomas Rice King is a model of this family foundation. He and his forebears, as well as his family, stand tall in the pages of time as common people, who through hard work and perseverance created a proud heritage for grateful descendants, perhaps not to be measured by political office, titles, or trophies, but by producing a legacy of honorable everyday people who excelled in building a religious and secular society within family, community, and country. While never part of the inner circles of the political, economic, or religious elite, Thomas and Matilda associated with them and worked to accomplish the same noble goals and objectives.

The known beginnings of the King family are rooted in seventeenth-century England with Edmund Rice and his family who joined the great migration to Puritan Massachusetts in the 1630s. Contemporary with the Rice family was the family of Thomas King; and within twenty years the two families were inseparably connected as three Rice sons married three King daughters. Bringing the two families even closer was the King family's adoption of a Rice grandson, Samuel Rice. Following the death of Elizabeth King Rice, the baby Samuel was adopted by Elizabeth's brother, Peter. Samuel became the heir of Peter and assumed the name of Samuel King, thus ensuring the continuation of Thomas King's name as there were no other male descendants than the childless Peter. Thomas Rice King, by his very name, symbolically links the two families together.

The Rice and King families built their homes, raised their families, and helped develop new communities in the undeveloped land they called New England. They were part of the stirring religious, economic, and political reformation of the day. They served their communities and church, fought the Indians, French, and later the mother country itself to help shape the destiny of a new nation.

In mid-nineteenth century, their Puritan and congregationalist beliefs gave way to a new religious system when Thomas Rice King, his father, and two older brothers, accepted both the profound excitement and frightening burden of Mormonism. This significant paradigm shift, second only to the familial emigration to the American colonies, sent the King family into a new dimension which became part of the development and settlement of the Mormon empire in the Great Basin in the western United States. Here many members of the family served Church missions, lived the economic communal United Order, and participated in the social experiment of plural marriage. The men knew the trials of becoming outlaws and served time in prison for their religious belief. They endured the prejudice and jealousy of neighbors causing them to move on and establishing a new home in the latter years of their life. Yet through it all, they were fortified by spiritual confirmation and experience.

The Kings were a proud and strong-willed people, enterprising, hardworking and independently minded, yet submissive to church and family leadership. There are also traces of stubbornness with a hardheaded temperament. Their souls were filled with a passion and vision of a new and better life. During the United Order period in Piute County, the Kings controlled the temporal as well as the ecclesiastical positions of leadership. Thomas was president and son, William, was bishop. Sons Culbert, John, Volney, and Edwin also played key roles. In the ensuing power struggle after the death of Thomas, William won out, but not without ill feelings. Behind their backs the Kings were referred to by their detractors as the "Kings of the Kingdom."

While they were never monetarily rich or achieved economic or political prominence, they counted their wealth in their posterity and by providing humble service to their church and community. Today a small southern Utah community still bears the name of Kingston in honor of Thomas Rice King, and it is the only remaining evidence of this failed early attempt to live a more perfect economic union.

The descendants of Thomas and Matilda have traveled differing roads, experiencing both humble and prominent circumstances. Coming out of the United Order experiences, the family has produced a fiery conservative U.S. Senator, and on the other end of the political spectrum, an ultra-liberal governor of California, and an internationally noted writer for socialism. Most descendants have remained active participants in the Mormon tradition, while others elected to adjust their religious focus.

In writing the account of early seventeenth- and eighteenth-century Rice and King families there are no known letters or diaries. Most information comes from public records and secondary sources. Of the Thomas Rice King family, a son, Volney King, was a diarist for several years; and a few family letters and writings have surfaced. From these records we do have an understanding of the basic landscape of their life, yet there are many instances where it would be nice to know their innermost thoughts and feelings and to better understand their marital and parent-child relationships. The Kings were not a perfect family and any attempt to portray them otherwise is a distortion of life. They were a great and wonderful people, devoted to family, church, and community, who made mistakes and exhibited excruciating human weaknesses. Many of them deeply agonized over plural marriage, living in the United Order, and being sent to prison. The matriarch, Matilda, a devoted member of the LDS faith was denied service in the Fillmore Ward Relief Society presidency because she could not give up her corn cob pipe, yet she spoke in tongues, had her prayers dramatically answered at critical times and experienced the transfiguration of Brigham Young to Joseph Smith in Nauvoo. Perhaps from these experiences there is a significant message to her descendents that we not take life too serious, that there is eternal hope for us all.

As a descendant of Thomas Rice King, I, today, enjoy the nobility of this birthright.

Acknowledgements

No work of any consequence is ever the effort of only one person. I would be remiss if I didn't acknowledge the contribution, encouragement, and help of several people who made the publication of this book a meaningful experience and who added immeasurably to the content, accuracy, and layout.

The people at the Utah State Historical Society, LDS Church Historical Department, Utah State Archives, and The Utah State Territorial Capital Museum all went beyond the call of duty to provide material and suggestions. It was fun to work with people like Susan Easton Black at the LDS Church's Nauvoo Visitors Center in Nauvoo, Illinois, and to share her enthusiasm for historical research. The delightful Olive Sudweeks of Kingston, Utah, had never met me but was willing to take me all over Circle Valley and point out important historical spots. Not to be left out is Mr. Leavitt Christensen, Kanosh, Utah, who graciously invited me into his home to show me his many beautiful paintings of historical spots in Millard County before giving of his time to introduce me around Kanosh.

Others who came to the rescue were Kay Watson, a friend of many years, who works as an Electronic Production Specialist and a commercial artist; and John Williams who is a technical writer. Both of these gentlemen provided many valuable suggestions on layout and format and who proofread the manuscript. The cover was designed by my son Robert King. Those providing encouragement and help were former Utah Congressman David S. King, Kensington, Virginia; Dwight King of Salt Lake City, Utah; my brother Paul King and my good friend James Carver, both of Cedar City, Utah. The list could go on. Thanks to everyone.

Most of all I would like to thank some very exceptional people who gave me encouragement and support through a very difficult and challenging time of my life while writing this book. A bouquet of flowers to my secretary, LaNan Garrido. A heartfelt tribute to my children: Kristy, Stephanie, Robert, David, Alan, and Jared whose blessing I treasure. Last but not least, a quiet but notable thank you to some very special friends whose Christlike example and encouragement simply made the difference.

Second Edition

In addition to the above, I would like to thank those who purchased and read the first edition of *Kings of the Kingdom* and who offered valuable suggestions and found further information for this second edition. A special thanks to Carol Sorensen of Tucson, Arizona whose tenacious research was most helpful in connecting critical pieces of information. The insight of Michael Landon of the LDS Church Family and Church History Department was incredible. I was always picking his brain when we were together planning a Mormon History Association conference in Casper, Wyoming. I think I always had ulterior motives in our meetings. My appreciation to William G. Hartley, associate professor of history at Brigham Young University and past president of the Mormon History Association, and Robert Rice, president of the Edmund Rice Association (ERA) who graciously read all or part of an early manuscript and offered suggestions and encouragement. Max Sudweeks, a good friend, who lives in Kingston, Utah, was most helpful in regard to the Kingston United Order. He patiently walked the ground with me and, in his home, shared with me much of his own research pertaining to the order. Much inspiration came from the wonderful people of the Mormon History Association whom I have been privileged to work with for the last several years. My particular thanks to Ron Barney, Ardis Parshall, and Lowell (Ben) Bennion, for their suggestions and for providing helpful material and references.

In recent years few publications in Mormondom have not been touched in some manner by Lavina Fielding Anderson, and this one is no exception. Her lively nature and sense of humor can make one feel good all over, while at the same time telling you all the things you need to correct. My hat is off to her for her wonderful friendship, patience, and comprehensive editing of this book.

Invaluable to this edition is my lovely wife, Alene, who has taught me by example what unconditional love is all about. She has spent many hours proofreading, offering suggestions, and giving timely encouragement when my own doubts found fertile ground.

I have learned by unfortunate experience the difficulty of producing a book of this type and magnitude without errors or mistakes. If any are found, they are my responsibility with deepest apologies.

Maps and Illustrations

Maps

Illustrations and Photographs

Genesis

("In the Beginning...")

T homas Rice King's beginnings are rooted in England, and by his very name bridges two families into one — the Rices and the Kings. His paternal fourth great-grandfather was Edmund Rice from Berkhampstead County, the first known member of a large family of Rices who now proudly number themselves in the thousands. His adopted and related fourth great-grandfather and namesake, Thomas King, came from Dorset County. Both families came to this country within a score of years after the first Pilgrims landed at Plymouth Rock and a decade after the Puritan settlement of Boston. By 1640 the Massachusetts Bay Colony near and around Boston was a thriving, moderately sized community of about 10,000 pioneering colonists.

When considering the history of an individual or individuals (fortunately or unfortunately, as the case may be), the amount of history or the place a person takes in the landscape of time is determined by the records that have been kept either by the individual, family, or community. Some people of greatness in both word and deed are lost due to the absence of adequate records, and the legacy of others who happen to have only filled time and space may be preserved for generations. Often descendants indulge in the halo effect, pampering an ancestor with comments supporting his/her superior character, position, and spiritual strength.

The known history of Edmund Rice is a mixture of the above traits. Several records give us a peek into his character as a respectable individual, yet there is still much that remains unknown about this esteemed man and his family. There are no known diaries or letters that reveal his personality, thoughts, or feelings. While most of the honors bestowed on him appear well deserved, some attempt to make more of him than he is. There is no evidence that he came from prominent English gentry or had the genes of royalty. Colonial records give him the upper middle-class rank of "yeoman," meaning land owner. If Edmund had been connected with people of title he would have been called or addressed as "Gentleman" or "Mister."[1] But what he did possess was a burning desire to improve his English middle class status and a willingness to face relentless trials and privations to better his life and the lives of his family members.

---

1   Elsie Hawes Smith, *Edmund Rice and His Family: We Sought the Wilderness* (Boston: The Meador Press, 1938), 12.

His legacy lives on in a multitude of descendants who not only carry on the family name of Rice, but a host of other common American names.[2]

Edmund lived at the dawning of the American dream of political and religious freedom. The economic advantages of land ownership were taking hold in early seventeenth century America as Pilgrims, Puritans, and people of all religious and political stripes by the thousands were looking for a new life. Tyranny and oppression had been their lot in life for generations in European cities and countrysides, and the new world filled them with hope and the vision to move on regardless of effort or cost.

England was also experiencing its Golden Age. The Spanish Armada had been defeated just fifty years earlier (1588) to establish Britain as a great naval power, and men such as Shakespeare, Sir Walter Raleigh, and Sir Frances Drake were shaping English society. To England the cultivation and settlement of its recently discovered American territory was essential in its competitive struggle with Spain and France who were energetically colonizing Central and South America, the West Indies, and western Canada. Economically the colonies would become an important outlet for English manufactured goods. Supplying in turn such raw materials as lumber, tobacco, furs, indigo and ship building products. And there was always the fleeting hope that the English would be as successful as the Spanish in finding gold and silver riches.

In spite of its social and military successes, England was racked with internal religious and political unrest. The unpopular King Charles I sat on a shaky throne and was at odds with his Puritan subjects over the "divine right of kings." This unrest eventually resulted in the Puritan revolt led by Oliver Cromwell in 1642 and to eighteen years of parliamentary government. The Puritans also wanted to "purify" the Church of England from such Catholic vestiges as elaborate ceremonies and priestly vestments. Their desire was to return society to more a modest and simple belief system and government. Yet by their intolerant ways and structured lifestyle, they created their own religious excesses.

Furthermore, there was a belief in the sixteenth and seventeenth centuries that England was overpopulated, and unemployment hampered the British economy as the old feudal and manorial system began breaking down. The economy experienced particular dislocations in the depression years of 1619 to 1624, from 1629 to 1631 and from 1637 to 1640. During the latter time frame, the Rice family came to Massachusetts.

From all appearances, the colonies provided an opportunistic

---

2   See Andrew Henshaw Ward, A.M., *Genealogical History of the Rice Family: Descendants of Deacon Edmund Rice* (Boston: C. Benjamin Richardson, 1858).

resolution to the economic problems of the day; and beginning in the 1630s, American settlements sprang up all over the Atlantic coast from Maine to South Carolina, including the Massachusetts Bay colony. An estimated eighty thousand people left England for the New World between 1620 and 1642.[3]

Edmund Rice left Berkhampstead, Hertford, England, and sailed to America in the summer of 1638. Thomas King left Dorset County, England, about the same time.

The Massachusetts Bay colony, well organized and well funded, started out as a commercial venture. In the first year of operation in 1630, seventeen ships carrying fifteen hundred people arrived to create the Boston settlement. Within five years, eight thousand settlers had arrived. This rate of growth continued until the end of the decade. Emigration began to subside as Puritans became more optimistic of their chances of survival in England with Cromwell coming to power.

Under English law all land in the American colonies was owned by the King who granted permits or colonial charters to groups to settle various regions. These proprietors laid out communities or plantations, distributing land to individuals and families, usually enough land near the village common area for a house, garden, and cow shed. A settler was also given a strip of farmland on the edge of the village, where he could raise other crops such as corn, rye, barley, wheat, hemp, and flax.

While land ownership was widely distributed and created the basis of a capitalistic society, the system created some inequities with

---

3   Everett Emerson, *Puritanism in America 1720-1750* (Boston: Twayne Publishers, 1977), 32.

political favors and land speculation becoming somewhat commonplace.

Irrespective of abuses, people settling the New World were quick to experiment with a whole new economic, political, and social order, thus sowing the seeds for an eventual and dramatic flowering of new political thinking and expectations.

Edmund's Beginnings and Family[4]

Edmund was born about 1594 possibly in Sudbury, Suffolk County, England[5] although no birth or parentage records have been found.[6]

---

4   An Edmund Rice (1638) Association was organized in 1912 and chartered on January 10, 1934, for the purpose of preserving the memory of Edmund Rice and fostering research into his posterity and ancestors. This interest was initiated by the research of Andrew Henshaw Ward who in 1858 published his groundbreaking book, *A Genealogical History of the Rice Family: Descendants of Deacon Edmund Rice*. This book has been reprinted by the association.

This work was further enhanced by Elsie Hawes Smith's book in 1938, *Edmund Rice and His Family: We Sought the Wilderness*, also written for the association.

Perhaps the most noted work on the history of Sudbury, Massachusetts, which also touches on the life of Edmund Rice is Sumner Chilton Powell's *Puritan Village: The Formation of a New England Town* (Middletown, CT: Wesleyan University Press, 1963). In 1964 Powell received the Pulitzer Prize in history for his book.

The Edmund Rice Association (ERA) maintains a well organized and documented website, http://www.edmund-rice.org/, for which I am grateful. Many of the details and family information herein are taken from this site.

Considerable information is also located on the websites of Sudbury, Massachusetts: http://www.town.sudbury.ma.us/archives/, and Marlborough, Massachusetts: http://freepages.history.rootsweb.com/~historyofmarlborough/contents.htm#CONTENTS.   It should be noted that no records have survived from Marlborough between 1665 and 1739. Information is available only from related sources such as the General Court records.

5   This date is determined from a deposition in the court files at Cambridge, Massachusetts, April 3, 1656, by Edmund stating his age to be "about 62 years," thus born about 1594.

6   Over the years, there has been considerable speculation on Edmund's parents. Charles Elmer Rice proposes quite an elaborate pedigree in his book, *By the Name of Rice: An Historical Sketch of Deacon Edmund Rice, the Pilgrim (1594-1663)* (Alliance, Ohio: The Williams Printing Company, 1911). Mary Lovering Holman (*American Genealogist*, 10:136) proposes that a Henry Rice who married Elizabeth Frost, Thomasine's older sister, could possibly be the father of Edmund or even a brother and that Edmund named his first son after his father, Henry, and his second son after his wife's father, Edward. The Ancestral File in the Family History Library of the Church of Jesus Christ of Latter-day Saints (LDS) suggests that Edmund's father is a Thomas Rice (b. 1568) who married Catherine Howard (b. about 1560) and that the above Henry is a brother to Edmund.

Charles Elmer Rice's argument is discredited by Donald Lines Jacobus, M.A., of New Haven, Connecticut in his article in the *American Genealogist*, "Pre-American An-

Thomasine, his wife, was born about 1600, the daughter of Edward Frost and Thomasine Belgrave. She was baptized on August 11, 1600, at St. James Church, in neighboring Stanstead.[7][8] Edmund and Thomasine were married October 15, 1618, at St. Mary's Church, in Bury St. Edmunds, Suffolk, England.[9] There they settled down for the first eight years of their marriage long enough to have their first four children: Henry, Mary, Edward, and Thomas, apparently losing one (Mary) in infancy. By 1627 they had moved to Berkhamstead, Hertfordshire (County) and between 1627 and 1638 they had five more children: Lydia, Matthew, Daniel, Samuel and Joseph with Daniel passing away right after birth. Edmund became a small land-owner with fifteen acres of land,[10] quite unusual as only a small percentage of English citizens ever acquired any land.

As a yeoman and landowner, Edmund would have assumed both personal and some community responsibilities in Berkhamstead. He also would have had at least a limited education, knowing how to read and write.

---

cestries," 11:14-21, Family History Library.

As to who is Edmund's father, no record has been found which has been accepted by any creditable organization. See "The Epistle," Rosemary E. Bachelor, Editor, no. 2, August, 1976; 3:44-45, and "A Treatise on the Rice Family," by Roger E. Rice, 1989 FHL 929.273 R36a. Quoting Mr. Rice: "Records of his exact date of birth or of his parentage have not been uncovered by researchers to date, and since all Rices do not descend from the founder of the second royal tribe of Wales, as some genealogical opportunists would have you believe, any such ancient pedigree given for Edmund Rice is not accepted by the Edmund Rice (1638) Association, and will not be until such irreproachable documentation surfaces, according to Miss Margaret S. Rice, Association past president/historian. Deacon Edmund Rice descendants are cautioned to make no claim of any pedigree farther back than the man himself, and to also be wary of any offers of coats-of-arm, all of which are unauthentic and for the most part phony."

In correspondence to the author from Robert Rice, President of the Edmund Rice Association, dated November 29, 2006, he indicated that Edmund's home town was probably Sudbury, Suffolk County. He goes on to say that "there is no evidence that Rices were around Berkhamstead before 1629. We think that he (Edmund) went there because monast(e)ry lands were opened for sale about that time. Recently it has been found from the 1841 England census that relatively large concentrations of Rices were located in south west Suffolk county which may someday allow us to find some of Edmund's family there."

7   Harold R. Porter, Jr., "The Paternal Ancestry of Thomasine Frost, Wife of Deacon Edmund Rice of Sundbury, Mass.," *The American Genealogist,* 63: July 1988, 3:134.

8   Charles Edward Banks, *Topographical Dictionary of English Emigrants to New England 1620-1650* (Baltimore: Genealogical Publishing Company, 1969), 34.

9   Mary Lovering Holman, "The Wife of Edmund Rice," *The American Genealogist,* 15:July 1938, 1:227.

10   Powell, *Puritan Village,* 23-24, 189.

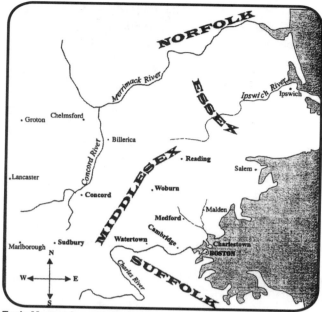

Early Massachusetts Bay colony. Sudbury was the nineteenth plantation (community) settled.

How long Edmund and Thomasine had made plans to leave England has not been recorded. Many people coming to America at this time came with or were preceded by a support group of friends, neighbors, fellow church members or family, thus enabling them to more effectively deal with the rigors of primitive travel and the monumental adjustments to an unseasoned way of life.

The Rices had the benefit of Thomasine's extended family. Two older sisters, Elizabeth and Alice, and their families had emigrated to the Boston area as early as 1635. Elizabeth, and her husband Philemon Whale, also joined the Rices in establishing and living in Sudbury. It is possible that other family and extended family members preceded Thomasine and Edmund and encouraged and assisted them in the move.[11]

Travel was also very expensive and could cost as much as £6 to £10 a person.[12] For the large Rice family a total of £72 would equal about two year's wages and most people had to sell everything they possessed to meet travel expenses. In 2006 dollars, this would equate to approximately $1,635 per person, or nearly $15,000 for the family.[13]

---

11   There is some evidence a brother of Thomasine by the name of Thomas emigrated to Boston, and at this same time there is also an Edmond Frost living in Cambridge. Edmond had a son, Thomas, who later lived in Sudbury, however, a connection between Thomasine and Edmond has not been made. In addition, Thosmaine's grandmother was a Scott and from that family came a Richard Scott who arrived in Boston in 1634 and later settled in Providence, Rhode Island.

12   Harold Underwood Faulkner, *American Economic History* (New York: Harper & Brothers, 1960), 72.

13   Due to the many variables involving inflation, monetary evaluation, and wages,

The sea trip itself must have been an ordeal beyond description for any individual, but was only accentuated for parents with a nursing baby and energetic children. Generally fifteen to twenty families plus a few single men were crowded together in only a few square feet of space below deck with little chance to experience the fresh air of the open sea or daylight above. The passenger ships of the day were no more than converted cargo vessels, about 100 feet long and 26 feet wide, weighing perhaps 180 to 200 tons. All together, perhaps as many as one hundred people plus captain and crew would occupy the ship.

Average traveling speed for these small three-masted sailing ships averaged no more than two to three miles an hour, depending on the direction of the prevailing wind and current. The thirty-eight hundred mile trip would take over two tedious and difficult months.

There were no real sanitation facilities on board except for small

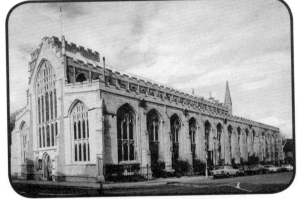

St. Mary's Anglican Church, in Bury St. Edmunds, Suffolk, England was rebuilt in 1424-45. Edmund Rice and Thomasine Frost were married here October 15, 1618.

buckets, and fresh water was too scarce for washing. They also had to share their limited space with hogs, sheep, and goats, and most ships were beset with rats and reeked of bilge water, spoiled food, human and animal waste, and most anything else on board. Sea sickness plagued the travelers as they were tossed back and forth to the degree that prevailing weather conditions imposed. In stormy weather, the little ship and its passengers

economists find it is very difficult to convert the purchasing power of 1638 pounds to 2006 dollars. This figure, however, was obtained by using the website "Measuringworth. com by Lawrence H. Officer and Samuel H. Willamson.

An early seventeenth-century passenger ship like that on which Edmund Rice, Thomas King and their families may have sailed to America. *(Edwin Tunis, Oars, Sails, and Steam, p. 32.)* The ship would have been a two or three masted sailing vessel, about 100 feet long, 26 feet wide and weighing about 200 tons. Living conditions would have been terrible at best.

must have taken a frightful beating.

Food was limited to unappetizing hard biscuits (hardtack), cheese, and perhaps some salted beef or fish. Each family was allowed a few meager household and personal possessions including tools, a flax spinning wheel, ammunition, and firearms, and perhaps a chest with blankets and linens. Furniture had to be left behind and would have to be fabricated upon arrival in their new settlement. But the magnetic dream of the New World kept the people motivated, and it must have been an immense relief when the call rang out, "land ahoy."

The Rice family — Edmund, 44, Thomasine, about 38, and seven children ranging in age from a three-month-old boy to a twenty-one-year-old son, probably set sail in April 1638, arriving three months later. The exact ship and departure date is uncertain; but from an analysis of the ships arriving in the New England area in 1638, it appears the Rice family could have been on the *Susan and Ellen* which left London April 11, 1638, and arrived in Boston July 17, 1638.[14]

---

14   In 1638 five ships of record arrived in New England: The *Susan and Ellen*, left London April 11, 1638, and arrived in New England (port unknown) with a very incomplete passenger list. *The Confidence* left Southampton April 11, 1638, (date of arrival and port unknown). The passenger list is extensive with about 73 people on board. *The Bevis (Beuis),* left Southampton May 1638, (arrival date and port unknown). The passenger list contains 61 people. *The Dilligent,* left Ipswich, England in June 1638, and arrived in Boston August 10, 1638 with about 100 passengers, all destined for Hingham, Massachusetts. *The Martin,* left England in 1638 and arrived in Boston before July 13, 1638. Port and date of departure are unknown and the passenger list contains a small and incomplete list of people going to Rhode Island.

Edmund and
Thomasine Frost Rice Family

Henry Rice
- (B) Abt 1617
- (C) 13 Feb 1621 Stanstead, Suffolk, England
- (M) 01 Jan 1644 Sudbury, Middlesex, Massachusetts
  Elizabeth Moore
- (D) 10 Feb 1711 Framingham, Middlesex, Massachusetts

Mary Rice
- (C) 18 Aug 1619 Stanstead, Suffolk, England
- (D) Bef 1638 England

Edward Rice
- (B) Abt 1622 Stanstead, Suffolk, England
- (C) 27 Oct 1622 Stanstead, Suffolk, England
- (M) 1647
  Agnes Bent
- (D) 15 Aug 1712 Marlborough, Middlesex, Massachusetts

Thomas Rice
- (C) 26 Jan 1626 Stanstead, Suffolk, England
- (M) Abt 1651 Sudbury, Middlesex, Massachusetts
  Mary King
- (D) 16 Nov 1681 Sudbury, Middlesex, Massachusetts

Lydia Rice
- (B) Abt 1627
- (C) 9 Mar 1628 Berkhamstead, Hertford, England
- (M) Abt 1645 Sudbury, Middlesex, Massachusetts
  Hugh Drury
- (D) 5 Apr 1675 Boston, Suffolk, Massachusetts

Matthew Rice
- (C) 28 Feb 1629 Berkhamstead, Hertford, England
- (M) 7 Jul 1654 Sudbury, Middlesex, Massachusetts
  Martha Lamson
- (D) 1717 Sudbury, Middlesex, Massachusetts

Daniel Rice
- (C) 01 Nov 1632 Berkhamstead, Hertford, England
- (Bu) 10 Nov 1632 Berkhamstead, Hertford, England

Samuel Rice
- (B) Abt 1634 Berkhamstead, Hertford, England
- (C) 12 Nov 1634 Berkhamstead, Hertford, England
- (M) 8 Nov 1655 Sudbury, Middlesex, Massachusetts
  Elizabeth King
- (M) Sep 1668 Sudbury, Middlesex, Massachusetts
  Mary Dix
- (M) 13 Dec 1676 Concord, Middlesex, Massachusetts
  Sarah White
- (D) 25 Feb 1685 Marlborough, Middlesex, Massachusetts

Joseph Rice
- (C) 13 Mar 1638 Berkhamstead, Hertford, England
- (M) 4 May 1658 Sudbury, Middlesex, Massachusetts
  Mercy King
- (M) Abt 1670
  Mary Beers
- (M) 22 Feb 1678 Dedham, Norfolk, Massachusetts
  Sarah Prescott
- (D) 23 Dec 1711 Stow, Middlesex, Massachusetts

Benjamin Rice
- (B) 31 May 1640   Sudbury, Middlesex, Massachusetts
- (M) 2 Jun 1661   Sudbury, Middlesex, Massachusetts
  Mary Brown
- (M) Apr 1, 1691   Sudbury, Middlesex, Massachusetts
  Mary Chamberlain
- (D) 19 Dec 1713   Sudbury, Middlesex, Massachusetts

Edmund and Mercie Hurd Rice Family

Lydia Rice
- (B) Abt 1657   Sudbury, Middlesex, Massachusetts
- (M) Abt 1678
  James Hawkins, Jr.
- (D) 26 May 1718

Ruth Rice
- (B) 29 Sep 1659   Sudbury, Middlesex, Massachusetts
- (M) 20 Jun 1683   Wethersfield, Hartford, Connecticut
  Samuel Wells
- (D) 30 Mar 1742   Glastonbury, Hartford, Connecticut

It is thought that, upon arrival, Edmund and his family went to stay with friends or extended family members, probably in Boston or Watertown, about ten miles west and up the Charles River from Boston.

Sudbury Plantation

Before the arrival of the Rice family, a new plantation settlement had been applied for in November 1637 by several of the leading citizens of Watertown; and on September 6, 1638 it was approved by the governor and the General Court, the governing body over the Massachusetts Bay Colony. The new settlement ten miles west of Watertown, was to be the nineteenth town in the colony, named Sudbury, apparently after the English community of Sudbury, Suffolk County, and former home of some of the first settlers.

The authorities agreed that the selected location was rich in meadowlands on either side of the Sudbury River with an adjoining abundance of woodland. It was said "that the early settlers found broad meadows wherein grew neither shrub nor tree, but as much grass as may be thrown out with a scythe, thick and strong, and as high as a man's middle (or more),

---

From the above list, no definite conclusions can be reached, but the best possibility by default appears to be the *Susan and Ellen*. The *Confidence* and *Bevis* left from Southampton located on the far sound end of England. London would have been a better port of departure. (For more information see http://olivetreegenealogy.com/ships/tousa_index.shtml and http://www.packrat-pro.com/shiplist.htm)

that a man may cut three loads in a day."[15] The forests on the west side were full of heavy pine for home construction and from which tar could be manufactured for roofing and sealants.

The country afforded a wide range of wild animals and was well stocked with game including deer, bear, and beaver. Wild fowl such as turkeys,

St. James's Church, Stanstead, England where Thomasine Frost was Christened August 11, 1600.

strutted in the lowlands and meadows, and flocks of pigeons and grouse were plentiful. Fish, including salmon, alewives, shad, and dace, graced the streams and rivers.

With these advantages came disadvantages. The little town was twenty miles over crude roads and bridges from a bustling Boston market to buy and sell needed products and produce, and the primary medium of exchange was barter as there was little coinage or currency in the colony. At first the roads were nothing more than a series of interlacing trails created over decades by wild game and Indians. In subsequent years, the famous Boston Post Road would go through Sudbury, placing the town on the map.

The settlers were also on the western frontier where packs of wolves would harass their livestock, and there was little protection against marauding bands of Indian. While technically at peace with their Indian neighbors, the town had to be constantly on the alert against sporadic attacks of a nature almost inconceivable to English farmers. These rural people were accustomed to wars being fought by professional soldiers with certain rules of engagement. The Indians knew no rules such as not fighting at night, in the rain, during harvests, or over the snow. They were as ready to slit the stomach of a pregnant woman as they were to scalp a man who crossed their warpath. The people of Sudbury had to steel themselves for such barbaric tactics, and each man was armed with a musket and ammunition.

Most of the new Sudbury settlers such as the Rices were recent arrivals

15   Samuel Adams Drake, *History of Middlesex County, Massachusetts* (Boston: Estes and Lauriat, 1880), 357.

A 1638 map of the first roads and house lots in Sudbury. Edmund Rice's first home and four acre lot is on the old Mill Road and identified by the arrow. (Alfred Sereno Hudson, *History of Sudbury, Massachusetts 1638-1889,* Sudbury: Sudbury Press, 1889: 77)

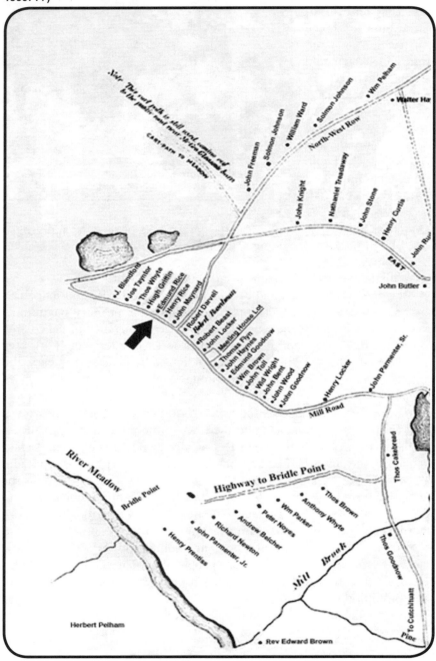

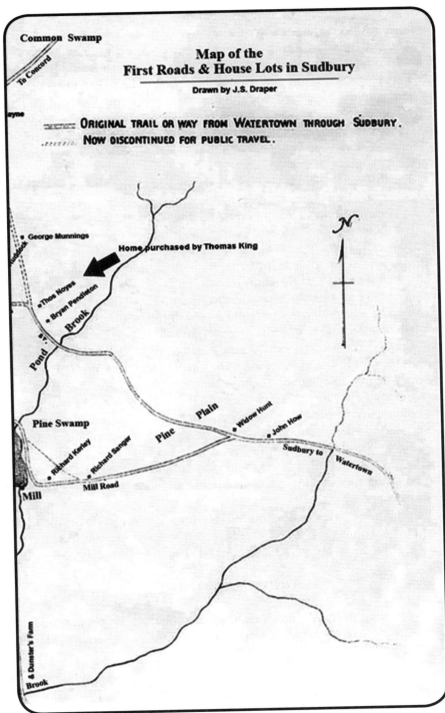

Map of the
First Roads & House Lots in Sudbury

Drawn by J.S. Draper

Common Swamp

To Concord

ORIGINAL TRAIL OR WAY FROM WATERTOWN THROUGH SUDBURY.
NOW DISCONTINUED FOR PUBLIC TRAVEL.

• George Munnings

Home purchased by Thomas King

N

•Thos Noyes
• Bryan Pendleton

Brook

Pond

Pine Swamp

Plain

• Widow Hunt
• John How

Pine

• Richard Kerley
• Richard Sanger

Sudbury to

Watertown

Mill Road

Mill

& Dunster's Farm

Brook

from England, with a few people from nearby Watertown. Soon there would develop a community of seventy-five or more families.

The initial Sudbury land grant was for five square miles and was purchased from an Indian dignitary called Cato or Karte. It is said that Cato was a man of sober tastes and philosophical bent. He took to heart the exhortations of the local preacher and became a practicing Christian.[16] The agreed purchase price was £5 in commodities and wampumpeag and was paid by a Walter Hayne and Hugh Griffin of Sudbury. A deed was sealed, acknowledged, and recorded.[17] Additional one mile and two mile grants were later added.

The little settlement was officially incorporated on September 4, 1639, and Edmund's leadership qualities quickly surfaced as he was called upon by the General Court to assist in the first division of land.

For their common defense, the first housing lots, comprising four to six acres, were closely knitted together for home and garden. There was also a large common area for cattle and share cropping. The General Court had decreed that no house should be built more than a half mile from the central meeting house of the community. To get to their new community, the only transportation was walking or riding horseback on a rough, muddy, and winding trail, described above.

The first houses were built on the east side of the Sudbury river, now within the city limits of Wayland. The first homes were crude small log cabins with no more than one or two rooms and a dirt floor. These would be temporary shelters as the winter of 1638-39 was fast approaching and the community worked together to help each other to secure housing and get established before snowy conditions dropped the temperatures into the 20s, 30s or possibly lower. No doubt these were busy days for all. Land had to be cleared, firewood cut, wild animals and fowl hunted and cured for the winter food supply, and simple household furniture made for eating and sleeping.

Edmund's first home was located on a four-acre parcel on the old Mill Road (now Highway 27) just northeast of the town meeting house and later the city cemetery. (See maps pp. 12-13)

Native Americans

Beginning in the sixteenth century, European explorers and traders frequented the coasts of eastern North America from Nova Scotia to Florida

---

16   Members of the Federal Writers Project, Works Progress Administration in Massachusetts, *A Brief History of the Town of Sudbury in Massachusetts 1639-1939* (Sudbury: Sudbury Historical Society, 1987), 5.

17   Ibid., 358.

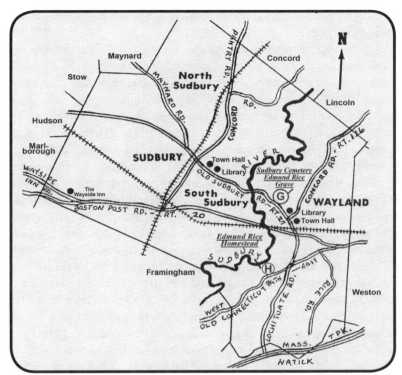

An early map showing the original township of Sudbury which now encompasses the towns of Sudbury, South Sudbury, North Sudbury, and Wayland. The first settlement was on the east side of the Sudbury river which is now in Wayland. The location of Edmund Rice's homestead (H) and grave (G) are so marked. The grave site is where the first town meetinghouse was erected, a short distance from Edmund's first home. (*A Treatise on the Rice Family* - Graphics, 1.)

without realizing the near genocidal infection they brought to the new, untouched world. Their ships carried rodents, fleas, and other insects, and the human contact brought diseases never experienced by the Indians such as smallpox, flu, and measles. The immune system of the Native Americans knew no such infections resulting in the deaths of hundreds of thousands. It is estimated by one researcher that up and down the coast and for 300 miles inland, 90 to 95% of the people died. Whole villages and tribes were lost.[18]

In Massachusetts alone the Indian population had been reduced from 30,000 to 7,000 inhabitants by the time the Pilgrims arrived. In 1633 in the Sudbury area another smallpox epidemic just about wiped out the few

---

18　E. P. Rice-Smith, "Essay III: Ashur Rice - Returned to Westborough. Amongst Family and a Member of the Church*," Edmund Rice (1638) Association Newsletter* 80, no. 4 (Autumn 2006): 19.

remaining tribesmen. As a result Indians could not effectively resist European settlement.

As historical memory is always short, the English immigrants to New England had long forgotten how their own people were once woodlanders and wilderness peoples. As a tribal people they had withstood for centuries countless invasions including the Romans who brought enormous social and political changes, and the establishment of the Christian Church.[19] In turn, little did the English invaders to North America realize their impact on the indigenous people and their society. To the Puritans they were the new Israel being given an inheritance in an unoccupied land, and at first the Native Americans were considered the lost tribes of Israel ripe for religious conversion. But as social intercourse between the two cultures continued and as the English needed the friendly assistance of the local people less and less to survive in the hostile environment, the Puritans began to change their view. Soon the Indians became regarded as agents of evil and their afflictions were the result of depraved deeds.

While the Indians of the various tribes in the Massachusetts Bay area were fairly peaceful in the 1640s, there was always a suspicious concern for the common safety of the community. A series of Indian wars in Virginia and other areas had left hundreds of settlers dead, and the 1637 war with the Pequot Indians across Massachusetts, Connecticut and Rhode Island was still fresh in the minds of the people. One skirmish had led to another until in June 1637, the colonists attacked a Pequot village near West Mystic, Connecticut, burning and massacring over 600 Indians and selling the remaining captives into Bermuda slavery. Cotton Mather, the Puritan scholar, wrote that the colonists thought this "a sweet sacrifice, and . . . gave the praise thereof to God."[20]

While brutality extended on both sides of the cultural divide, many of the New England settlers tried to create a peaceful atmosphere and in many cases bought the land from the natives. Fortunately, Edmund would escape the hostilities and privations that would fall upon many of his children and grandchildren through the bloody King Philip's war of 1675-76 and the several French and Indian wars that soon followed.

Community and Family Life

Life was not easy on the fringe of the frontier; but with hard work and planning, a simple but good life, by early American standards, could be achieved. In the words of one author:

---

19   Ibid., 19-20.

20   "Indian Wars," *The World Book Encyclopedia*, 20 vols., (Chicago: Field Enterprises Educational Corporation, 1970), 10:145.

With the exception of a few dollars' worth of salt and iron, many a New England farmer was practically self-sufficing. From his field he obtained grains, from his orchard fruits, and from his pasture land meat and dairy products. Flax from the field and wool from the sheep were spun and made into clothing by his wife and daughters. From honey and maple sap

A depiction of one of the first Sudbury homes of the Edmund Rice family. Note the thatched roof. (Powell, *Puritan Village*, Figure 13, n.p.)

he obtained ingredients to sweeten his food; corn whisky and cider furnished him with strong drink. Every farmer had to be a Jack-of-all-trades, and his wife had to be just as able to turn her hand to anything.[21]

Prosperity for these people was usually measured in terms of a warm, comfortable home, an adequate but simple food supply, clothes to wear, good health, and safety. This economic existence would have been supported by such things as their farming tools, cattle, household furnishings, spinning wheels, and their means of defense such as muskets and swords. Above all, these people had a thirst for land, and most of a person's wealth would be calculated by how much land he owned.

Besides becoming a prosperous farmer, an abundant life was within the reach of most men; and was recognized by marrying well, having children, and achieving the respect of one's neighbors and the blessings of God.

When spring awoke after the first winter in Sudbury there was much to be accomplished. Homes were enlarged and improved, barns and fences constructed, roads laid out, and an all-important first grist mill for the grinding of corn meal and flour was erected by none other that Mr. Cakebread. No mention is made in the records for the construction of a sawmill; but with many homes and a community to be built, one must have been made available on one of the many streams of water flowing through the area. Of the other necessary services to build a community, a blacksmith would not be available for some fifteen years. In 1663 an offer was made that if the smith agreed to stay for four years he would be paid in land and timber.

---

21   Faulkner, *American Economic History*, 64.

A depiction of the first Sudbury River bridge constructed in 1642. (Powell, *Puritan Village*, Figure 16. n.p.)

With all of this activity, it would be several years before Edmund and the other city father's could address other pressing issues. In 1642 a cart bridge was finally constructed over the ever-flooding Sudbury River providing greater access to the property on the west side of town. Although a church was organized as early as 1640, a contract for the construction of a meeting house was not awarded until February 1642. The church was to be 30 feet long by 20 feet wide, or 600 square feet — not large by most standards, but adequate to meet the immediate needs of a small community. It was to be located just south of Edmund's home and for several years would be the center for town activities.

Besides the above-mentioned home, Edmund also received grants of 48.5 acres of meadow, 64 acres of upland, and later 130 acres in a two-mile land extension to the Sudbury community.[22] Edmund, as a settler and for his community service, ranked sixth in the amount of land granted to him by Sudbury. Besides this acreage, Edmund would have shared in the "cow commons" and grazing land held by the Sudbury community. There were also planting fields held in common, and by 1642 the records speak of five planting fields located in various parts of town. These fields required vigilant watching for protection against marauding beasts and birds and participating towns people were required to take their turn standing guard.

For Edmund land ownership did not stop with these allotments and eventually he became the largest land owner in Sudbury.[23] In September 1642, he sold his home on old Mill road and bought another home and six acres from Mary Axdell. He also leased for six years, the six hundred acre farm of Henry Dunster, first president of Harvard College. It was agreed

---

22   This information is taken from the early Sudbury town records located on the Sudbury website. The total agrees with the ERA web page. Powell, *Puritan Village*, 189, gives the figure of 87.5 acres.

23   "Presidents Column," by Robert V. Rice, *Edmund Rice (1638) Association Newsletter*, Autumn 2003, no. 4, 77:1.

that Edmund would pay thirty bushels of corn for two years, fifty bushels each for the next two, and one hundred bushels each for the last two in equal proportions of wheat, Indian corn and rye. At the end of the lease, Edmund bought the farm. Later he bought another nine acres and a house near a place called the "Spring" which

A rendition of the second church built in Sudbury in 1653 when Edmund was serving as deacon. This building replaced the first one built in 1642 and was much larger than the first one. One of the two contracting parties to build the church was Peter King as noted on page 47. (Powell, *Puritan Village,* Figure 18, n.p.)

adjoined the Axdell property. These parcels of land with some additional acres made up the Rice homestead where six Rice generations lived and the old house stood until recent years.[24] (See map on page 15.)

With the acquisition of the Axdell home, the living conditions of the Rice family were enhanced significantly. The original Rice home probably began as a one-room log cabin with a dirt floor and a sleeping loft for some of the older children. The overall size would have been no more than about 300 square feet — not much room for a family of nine people with a tenth soon to follow. However, with Edmund's energy and determination, improvements in the basic structure would have been made over the years. Perhaps a wooden floor and a second room began the expansion project.

In 1650, Edmund made another step forward in his family's living conditions when he built a new home. The construction of this home would also reflect his improving economic affluence, and it would follow the developing and innovative style of a New England saltbox style reserved for the more successful members of society.[25]

The colloquial term "saltbox" came from the shape of the house. Salt was a precious commodity in Colonial America and was carefully stored

---

24   Smith, *Edmund Rice and His Family*, 18-19.

25   Figures 13, 16, 18 come from Powell, *Puritan Village*. Credit is given to Kenneth Conant, a professor at Harvard University, and Charles Strickland, an architect of Boston, who assisted with the sketches. Since 1952, when some of these drawings appeared in the *Journal of the Society of Architectural Historians,* no one has questioned the reconstructions. See p. xv.

An old photo of the actual Edmund Rice farm home built in 1650 on the old homestead by the spring. The home stood until it burned in the late 1800s. (Photo courtesy Edmund Rice Association)

in a wooden box hung on the fireplace to keep it dry and to prevent caking.

The size of the Rice home could have been about 30' by 40' or 1,200 square feet on the main level and another 800 square feet on the second level, not counting the storage area. The frame would have been hewn from oak trees, the outside would be a riven siding and the inside would be a whitewashed lath and plaster. The main level would include the living rooms in front, including a parlor, and the kitchen or great room called a hall in colonial times. The upstairs would contain the bedrooms and storage. A large chimney rose in the middle of the home for wintertime heat and to accommodate the flues for an oven and a large fireplace in the kitchen.

To this house would have been added additional outbuildings such as a springhouse for cooling dairy products and other perishables, a root cellar for fruits and vegetables, a woodshed, and a privy. Water for cleaning and bathing would have been obtained from a nearby spring.

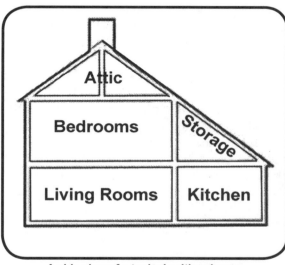

A side view of a typical saltbox home.

Other trappings of affluence that began to show up in the Rice home were chairs, rugs (bedspreads), curtains and linens.

The life of Thomasine as a colonial housewife was physically and emotionally exhausting, but also rewarding and fulfilling. The two-year compressed cycles of pregnancy, childbirth, and lactation did not provide much of a breather while other small and fussing children tugged at her apron strings. In small homes, privacy for mother and father was limited. Parental copulation and breast feeding were commonplace and, for the ever present children, not much different than what they observed every day in the barnyard. Chamber pots were also used during evening hours and other critical times.

In each home there was a "walk-in" fireplace where a fire was kept going most of the time for boiling and coals for broiling. Pots were hung by pothooks or trammels from a lug pole across the throat of the flue from which emerged the New England staple of stews, pot roasts, and vegetables; puddings (bread or plum) could be steamed in a fabric bag hung over the pot. Beef and pork were the primary meats and beer was the principal drink. Colonial beer was only about 1/2 to 1% alcohol, enough to kill the bacteria that might infect the water, yet potable for all to drink including small children.[26] Their beer was akin to the ale they were accustomed to in England.

Ovens were also built, mostly outside, for breads and pastries. Because of the dangers of the open fire when cooking, Thomasine would have hitched up her skirts, petticoats, and aprons, tucking them into her waistband. She may have also elected to work in a state of undress, meaning working in her shift or as some called it, a chemise. This was nothing more than a ankle-length linen nightdress with drawstrings at the neck and wrists and was the standard undergarment. In her shift alone a woman was considered naked.[27]

The day's activities for both men and women were driven by natural light, not the clock as we have today. Artificial light, including candles, was expensive and people arose and went to bed with the sun.

Thomasine would have also helped with the twice-a-day milking, churning the butter, making cheese, and slaughtering the pigs. With only one daughter to help, she may at some point have had servant girls to assist her. Girls, like young men, often times were apprenticed out, or a single girl may have been brought in from one of the poorer families to earn her keep.

Neighborly sharing and borrowing were all part of the social fabric, and friends and neighbors became close; but any strength can become a weakness. Friendships could easily turn to gossip and petty differences as everyone would know everyone's business, history, and idiosyncrasies. Through the early trials of settlement in Sudbury, Thomasine must have

---

26   Dale Taylor, *A Writer's Guide to Everyday Life in Colonial America from 1607-1783* (Cincinnati, Ohio: Writer's Digest Books, 1997), 87.

27   Ibid., 107-108.

A plaque identifying the location of the Edmund Rice homestead in Wayland, Massachusetts, just south of the intersection of highway 126 and 27.

DEACON EDMUND RICE
BORN IN
BUCKINGHAMSHIRE ENG
1594
SETTLED IN SUDBURY 1638
BUILT HIS HOUSE BY THE
SPRING NEAR THIS SPOT
APPOINTED TO APPORTION
LAND 1639 DEPUTY TO THE
GENERAL COURT - MAGIS
TRATE 1641 - SELECTMAN 1644
AND FOLLOWING YEARS - A
PETITIONER FOR THE INCOR
PORATION OF MARLBOROUGH
1656 - WHERE HE DIED MAY
3, 1663 HIS GRAVE IS IN
WAYLAND
ERECTED BY HIS
DESCENDANTS
SEPTEMBER 13, 1913

enjoyed having her sister, Elizabeth, nearby until her death in 1647.

Within the colonies there developed early a limited aristocratic social system; however, this system would not have been evidenced as much in the outlying and smaller farming communities, such as Sudbury, as in the social and economic centers such as Boston and Philadelphia. Never-the-less social rank among women was still recognized with the wives of magistrates or ministers at the top, wives of small land-owners and crafts-men, and then, at the bottom, the wives of those living in rented houses and semi-dependent upon employers or parents. A fourth group could be classed as unmarried girls working as servants.

Commensurate with Edmund's political and economic success, Thomasine would have received recognition within the community and religious circles. Even her dress would have reflected this distinction as well as the seating arrangement in the church.

AS THE FOUNDATION of this small New England community con-tinued to grow, Edmund's organizational and leadership influence grew with both church and community. As a test of church and political loyalty and to make himself voter eligible, Edmund took the Freeman's oath May 13, 1640. This may have been Puritan country, yet only about 10 percent of the New England population were church members and able to vote.

On June 2, 1641, he was appointed one of three individuals as "an assosiate for the Courts and comission'r for the tourne of Sudberry," or a modern day justice of the peace. The term of office was for one year and he was reappointed to serve in this capacity May 6, 1646. In 1648 the procedure changed and the position was made available through a general election of the town's voters, Edmund was elected to the post on May 10, 1648, and again in 1654. The job required him to deal with money issues under £2 and to hear small local cases involving infringements of regula-tions regarding personal behavior and welfare. These were Puritan people who adhered to a strong code of ethics and morality. And while they fer-vently sought religious freedom, they frequently denied the same rights to others of a differing persuasion, expelling such people from their midst. Common regulations were passed limiting the use of tobacco, the buying and selling of produce, and the establishment of a dress code.

> No Garment shall be made with short sleeves whereby the nakedness of the arms may be discovered in the wearing thereof, and such as already have garments made with short sleeves shall not hereafter wear the same unless they cover their arms to the wrist with linnen or otherwise.[28]

While they were a sober and solemn people, they did have a love for laughter and fun, but moderation in all things was the rule. Fancy dress pants, slit sleeves, double ruffs, and other marks of vanity in clothing were not allowed. Idleness was considered the first step toward excess and mischief, and laws were passed to prevent such evil. Playing cards, dice games, swearing, and drunkenness were punishable by law. Capital crimes

---

28   Smith, *Edmund Rice and His Family*, 21.

included idolatry, witch-
craft, blasphemy, and smit-
ing one's father or mother.

Edmund's duties also
included the performing of
marriages. As a result, he
may have performed the
marriage of one or more
of his children. Marriage
at this time was a civil
ceremony, and ministers
were not allowed to offici-
ate until a much later date;
however, where possible,
intentions were read in
the churches. If one was
not available a notice was
nailed to a post for fourteen days before the day of
the ceremony.

The Freeman's Oath

*I, being by God's providence an In-
habitant within this Jurisdiction doe tru-
ely and solemnly acknowledge myselfe to
be subject to the government of the same,
and therefore doe here sware by the great
and dreadfull name of the ever livinge
God that I will be true and faithful to the
same and will accordingly yield Assistance
thereunto with my person and that as in
equity I am bound. And I will all soe tru-
ely endeavour to maintayne and preserve
the libertyes and privileges thereof sub-
mittinge myselfe to the wholesome lawes
made and established by the same. And
further that I will not plott or practice any
eveill against it nor consult with any that
shall soe doe, but will tymely discover the
same to lawfull Authority now here established for the suppressinge of the same soe
help me God and the Lord Jesus Christ.*

Furthering his involvement in the community, Edmund was elected a
selectman for eleven one-year terms between 1639 and 1656.[29] This would
be the equivalent of today's city councilmen to help regulate the affairs of
the village. Responsibilities included matters pertaining to the division of
land, taxation, fees, and fines, and town ordinances such as the building of
fences, roads, bridges, and the regulation of cattle.

In addition to these responsibilities, Edmund also functioned in other
capacities such a fence viewer, an insurance taker, and a surveyor of highways. A good degree of attention was given to fences. Surveyors and
fence viewers held considerable authority and were appointed to judge
the sufficiency of the fences about men's particular properties in cases of
damage and difference.

In the study made by Powell in his book *Puritan Village,* it appears
that only four other men between 1638 and 1655 served more frequently
than Edmund in community responsibilities. The political power of the

---

29   In reviewing the Sudbury records identified by the Sudbury website the following dates have been found for Edmund's selectman service. The information that he was
elected eleven times is taken from Powell's *Puritan Village,* 189.

June 25,	1644	February 19,	1651
September 19,	1647	February 19,	1652
October 1,	1648	March 7,	1654
December 4,	1649		

community primarily rested with six individuals.[30]

Besides his devotion to family and community, Edmund was a leader in his Puritan church and was selected as a deacon in 1648, a position of respect and honor. He later became known as "Goodman Rice," not a unique title for the day, but one denoting a person of excellent character.

The responsibilities of a deacon included assisting with the sacrament, visiting the sick and needy, and taking a collection for benevolent objects.

In the midst of building a new home in a new land, the Rice family continued to grow with the addition in May 1640 of a tenth child and eighth son, Benjamin. This was Thomasine's last child, and to her the joys and burdens of children were many. She was fortunate enough to experience her own children having children as four of her own children married before her death on June 12, 1654, at the age of fifty-four, leaving a grieving husband, children, and grandchildren. At home were still two teenage children, Joseph, age 19, and Benjamin, age 14. Her burial was five days later at the old Sudbury cemetery.

The delay in burying the dead was a colonial custom. The body was laid in state in the home of the deceased allowing time for a person pronounced dead in error to come back to life.

Thomasine was fortunate to have lived as long as she had. Fifty-four by modern standards is still young, but for her day the mortality rate among women was very high. Well over 25% of the women died from complications incident to child-birth, and another 25% died from cooking accidents, notably burns when their long dresses caught fire.[31] Not an emotionally encouraging lifestyle for a young bride.

For others, smallpox, measles, and fever epidemics would sweep across the colony with almost diabolical regularity. Parents had little hope of protecting their children from the approaching menace. Many tried by sending susceptible children to neighboring towns to stay with relatives or friends, only to further spread the disease. Early deaths of fathers often were the result of many of the same diseases, farm accidents, and armed conflicts. It was not uncommon for many families to be completely wiped out, or for men and women to marry three and four times in a lifetime, yet Edmund and Thomasine lost only two of their ten children in England before arriving in America.

IN COLONIAL TIMES, marriage was more a negotiated, economic, business arrangement than a romantic or even a sacramental (religious)

---

30   Powell, *Puritan Village,* 189. The six men were Peter Noyes, Edmund Goodnow, William Ward, Walter Haines, John Goodnow, and Edmund Rice.

31   Taylor, *A Writer's Guide,* 81, 129.

institution.   The mind-set of today would look on this arrangement as giving the woman little power or opportunity to be something other than a homemaker and mother.   She became part of the man's identity and usually had no independent existence apart from her husband.   However, through the eyes of seventeenth century New England, this situation was not considered discrimination but one where the sexes had distinct roles.   Women had their own sphere of influence within the home and appendages thereto.   Men's influence became external including politics, business, land ownership, and managing a labor-intensive farm, although, many women became very successful in running the affairs of the farm or business upon the absence or death of their husbands.

Women also exerted considerable influence in church affairs.   The men may have sat on the board, hired and paid the minister, and served as deacons and tithing men; but over time, more women than men participated in church services, and they could make or break a minister with back-fence gossip.

Women were the care givers and nurturers not only to their own family, but to neighbors, other women at childbirth and other families in need. In general women did not have a strong literary education, but were "street wise" as homemakers and caregivers.

While marital love by some was considered unimportant, from several Rice and King wills tender and loving feelings are expressed toward a "beloved wife."

Due to this division of labor, it would have been difficult for Edmund to continue to manage his affairs without a spouse.   Edmund married the forty-two-year-old widow Mercy (Hurd) Brigham of Cambridge on March 1, 1655, ten months after Thomasine's passing.   Mercy's first husband had come to America in 1635 and had been a prominent pioneer in Cambridge. Mercy also brought to the marriage five children, the youngest only three. The oldest, Thomas Hurd, later married Mary Rice, Edmund's granddaughter through his oldest son Henry.

From Edmund's second marriage came two more daughters, Lydia in 1657 and Ruth in September 1659.   Their birth gave Edmund twelve children with ten of them growing to adulthood and having families.

General Court

The colonial government of early Massachusetts began as a political experiment, not by intention, but out of circumstances that neither England nor the citizens of the colony could foresee the end result.   At first the Massachusetts Bay Colony was founded and chartered by the British government not as the founding of a state, but as a commercial venture. The king claimed no jurisdiction in its internal affairs.

The governor was appointed and the company was formed. It purchased a tract of land "three miles north of any and every part of the Merrimac River and three miles north of any and every part of the Charles River and extending westward to the Pacific Ocean,"[32] essentially a fifty to seventy-five-mile wide strip of land 3,000 miles long. The company also agreed to pay the Crown 1/5th of all discovered gold and silver. Certainly, as it turned out, the venture was not as lucrative as what the Spanish found in the Americas.

To manage their affairs at the lowest level of government, the people soon introduced the concept of a town meeting. This was unlike any other political assembly of the day and was patterned after the New England Congregational Church meeting. With freedom and equality, each community soon became its own little democracy.

From this beginning grew the spirit of representative government; and in 1634, a governor, a legislature, and a judiciary were elected. Communications with the mother country took months, and the people soon came to enjoy the democratic process. Both the towns and the Massachusetts central government came to depend on each other. Whatever laws needed were passed, and offices were filled.

Each town was permitted to elect two representatives to the legislative body soon known as the General Court, which carried considerable influence and prestige. The people still considered themselves loyal British subjects as Massachusetts was part of *New* England.

As more and more people arrived from Europe, new towns and governments were organized and delegates were chosen to gather in Boston to regulate the affairs of the colony. The General Court was not organized into political parties as we know them today, and it usually conducted most of its business in committees who then made their recommendations to the assembly for action. The voice of the people was heard most everywhere, and the legislature allowed most provincial problems a hearing.

Besides these issues, budgets, taxes, and the safety and the defense of the colony were always pressing items.

At first the General Court met in many different buildings, churches, and/or taverns. The first Town House was not built until 1657 and the old Statehouse, still standing, was not built until 1712. Sessions could last for several weeks at a time, and representatives were usually supported by the represented community during their term of service.

---

32   Alfred Sereno Hudson, *The History of Sudbury, Massachusetts* (Sudbury, Massachusetts: Town of Sudbury, 1889).

28   *The Kings of the Kingdom*

It was here in the General Court that Edmund's influence extended beyond Sudbury. He served as its representative for five terms between 1640 and 1654.[33] On the list of General Court members in which Edmund first appears in May 1640 twenty-seven men were addressed as Mister and three as Captain or Lieutenant. Edmund was one of thirteen without any title.

The General Court eventually included several Rice descendants and related family members. In the legacy of the institution such notables as John Hancock, James Otis, and Samuel and John Adams would, decades later, rise to prominent leadership.

Puritanism in Massachusetts

The militant conflict for religious dominance in England had been going on for years. The first spark of reformation against the established Catholic Church was by John Wycliffe in the latter part of the fourteenth century, but the movement did not gain an appreciable foothold until the early 1500s during the rule of King Henry VIII. Henry's desire for a church sanctioned divorce was denied by the Pope so Henry eventually established his own church, the Anglican or Church of England. The violent struggle to return England to the Catholic faith was renewed by Henry's daughter. Mary's five-year rule was marked by so much bloodshed that she became known as "Bloody" Mary; but following her death in 1558, her Protestant sister, Elizabeth, brought the country back into the Reformation fold.

To the Puritans, a subset of reformation minded people, the cleansing of the church from many of the sophisticated and portentous rites and rituals of Catholicism was either not significant or not moving fast enough. Their principled zeal created their own friction and disfavor with the established clergy and political leaders; and as the fervor of their movement gained momentum, the establishment of the Massachusetts Bay Colony became a hotbed for the extension of their philosophy and ideals in the Americas. While people came to the colony for many reasons already noted, the religious zeal of the Puritans dominated the New England political and social fabric of the time. They firmly believed in welding both the

33   Edmund attended the General Court the following years:

October 7,	1640
	1643
May 27,	1652
May 18,	1653
May 3,	1654

See ERA website: http://www.edmund-rice.org/edmund.htm and the *Edmund Rice (1638) Association Newsletter,* 77:4, Autumn 2003.

political and church functions together. They were building a new Israel and they saw themselves, like the Hebrews, in a covenant with God. The seals of the old covenant were circumcision and the Passover, and those of the new covenant were baptism and the Lord's Supper. They were building the "city on a hill" in preparation for Christ's second coming. The millennium was at their doorstep.

Being God's people required that they live a prescribed way of life and receive the grace of God into their hearts. This lifestyle governed their daily activities and how they acted and dressed. The Sabbath was strictly observed from Saturday afternoon until Sunday evening. A high standard of morality was enforced, and each church member was expected to watch over the others including the less than active attendees. Church attendance was expected of all whether they had been accepted as church members or not, but only church members could partake of the sacrament.

None questioned the presence of God and the devil in their midst as manifest by sudden deaths, earthquakes, eclipses, and strange lights in the night sky. All natural phenomena were believed to be providential signs or warnings whereby the divine will was revealed.

As the political franchise only extended to those in good church standing, the unchurched, who comprised a goodly part of the overall population were relegated to a society of second-class-citizens. They could neither vote or hold public office. It was not a Puritan goal to establish a free church, or tolerance for an inter-religious society. Rather it was their goal to establish their own freedom from the tyrannies, persecutions, and corruptions of a religious monarchy. They would conform to this new society and require conformity from others as well.

One of their main objectives was to build a community of peace and tranquillity but anything that interfered with this ideal was dealt with quickly and harshly. These people were not strangers to the use of torture, decapitation, dismemberment, and the use of stake and fire. Corporal punishment was not uncommon for crimes against their society. A policy of exclusion was strictly enforced; and Baptists, if found, were whipped or fined. Any Quaker who came into the colony was fined £100, arrested, whipped, and transported out of the territory. Any colonist possessing a Quaker book was fined £5. The culmination of many of these excesses resulted in the infamous Salem witch trials. During the "witch hunt" of 1692 nineteen people were hung and one pressed to death after being accused of being in league with the devil.

The attempt to build their peaceable society did not stop at excluding outsiders. They also dealt summarily with internal strife. Most notable was the expulsion of Roger Williams in 1636 for his views on religious intolerance and the importance of the separation of church and state. Following Williams the very next year came Ann Hutchinson. Her kindness and generous care of the sick made her a popular colonial figure, but she quickly fell out of favor with political and church leaders by taking the explosive position that a person could have direct and personal contact with the divine grace and love of God, this without regard to church or minister. She was summarily expelled from the church and moved with her family to Rhode Island.

The fallout of these challenges to the hierarchal claims of the ruling class in Massachusetts must have been met, and not gone unnoticed, by Edmund on his arrival.

In Sudbury the church was Congregationalist in government and Calvinist in doctrine. The beating of drums twice each Sabbath day by a selected towns-person, before a bell was installed, summoned the Sudbury Puritans to Sunday worship. They all came by foot as even their beasts of burden were given the day of rest. There was both a morning service and an afternoon meeting, and the ever-present "tything" men bearing long poles tipped with feathers tickled the faces of sleepy ones ensuring the full attention of the congregation.

Records are silent as to Edmund's conversion to Puritanism. He and Thomasine were married in the Anglican Church and all of their children, including Joseph who was born as late as March 1638, were baptized in the same church. Yet the Rice family emigrated to Puritan Massachusetts rather than some other colony, and Edmund became a political and church leader. Perhaps his religious sentiments were changing by the time he left England as there were Puritan groups forming in the Berkhampshire area, or once in New England, he may have converted out of expediency. The fact that many generations of Rices followed in their father's footsteps as deacon of the church is one indication that his conversion was sincere and genuine.

Education and Early Schooling

Education was vitally important to the citizens of the Massachusetts Bay Colony. At first, schooling was conducted in the homes, and the parents who could, taught their children how to read and write. Most parents gave instruction in the principles of obedience, religious beliefs, and the skills needed in daily life. As early as 1642 a law was passed:

> Forasmuch as the good education of children is singular behoof and benefit to any Common-wealth; and whereas many parents & masters are too indulgent and negligent of their duty in that kinde. It is therefore ordered that the Select men of everie town, in the severall precincts and quarters where they dwell, shall have a vigilant eye over their brethren & neighbors, to see, first that none of

them shall suffer so much barbarism in any of their families as not to indeavour to teach by themselves or other, their children & apprentices so much learning as may inable them perfectly to read the english tongue, & knowledge of the Capital Lawes: upon penaltie of twentie shillings for each neglect therin.

To emphasize the importance of their religion the law further stated:

Also that all masters of families doe once a week (at the least) catechize their children and servants in the grounds & principles of Religion, & if any be unable to doe so much: that then at the least they procure such children or apprentices to learn some short orthodox catechism without book, that they may be able to answer unto the questions that shall be propounded to them out of such catechism by their parents or masters or any of the Select men when they call them to a tryall of what they have learned of this kinde.[34]

The first public school system in the country supported by public taxation was set up in Massachusetts in 1647 and called for every town with at least fifty families to establish an elementary school. Larger towns were to establish secondary schools.

The degree in which Sudbury complied with these requirements is not clear. Compliance rested upon the availability and afford-ability of a competent schoolmaster. The first recorded event for a school was not until 1664 when a Mr. Walker was encouraged with a land grant to establish a free school.

External Influences

Besides the many internal factors of family and community there were many external influences that had an effect on the lives of the Rice and King families, some more directly than others. As neighboring Boston grew and developed, it enjoyed considerable economic prosperity as a major seaport exchanging products with England, the West Indies, and other trading partners. To raise the educational standard of the colony, Harvard College in Cambridge was founded in 1636. The first printing press in America was also set up in Cambridge three years later and communications improved with the inauguration of the first mounted mail service between Boston and New York. The post road came right through Sudbury in 1673.

Hurricanes were a problem from time to time, hitting the Boston area in 1638 and in 1675. The first large-scale outbreak of smallpox occurred in 1648-49 and again in 1666. An outbreak in 1677-78 killed as many as thirty people a day in Boston.

---

34   Marlborough, Massachusetts town records: Rootsweb.com(http://freepages.history.rootsweb.com/historyofmarlborough/earlyschool.htm).

In England, civil war broke out in 1642 between the royalists and the separatists (Puritans) led by Oliver Cromwell. In Puritan Massachusetts anxieties and jubilation ran high as Cromwell assumed power, and established an English republic. There is evidence that a small number of Puritans returned to England to support the cause.

Inspired by these events, Massachusetts stated its own democratic aspirations in 1652 when it declared itself an independent commonwealth. However, with the reestablishment of the English monarchy in 1660, the political winds shifted. The charter of Massachusetts was revoked in 1684, and it became a royal colony. It wasn't until seven years later that a new, more limited charter was issued. This now included the territories of Nova Scotia, New Hampshire, Plymouth, and Maine as well as Massachusetts. The governor was appointed by the king and given veto power over the General Court.

Thomas King Family

Contemporary with the Rice family and the settlement of Sudbury was the Thomas King, Jr. family,[35] one of many King families emigrating from England. Arriving from Shaftsbury, Dorset County, about the same time and in much the same manner as the Rices, the two families were eventually and inseparably joined together.

Thomas was born about 1599 (christened September 5, 1599) in Tarrant Hinton, Dorset, England, the son of Thomas and Agneta King. He and Anne Collins, the daughter of Henry Collins and Maude Whittacker, were married about 1625. Before emigrating, they had five children, and after they settled in Sudbury, two more followed.

The King family emigration date and ship of passage have been lost in time, but a daughter, Mercy, was born in Sudbury in February 1639, giving reason to believe that the King family emigrated in 1638. It could be speculated that Thomas came at the encouragement of or even with Thomas Goodnow, also from Shaftsbury, who set sail on the ship *Confidence* April 11, 1638.[36] The two Thomases may have been friends; although later

---

35   Much of the genealogical information on the King family for the next five generations is taken from an unpublished manuscript, "A Genealogy of the Family of Rice and King alias Rice, Descendants of Deacon Edmund Rice and Thomas King of Sudbury and later of Marlborough, Massachusetts, and from which the family of 'King' alias Rice descended," by George Oscar King, Corry, Pennsylvania, copy in my possession. Mr. King's passion for twenty-two years in the later part of the nineteenth and early twentieth century was researching the King family.

36   See Footnote 13 for a list of the ships arriving from England in 1638. From the list no conclusion can be reached as to which one might contain the King family. One argument might be made that they came on the ship *Confidence* leaving England in April

in the settlement of Marlborough, they would become very much at odds with each other.

It would also be interesting to know the financial means of Thomas. The cost of the trip from England was no small matter, and many people were supported by religious congregations for the purpose of settling the new world, or simply became indentured. The fact that Thomas had the resources to purchase land in Sudbury soon after arriving is an indication that he must have been a land owner or proprietor in Shaftsbury and paid the way of his family with money to spare to purchase needed land. There are no surviving records revealing this information.

St. Mary's Church, Tarrant Hinton, Dorset, England where Thomas King and probably his first four children were baptized. The church dates to the twelfth century with additions in the thirteenth, fifteenth, and seventeenth centuries. In 1874 the church was partially rebuilt.

After arriving, Thomas King did not immediately receive any land grants but purchased in 1642 a house and seven acres of upland property on the east side of the Sudbury River from Thomas Noyes (See map pp. 12-13). In addition he purchased eight acres of meadow on the west side of the river. In 1649 Sudbury received a two-mile extension to the west

---

1638. Although the passenger list appears to be a comprehensive number with about 73 people, conceivably it could be incomplete as some ships held over 100 passengers. The *Confidence* left from Southampton, close to Shaftsbury; the ship had other passengers from Dorset County including Thomas Goodenowe, who was also from Thomas King's home town of Shaftsbury and also went to Sudbury; the ship had several other families going to Sudbury including the Bents, Noyes, and Biddlecombes.

Thomas and
Anne Collins King Family

Anna King
	(B)	Abt 1626	Dorset, England
	(M)	6 Oct 1646	Sudbury, Middlesex, Massachusetts
		William Kerley, Jr.	
	(D)	18 Feb 1698	Marlborough, Middlesex, Massachusetts

Peter King
	(B)	Abt 1627	Dorset, England
	(M)	Abt 1660	Prob Sudbury, Middlesex, Massachusetts
		Sarah	
	(D)	27 Aug 1704	Sudbury, Middlesex, Massachusetts

Mary King
	(B)	Abt 1630	Dorset, England
	(M)	Abt 1651	Sudbury, Middlesex, Massachusetts
		Thomas Rice	
	(D)	22 Mar 1715	Sudbury, Middlesex, Massachusetts

Sarah King
	(B)	Abt 1632	Dorset, England
	(M)	1656	
		Nathaniel Joslin	
	(D)	2 Jul 1706	Marlborough, Middlesex, Massachusetts

Elizabeth King
	(B)	Abt 1635	Shaftesbury, Dorset, England
	(M)	8 Nov 1655	Sudbury, Middlesex, England
		Samuel Rice	
	(B)	30 Oct 1667	Marlborough, Middlesex, Massachusetts

Mercy King
	(B)	26 Feb 1639	Sudbury, Middlesex, Massachusetts
	(M)	4 May 1658	Sudbury, Middlesex, Massachusetts
		Joseph Rice	
	(D)	4 Jan 1668	Marlborough, Middlesex, Massachusetts

Thomas King
| | (B) | 4 Dec 1642 | Sudbury, Middlesex, Massachusetts |
| | (D) | 3 Jan 1643 | Sudbury, Middlesex, Massachusetts |

of the township. In January 1658 this land was divided among the town's citizens in the form of additional grants. Thomas received 130 acres in the far southwest corner adjacent to the cow pens. Perhaps it was not the most favorable spot, but the lots were usually determined by lottery.

The last child and namesake of Thomas was born December 4, 1642. However, the birth was too much for Anne and she passed away on Christmas eve three weeks later. She would only have been thirty-four-years of age. Unfortunately, young Thomas III was also not able to survive. He died ten days later on January 3. This left Thomas with six children to raise, ranging in age from three to sixteen years. No doubt the older children shared in the responsibility of caring for the home and younger children.

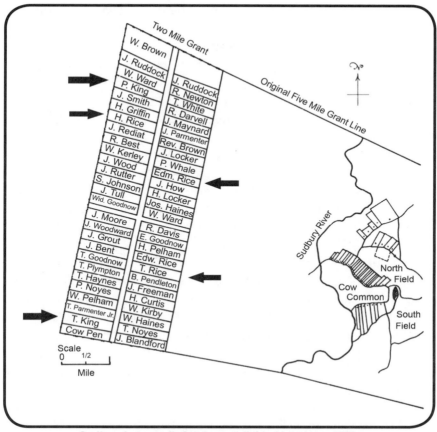

Sudbury's two-mile land grant divided into lots , 1758.
(Powell, *Puritan Village*, 108).

In spite of this personal setback, Thomas continued to be active in his community. He took the Freeman's Oath on July 9, 1645, and by February 1649 he was being referred to as "Goodman Kinge."[37]

In November 1643 he was authorized by the town together with four individuals "to view the river at Thomas Kinges and to agree with work-men to build a cart bridge over the river accordinge as they shall see inst. occasion."[38] Then in February 1849[39] he was given three acres of meadow for his costs to have the bridge built.

37   Sudbury Town Document #238, Sudbury, Massachusetts website.

38   Ibid., #197.

39   For the purpose of this book, I have eliminated any reference to the practice of double dating to accommodate the calendar change in 1752. All dates prior to 1752 be-tween January 1 and March 25 are registered in the current equivalent year.

On May 22, 1649, Thomas was one of two surveyors of highways appointed for a year by the town. They were given the authority to call men to work. Besides surveying the land for lots and roads, it appears that town surveyors were also responsible for helping to maintain the public fences.

By March 1653, Thomas's community leadership continued to develop as he was elected as town selectman. He was elected again in March 1655 and March 1661.

Under the selectman's tutorage nearly every aspect of community life was governed. Appointments were made to see that the children and servants were employed in work and in the ways of God according to the order of the General Court. And, by order of their governing council every swine that "shall bee found within the meadowes without a ringe or a yoake . . . shall forfeit for every hogge found twelve pence"[40]

For thirteen years Thomas raised his family and participated in community life and affairs as a single parent, quite unusual for the day. However, in 1655 he met and married Bridget Loker Davis, widow of Robert Davis, who had been killed by the Indians the previous July. She had one daughter, Sarah, whom Thomas helped raise to adulthood.

As family and community life continued to develop in this small and fragile community, the friendship between the Rice and King families moved to a new level as marriages began to occur, not once but three times between three Rice sons and three King daughters. The first was Thomas and Mary in about 1651, followed by Samuel and Elizabeth on November 8, 1655, and Joseph and Mercy on May 4, 1658. Edmund and Thomas were now sharing children as well as grandchildren. However, the full extent of the welding of these two families has yet to be fully played out.

Marlborough Community

For a dozen years after the founding of Sudbury, a certain degree of community harmony prevailed and was enjoyed. The town book contains few records of quarrels, refusals to pay taxes, or misdemeanors compared to neighboring communities, a testament to the quality of the people and their leadership. But history records over and over again the difficulty of established leadership to make needed adjustments. Generational changes and expectations are many times hard for older people to understand. Pride and arrogance of age and rank can also play a major attitudinal role, and often the stronger the establishment the greater the rupture and societal division.

40　Sudbury Town Document #163.

At first it was the size of the meetinghouse. The elders wanted to avoid the expense of a larger building to accommodate a growing population by putting galleries in the old church. The younger people disagreed as they would be the ones shoved up near the thatched roof. Then there were the established land policies that were limiting the new generation from acquiring land. By now there were six large open fields demanding the strength and cooperation of the younger people but without giving them the benefit of ownership. This may have been the accepted and traditional system in England, but as the younger and new people saw the opportunity of land ownership in the colony, it wasn't good enough. They wanted a change. In addition, several of the people who were enjoying the freedom of land ownership were starting to feel crowded — an ironic twist as Sudbury's population was probably fewer than three hundred fifty people. As feared by many Puritan leaders, the economic spirt of self-interest was rapidly spreading to Sudbury.

Edmund appears to have been a shrewd politician at first as he abstained from any heated debates and voting, yet with five sons acquiring families he knew something had to be done. Both he and Thomas King eventually used their influence to leave Sudbury. They became two of thirteen men who petitioned the General Court for a new plantation eight miles further west. Included with Edmund and Thomas in signing this petition were two of Edmund's sons, Henry and Edward.

> God hath beene pleased to increase our children, which are now divers of them grown to man's estate, and wee, many of us, grown into years, so as that wee should bee glad to seee them settled before the Lord take us away from hence, as also God, having given us some considerable cattle, so that wee are so streightened that wee cannot so comfortably subsist as could bee desired; and some of us haveing taken some pains to view the country: we have found a place which lyeth westward, about eight miles from Sudbury, which wee conceive might bee comfortable for our subsistence.[41]

Edmund was serving in the General Court at the time and with his influence a new community was approved on May 14, 1656. This would be a significant move for both Edmund and Thomas. Edmund was now sixty-two years old and Thomas was only five years his junior. They would be leaving comfortable homes, established farms, and many friends. Again land would have to be cleared and again they were pushing farther into the western wilderness. But again the dogged determination that brought them to this country in the first place would see them through any new challenges.

---

41   "Colonial Records of Marlborough, Massachusetts," 3, ttp://freepages.history.rootsweb.com/~historyofmarlborough/contents.htm#CONTENTS.

The settlement was first known by the Indian name of Whipsuffenicke. The land grant was for a little over six miles square or 29,419 acres and in September of the same year, the first town meeting was held with Thomas being appointed one of four people to put the affairs of the new Plantation in order. To facilitate the settlement, lands were divided among the proprietors based on wealth, ability to improve the land, and participation in the founding of the community. In the first division for housing lots Edmund was one of three who received fifty upland acres and Thomas received thirty-nine and one half upland acres, the next highest level. The home of Edmund was located where the Marlborough City Hall now stands. In subsequent divisions of land Edmund received sixty-two and one half acres of upland, a little over forty-five acres, of meadow and twenty-five acres of swamp. Thomas received a total of forty-nine acres of upland, thirty-six acres of meadow, and not quite twenty acres of swamp. The value of upland and meadow lands is apparent, but the value of swamp land could be questionable. Again, Edmund appears to be one of the largest land holders in Marlborough with Thomas in the second tier.

At the outset, there appeared to be a problem with people signing up, but not moving to Whipsuffenicke as first planned. In the meantime, the new town was incurring operational expenses. In December 1659, the selectmen took action by ordering "that all such as lay clayme to any interest in the new Plantion at Whipsuppenicke are to perfect their house lots by the 25th of March next ensuing, or else loose all their interest in the aforesaid Plantation." It was also ordered that anyone with a lot in Whipsuffenicke was to pay twenty shillings to the town by March 25, 1660 or they would "loose all theire Interest in the ffores Plantation."[42]

As the town grew during the next four years, it was incorporated on June 12, 1660, and renamed Marlborough, after its namesake in Wiltshire, England. At the first town meeting, Edmund and Thomas were elected two of the seven selectmen and became busy helping this fledgling frontier community. In the words of one historian:

> Before the duties of town officers were clearly defined, the Townsmen, or Selectmen, exercised a great variety of powers. Any thing and every thing, not expressly provided for, fell by custom at least, within their jurisdiction; and when any perplexing question arose in town meeting, almost as a matter of course, it was handed over to the Selectmen without instructions, as though they were the fountain of power, if not of wisdom. The practical effect was, that in the choice of those officers, the people were more particular than they are at this day, when the powers of town officers are more limited and better defined. To be selectman in those days – to be regarded as one the "fathers of

---

42   "Colonial Records of Marlborough, Massachusetts," 9.

the town," and a depositary of almost unlimited power – was considered no small honor.[43]

Specifically, the selectmen busied themselves with land allocation and ordinances were passed attending to the affairs of the town. Cattle should be provided with a keeper and every man should have his fences properly made up and finished; no person was to put any flax or hemp into any pond or brook where cattle drink, and any violation of these provisions resulted in fines. Public work projects were also incorporated with roads for public travel "with a width of four rods" (66 feet). They also provided for a road to Sudbury and contracted for a bridge over the Sudbury River for "horse and man and laden carts to pass over at all times."[44]

As evidence of the closeness of church and state, a tax was also imposed in May 1661, of three pence half penny per acre upon house lots and the same per pound upon cattle for the support of the ministry, including the construction of a manse.

Both Edmund and Thomas were elected to five successive terms as town selectmen and served from 1660 to 1664. Thomas was also reelected again in March 1665 for a sixth term.[45] However Edmund died in office when he passed away on May 3, 1663[46] at the age of sixty-nine. The forty-five-year-old Mercy was again left a widow with two small children, Lydia, age six, and Ruth only four. Mercy married for the third time a year and a half later in October 1664 to William Hunt.

The death of Edmund was a shock to both family and community. By colonial standards, he had provided well for his family and had been instrumental in founding and shaping the destiny of two communities. His influence had reached as far as helping to settle the affairs of the Massachusetts colony.

After the funeral and the paying of respects by family and friends, Edmund was transported back to Sudbury where he was buried in the old Sudbury burying ground next to Thomasine. No doubt the trip was an arduous one as people would have to ride horses or walk, carrying the casket for eight miles.

---

43   Charles Hudson, *History of the Town of Marlborough* (T.R. Marvin & Son, Boston, 1862), 279.

44   "Colonial Records of Marlborough, Massachusetts," 16.

45   Ibid.,3-31.

46   There is some confusion as to Edmund's death year. All ERA records give the year as 1663, but "Marlborough Colonial Records," p. 28, and estate documents identify "Edmond Rice" as being elected a selectman March 6, 1663/4. This would put Edmund's election ten months after his death. The problem may be in the conversion of dates from the old double dating system used until 1752.

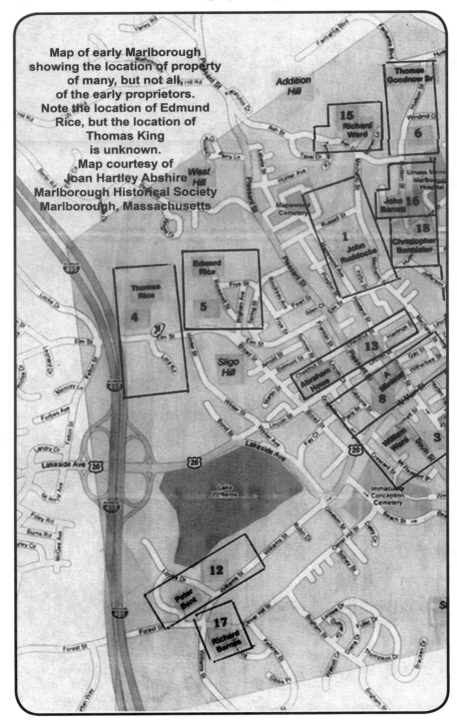

Map of early Marlborough showing the location of property of many, but not all, of the early proprietors. Note the location of Edmund Rice, but the location of Thomas King is unknown. Map courtesy of Joan Hartley Abshire Marlborough Historical Society Marlborough, Massachusetts

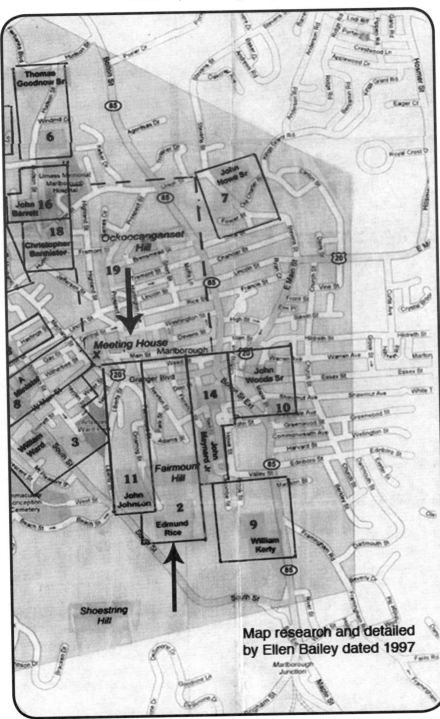

Map research and detailed by Ellen Bailey dated 1997

The Edmund Rice grave marker in the old burying ground, Sudbury (Wayland), Massachusetts. The site was marked by this monument and dedicated by the Edmund Rice Association August 29, 1914; however, the exact site of his grave in this cemetery is unknown.

Edmund died intestate (without a will) which suggests that his death might have been somewhat sudden and unexpected. Shortly after his death, Thomas was one of four appointed to inventory the estate. It appears that a fairly quick settlement was made of the first distribution of property with each of ten living children receiving from £10 to £40; however, the final settlement languished for another fifty-three years until March 1716. Due process of law was no quicker then than it is today.

From the inventory taken of Edmund's estate, it again appears that Edmund did well economically.[47] Besides his extensive land holdings, a mark of wealth in English society, his home in Marlborough was every bit as nice as the one in Sudbury with two parlors and a hall. It also appears that before his death he had started to provide for his children by conveying to them part of his assets.

He still possessed four oxen, a horse, mare and a colt. His oxen were the preferred beast of burden over horses due to their strength, consistency,

47   The amount of Edmund's estate was £566.00.07 (see Appendix 1). Family historians have tried to convert this to current dollars. For example Michael A. Rice writing in the *Edmund Rice (1638) Association Newsletter,* (Fall 2007, no. 4, 81:19) estimates the value at $2.33 million. This calculation is based on the amount of land Edmund had, compared to the price of silver, and then making adjustments between the British pound and the U.S. dollar, plus using the Consumer Price Index; but a person must be careful in using such a comparison. The standard of how people judged wealth in the middle sixteen hundreds is much difference than today; and as the value of the estate is based on land, the old cliche "land rich, but dirt poor" may have some application.

and docility. Horses were a means of transportation but were easily spooked, could break a plow by their quick movement, and would more quickly wear out physically.

For food and dairy products, he possessed a bull, eight cows, six calves, and three heifers, four yearlings and several swine. His house was well furnished; but missing from his estate are such items as chickens, a spinning wheel, a loom, and a wagon or carriage. Perhaps milk was traded for eggs and cloth, and the roadways had not yet developed within his lifetime to require a wagon or carriage.

In the inventory were also listed books at £1. This would not be an extensive holding, but might be a ledger book, a Bible, and other reading material — again, a sign of some literary accomplishment.

Edmund's greatest asset was his family, a devoted wife and daughter responsible for the internal affairs of the home and seven healthy sons to assume the responsibility of the external affairs of the family economy. No doubt this was one of the reasons he could devote so much time to political and church pursuits and still prosper financially.

FOLLOWING EDMUND'S DEATH, a hidden hostile undercurrent began to erupt into the open. Whether the passing of Edmund had anything to do with the surfacing of this antagonism is hard to tell; but after their father's death, Edward, Thomas (Mary King), Samuel (Elizabeth King), and Joseph (Mercy King) Rice all moved to Marlborough. Many people had received an allotment of land and there was considerable trouble over paying the 20 shilling assessment mentioned earlier. No doubt as selectmen, both Edmund and Thomas King had been responsible for the eviction of some people from their land, and there were differing opinions about how and to what degree the regulations should be administered. Among strong-minded people there is always some conflict; and Edmund, Thomas, and their associates were no weaklings.

Included in this dissension was Thomas Rice, Edmund's son. Apparently Thomas had refused to pay his assessment and legal action was started against him by the town of Marlborough in the county court at Cambridge. The court ruled in favor of the city, and Thomas was directed to pay £3 for the delinquent claim. The court further advised all the other citizens of Marlborough in the same predicament to pay their assessments and "that they all Joyntly concurre in such waies as might lead to the furtherance of peace among themselves."

It appears that several in the community were not able to follow the court's advice, and apparently there was still a dispute over how the city was to compensate for property improvements in the event of foreclosure. A petition was made to the General Court which sent out a committee to inquire into the facts of the case. The committee recommended in 1663 that, in all such cases, the city should compensate property owners for all improvements on forfeited estates.

Rather than putting the matter to rest, another petition was filed with the General Court "to appoint a committee, with full power to hear and settle all their difficulties. They declared that their differences are such as to render them incapable of carrying on their affairs." Apparently, the disputes involved both church and state matters as the petitioners admitted that their troubles have "arisen partly from our own corruption, and the temptations of Satan, hindering their own good feelings in matters both civil and ecclesiastical, which have been and are very uncomfortable to them and their friends."[48]

This latest petition apparently was led by a group of seventeen prominent families such as the Wards, Ruddockes, and Goodnows against a coalition of eighteen led by the Kings and Rices who opposed the petition.[49] The contest this time had something to do with the "Town Book" and the recordings contained therein. Apparently the Kings and Rices wanted to make some changes that were opposed by the first group. There was also the charge that the Kings and Rices were "trying to root out the minister."

The nature of the ecclesiastical conflicts are unknown, only that the minister, a Mr. Brimsmead, was disheartened by the distracted state of affairs in his parish. He left for a couple of years and settled in Plymouth; but returned in October 1666. Evidently Mr. Brimsmead, though well respected, may have been part of the problem as his Puritan orthodoxy may have been somewhat extreme even for his parishioners. He never married, and it is reported that he uniformly refused to baptize children who were so "irreverent" as to be born on the Sabbath. This position was not unique among the Puritan clergy.

When Mr. Brimsmead left, the King/Rice coalition petitioned the Magistrates for a church to be organized in Marlborough. While Mr. Brimsmead had lived in the community and had a house provided at community expense, no formal church had been organized. The petition set forth:

> ... that their distance from the church at Sudbury, of which they were members, rendered it inconvenient to go there to enjoy church privileges; that there were several aged sisters residing in Marlborough, who were almost entirely deprived of the privileges of communion; and that there were others in town who would gladly unite with the church, if one were established in the place.[50]

---

48   Hudson, *History of the Town of Marlborough,* 46.

49   Ibid., 46.

50   Ibid., 49.

In answer to this request and upon the return of Mr. Brimsmead, the church was formed on October 3, 1666, and Mr. Brimsmead was ordained as pastor.

The committee's report back to the General Court dragged out for another seven and a half years until May 27, 1674. The committee reported that, after much deliberation,

> . . . the result of all which is now mostly contained in the New Town Book, which we have caused to be finished, wherein not only their fundamental orders and grants are recorded, but also the particular stating and bounding of all those lands that are already laid out to the several inhabitants there. This New Town Book, as it now stands under the hands of Mr. John Green, we have by our order publicly approved, enstamping upon it what authority is with us to convey, humbly representing to this honored Court.[51]

Again one would have to wonder if this wouldn't put matters to rest and end all strife; but as soon as the report was filed by the commission, one writer reported that "Thomas King, who appears to have been fond of the bitter waters of strife, together with other inhabitants of the town, preferred another petition, reflecting upon the Committee, and demanding another hearing."[52] The "other inhabitants" were probably the Rices.

The Court passed on the petition May 12, 1675; but due to the coming Indian troubles, findings were delayed for another four and a half years.

Thomas, now seventy-seven, was failing fast; and on January 12, 1676 he made out his will. He indicated that he was in poor health:

> It having pleased God to cast me, Thomas King, of Marlboro, upon the bed of sickness and being weak, yet in perfect understanding, considering that God and his providence and dispensation towards me at this time, calls for me to set my house in order, and to dispose of the estate that God in his mercy hath given me, to my beloved wife, children and relatives.[53]

Thomas died a few days later, but before January 24. Little else is known of his passing, and he is probably buried at the old churchyard in Wayland close to his wife, Anne, and his friend, Edmund Rice. Bridget passed away nine years later on March 11, 1685, in Marlborough.

From Thomas's will it is hard to determine the complete lifestyle of the King family. With assets of £383, and with a home and sixty acres of land in Marlborough listed at £200, he must have had a reasonably comfortable living, although his list of assets does not include items that

---

51   Ibid., 47.

52   Ibid., 48.

53   See Appendix 1.

would indicate an upscale lifestyle or trappings of any degree of affluence such as Edmund had. It does mention £12 of household goods not itemized and bequeathed to his three daughters. Outside of his real estate, he had four head of oxen, two horses, two mares, two saddles, pigs, and three cows.

Another key to Thomas's activities are the butchering tools he gave to his son Peter. Thomas must have spent part of his time as a butcher. Also, Thomas appears to have had some type of store in his home. Most estate inventories do not list commodity items, however, his inventory lists a large stack of hay in the barn, £12 of flax, four barrels of beef, £5 of yarn, twenty bushels of Indian corn, seven bushels of wheat, six bushels of rye, four bushels of barley, and bacon.

For his protection, he owned a fowling piece, musket, and sword. No books are listed.

King Philip's War

As the colonists continued to push westward, strong cultural differences and the proverbial land disputes with the Indians continued to mount. At first Massasoit, the chief of the Wampanoag Indians, had been a great friend of the Plymouth colonists, but his two sons Alexander and Philip did not share their father's friendly relationships. When Philip became chief in 1662, he began plotting against the colonists. He felt that Indian survival depended on driving the white men out of the country, and he secretly began to build alliances with many of the native tribes.

In June 1675 a series of brutal attacks began; and the community of Swansea, Massachusetts, sixty miles southeast of Marlborough, was the first to fall. Before the war was over a year later, more than a thousand colonists had been killed and twelve English communities were destroyed. Philip's wife and son were captured and sold into slavery, and Philip was killed in August 1676 in South Kingston, Rhode Island. It was a very costly struggle for both sides.

Marlborough was not without its fault in antagonizing the Native Americans. When the town was first proposed, the original plan called for the annexation of 6,000 acres of Indian land. The General Court wisely refused to convey this land to the settlers; however, the new church was built over the line on Indian land, and the natives were left to negotiate the best deal they could before conveying the land to the citizens of Marlborough.

As the animosity between the Indians and the whites grew, Marlborough was a high-risk community. At the direction of the General Court and with the support of the community, the citizens, including the Kings and the Rices, began in October 1675 to build garrisons and to fortify their community.   Thirty-seven militia soldiers with weapons and ammunition were added to their defense. The Indians of the area, friendly or not, were marched to Boston and interned in the harbor on Deer Island.   Here they suffered from cold and lack of food, but a few managed to escape and join Philip.

Of the eight garrison houses that were established, two were at Joseph and Thomas Rice's homes. For weeks these frightened people waited and watched and tried to carry on life the best they could, yet having to share their small and crowded homes with soldiers and military provisions. There was always a fear about venturing out very far for water and to care for fields and cattle.

King Philip, son of Chief Massasoit, made war on the New England settlers in 1675-76. Marlborough was one of several communities destroyed during the conflict. (Picture found on the Connecticut River Website, University of Massachusetts Amherst.)

After several weeks, Captain Samuel Brocklebank of Rowley, Massachusetts, who headed the militia unit in Marlborough, began to feel there wasn't much more he could do. Thinking that perhaps the threat of attack had been over-estimated, he ordered the soldiers to withdraw to their own communities, but this was just what the Indians were waiting for. Four days later, they attacked. On Sunday morning, March 26, 1676, the 225 people of the town were assembled in church. The pastor had just prayed for safety and protection and a hymn had been sung, when the cry went up, "the Indians are upon us." At once the people ran to the nearest designated shelter. While they could protect themselves, they could not save their property. The Indians, numbering about three hundred, made quick work of tearing down fences, burning homes and barns, including the church house, peeling and hacking fruit trees, and killing cattle.

After the raid and unable to inflict any further damage, the Indians retired to the woods and camped for the night. However, the citizens of Marlborough still had some fight in them; and under the direction of their garrison commander, a Lieutenant Jacobs, they counter-attacked in the middle of the night, killing or wounding about forty of the native warriors.

This attack on Marlborough essentially destroyed the town, and the survivors fled to neighboring and more established towns for safety. Most went to Sudbury, Concord, or Watertown. Many of the Rices moved back to Sudbury where they found shelter with extended family members.

Four weeks after the initial attack on Marlborough, the Indians determined to further punish the whites. Several hundred warriors again attacked Marlborough, adding to the destruction of the previous assault.

Three days later on April 20, 1676, they attacked the east side of Sudbury (Wayland). The following day, the battle extended out three miles from the center of town on the west side of the Sudbury River at a place called Green Hill. By setting fire to the woods, the Indians were able to rout the defenders, causing additional loss of life and property.

Although the war technically was over within a short fourteen months, the impact on the citizens lasted for years. Over 10 percent of the white adult males of the colony were killed,[54] and the trauma of the many homes and communities destroyed was without measure. The aftermath of the war also included the disruption of the economy and the draining of precious governmental coffers. Of course the clergy had a field day with guilt and God's displeasure with His chosen people. The ravages of the war were a consequence of their backsliding ways.

Unfortunately, this would not be the last encounter with Indians for the King/Rice family as hostile relations with the Native Americans was an issue for the next seven generations. The descendants of Edmund and Thomas, the ancestors of Thomas Rice King, were pioneers filled with a passion for freedom and adventure. No single individual in the family was born and died in the same locality. They were always pushing into new frontiers. They fought the Indians for the land, the natural elements for their food, primitive conditions to bring their families into the world, and the French and British for their freedom. They knew the privations of frontier life and the joys of success as they carved out new homes and farms in a wilderness filled with opportunity. While many participated in the social, political, and religious activities of their society, they were common people facing extraordinary challenges and a destiny to achieve an ideal for generations to follow.

---

54   Michael J. Puglisi, *Puritans Besieged: The Legacies of the King Philip's War in the Massachusetts Bay Colony* (New York: University Press of America, 1991), 59.

Samuel Rice

Samuel was only a small four-year-old when his family came from England, and Sudbury was the only home he really knew. Also, growing up in Sudbury was Elizabeth King, the daughter of Thomas King. Like Samuel, she was born in England and came to the colony as a youngster.

Very little can be said about their childhood except that they grew up as a new community grew with them. They experienced the hard work of farm and home and were trained in the Puritan faith.

Samuel was twenty-one years old and

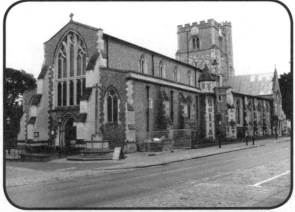

Samuel Rice was Christened November 12, 1634 in St. Peter's Church, Berkhampstead, Hertford, England.

Elizabeth twenty when the two were married. There is no record of Samuel owning property in Sudbury, but he probably worked and established his home on part of his father's estate. Three of his six children were born in Sudbury before he moved in 1664 with the Rice and King families to Marlborough. Here Samuel's name appears as one of the original inhabitants who received an allotment of twenty-six acres for a household lot, a little less than the average that others received. He also received in Marlborough additional land grants of nineteen and a half acres of meadow and thirteen acres of swamp land.[55]

From all appearances, Samuel did not actively participate in community affairs as had his father and some of his brothers; but he sided with the Kings and Rices in the previously mentioned controversy that embroiled

---

55   Colonial Records of Marlborough, Massachusetts, 33.

Samuel and
Elizabeth King Rice Family

Elizabeth Rice
- (B) 26 Oct 1656   Sudbury, Middlesex, Massachusetts
- (M) 2 Jan 1677   Sudbury, Middlesex, Massachusetts
  Peter Haynes
- (D) 22 Dec 1727   Sudbury, Middlesex, Massachusetts

Hannah Rice
- (B) 1658   Sudbury, Middlesex, Massachusetts
- (M) 15 Mar 1682   Concord, Middlesex, Massachusetts
  Jonathan Hubbard
- (D) 9 Apr 1747   Concord, Middlesex, Massachusetts

Joshua Rice
- (B) 19 Apr 1661   Marlborough, Middlesex, Massachusetts
- (M) Abt 1690   Sudbury, Middlesex, Massachusetts
  Mary Sawyer
- (D) 23 Jun 1734   Marlborough, Middlesex, Massachusetts

Edmund Rice
- (B) 1663   Sudbury, Middlesex, Massachusetts
- (M) 15 Nov 1692   Roxbury, Suffolk, Massachusetts
  Ruth Parker
- (M) 23 Jun 1720   Sudbury, Middlesex, Massachusetts
  Hannah Brewer
- (D) Sep 1726   Westboro, Middlesex, Massachusetts

Esther Rice
- (B) 18 Sep 1665   Marlborough, Middlesex, Massachusetts
- (M) 1 Nov 1683   Hadley, Hampshire, Massachusetts
  Daniel Hubbard
- (D) 11 Feb 1737   Hadley, Hampshire, Massachusetts

Samuel "King alias Rice"
- (B) 14 Oct 1667   Marlborough, Middlesex, Massachusetts
- (M) 30 Oct 1693   Milton, Norfolk, Massachusetts
  Abigail Clapp
- (M) Sep 1668   Sudbury, Middlesex, Massachusetts
  Mary Dix
- (M) 13 Dec 1676   Concord, Middlesex, Massachusetts
  Sarah White
- (D) 4 Mar 1713   Sudbury, Middlesex, Massachusetts

Samuel and
Mary Dix Rice Family

Mary Rice
- (B) 6 Aug 1669   Marlborough, Middlesex, Massachusetts
- (M) 15 Nov 1692   Marlborough, Middlesex, Massachusetts
  Benjamin Rice
- (D) 22 Oct 1736   Marlborough, Middlesex, Massachusetts

Edward Rice
- (B) 29 Jun 1672   Marlborough, Middlesex, Massachusetts
- (M) 25 May 1702   Sherborn, Middlesex, Massachusetts
  Lydia Fairbanks
- (D) 20 Jul 1741   Marlborough, Middlesex, Massachusetts

Abigail Rice
- (B) 10 Mar 1674   Marlborough, Middlesex, Massachusetts
- (D) Aft 1684

Samuel and
Sarah White Rice Family

Joseph Rice
  (B) 16 May 1678 Concord, Middlesex, Massachusetts
  (M) 25 Jun 1701 Boston, Suffolk, Massachusetts
  Mary Townsend

the community. He also joined with his father-in-law and brothers in petitioning for a new church in Marlborough. There is no record of his taking the Freeman's Oath or holding any public office.

In Marlborough three more children were born; the last was Samuel's namesake born on October 14, 1667. However, two weeks after the birth of this child, Elizabeth died. She was only thirty-two and left Samuel, Sr. with the challenge of trying to raise a two-week-old baby without a mother. As a result, the childless Peter King, brother of Elizabeth, and his wife, Sarah, took the child and adopted him as their own. His name was changed to "King alias Rice," and he became the sole heir to Peter's sizable estate.

Family records show Samuel taking Elizabeth back to Sudbury for burial in the Old Churchyard where both his father and mother were buried. Marlborough may have been their home, but it appears that Sudbury was still where the heart of the family resided.

A year after Elizabeth's death, Samuel married the widow Mary Dix Browne in Sudbury (Wayland) and moved back to Marlborough. Mary was born in Watertown, the daughter of Edward and Jane Wilkerson Dix, and Mary had married Abraham Browne in 1662. There were no children from her first marriage, but she and Samuel had three children of their own, all born in Marlborough: Mary, Edward, and Abigail. Sadly, however, Mary unexpectedly passed away on June 18, 1675, two years after the birth of Abigail leaving Samuel a widower a second time, now with eight children.

Samuel and his large family were all residing in Marlborough when the Indians attacked in March 1676. Like the rest of the citizens of the community, they fled for their lives that tragic Sunday morning. Following the attack and as the Marlborough citizens moved to safer communities, Samuel retired to Concord where he met and married on December 13, 1676, the thirty-three-year-old widow Sarah White Hosmer. Sarah was born April 9, 1643, at Salem, Massachusetts, the daughter of John and Joane West White. She had earlier married James Hosmer and it appears there were no children from this marriage. James was a member of the militia that was attacked by the Indians just outside of Sudbury and was killed when the Indians overran his position. Sarah and Samuel had one child, a son named Joseph.

Following the Indian hostilities, Samuel, Sarah and their family moved back to Marlborough to rebuild their destroyed home and farm. His physical losses must have been considerable. Eight years later, Samuel passed away at the age of fifty-one, leaving a large family and a two-time widow. His passing may have been somewhat expected. A brief will was made out on January 10, 1684, a year before his death, but it contained only a few short, cryptic statements.

Sarah later moved to Woodstock, Connecticut, where she died in 1711. It is not known for sure just where Samuel is buried, but with parents and Elizabeth all buried in Sudbury, chances are that Samuel was returned to Sudbury (Wayland) for interment.

Unfortunately this would not be the last of the Indian troubles for these families on the western frontier. There was always the fear of attack and a concern about just how far to venture from the safety of home or other people.

One such occurrence directly affected the family of Samuel and Elizabeth, although some time after their death. On August 8, 1704, tragedy struck the family of their son Edmund, and his wife Ruth.

The quarrels of France and England continually spilled over to the Americas, and in 1702, one of a long series of French and Indian wars broke out. Many of the Indian tribes sided with the French; and while Massachusetts was spared much of the fighting, Deerfield, a few miles northwest of Marlborough, was attacked and destroyed. Several times Indians on the war path attacked other outlying settlements killing unsuspecting men and carrying off sobbing and frightened women and children. Many of these prisoners were either taken to Canada and later ransomed, adopted into the various tribes, or simply killed.

Unaware of what was about to happen, Edmund and Ruth's children, Silas, age nine, Timothy, age seven, and five-year-old Nahor, were out in the fields with two of their cousins, Ashur and Adonijah Rice, when a group of eight to ten Indians sprang from the woods. They grabbed Silas, Timothy, Nahor, and the other two children and fled back into the dense forest. As they left, they smashed the head of little Nahor on a rock, immediately killing him. Regardless of pursuit by the men of the community, the Indians and their captives were not to be found.

It was several years before the worried Rice parents learned the fate of their children. A ransom was paid for Ashur, but it is not known why Silas, Timothy and Adonijah were not returned. Later they learned that the boys had been adopted into the tribe, eventually married Indian wives, and

The Rice Memorial in Westborough, Massachusetts on location where four Rice boys where captured by Indians August 8, 1704.

fathered native families. To Silas, the Indians gave him the name of Too-kanowras, and Timothy was called Oughtzorongoughton. Timothy rose within the tribe and became the third of six chiefs of the Cognawaga tribe. In that capacity, he addressed Colonel (later General), John Burgoyne who was employed in an expedition against Canada in the French war of 1755.

The Indians had trained Timothy to be a tribe spokesman with the English. His fair skin and knowledge of the white man's ways were not lost on the British. In his encounter with Burgoyne, he was pleading for the safety of his adopted people who wanted to remain neutral in the coming hostility.

Later in September 1740 Timothy visited Westborough (Marlborough) and, with the help of an interpreter, viewed the place of his capture and met many people whom he still recognized. He still had a clear remembrance of the circumstances in which he was taken, but nothing could induce him to stay. He had lost his native tongue, and the lifestyle he had become accustomed to for thirty-six years had stronger emotional ties than the few tender years as a white boy. He returned to Canada where it was reported that he and his brother Silas were still living in the summer of 1790.

An interesting follow-up note to this saga comes from the Edmund Rice Association. In the last few years, they have been conducting DNA tests with the Mohawk tribe in Canada and have discovered a link of several members with the Rice family. The association is now working with tribal members to reconstruct an accurate pedigree.

Peter King

Of all the Rice and King parents and siblings of this period, Peter stands out as perhaps the person with the most financial and political success. He must have been an astute businessman and farmer. His estate at his death was over £17, 221. This compares to other King and Rice family members as follows:[56]

Edmund Rice	£566
Thomas King	£383
Samuel Rice	£349
Peter King	£17, 221
Samuel King alias Rice	£720
Ezra King	£950

In reviewing several estates of this time period, it appears that a person with an estate of £500 to £600 was fairly well off and above average. Less than £300 was at a subsistence level and over £1,000 would be considered fairly well-to-do. Beyond this broad generalization, it is difficult to compare their standard of living one to another.

The smaller estate of Samuel Rice was no doubt influenced by the loss of home, buildings, fences, and cattle during the war in 1676. The interesting part of an estate inventory during this time period is the detail — right down to each pot & pan and items of clothing. Nothing was left out.

The size of Peter's family may have also played a part in his financial and political successes. He and his wife Sarah were able to have only one child, Thomas, who was born and died in 1662. Their only living heir was their adopted son, Samuel.

From these circumstances originated the families of Kings that for two generations signed their name "King alias Rice" after which the "alias Rice" was dropped and the family name of King continued. Had it not been for the adoption of Samuel Rice, Jr. by his uncle, the family name of King, descendants of Thomas King, would have become extinct upon the death of Peter. He died childless and was the only son of Thomas who lived to manhood.

Peter was born in Dorset, England, and came to America with his family in

---

56   See Appendix 1 for a listing of known estates and inventories.

his early teens. He and Sarah were married about 1650. Sarah is somewhat of a mystery person as no record can be found of her parentage or even her last name, let alone her birth or death dates. She just seems to have appeared and then disappeared. Some have speculated that she was another daughter of Edmund Rice, but there is no evidence except for a statement in Samuel Rice's will that he gave his son Samuel "to my brother and sister King for their own." There also was no provision in Edmund's estate for a daughter, Sarah.

As an energetic young man, Peter's enterprising skills became evident early in life. At the age of only twenty-four, he and a friend, Thomas Plympton, contracted with the community to build a new meetinghouse. It was to be forty feet long and twenty feet wide, and they were to be paid in corn, wheat, butter, cattle and money. Three years later they contracted to build the seats in the meeting house at a rate of one shilling and eight pence per seat, payable in wheat and rye. Coincidentally, Peter would buy the building back for £6 thirty-six years later.

Peter acquired 160 acres in Sudbury in the two-mile, west-side grant in 1658 (see map p. 35), but settled on the east side of the river near a place that is still called "King's Pond." He also participated in the founding of Marlborough and received there grants of twenty-two acres and fifty-eight acres. But apparently by April 1665, his Marlborough holdings had been sold or in some manner passed to a Nathan Johnson, and his participation in Marlborough affairs essentially ended.

As the clouds of war began to appear in Sudbury, Peter was one of thirteen petitioners asking the General Court for a militia of twenty men be sent to assist in their defense and to act as scouts in the "woods and about our towne." Following King Philip's War in 1676, a modest gift of money was made by "diverse christians in Ireland, for the relief of such as are impoverished, destitute, and in necessity by the last Indian Wars" sent by the good ship called *Katherine of Dublin*. In the list of losses, Peter puts his losses at £40, considerably less than the claims of other citizens which ranged as high as £180 to £200, but more than the £10 to £15 others sustained.[57]

Peter's industrious and active style not only brought him financial rewards, but he went on to achieve some prominence in the community. He took the Freeman's Oath and began to serve in committee assignments for the town of Sudbury, including such menial tasks as repairing and maintaining the local animal pound, acting as town surveyor, and mending and repairing roads and fences. Later he was called on to help lay out the highway through the new grants within the town boundaries.

---

57   Hudson, *The History of Sudbury, Massachusetts*, 255-257.

In January 1664 he was elected as a town selectman. He was re-elected to this position nine times in an eighteen-year period.[58] He also served as constable in 1665 and 1666.

As the need for lumber was always evident in a growing community, Peter and four other men were authorized in March 1677 to build a saw mill and they were authorized "twenty tons of timber of the Common and for the building thereof & earth for their Damme, & also they are to make a small damme or sufficient causye so as to keep the water out of the swamp lands there."[59]

The financial abilities of Peter were also recognized by the community. Over the course of the years he helped collect the taxes and assessments due the city and he helped raise money for Harvard College. He was elected town treasurer in March 1700 and served for two years.

His support and closeness to the church was also evident in his life. When the pastor of their church became too sick to function, Peter was part of a committee in 1678 to ensure "that the town be supplied with able preachers."[60] Another document called for the committee to "provide an able orthodox preacher, to prech in this Towne during the Pastors weaknesse,"[61] and the records show that Peter was compensated 5 shillings a week by the community for providing temporary lodging for the replacement minister.

As his stature increased, by 1682 the records of Sudbury began to refer to him as "Goodman Peter King,"[62] and in November 1685 he became one of six "tythingmen" for the town. In this capacity he was responsible for the collection of the tithing (tax) for the support of the church. He served in this capacity for three terms.

Peter went on to become the deacon of the church by 1697, at the age of seventy. As such and in his role as selectman, he would play a part in ensuring that the children of the community "are in a forward and growing way as to reading & catechizing, & as to work & employment."[63]

In 1688 and again in 1700, Peter's political career reached its zenith when he was appointed to the General Court in Boston to represent Sudbury. During his term of office in May 1689, he was called upon to represent his community during the Massachusetts Bay Colony's fight

---

58   The actual years Peter was elected are 1670, 1672, 1676, 1680, 1682 1685, 1687, and 1688. See Sudbury, Massachusetts website.

59   Sudbury Town Document #396.

60   Ibid., #399.

61   Ibid., #403, 404.

62   Ibid., #436.

63   Ibid., #425.

with England over the colony's charter. In the ongoing political battle with the Puritans, the crown had revoked the royal charter in 1684, and in 1686, a new royal governor, Sir Edmund Andros, was appointed. His arbitrary acts, including imprisonment without trial and oppressive taxation, inflamed the people. When the people were informed that they might not have good title

> ## The Tythingmen Oath
>
> *Whereas you are chosen a Tythingmen within the Town of_____ for one year untill others bee chosen & sworn in your roome & stead, you doe heer swear by the living God that you will dilligently endoavor & to the utmost of yoar ability perform & intend the duty of your place according to the particulars specified in the laws perculiar to the office, so help you God.*

to their property, there was open rebellion and the taking up of arms. Peter was one of the delegates who voted not to push the matter any further and to appeal to England for redress. Several years later in 1692, when the colony agreed to submit to the king's directives, a new charter was issued.

It is interesting that in all of Peter's activities, his name does not appear on any of the petitions involving the community squabbling that embroiled other members of the King and Rice families in Marlborough.

Peter died August 27, 1704, at the approximate age of seventy-seven. His will is a testament to his love and loyalty for his church and family. "I resign my spirit unto my dear Lord and Savior Jesus Christ, and my body to be decently buried." To his pastor, James Sherman he bequeathed "forty shillings as [a] gift of my love to him."

To his "well and beloved" adopted son, Samuel, he conveyed the whole of his estate with provisions that "my dearly beloved wife Sarah King . . . be carefully, comfortable and constantly with all tenderness, helped, relieved and supplied during her life." He also provided for his "beloved kinsman Thomas Rice" and for the children of his three sisters.[64]

Unfortunately, no further information is available on Peter and Sarah, but no doubt both are buried in the old cemetery in Sudbury (Wayland).

Samuel King Alias Rice

As previously noted, Samuel was raised by his adopted parents, his uncle Peter and wife Sarah, and as such was Peter's sole heir to a very wealthy estate. He was born October 14, 1667, in Marlborough and, as a young boy, experienced the Indian uprising and the forced evacuation of Marlborough in 1676.

---

64   See Appendix 1.

Although mostly raised in Marlborough, when married he moved to and sired his family in Sudbury. At the age of twenty-six, he met and married Abigail Clapp, who had been raised in Milton, just a short ten miles south of Boston. Her parents were Ezra and Abigail Pond Clapp and it was her grandfather, Edward Clapp, who had emigrated to New England in 1633 from Devonshire, England.

Samuel and Abigail were married in Milton October 30, 1693 before moving to Sudbury. While it is not known what conditions took Samuel to Milton to meet and marry Abigail, in the next twenty years they had eight children.[65]

Soon after his marriage and settling into family life, Samuel begin to follow his adopted father's footsteps by becoming active in the community. In March 1694 at age twenty-seven, he was elected constable for the east side of the river and, again in May 1698, and for a third term in November 1698. He was a surveyor in 1698, and the following year in March, he was elected a town selectman. He held this same post again in 1700, 1703, 1705, 1707, and 1709.

Besides his political career, Samuel pursued an interest in military affairs. By May 1698, he was a sergeant in the militia and by 1707 was an officer with the rank of ensign. In 1710 he was known as lieutenant Samuel King and probably responsible to a captain who commanded the local militia.

Given his involvement with the militia, Samuel would have been very much responsible for the over-all defense of the community during the period of the French and Indian wars. Indians were still very troublesome; and in neighboring Marlborough in August 1704, his nephews Silas and Timothy were abducted and Nahor was killed. Later in July 1707, there were further attacks on Marlborough in which several people were injured or killed.

Samuel also participated in his community by serving on several town committees — one to "prosecute those who have or shall trespass in falling of wood or timber in our undivided lands," and others involved in settling town conflicts.

One issue the town soon faced was the natural division of the community by the Sudbury River. By 1707 the growth on the west side of the river had substantially enlarged the community and there were sentiments to divide the town. A formal petition for such action was soon drawn up

---

65   In the Ancestral File, Peter King is listed as the second son born in 1701. Again, this is wrong as he was the eldest son born in 1695. Another daughter is purported to have married a Moses Rice. Again, it is an erroneous connection. Moses Rice married a Sarah King, but she was the daughter of a Thomas King and Elizabeth Clapp, who are a different King family. See further notes on the family in Appendix 1 under Samuel King.

Samuel and Abigail Clapp
King alias Rice Family

Ezra King
- (B) 22 May 1697 Sudbury, Middlesex, Massachusetts
- (M) Abt 1719 Worcester, Worcester, Massachusetts
  Silence Rice
- (D) 14 Jan 1746 Cape Breton, Nova Scotia, Canada

Sarah King
- (B) Abt 1699 Sudbury, Middlesex, Massachusetts

Peter King
- (B) 24 Mar 1701 Sudbury, Middlesex, Massachusetts
- (M) 15 Feb 1720 Weston, Middlesex, Massachusetts
  Elizabeth Flagg
- (M) 25 Mar 1723 Sudbury, Middlesex, Massachusetts
  Elizabeth Graves
- (D) 9 Apr 1739 Sudbury, Middlesex, Massachusetts

Samuel King
- (B) 24 Mar 1701 Sudbury, Middlesex, Massachusetts
- (M) 29 Feb 1728 Springfield, Hampden, Massachusetts
  Abigail Hitchcock
- (D) 11 Aug 1774 Monson Hampden, Massachusetts

Thomas King
- (B) 25 Mar 1703 Sudbury, Middlesex, Massachusetts
- (M) 4 Aug 1726 Brimfield, Hampden, Massachusetts
  Lydia Moulton
- (D) 3 Aug 1738 Brimfield, Hampden, Massachusetts

Edward King
- (B) 4 Aug 1705 Sudbury, Middlesex, Massachusetts
- (M) 26 Apr 1733 Cumberland Center, Cumberland, Maine
  Mary Scales

Elizabeth King
- (B) 29 Apr 1707 Sudbury, Middlesex, Massachusetts
- (M) 22 Oct 1723 Stow, Middlesex, Massachusetts
  Amos Brown

Mindwell King
- (B) 16 May 1709 Sudbury, Middlesex, Massachusetts
- (D) 19 Feb 1730

Abigail King
- (B) 1713 Sudbury, Middlesex, Massachusetts
- (D) 17 Feb 1730 Sudbury, Middlesex, Massachusetts

and presented to the General Court. Samuel was one of several east-side inhabitants who opposed the proceedings, arguing that the community could financially ill afford such a move. It would not only create increased administrative costs but also increase the cost of defense and the support of two ministers. In his opposition, he was a member of the committee that successfully argued the case before the General Court.

Whether any of these many activities had a bearing on his health is not known, but Samuel died unexpectedly at the early age of forty-five on March 4, 1713. His untimely death left the thirty-seven-year-old Abigail with eight minor children Again, circumstances are not known; but four months after the death of Samuel, Abigail passed away on July 6, 1713.

Due to the premature death of both parents, one can only speculate that they perhaps contracted some contagious illness such as smallpox. Certainly these deaths were a tragic and substantial loss for the family.

To care for the children, John Rice was appointed guardian of Ezra and the other children. John was a cousin to Samuel and had also married Abigail's sister, Elizabeth — another family intermarriage.

Samuel died intestate (without a will) and it is interesting to note the amount of his estate at his death. His inventory at death was £720, a respectable amount, and one that would provide for a comfortable living for his family, but far short of the amount he had inherited from his adopted-father.

Samuel also left considerable indebtedness, £125 to thirty-three creditors, and it took over five years for the administrators to finally settle all the affairs.[66] There is no information about how Samuel incurred this indebtedness except for one note for £40 to a gunsmith in Charlestown. This may have been tied to his military service except that the inventory of assets make no mention of firearms.

Another interesting item in his estate is his "library of books." Besides the normal emphasis placed on reading and writing by the Puritan culture, Samuel must have been a man of some literacy.

Ezra King

Ezra King, the eldest son of Samuel and Abigail, was born in May 1697 and named after his grandfather, Ezra Clapp. He was only in his sixteenth year when his father and mother died and until he reached legal age he lived with his cousin and aunt.

When he became of age he again pushed the family into uncharted territory by moving twenty-eight miles farther west to Worcester, Massachusetts. This move was perhaps influenced by several Rice cousins who were some of the first settlers of the region and later a younger brother, Peter, who also moved to Worcester.

At the age of twenty-two, Ezra married his second cousin, Silence Rice, the daughter of Jonas Rice, who had been the first pioneer of Worcester in October 1713. This was the third attempt to settle this area; and thanks in large part to the efforts of the Rice family, the community finally took hold. Jonas and his family were the only inhabitants for about eighteen months. After about five years, the population had reached between 200 and 300 people with fifty-eight homes, including four garrison houses for the common defense of the settlement.

---

66   See notes in Appendix 1 under Samuel King.

As a young family just starting out, Ezra and Silence cleared the timber and built their home from what they could obtain from the land. However, soon after their marriage, Ezra begin to assist in petitioning for and forming a new community another twenty-eight miles southwest of Worcester. Based on the births of their children, it appears that they moved to Brimfield in about 1730. Their first four children were born in Worcester between 1720 and 1728. The birth of a fifth child went unrecorded, and the rest of their thirteen children were born in Brimfield starting in July 1731.

In the creation of the Brimfield community, Ezra and his two brothers, Samuel and Thomas, played key roles. Ezra received a couple of sizeable land grants, one for 120 acres and another for twenty acres. In 1732 a stream of water on Elboe Brook was added for the construction of the first grist mill. It is interesting to note that wheat was never raised to any extent in Massachusetts and rye was the grain of choice. Women made all their breads and pastries out of rye flour. The economical house-keeper would use rye meal in making her pie crusts and then layer the upper part of the crust with wheat flour, or as the saying goes, the "upper crust."

Following the Rice and King family tradition, Ezra was active in community affairs and was voted in as one of the first five selectmen of the community in March 1731. He was reelected for an additional five years to 1737.

The first church in Brimfield, the First Congregational Church, was built in about 1721. However, many of the early records were destroyed by fire in 1748 and church membership information is lacking. It can only be surmised that Ezra and Silence were active in church affairs due to his leadership roles in community and military affairs.

As war clouds again hung over the colony, Ezra and his oldest son Jonas volunteered to participate in the "Third French War," one of a long series of wars between the French and British for control of the New World. The French had become a threat to the New England colonies, principally Massachusetts. Fishing had been interrupted and many merchant ships had been attacked and destroyed. At the urging of Governor William Shirley of Massachusetts, a 4,000-man militia force assembled from Massachusetts, Connecticut, Rhode Island, and New Hampshire. Their objective was the capture of Cape Breton and the adjoining town of Louisbourg, Nova Scotia, a strong fortress guarding the sea approach to the St. Lawrence River. It was considered the Gibraltar of North America.

It would be interesting to understand why Ezra joined this military venture? He was forty-eight-years-old and had small children. Was he going out of a sense of patriotism, did he have aspirations of a war bounty or land grants, or was it to look after his son Jonas who had also joined

The Kings of the Kingdom

Ezra and
Silence Rice King Family

Abigail King
- (B) 23 Oct 1720   Worcester, Worcester, Massachusetts
- (M) 11 Jun 1741   Brimfield, Hampden, Massachusetts
  Joseph Hitchcock
- (D) 10 Jul 1743   Brimfield, Hampden, Massachusetts

Jonas King
- (B) 13 Oct 1722   Worcester, Worcester, Massachusetts
- (M)   Brimfield, Hampden, Massachusetts
  Mary
- (D) 12 Feb 1746   Cape Breton, Nova Scotia, Canada

William King
- (B) 24 Oct 1724   Worcester, Worcester, Massachusetts
- (M) Abt 1756   Maine
  Elizabeth Cushing
- (D) 8 Nov 1793   Brattleboro, Windham, Vermont

Mary King
- (B) 9 Jul 1726   Worcester, Worcester, Massachusetts
- (M) 30 May 1751   Littleton, Middlesex, Massachusetts
  Charles Baker
- (D) 8 May 1803   Littleton, Worcester, Massachusetts

Ezra King
- (B) 3 May 1728   Worcester, Worcester, Massachusetts
- (M) 1753   Worcester, Worcester, Massachusetts
  Prudence

Silence King
- (B) Abt 1730   Prob. Brimfield, Hampden, Massachusetts
- (M) 21 Nov 1751   Worcester, Worcester, Massachusetts
  John Bond, Jr.
- (D) Dec 25, 1812 Conway, Franklin, Massachusetts

Experence King
- (B) 27 Jul 1731   Brimfield, Hampden, Massachusetts
- (D) 20 Nov 1731   Brimfield, Hampden, Massachusetts

Elizabeth King
- (B) 16 Nov 1732   Brimfield, Hampden, Massachusetts
- (M) 27 Mar 1750   Worcester, Middlesex, Massachusetts
  Cyrus Rice
- (D) Bef 1767

Adonijah King
- (B) 18 Jul 1734   Brimfield, Hampden, Massachusetts
- (D) 14 Oct 1753   Worcester, Worcester, Massachusetts

Bulah King
- (B) 23 Sep 1735   Brimfield, Hampden, Massachusetts
- (M) 8 Jan 1760   Petersham, Worcester, Massachusetts
  James Pierce

Nehemiah King
- (B) 27 Jul 1737   Brimfield, Hampden, Massachusetts
- (D) 30 Jul 1738   Brimfield, Hampden, Massachusetts

Eunice King
- (B) Abt 1739   Brimfield, Hampden, Massachusetts
- (M) Abt 1760   Brimfield, Hampden, Massachusetts
  John Barrett

Mindwell King
- (B) Abt 1741   Brimfield, Hampden, Massachusetts
- (D) Aft 1764

Ezra King died at Cape Breton in January 1746 while serving as part of the militia force sent to fight in the "Third French War."

the cause? Furthermore, he left knowing he was going into battle, but for some reason he did not take the precaution of first making out a will.

The military force sailed from Boston in a fleet of 110 ships, including ten ships-of-war. Ezra served as a sergeant in Captain William William's 2nd Company, 8th Regiment, and Jonas was a private in the same company which lay siege to the fort April 30, 1745. When the fort fell to the New Englanders and their British allies in June, there was much jubilation in the colonies. Besides the usual "praise be to God," the nationalistic self-esteem of the colonists soared. A group of rag-tag militia had gone up against the French regulars and had won the day.

They had won the battle, but the real war was yet to be fought. The colonial militia had suffered only a few casualties in taking the fort; but for the soldiers, the victory proved fleeting. Winter was soon upon them and they were poorly clothed with limited rations, and sickness and disease running rampant. Louisbourg at best was a town of narrow streets and the interruption of ordinary life during the siege had left an accumulation of filth of staggering proportions in the town.

Besides these deplorable conditions, there was no booty or prize money for the victors. They longed for their families, and with the intense boredom, came alcoholism and a spirit of mutiny. To silence the discontent among the troops, Governor Shirley made a quick visit to Louisbourg and assured the garrison that supplies and reinforcements were on the way. However, by spring, the effects of these deplorable conditions were measured by the number of dead soldiers. Over 1,200 men perished,[67] nearly 50 percent of the militia. Included in this count were both Ezra and Jonas — Ezra on January 14, 1746, at age 48, and Jonas a month later. They were noble but waisted deaths for in the peace treaty that followed, England gave Cape Breton back to the French.

Three years following her husband's death, and with children under the age of eighteen, Silence married a widower John Bond, Sr., who was also the father-in-law of her daughter, Silence – two Silence Kings and two John Bonds. She is believed to have died in Worcester or Brimfield.

At his death, Ezra had amassed a fairly respectable estate of over £1,000. His biggest holdings were in property. He owned 354 acres and also had one yoke of oxen, a horse, three cows, three heifers, swine, eight sheep, and twenty-three goats plus farming implements and household items.[68]

From the estate documents, it is interesting to see how the family divided up the real property. As they sliced and diced it, no one would have anything of value unless one sibling bought out another. Silence was even awarded a third of the barn "and liberty to come to Barn." One can only imagine that, as brothers or sisters wanted to move on with their life, they would have to abandon their interest, hoping that someone would come along and buy their dissected piece of property. The more efficient way of selling the entire parcel and paying each sibling in cash, as it is done today, was not available at the time. Money was scarce and it was hard to liquidate real property.

The time required to settle estates would also be an issue. Within the six and a half years to settle the estate, animals would have lived, reproduced and died, equipment would have worn out, and fences and outbuildings would have fallen into disrepair. Though technically fair, it was not a very efficient way of dealing with scarce resources.

---

67   G. A. Rawlyk, *Yankees at Louisbourg* (Orono, Maine: University of Main Studies No. 85, University of Maine Press, 1967), 157.

68   See Appendix 1.

The Great Awakening

During the latter part of the seventeenth century, social, religious, and political attitudes began to change irreversibly within the colonies. Historians call this remarkable shift the "Great Awakening."

Specifically the power and influence of the Puritan movement began to dramatically decline in Massachusetts as the influx of outsiders and commercialism further diluted the Puritan position. Attitudes and allegiance to former political and religious institutions soon changed, and cultural and social classes began to break down as new generations followed. As many of the older institutions began to give way to the new, the impact of this movement was felt by the King family, particularly the William King family and for the next two generations.

With the dawn of the eighteenth century, a new wave of zealousness and enlightenment invoked a political and religious belief system that all men (except slaves and Indians) were equal under God. The culmination of this new attitude caused a small unorganized and ill-prepared group of people to declare their political independence and to militarily take on England, the super-power of the day.

William King

The chronicle of William King appears to be a history of contrast with many records clouded and incomplete. For four generations, the Rices and Kings exhibited themselves as high-profile and strong-willed community and church leaders. In contrast, William appears to be more reserved; and while the circumstances of the day required a certain degree of tenacity and self-determination, there are no records of William assuming any leadership roles in community or church affairs, or even holding membership in a church. Vital records to reconstruct the formation of his family are scarce or non-existent, and a certain obscurity followed him throughout his life. Whenever the Rices or Kings moved to a new locality, there seemed to be a degree of support from other family members and friends. William's move northeasterly from the Massachusetts frontier society to the coast of Maine appears to be by himself and out of context. The few exceptions were a younger brother, Ezra who went to Wiscussett, Maine, a few miles from Meduncook and his Uncle Edward who settled in Cumberland, Maine.

William was twenty-two years old when his father died and for the next eight years, his life is absent from the records. He may have stayed in Brimfield for a time or moved to one of the centers of population like Boston or Plymouth. In any event by February 1754 at the age of thirty,

William is discovered in a small village called Meduncook, Maine (now called Friendship).[69]

Meduncook was founded by General Samuel Waldo in the early 1730s and located on the southeast coast of Maine at the outlet of the St. George River. He had secured a patent on a large tract of land and used various and ingenious if not questionable methods to promote the sale of land. His come-on was an offering of 100 acres of free land. "Land is extraordinary good and lyes upon a pritty little River." Further, Waldo claimed "a number of families [had already] settled . . . and [he soon anticipated having] a thousand families on the spot." He even offered transportation by boat from Plymouth to Meduncook.[70]

By 1750 the first settlers began to arrive, many from Scotland, and by 1754 there was a small community of twenty-two families. Included in this number was William[71] who purchased an additional sixty-one acres worth £35. Other settlers at this time included several members of the Cushing family. Perhaps the most notable was Captain Ignatius Cushing and family, including a daughter, Elizabeth,[72] and a son Zattu, and cousins Joshua Cushing, both senior and junior. The neighboring community of Cushing was named after Thomas Cushing, a prominent Massachusetts political leader and later lieutenant-governor of Massachusetts. It is said that Ignatius "was a man of peculiar habits and manner, not unconnected with stubbornness. He derived his title of Captain from the mastery and owner-

---

69   Hampden County, Massachusetts Property Records, deed dated February 7, 1754 and recorded May 28, 1761.

70   Records of the Lower St. Georges and Cushing, Maine 1605-1897, Transcribed and Edited by Ruth J. Aiken, (Cushing, Maine: Driftwood Farm, 1987), 174.

71   *A List of the Settlers in St. George's River, Meduncook and Broadbay*, "The New England Historical and Genealogical Register" 46: 1892, 120.

72   The parentage of Elizabeth has long been in dispute by family members. For example, many King family records and the Ancestral File identify Elizabeth Cushing as the daughter of Caleb Cushing (b. Salisbury, Massachusetts, 1703). However, there are many problems with this connection including that Caleb Cushing had two daughters, both named Elizabeth who both died at a young age. Other family members have concluded that Elizabeth is the daughter of Ebenezer Cushing (b. Boston, Massachusetts, 1710) and wife Elizabeth Daniels. This argument is primarily from the George O. King family in Corry, Pennsylvania. (See letter from Mary Porritt of St. George, Utah, September 17, 1995 in my possession.) If this is correct, this Elizabeth would have been only fifteen years old when she and William married. Ebenezer also had another daughter by the name of Elizabeth who was born in July 1733. She fits the correct profile but died before 1741. Besides these issues there are other problems with this connection. Short of a definitive record to the contrary, I believe that Elizabeth is the daughter of Ignatius Cushing (1689). She is the only Elizabeth not accounted for in James Cushing's work, (See Cushing footnote #76 below, page 69), she fits the profile, and she and her family can be placed in Maine at the time of William's presence.

Garrison Island off the coast of Meduncook, Maine. It was here that the early settlers built their blockhouse fortifications for protection against the Indians. Access by foot was available only at low tide.

ship of a small boat, said not to sail in any way except before the wind, which was a sport in which the captain was pleased to indulge."[73]

The harsh reality of Meduncook soon became apparent as Waldo had over-sold the primitive and inhospitable environment of the rocky and foggy coastline. The soil was not conducive to farming, and only meager crops could be raised in the short growing season cut off by long terrible winters. Subsistence was primarily gained from potatoes, wild game, and fish.

The Indians were also troublesome, so a small blockhouse fort was constructed. As an early settler at Meduncook, William would have helped build and maintain the fortification located on a small, but strategically situated twelve-acre island. Known as Garrison Island, it was connected to the mainland at low tide by a bar of sand and rocks.

The Indians again were closely allied with the French, and in 1755, the fourth in a series of wars between the English and French broke out. The threat to the several villages up and down the Maine coastline was substantial, and the vulnerability of Meduncook became obvious by an attack in May 1758 in which a Bradford family was caught outside the fort and killed. Furthermore, in September 1758, several members of the community were captured by the Indians and held for ransom including Zattu Cushing.

---

73 Melville Bradford Cook, *Records of Meduncook Plantation and Friendship, Maine 1762-1899* (Shore Village Historical Society, Rockland, Maine, 1985), 7.

William and
Elizabeth Cushing King Family

Adonijah King
  (B)   18 Feb 1757   Near Scarborough, York, Maine
  (M)   Abt 1782   Guilford, Windham, Vermont
        Diadema Marsh
  (M)   1 Jun 1786   Royalston, Worcester, Massachusetts
        Rachel Bliss
  (D)   25 Jul 1825   Hatch Hollow, Erie, Pennsylvania
Elizabeth King
  (B)   19 Mar 1759   Near Scarborough, York, Maine
  (M)   Samuel Marsh
William King
  (B)   29 Jan 1762   Brattleboro, Windham, Vermont
  (M)   Abt 1787
        Lydia Goodell
  (D)   19 Dec 1844   South Newfane, Windham, Vermont
Ezra King
  (B)   29 Jan 1762   Brattleboro, Windham, Vermont
  (D)   12 Nov 1812
Cushing King
  (B)   18 Feb 1764   Brattleboro, Windham, Vermont
  (M)   Abt 1789
        Chloe Warriner
  (D)   19 Nov 1843   Edinburg, Saratoga, New York
Polly Lucy King
  (B)   5 May 1767   Brattleboro, Windham, Vermont
  (M)   Abt 1791
        Joseph Goodell
  (D)   17 Mar 1856
Thomas King
  (B)   20 Oct 1769   Brattleboro, Windham, Vermont
  (D)   1770   Brattleboro, Windham, Vermont
Thomas King
  (B)   16 Oct 1770   Brattleboro, Windham, Vermont
  (M)   13 Jan 1795   Prob Pittstown, Rensselaer, New York
        Ruth Hyde
  (M)   28 Jun 1839   Brattleboro, Windham, Vermont
        Elizabeth Warriner
  (D)   31 Jul 1845   Montrose, Lee, Iowa
Ruth King
  (B)   2 Dec 1775   Brattleboro, Windham, Vermont
  (M)   William Reed

Whether due to the unfavorable conditions or the outbreak of war, By 1756, William appears to have moved seventy miles south to the Portland area. His move may have been in haste or discouragement, for in 1765 a judgment was rendered against him for £26.13.04 for nonpayment on his abandoned Meduncook property.[74]

Also fleeing to Portland was the Cushing family. Ignatius took all his

---

74   Lincoln County, Maine Indexed Deeds, vol. 1 (1761-1784) 4:94.

family, except Zattu, to live on Long Island.[75] Ignatius's brother Ezekiel was a substantial and prosperous business, political, and military leader in Falmouth and Portland. He also owned a fleet of "schooners and sloops" as well as all of Long and Cushing Islands.[76]

William and Elizabeth were married in 1756. No marriage record has been found to identify whether they were married before or after the move, only that their first child, Adonijah, was born February 18, 1757, "near Scarborough,"[77] a small community a short distance south of Portland. Daughter Elizabeth was born two years later in March 1759.

Soon after the births of these first two children, the King family pulled up stakes and made a significant 165 mile move west to a promising development in southern Vermont. At the conclusion of the war in 1760, the Indians were no longer a threat in Vermont and the new town of Brattleboro located on the Connecticut River in Windham County was laid out. Again land patents had been obtained by a few speculators and they were selling the land to all comers. The soil was fertile, but Brattleboro was a densely forested area, and the land had to be cleared. The first roads were hardly more than footpaths until they could be enlarged for ox sled or cart. Life was hard; but as homes were built and farms laid out, a community spirit developed.

It should also be noted that this seemed to be the end of free land grants to help settle a new community as had been known for four generations. It was now necessary for William to purchase his farm. In addition, Vermont was considered part of New Hampshire but claimed by New York. In 1777 it declared itself an independent republic and until 1791 called itself New Connecticut when it was brought into the Union as the fourteenth state.

The early land records are incomplete, but to begin with, it appears that William may have rented farm land to support his young family. The records of Brattleboro speak of him on property known as the "Rufus Clark place" or "on property where [the] Lorenzo Thayer's farm is."

---

75   Will of Ezekiel Cushing located at the Maine Historical Society, Portland, Maine. A copy is in my possession.

76   James S. Cushing, *The Genealogy of the Cushing Family* (Montreal: The Perrault Printing Company, 1905), 38-41.

77   Sons of the American Revolution membership application for John Hollis King, born Corry, Pennsylvania, July 30, 1880, a descendant of Adonijah King. See also Norman Thomas King Newton, "The Forebears of George Oscar King (1842-1917)," an unpublished manuscript at the New England Historic and Genealogical Society Library, Boston, Massachusetts, 19. Other family records give the place of birth as Meduncook, but this is highly unlikely. From all appearances, William and Elizabeth were married in the Portland, Maine area.

Fort Ticonderoga, New York, where the Continental Army with William King and his two sons, William, Jr. and Ezra, temporarily held back the British in June 1777 during the Revolutionary War.

The first recorded purchase of property was in October 1772 when he bought fifty acres for 40 shillings. He later added another fifty acres. His farm was located where the Austine School for the Deaf is now located on the border of Brattleboro and West Brattleboro.[78]

His circumstance for renting may have resulted from the economic loss at Meduncook. He was, however, able to sell additional inherited property in Brimfield which may have given him the resources to make his first purchase.

Within a few years the spirit of revolution and freedom also began to prevail throughout the colonies. William and four of his sons (Adonijah, William Jr., Ezra, and Cushing) all enlisted as privates in the Continental Army. A fifth son, Thomas, was too young to serve.[79]

William's first enlistment came on June 9, 1777. Both he and his six-teen-year-old twins, William, Jr. and Ezra, joined the third New Hamp-shire Continental Regiment at a time when the colonials were desperately trying to reinforce their garrison at Fort Ticonderoga in New York. British

78　　Norman Thomas King Newton, New York, New York, to Gertrude S. R. Thayer, Brattleboro, Vermont, January 4, 1930. See note at the bottom of letter believed to be in the handwriting of Mrs. Thayer found in the Newfane, Vermont Historical Society archives. A copy is in my possession.

79　　Volney King reports that his father, Thomas Rice King, had told him that "his father [Thomas] had served in the War." There are no records to support this claim and Thomas would have been only eleven by the war's end.

forces under command of General John Burgoyne were moving south out of Canada for the tactical advantage of cutting the colonies in half, and the Americans seriously needed to blunt his advance.

The New Hampshire regiments began moving into Ticonderoga the latter part of May 1777; however, on July 6, 1777, the colonists were forced to make a sudden retreat. Burgoyne surprised the garrison through a military maneuver, gaining control with his cannons of the hillside overlooking the fort. As William and the Continental army retreated south towards Saratoga, New York, Burgoyne pressed the attack. However, the Americans were able to turn the tide and in battles on Sep-

William King's cemetery marker located in the small Old Brattleboro Village Cemetery in West Brattleboro, Vermont, now over 210 years old. A Daughters of the American Revolution (DAR) marker also distinguishes the grave.

tember 19 and October 7, they forced Burgoyne to surrender. The Kings were unhurt through this engagement, and William was discharged on October 23.

The significance of this victory not only prevented the British from achieving their strategic advantage, but it brought France into the war allied with the desperate Americans.

William again joins the army on February 14, 1778 for an undetermined period of time. The two boys, William, Jr. and Ezra, spent the balance of a three-year enlistment, including an inhospitable winter at Valley Forge huddled in makeshift shelters and huts. The horrors of the six-month engagement are evident by the bold statistic that an estimated 2,500 men perished out of a force of 10,000. Many other struggles and battles were encountered by the King boys. Fortunately at the war's end, all returned safely home.

At the beginning of the war, William was getting along in years at age fifty-two and it appears that, after his first engagements at Ticonderoga and Saratoga, his involvement was for short periods of time.[80] The service records provide no further information.

During the course of the war, Adonijah was the first to join the ranks of the military in November 1776 for five months of service in Hull, Massachusetts, and Cushing was the last to join in January 1781 for six months' service with the Massachusetts 6th Regiment.

It is also interesting to note the physical descriptions of the King boys given in the military registers. Ezra, age eighteen (July 1, 1780), was five feet four inches tall with a light complexion. Cushing, age sixteen, (July 1, 1780), was four feet eleven inches tall with a light complexion.[81] If this is representative, the Rice and King families were fairly short people, and it wasn't until later generations that they became a much taller family.

William passed away at age sixty-nine, November 8, 1793, and is buried in the West Brattleboro Village Cemetery. Elizabeth continued to live for another twenty-four years, passing away at age eighty-four in 1817, probably in Brattleboro or Newfane. William died without a will; and there is no record of an inventory or probate, but with a hundred-acre farm, home, farm animals, and tools, he would have had a modest but respectable estate at his death.

Thomas King

Thomas, the youngest son of William, at maturity moved to Pittstown, Rensselaer, New York, just north of Albany in about 1794. Pittstown was a more established community of about 3,000 people. Here he met and married Ruth Hyde and eventually fathered eight children. The youngest was Thomas Rice King, who was born March 9, 1813.

The Hyde family had migrated from Connecticut to Vermont and then to New York. Ruth's father, Eliphalet, was also a Revolutionary War soldier, a Congregationalist, and one of the early settlers of Whittingham, Vermont, where he became the first town clerk before moving on to New York.

At the time of his marriage, Thomas was twenty-four and Ruth not quite eighteen. It is reported that Thomas and Ruth became Baptists in faith, and in politics, Thomas was first a Jeffersonian Democrat and later a

---

80   The *Vermont Historical Gazetteer*, 5:54, published in 1891, tells a story of William King's military service that is so full of exaggerations and errors that it is only mentioned here to warn against using it as a reference.

81   Mary R. Cabot, comp. ed., *Annals of Brattleboro, 1681-1695*, 2 vols., (Brattlebor, Vermont: E. L. Hildreth & Company, 1921) 1:154.

Thomas and Ruth Hyde King Family

Abigail King
- (B) 17 May 1796 Pittstown, Rensselaer, New York
- (D) 14 Dec 1817 Onondaga, Onondaga, New York

Zattie King
- (B) 17 Nov 1797 Pittstown, Rensselaer, New York
- (D) 6 Apr 1798 Pittstown, Rensselaer, New York

Zina King
- (B) 8 Feb 1799 Pittstown, Rensselaer, New York
- (D) 26 Nov 1820 Onondaga, Onondaga, New York

Volney King
- (B) 9 Nov 1800 Pittstown, Rensselaer, New York
- (M) 12 May 1822
  Salina Chapman
- (D) 19 Feb 1890 South Onondaga, Onondaga, New York

Timothy Hyde King
- (B) 22 Aug 1803 Pittstown, Rensselaer, New York
- (M) 15 Aug 1833 Cicero, Onondaga, New York
  Mary Fay
- (D) 13 Oct 1867 Fillmore, Millard, Utah

Naomi King
- (B) 24 May 1806 Marcellus, Onondaga, New York
- (M) 22 Oct 1823 Onondaga, Onondaga, New York
  Abner Leslie
- (D) Jun 1859 Grand Travis County, Michigan

Rufus King
- (B) 25 Sep 1808 Marcellus, Onondaga, New York
- (M) 5 Jan 1831 Lysander, Onondaga, New York
  Elizabeth Fidelia Parker
- (M) 18 Jun 1851 South Milford, LaGrange, Indiana
  Elizabeth Dodge
- (M) 11 Feb 1866 Unionville, Putnam, Missouri
  Margaret E. Wagoner
- (D) Aft 1870

Thomas Rice King
- (B) 9 Mar 1813 Marcellus, Onondaga, New York
- (M) 25 Dec 1831 Cicero, Onondaga, New York
  Matilda Robison
- (D) 3 Feb 1879 Kingston, Piute, Utah

Whig.[82] In modern terminology and in very general terms, he went from a more a progressive liberal to a more conservative position.

After the birth of five children, the King family moved from Pittstown to north central New York, in the Syracuse area, and settled in the small village of Marcellus. The first settlers had arrived just a few years earlier and the area was still heavily timbered with dense undergrowth, but the stage was set for considerable economic development. By 1825 the vision of an inland waterway between the great lakes and the Atlantic Ocean was

---

82   Carol Gates Sorensen, Tucson, Arizona, notes on Thomas King/Ruth Hyde sent to me, June 2006, but researched in June 1980. Her information is taken from an article on Volney King (brother of Thomas Rice King), Volney King Papers, Utah Historical Society, Salt Lake City, Utah.

completed in the form of the Erie Canal. The canal ran through Syracuse between Albany and Buffalo and was the first important waterway built in the United States. The economic impact was significant as manufactured goods could easily move West and raw materials could be discharged into the East. To the farmer, the canal introduced a period of relatively stable agrarian maturity, and for people like Thomas, it provided a greater opportunity to make a living. It is hard to tell just what Thomas may have done as there is no record of him owning land in Marcellus. Perhaps he may have been some kind of a hired hand or an itinerant farmer, however, it was here that his last three children were born.

Contemporary with the Thomas King family was the family of the Mormon Prophet Joseph Smith, who moved to Manchester just a short sixty miles to the west of Marcellus in 1811. Shortly after the move, Joseph had his "First Vision" in 1820 of God the Father and His Son, Jesus Christ. This landmark experience was followed by several angelic visitations which produced the Book of Mormon in 1829 and the organization in Fayette of The Church of Jesus Christ of Latter-day Saints (LDS) on April 6, 1830.

Word of agitation against the Mormons soon reached Marcellus, which was frequently visited by early missionaries. Marcellus and Manchester were also in the middle of what is called the "Burnt-Over District," a geographical area west of the Catskills and Adirondacks in New York. This area experienced a variety of social experiments and religious novelty unparalleled in American history during the quarter century following 1825. Spiritualism and religious revivals involving several religious movements, including the Presbyterians, Methodists, Baptists, and many of their offshoots, were frequent and intense. The breadth and width of this movement also included such issues as the anti-slavery, anti-masonry, and temperance crusades. Opponents to these social movements used the term the "Burnt-Over" to suggest spiritual exhaustion while advocates took it up to indicate the heavy concentration of piety, which, in their view, resulted from commendable religious enthusiasm.

Caught up in this movement were the Mormons and their church with Joseph Smith as prophet-leader. He was one of many claiming divine gifts, experiences, and purposes, but Joseph was unique in that he brought forth a new book of scripture and a claim to priesthood authority. Other scripture followed; and with these divine gifts, persecution stalked the Mormons wherever they went.

Thomas will perhaps be best known for accepting the Mormon missionaries and joining the LDS Church. He was baptized in 1838 in Marcellus. Ruth, his wife, had just passed away, and he and three of his five living children, Timothy Hyde, Rufus, and Thomas Rice, over the course of two years joined the Church.

Ruth died on March 20, 1838 in Palermo after forty-three years of marriage and the births of eight children. Thomas then married the twice-widowed sixty-two-year-old Elizabeth Warriner. Elizabeth and Thomas had grown up together in Brattleboro, and her father held many important positions in the community: justice of the peace, moderator of a town meeting (1778), coroner (1778-80), and deacon in the Congregational Church.

After Thomas left to go to New York, Elizabeth had married David White and, following his death she married Samuel Keep who died in 1825 in Brattleboro. It was another fourteen years before Thomas went back to Brattleboro and married Elizabeth on June 28, 1839. It is interesting that, after all the years that had gone by, Thomas went all the way back to Vermont to get Elizabeth. One can only speculate as to what may have transpired over the years. Could there have been periodic trips back to the homestead, a special relationship between the King and Warriner families, or perhaps a teenage relationship between Thomas and Elizabeth that never materialized?

It also appears that Elizabeth may not have had a happy experience with her marriage to Keep. In November 1813, she and her family received a "warning out" from the town of Brattleboro. Again five years later Samuel Keep received a "Warning" from Castleton, Vermont. It cannot be said categorically that a warning-out was due to the recipient's undesirable social or economic status in the community, but a pretty good indication. At this time many communities were sensitive to people who might become chargeable to the town (on public welfare) and were anxious to avoid the responsibility by asking people to move on.

Little is known of Elizabeth's children as the records are silent except to say that she had two: Sophronia White by her first husband (b. about 1801) and William Keep (b. about 1812) by her second. Elizabeth also helped raise the four living children of Samuel Keep by his first two marriages.

Elizabeth also joined the LDS Church; and following her conversion she and Thomas moved to Montrose, Iowa, just across the Mississippi River from the Mormon settlement of Nauvoo, Illinois. Here the seventy-four-year-old Thomas died on July 31, 1845, prior to the Mormon exodus in the spring of 1846.

Elizabeth, now alone for the third time, faced the daunting task of moving west as an elderly lady of sixty-nine. Assisted by family members, she moved to Winter Quarters (Omaha), Nebraska where she and so many others died the following year. She is buried in a simple grave among the hundreds of graves that stand as a tribute to the sacrifice and destiny of an unshakable faith in their new-found religion.

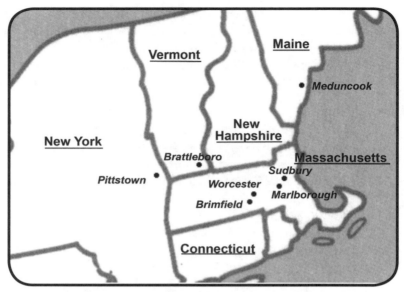

The King Family moved from Sudbury, Marlborough, Worcester, and Brimfield, Massachusetts, to Meduncook, Maine; Brattleboro, Vermont; and then to Pittstown, New York, in the space of six generations.

A Mayflower Connection

Most families are excited to find connections to people of prominence or distinction and rumors of such a nexus abound in many family circles. The King family is no exception as family tradition for years has supported the idea of a link to one of the *Mayflower* notables. The problem many times in making such a connection is going through the maternal rather than the paternal lines. In earlier years, the families of many of the wives were not as well known as those of the husbands; and as a result, the connections through the women should be looked upon with a certain degree of skepticism and a higher probability of error.

The rumored King family relationship with the *Mayflower* is just such an example, and is presented here only as a matter of interest and not a proven fact by what some might call "hard evidence." While the first six generations (page 79) are accepted by the *Society of Mayflower Descendants* in Plymouth, Massachusetts,[83] there are still questions that can be raised as to the authenticity of some of the connections. Any discussion of the matter should be given with such a disclaimer.

The purported King connection to Francis Cooke is through Ruth

---

83   Ralph V. Wood, Jr., *Francis Cooke of the Mayflower: The First Five Generations* (Rockport, Maine: Picton Press, 1996), pp. 1, 26, 29, 35, 72, 73, 102, 103, 249, 250.

**A modern replica of the Francis Cooke home in
Plimouth, Massachusetts.**

Hyde King, the daughter of Eliphalet and Abigail Washburn Hyde.

Francis and his son John embarked on the ship *Speedwell* at Delf-shaven, Holland, in July 1620, leaving behind Francis's wife Hester and the other children. At Southampton or Plymouth, England, they transferred to the *Mayflower* and set sail on Wednesday, September 16, 1620 to America with 102 passengers.

Cooke was one of the signers of the *Mayflower* Compact on November 21, 1620, and he and John received a parcel of ground in "Plimouth" for their first home and a garden plot. Unlike many of their fellow travelers, they survived the first terrible winter when sickness or death took a heavy toll on the small population. Hester and the rest of the family finally arrived on the ship *Anne* and joined them two and a half years later in August 1623.

Of the seven children of Francis and Hester, Jane was the oldest and was probably born in Leyden, Holland, in about 1604. Jane was married to Experience Mitchell in Plymouth soon after May 22, 1627. No verifiable vital records have been found for Jane, but some researchers think that she died in the mid-1630s. Jane and Experience had three children. The oldest was a daughter, Elizabeth.

Elizabeth was born about 1629 and died between November 1, 1681, and December 5, 1684. She married John Washburn in Plymouth on December 6, 1645. It is here that the family trail starts to have underbrush and be littered with boulders. The evidence that this Elizabeth is the daughter of Jane Cook is circumstantial, and historians have found only a

Mayflower II

veiled reference that Elizabeth is the granddaughter of Francis.

From Elizabeth and John Washburn the trail clears up for a while before getting cluttered again. They were blessed with eleven children, seven sons and four daughters. The second son, Thomas, was born about 1649, probably in Bridgewater and died there before December 4, 1732, the date his will was proved. Thomas married the first of three wives, Deliverance Packard, before October 29 1684. From this marriage, it appears that seven children were born, one being Timothy about 1694.

Timothy married Hannah (surname not known) about 1700. While no birth record is available, Timothy is mentioned in his father's will, and while there are no probate records for Timothy, various Plymouth County deeds describe him as "husbandman," "yeoman," and "tanner."

From here the trail again starts to grow a little cold, but still possible. Timothy and Hannah appear to have had nine children. The oldest, Timothy, Jr., was born October 26, 1721 in Bridgewater, Massachusetts; and baptized as a young man in Bolton, Connecticut, September 29, 1734.[84]

Timothy, Jr. married Kezia Guild, the daughter of Israel and Sarah Guild.[85] Kezia was born May 26, 1719, in Lebanon, Connecticut.[86] The records report eight children, four sons and three daughters including Abigail, the oldest, born August 2, 1747.[87]

---

84   *Vital Records of Bridgewater, Massachusetts to the year 1850,* Vol. 1 - Births, p. 336. *Bolton Congregational Church, Baptisms, Admissions to Membership & Marriages 1725 to 1763* (Hartford, Connecticut State Library, 1923), p. 235.

85   Walter Kingsley (Town Clerk), *Index to Marriages Lebanon, Connecticut 1671-1635, Females 1671-1875*, Hartford Connecticut State Library, 1946.

86   *The Barbour Collection of Connecticut Town Vital Records,* Lebanon, Vol. 1 & 2, 1700-1854, Compiled by Nancy E. Schott, Lorraine Cook White, General Editor, n.p.: Genealogical Publishing Co., Inc. p. 94.

87   The birth of their children occurred in three separate communities: Hebron, Coventry and Lebanon.

A Purported King Family
Connection to the Mayflower

(1) Francis Cooke
- (B) Aft 1582   England
- (M) 30 Jun 1603   Leiden, Zuid-Holland, Netherlands
-        Hester Mahieu
- (D) 7 Apr 1663   Plymouth, Plymouth, Massachusetts

(2) Jane Cooke
- (B) Abt 1604   Leiden, Zuid-Holland, Netherlands
- (M) Aft 22 May 1627   Plymouth, Plymouth, Massachusetts
-        Experience Mitchell
- (D) Aft 1630   Plymouth, Plymouth, Massachusetts

(3) Elizabeth Mitchell
- (B) Abt 1629
- (M) 6 Dec 1645   Duxbury, Plymouth, Massachusetts
-        John Washburn
- (D) 5 Dec 1684   Bridgewater, Plymouth, Massachusetts

(4) Thomas Washburn
- (B) Abt 1649   Bridgewater, Plymouth, Massachusetts
- (M) Bef 29 Oct 1684
-        Deliverance Packard

(5) Timothy Washburn
- (B) Abt 1694   Bridgewater, Plymouth, Massachusetts
- (M) Abt 1720   Bridgewater, Plymouth, Massachusetts
-        Hannah
- (D) Aft 11 Jun 1729

(6) Timothy Washburn
- (B) 26 Oct 1721   Bridgewater, Plymouth, Massachusetts
- (M) Abt 1746   Lebanon, New London, Connecticut
-        Kazia Guild

(7) Abigail Washburn
- (B) 2 Aug 1747   Hebron, Tolland, Connecticut
- (M) Abt 1774   Lebanon, New London, Connecticut
-        Eliphalet Hyde
- (D) Bef 1816   Pittstown, Rensselaer, New York

(8) Ruth Hyde
- (B) 12 May 1777   Whitingham, Windham, Vermont
- (M) 13 Jan 1795   Prob Pittstown, Rensselaer, New York
-        Thomas King
- (D) 20 Mar 1838   Palermo, Oswego, New York

Thomas Rice King,
1813-79
(Courtesy Territorial Statehouse
Fillmore, Utah)

At this point the trail really becomes cluttered as there is no specific record that positively identifies this Abigail Washburn, the daughter of Timothy, as the same Abigail that married Eliphalet Hyde. Land and vital records put the Washburns and the Hydes in the same community at approximately the same time and Abigail is three years younger than Eliphalet, but the marriage record of Eliphalet and Abigail simply states they were married.[88]

It should also be noted that this was a second marriage for Eliphalet. He had married Naomi Flynt May 20, 1766,[89]

The Barbour Collection of Connecticut Town Vital Records, Lebanon, Vol. 3, 1700-1854, Compiled by Nancy E. Schott, Lorraine Cook White, General Editor, n.p.: Genealogical Publishing Co., Inc. p. 215.

The Barbour Collection of Connecticut Town Vital Records, Hebron 1708-1854, Compiled by Dorothy Wear, Lorraine Cook White, General Editor, n.p.: Genealogical Publishing Co., Inc. p. 269.

Barbour Collection, Connecticut Vital Records to 1850, Compiled by Lucius A. Barbour and Lucius B. Barbour, (Connecticut State Library), W - Was, LDS Church Family History Library film #2,960.

88   Walter Kingsley (Town Clerk), *Index to Marriages, Lebanon, Connecticut 1671-1835* (Hartford, Connecticut State Library, 1946), Females 1671-1875, LDS Church Family History Library film #4,727.   There is some disagreement within the family over the correct Abigail Washburn.   For many years it was believed that Abigail (born July 7, 1745) was the daughter of Solomon Washburn and Martha Orcutt of Stafford, Connecticut.   This error has been perpetuated by the Ancestral File at the LDS Church Family History Library and temple sealing records. However, the records of Stafford identify a marriage on August 25, 1768 for Abigail Washburn and Eleazer Walbridge; and Stafford is thirty miles north of Lebanon.   (*The Barbour Collection of Connecticut Town Vital Records,* Stafford 1719-1850, Compiled by Jan Tilton, Lorraine Cook White, General Editor, n.p.: Genealogical Publishing Co., Inc. p. 157.   See also the findings of Brenton P and Robin P. Washburne, *The Washburne Family in America,* Vol. 1, Second Edition (n.p. 1997).   A copy can be found in the Family History Library, Salt Lake City, Utah.

89   *The Barbour Collection of Connecticut Town Vital Records,* Lebanon, 115.

and had one son, Abel, before she died on March 21, 1768.[90]

As a result, let the reader be somewhat careful with this information. From all accounts it appears to be accurate, but in a few spots the records can be disputed.

Thomas Rice King

Thomas, like his forefathers, was a tenacious, hardworking individual with a farming background. At the early age of eighteen, he married his sweetheart, twenty-year-old Matilda Robison, on Christmas Day, 1831. Matilda was the daughter of Joseph Robison and Cornelia Guinal. For at least four generations, the Robison family had lived in Montgomery County, New

**Matilda Robison,
1811-94
(Courtesy Territorial Statehouse
Fillmore, Utah)**

York. Matilda's grandfather, Lieutenant James Albert Guinal, had been killed in August 1777 at the Battle of Oriskany during the Revolutionary War.

The marriage of Thomas Rice and Matilda took place in Cicero, a small community ten miles outside of Syracuse, where the Thomas King family had moved prior to 1830. Thomas and Matilds's first child, William Rice King, was born in April 1834.[91]

Cicero was a fledgling and successful community, but located more in a large swampy district. Nevertheless, just prior to his marriage, Thomas and his brother Rufus purchased a fifty acre parcel from their older brother Timothy for $1,100 in July 1830. Here they lived for the next five years until Thomas and Matilda moved to Onondaga. He purchased another seventy-two acres for $1,800 and commenced raising wheat, potatoes, and fruit, the crops of the area. While they were here, their second child,

---

90   Ibid., p. 114, 116.

91   See Appendix 2 for a complete and detailed listing of the family of Thomas Rice King.

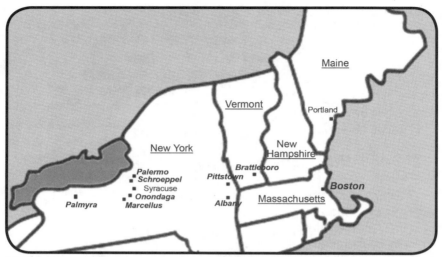

After their marriage, Thomas Rice and Matilda Robison King moved several times within the Syracuse area of New York. Cicero (twice), Onondaga, Palermo (twice), and Schroeppel were all called home.

Culbert, was born January 31, 1836.[92]

They sold their acreage the following July for a $366 profit and moved back to Cicero. Thomas also sold his interest in the partnership with his brother for what appears to be a $200 profit. In Cicero he went into partnership with forty-seven other men to purchase three-fourths of an acre. Such a small tract must have been a business property for retail or manufacturing purposes rather than agricultural land. However, Thomas's good fortune did not last long. In 1837 a severe country-wide economic recession occurred, known as the Panic of 1837. It was caused by unreasonable land speculation and excessive public and private debt (the usual reasons for most economic downturns). During this time Thomas must have lost most of what he had, for when he moved to Nauvoo he reported that he had only a few dishes and blankets and had made the move with a borrowed wagon.

Following the recession, his life now seemed to turn more into the life of a vagabond and his home was in rented quarters. By September 1837 he was living in Palermo, where John Robison was born. Two years later Thomas and Matilda were in Schroeppel, where Thomas Edwin was born, and by 1840 they were back in Palermo, where they joined the LDS

---

92   There are many historical references in LDS Church, and family documents that point to Culbert's birth in either Oswego, Onondaga, or Otisco, New York. The fact is that his parents owned land in Onondaga, and when they sold the land a year later, the deed indicates that Thomas Rice was "of Onondaga." This is a good indication they were living there at the time of Culbert's birth.

Church. This defining moment would change the entire course of their lives and the lives of future generations. It would also take Thomas and Matilda over two thousand miles from the place of their birth.

The Generations of Kings from Edmund Rice and Thomas King to Thomas Rice King

Edmund Rice
1594 - 1663
Thomasine Frost
1600 - 1654
|
Samuel Rice
1634 - 1685
Elizabeth King
1635 - 1667
|

Thomas King
1599-1676
Anne Collins
1608 - 1642
|
Peter King
1627 - 1704
Sarah
|

Samuel King alias Rice
1667 - 1713
Abigail Clapp
1676 - 1713
|
Ezra King
1697 - 1746
Silence Rice
1703 - 1763
|
William King
1724 - 1793
Elizabeth Cushing
1733 - 1817
|
Thomas King
1770 - 1845
Ruth Hyde
1777 - 1838
|
Thomas Rice King
1813 - 1879
Matilda Robison
1811 - 1894

Deuteronomy

(Gospel Acceptance)

L ittle did Thomas know the day he was baptized into the Church of Jesus Christ of Latter-day Saints how significantly his life would change. His Church membership dramatically affected his remaining thirty-nine years. He would thrice be uprooted from his home and asked to move under the most adverse conditions. He would experience persecution, privation, and the deaths of loved ones on the trail. He would be called to return to the land of his forefathers to preach his newfound faith, and he would also become the father of a large and noted posterity and a respected religious and community leader. He would learn to deal with aspects of a hostile environment ranging from a barren desert and voracious grasshoppers to vexing Indians.

Thomas was baptized July 19, 1840, in Palermo, Oswego, New York, however, some family records have Matilda being baptized eight days earlier.

CHRONOLOGICAL EVENTS

Jul 19,	1840	Thomas and Matilda are baptized members of the LDS Church.
Oct 4,	1840	Thomas ordained a priest.
Jun 6,	1841	Thomas & family leave Palermo, New York for Nauvoo.
Jul 10,	1841	Delilah Cornelia King born.
Aug 2,	1841	Thomas & family arrive in Nauvoo and settle outside of Montrose, Iowa.
Mar	1842	Move to Zarahemla, Iowa.
	1842	Matilda joins the LDS Relief Society.
Aug	1842	Thomas helps Joseph Smith and Porter Rockwell escape from their enemies.
Sep	1842	Thomas ordained an elder.
Sep 12,	1842	Thomas leaves Nauvoo for a short-term mission to Michigan.
Feb 20,	1842	Thomas returns to Nauvoo.
Mar 9,	1843	Thomas ordained a Seventy.
Summer	1843	Sickness in the King home followed by miraculous recovery.
Summer	1843	Matilda performs baptisms for the dead.
Jan 2,	1846	Thomas becomes a member of the Nauvoo Masonic Lodge.
Mar 25,	1845	Matilda Emily King born.
Jul 13,	1845	Thomas King, father of Thomas Rice, dies in Montrose, Iowa.
Jan 5,	1846	Thomas appointed one of seven presidents of his seventies quorum.
Jan 12,	1846	Thomas and Matilda go through the Nauvoo Temple and receive their endowments.
Jan 27,	1846	Thomas and Matilda sealed in the Nauvoo Temple.

Thomas was one of three brothers (Timothy, Rufus, and Thomas) who joined the Church, and Matilda was one of six brothers and sisters (William, Joseph, Matilda, Delilah, Peter, and Margaret) who became converts. Two years earlier, Thomas Rice's father, Thomas, had been baptized, and no doubt these families influenced and supported each other in making the transition to this new religious experience.

To these new converts the spiritual testimony of their religious convictions brightly burned in their searching hearts. They had been introduced to an expansionary gospel of ideas filled with biblical antiquity and theological innovations. Prophets, apostles, divine revelation, new scripture, and a holy priesthood were now commonplace having been previously lost to Christianity through an ancient apostasy. Joseph Smith was revered as a prophet, like unto Moses whose pronouncements were considered lawfully binding on man from God. The Book of Mormon, a sacred record of ancient America, was now a companion volume of scripture to the biblical record and a second testimony of the divinity of Jesus Christ. Priesthood ordinances such as baptism could be performed by divine authority and have the approval of heaven.

For these obscure people it was an exciting and glorious period of time. This restoration of gospel truth was the final phase in the preparation of apocalyptic events. The awaited return of Jesus Christ was now imminent, and the gospel was clearly to be preached to the world. Those who called themselves Saints were to be gathered out from among the wicked and flee unto Zion.

Thomas's remarkable destiny began to unfold as he embraced this new religion. He was first ordained a priest on October 4, 1840,[93] followed by plans to gather with the Saints in Nauvoo, Illinois. This was in fulfillment of a proclamation issued by the First Presidency of the Church May 24, 1841, for all the Saints to gather to Hancock County, Illinois, and Lee County, Iowa. "Here the Temple must be raised, the University built, and other edifices erected which are necessary for the great work of the last days, and which can only be done by a concentration of energy and enterprise."[94]

The original site for the "City of Zion" was Independence, Missouri, founded in 1831. However, with the final expulsion of the Saints from Missouri in the winter of 1838-39, plans were suspended and the Nauvoo area became a transitory substitute.

---

93   Within the LDS Church there are two priesthoods, the Aaronic and the Melchizedek. The Aaronic Priesthood has three offices: deacon, teacher, and priest.

94   Joseph Smith, et al., *History of the Church of Jesus Christ of Latter-day Saints*, edited by B.H. Roberts, 7 vols., 2nd ed. rev. (Salt Lake City, Utah: Deseret Book Company, 1957), 4:362.

To the persecuted and despised Mormons, Nauvoo was known as the City Beautiful. It was located in Hancock County on the banks of the Mississippi River in central Illinois. Partially built on a hill, the city sloped toward the river through disease-infested swamps that had to be drained before habitation. But the view over the adjacent country was one of beauty with lush vegetation and grandeur. The great river flowed around the city

Nauvoo, Illinois in 1844
(Courtesy LDS Church Historical Department)

in a large crescent. At first the city was built with log homes and shanties, but by 1842 these structures began to gave way to more permanent dwellings made of brick and stone.

The city was well laid out and divided into blocks of four acres each and then subdivided into four lots per block. Residents were to have space for gardens, orchards, and domestic animals. Farms were to be maintained outside the city. Also, to court the partisan favor of the Mormons, the politicians had granted to Nauvoo a most liberal charter, giving it an elaborate municipal court system, a university, and its own militia with Joseph Smith commissioned a lieutenant general. The few hundred early settlers would soon swell to some fifteen thousand, making it one of the two largest cities in Illinois at its 1844 zenith.

Without means of any kind, Thomas and Matilda packed up their convictions, their children, and what few dishes and bedding they owned, to begin the long trek to Illinois. They left Palermo June 6, 1841, no doubt with other converts, and traveled with a family who provided a wagon for transportation. Their four sons ranged in age from two to seven (William Rice was age seven, Culbert was five, John Robison was nearly three, and Thomas Edwin was two), and Matilda was eight months pregnant, with her fifth child. Under these difficult circumstances, the small children and

Matilda must have been very uncomfortable during their 900-mile, two-month-long journey.

The route wound westward across a major part of New York, perhaps through Buffalo — a major port city at the time — on to Cleveland and to Toledo, Ohio. It was just beyond Toledo in the small town of Sylvania that a little daughter was born on July 10, 1841. Thomas and Matilda named her Delilah Cornelia, no doubt after Matilda's mother, Cornelia Guinal. They must have felt a delight to have her born healthy and safe. Even with a new baby, they continued their journey on across Indiana and Illinois until they finally reached their destination on August 2.

Upon arrival they found much of Nauvoo under construction, and Joseph had also negotiated the purchase of twenty thousand acres of land on the Iowa side of the river for settlement. The Saints were gathering from all quarters, and it was felt that this land was necessary to support the burgeoning population. The city of Montrose, located directly across the river from Nauvoo, was enlarged, and a new community by the name of Zarahemla was established a couple of miles northwest. The Zarahemla Stake was organized, and many inbound Saints were encouraged to take up land and build their homes in this area. Attention to the Iowa side of the Mississippi was reinforced prior to Thomas and Matilda's arrival by a revelation in March 1841 when the Lord declared, "Let them build up a city unto my name upon the land opposite to the City of Nauvoo, and let the name of Zarahemla be named upon it."[95]

However, due to some very complex land issues, the growth of Zarahemla was far below expectation with only a few hundred people establishing homes and farms. The Iowa settlements had been founded on what was known as half-breed lands, and were part of a large tract of 119,000 acres set aside by the federal government for the benefit of the half-breed offspring of frontier traders, trappers, soldiers, and other assorted whites who had fathered and left children with their Indian mothers. Speculators and an assortment of dishonest people had obtained possession of much of this land; and without proper surveys and valid titles, they were selling the land to unsuspecting and naive individuals. Unfortunately Joseph Smith was also misled into buying this land and later in April 1843 admitted that the whole Mormon development in Iowa was a failure.[96]

It was in this locality that Thomas and Matilda settled. In his journal,

---

95   Ibid., 311-312. See also Doctrine and Covenants of the Church of Jesus Christ of Latter-day Saints, Section 125.

96   Robert Bruce Flanders, *Nauvoo: Kingdom on the Mississippi* (Urbana: University of Illinois Press, 1975) 142.

Thomas Rice King and his family traveled by wagon some 900 miles in over two months to arrive in Nauvoo August 2, 1841. The exact route across Indiana and Illinois is not known. A daughter, Delilah, was born en route at Sylvania, Ohio, July 10, 1841.

he records that "many of the brethren who came in the same company having friends and acquaintances in Iowa crossed the river and myself with them and stopped about six miles from Montrose where I stayed until March 1842."[97] There was not a lot of time to plant crops and build suitable housing this late in the season, and out of necessity they were perhaps forced to live in a dugout, a makeshift shanty, or their wagon. This would certainly not provide much safety and security against the elements for a young family with a new baby. The following spring, Thomas moved his family to Zarahemla, where he was able to obtain a lot and put up a small house. He also joint ventured with others in fencing and planting a crop on five acres of land.

Prior to Thomas Rice and Matilda's move to Nauvoo and Zarahemla, Thomas Rice's father, Thomas, with his wife Elizabeth, had moved a year earlier to Montrose and Thomas Rice's brothers Timothy and Rufus moved from New York, probably the following year. Timothy purchased property in Nauvoo a few blocks northwest of the temple. There is also a good possibility that several of the Robison converts also settled in the Montrose area.

Shortly after arriving in Zarahemla, Matilda became one of the early members of the Female Relief Society and enjoyed and participated in their activities and meetings. The Relief Society was first organized March 17,

---

97 "Autobiography of Thomas Rice King," a handwritten letter to Elder George A. Smith, January 6, 1868. This letter is found in the family records of Volney King, a copy is in my possession, and a copy can also be found in the Church of Jesus Christ of Latter-day Saints (LDS) Historical Department Archives, Salt Lake City, Utah.

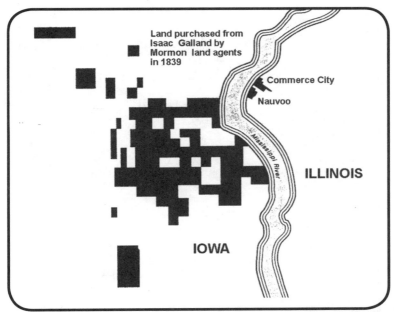

Land purchased from
Isaac Galland by
Mormon land agents
in 1839

Commerce City

Nauvoo

ILLINOIS

IOWA

Joseph Smith purchased large tracts of land in Iowa which encompassed Montrose and Zarahemla. This land was known as "Half-Breed Tract.", but the Saints were never able to obtain title to the land after settlement. (*Church History in the Fulness of Times*, p. 216.)

1842, by Joseph Smith and by the year-end had grown to a membership of eleven hundred women[98] and to more than thirteen hundred by the time of the martyrdom of Joseph Smith.[99] Joseph declared on the day of organization that "I will organize the sisters under the priesthood after a pattern of the priesthood."[100] Emma Smith, wife of the Prophet, was elected president, and the women had the opportunity of choosing the name of their organization.

Emma and Joseph together outlined the purposes of the society: "to provoke the brethren to good works, to look after the wants of the poor, to do good, to deal frankly with each other, and to correct the morals of the community."[101] Membership was not automatic by simply being a member of the Church. Each sister had to make application and be approved by the general membership of the society attesting to the applicant's high moral character and integrity.

98 Linda King Newell and Valeen Tippetts Avery, *Mormon Enigma: Emma Hale Smith* (Garden City, New York: Doubleday, 1984), 117.

99 LDS Church Educational System, *Church History in the Fulness of Times* (Salt Lake City, Utah: Church of Jesus Christ of Latter-day Saints, 1989), 249.

100 Newell and Avery, *Mormon Enigma*, 106.

101 Ibid., 108.

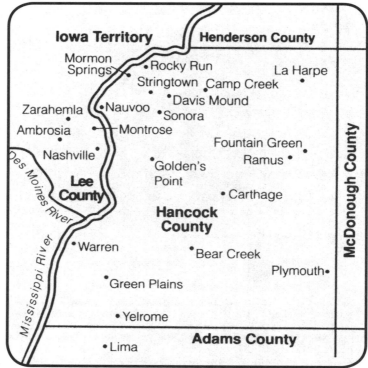

A number of Mormon communities grew up in Hancock County, Illinois, and Lee County, Iowa, during the Nauvoo era. Thomas Rice King and his family settled at Zarahemla. (*Church History in the Fulness of Times*, p. 222.)

Joseph Smith

In August 1842 Thomas Rice probably had his closest and most notable encounter with the Prophet. Earlier in May, an attempt had been made on the life of the former governor of Missouri, Lilburn W. Boggs. Governor Boggs was an avowed enemy of the Saints and was the person responsible for the issuance of the infamous Extermination Order in October 1838 resulting in the expulsion of Church members from Missouri. He blamed this assassination attempt on Joseph Smith and his bodyguard Orrin Porter Rockwell, and issued a warrant for the arrest of Smith and Rockwell. In compliance with this subpoena Joseph was arrested by three deputy sheriffs from Adams County, Missouri on August 8, but in a legal maneuver, he was able to secure a temporary release and went into hiding for three weeks.

It was during this time that Thomas reports in his brief autobiography that Joseph and Porter came to his house about dusk, being hunted by their enemies. They asked for shelter and if Thomas would take them across the river. By all accounts from Joseph Smith's history this would have been Wednesday, August 10, 1842.

Joseph Smith, 1805-1844, the charismatic leader of the Mormons. (Courtesy Utah State Historical Society.)

> We took a bye way down to the river by the old apple orchard where they remained until I went up to the town Montrose to obtain a skiff to cross with. I found the town full of strangers (mobocrats) but after a little maneuvering I found a chance to speak to Captain Davis unobserved. He gave me the key and told me where to find the skiff and oars. I said he must not be seen going to the skiff himself as he was being closely watched. After a little delay I managed to get away unobserved and crossed them over landing near the little red house near the old printing office. Joseph went to Bishop Whitneys and from there home by some back way. About 2 o'clock a.m. we started back . . . [but before leaving] . . . bro. Joseph put his arm around my neck and said I have found another true friend and I will yet take you to the Rocky Mountains where we will eat fish and get fat. The next day [Thursday, August 11, 1842] bro. Joseph with some others were at my house. We discovered some horsemen coming very fast [and] we had barely time to escape to the corn field. Joseph considering it not safe to stay longer where he was, went that night to the Island but I did not go with him.[102]

Captain Davis has not been specifically identified but appears to be a member of the Church and Iowa Militia.[103] The little red house is probably the red brick store, and the old printing office is probably the one that was

---

102   The way these events are recorded in Thomas Rice King's "Autobiography," it gives the impression these events occurred in the summer or fall of 1843. However, in reviewing Joseph Smith's *History of the Church* for this period of time; the *Church Chronology: A Record of Important Events Pertaining to the History of the Church of Jesus Christ of Latter-day Saints* by Andrew Jenson, 2d ed (Deseret News, Salt Lake City, Utah, 1914); the biography of *Porter Rockwell* by Richard Lloyd Dewey (Paramount Books, New York, 1986); and *Nauvoo: Kingdom on the Mississippi,* by Robert Bruce Flanders (Chicago, Illinois: University of Illinois Press, 1975) it appears that the events spoken of by Thomas must have occurred in August 1842.

103   Smith, *History of the Church*, 4:502.

located a short dis-
tance west of the store.
The Island was origi-
nally on the Montrose
side of the river but
is now under water
and no longer visible.
From Joseph Smith's
history Joseph indicat-
ed that he was spend-
ing Thursday with
"Uncle John Smith's
in Zarahemla." This
would put the King
family residence also
in Zarahemla rather
than Montrose.

Joseph Smith's red brick store (a replica) was built in 1841 on the corner of Water and Grange streets near the Mississippi River. This is probably the "little red house" spoken of by Thomas when he helped the Prophet escape from his enemies.

Thomas's experience of rowing Joseph and possibly Rockwell over to Nauvoo and back in the same evening must have been a rewarding but physically exhausting experience — rewarding with the emotions of a face-to-face conversation with the Prophet. Joseph must have thought enough of the experience that the next day, when he again needed help, he went back to the King home.

These were desperate days for Joseph, and he found solace with family and friends. Loyalty and friendship were most important to him. A few days later in his journal he listed fifteen men by name and one un-named oarsman.

> Many were my thoughts that swelled my aching heart, while they were toiling faithfully with their oars. [Of all his friends, he said], My heart shall love those; and my hands shall toil for those, who love and toil for me, and shall ever be found faithful to my friends. . . The still small voice whispered to my soul: These, that share your toils with such faithful hearts, shall reign with you in the kingdom of their God."[104]

Members of the King family may wonder if the unnamed oarsman might have been a reference to Thomas whose name Joseph could not remember after a week of dodging the mobs day and night.

First Missionary Journey

Shortly thereafter a large general conference of the Church was held on Monday, August 29, in Nauvoo. The elders of the Church assembled

---

104   Smith, *History of the Church,* 5:109.

Nauvoo as seen from Montrose, Iowa
(Courtesy LDS Church Historical Department)

in the grove near the temple at 10:00 A.M. and listened to an impassioned Hyrum Smith, the Prophet's brother, and Joseph talk about the many injustices and persecutions they and the Saints had endured and the many falsehoods that were being perpetuated by the apostate John C. Bennett. Bennett had been an early confidant and friend of Joseph Smith in the formation of Nauvoo City. He assisted in obtaining the charter for Nauvoo and quickly established himself in the inner circles of the Church. He was elected the first mayor of Nauvoo and became an Assistant President in the First Presidency of the Church. However, by May 1842, after only a few short months, he turned against the Prophet and became one of his bitterest enemies.

> President Hyrum Smith introduced the object of the conference by stating that the people abroad had been excited by John C. Bennett's false statements, and that letters had frequently been received inquiring concerning the true nature of said reports; in consequence of which it is thought wisdom in God that every elder who can, should go forth to every part of the United States, and take proper documents with them, setting forth the truth as it is, and also preach the gospel, repentance, baptism, and salvation, and tarry preaching until they shall be called home.[105]

The result of this call to serve was the enlistment of 380 elders who agreed to carry out such a mission.[106] Among those who volunteered

105   Ibid., 5:136.

106   Ibid., 5:139.

Thomas Rice King and his missionary companion traveled four hundred miles on foot to preach the gospel in Michigan. The exact route of travel is unknown. They were gone from September 1842 to February 1843.

was Thomas Rice. He was ordained an elder under the hands of Wilford Woodruff, one of the twelve apostles and a future president of the Church. As soon as his affairs were in order and leaving the farm to be cared for by Matilda and his young family and others, Thomas left on his first mission September 12 in company of Rufus Fisher, his companion.[107]

> To arrive at their field of labor in Michigan, they traveled 400 miles on foot in just fourteen days before arriving in the village of Gilead in Branch County, bordering on the Michigan/Indiana state line in central Michigan. They left their homes without "a penny," and when they arrived at Gilead they had been well cared for and each had $.25 in his pocket.[108] They consecrated their efforts for the next four months in the general area, traveling back and forth over a thirty-mile area. At first they met a lot of opposition to their message "until mountains of prejudice began to fall, and the people began to come out and investigate the subject for themselves." The result was they had as many calls for preaching as they could attend to. "A few presented themselves for baptism, others acknowledged [they] preached the truth, and if [they] would work a miracle they would believe it was of God."[109]

---

107   "Autobiography of Thomas Rice King."

108   Ibid.

109   A report of their mission is published in the newspaper, *Times and Seasons,* 4:194-195. A copy is in the LDS Church History Department library, Salt Lake City, Utah.

The success of their preaching is evidenced by the fact they baptized fourteen people, organized a branch of the Church, and ordained two elders, and one priest, teacher, and deacon. They left their little branch prospering and growing and began their return home the first of February 1843. They arrived in Nauvoo on the 20th. Unfortunately, the trip home was most difficult and arduous. Thomas reported that it was the coldest weather he had ever experienced. Traveling 400 miles by foot for fifteen days in both cold and snow must have been an experience that would have taxed the most experienced frontier traveler or outdoorsman.

With his return, Thomas, had now completed his apprenticeship in one of the basic requirements expected of any faithful brother in the gospel of Christ. No struggle was too great and no sacrifice was beyond expectation to build up the kingdom and to prepare the people for the return of the Savior. In recognition of faithful service, Thomas was rewarded the following year by being ordained a Seventy[110] and admitted to the 18th Quorum of Seventies on March 9, 1844.[111] He met with his quorum regularly, participated in missionary-related activities, and made frequent contributions ranging from a few cents to a couple of dollars to support missionary and temple work. On January 5, 1846, he was honored by being appointed one of the seven presidents of his quorum,[112] which position he held until 1869 when he was ordained a high priest.

Only one further step was now required and it was to help build the temple, now under construction. Every faithful person was expected to provide a generous tithe of his means, income, and labor.

Family Crisis

The cold weather during the winter of 1842-43 continued on through the early spring; and in April as Thomas attended the general conference

---

110   Within the Melchizedek Priesthood of the LDS Church are three offices: elder, seventy, and high priest. In the early days of the Church, the office of seventy was associated with missionary work, and missionaries who served faithfully were usually ordained to this office. The office of high priest was reserved for people in administrative functions and the office of elder was the introductory office for newly ordained members of the Melchizedek priesthood.

111   "Seventies Quorum Records 1844-1975," LDS Church Historical Department Archives. The record also reports that Rufus was a member of the 28th Quorum and Timothy a member of the 18th Quorum. An obscure entry in the Autobiography of Norton Jacob for September 28, 1846, states that Timothy served a mission to England. (See "Norton Jacob Autobiography," L. Tom Perry Special Collections and Manuscripts, Harold B. Lee Library, Brigham Young University, Provo, Utah.)

112   Ibid.

of the Church, he and many of the brethren crossed the river to Nauvoo by simply walking on the ice. Joseph Smith reported in his *History of the Church* that the ice was about two feet thick. The conference convened on the floor of the temple with the walls rising from four to twelve feet above the floor.

The Seventies Hall (a replica) was built during 1843-1844 and might be considered the first Missionary Training Center (MTC) of the Church. As a Seventy, Thomas would have participated in the activities and events conducted in this building.

Among the topics covered in the conference were the Prophet's comments about conditions in Iowa. It was nearly impossible to obtain title to the land that had been purchased, and Joseph asked forgiveness of all whom he had advised to go there.[113] This must have been a devastating blow to Thomas and Matilda. They had come from New York with the hope and dream of obtaining property and building a home. Now there was no hope of laying claim to all the work and improvements they had labored so hard to accomplish. Again they would have to start over, although it appears they stayed there for the next three years. There is some evidence, however, they may have moved to Montrose. The Seventies records identify Thomas's home as Montrose. Whether this was referring to the general area or to a specific area is not known.

The summer also brought another crisis and test of faith for the King family. Considerable sickness was experienced, especially with the children; and while it was a difficult period of time, their faith and devotion were rewarded. Thomas Edwin, only four years old, came down with an inflammation of the brain. After two to three days, John Smith, who lived in Zarahemla and was the branch president, and his son George A. Smith were asked to give Edwin a blessing. (John was also an uncle to Joseph Smith. George would later become an apostle and counselor in the First Presidency.) Within thirty minutes after the blessing, the boy was up and playing with the rest of the children.

Following Thomas Edwin's illness, John Robison, age six, was afflicted

---

with the ague and fever. Ague is a malarial type fever marked by recurring chills and shivering. One day he was shaking very hard, and again John Smith was called upon to give a blessing. John Robison was promised the ague would cease, and Thomas records that John was never afflicted again.

As the Saints were doing all that they could to finish the temple in order to do the promised ordinance work, permission was granted that part of the temple ordinance work could be temporarily performed outside the temple. Specifically they were permitted to perform baptisms for their deceased ancestors in the Mississippi River up until October, 1841. Afterwards baptisms were performed

John Smith, an uncle to Joseph Smith, was a good friend of the King family. He gave both Thomas and Matilda their patriarchal blessings November 17, 1845 -- See Appendix 10. (Courtesy LDS Church Historical Department.)

in the basement room in the unfinished temple in a temporary font built for that purpose. This was their first introduction to the principle of salvation for the dead, and Mary and Fidelia King, wives of Timothy and Rufus, and Matilda all participated in this ordinance. Only one reference can be found of Matilda doing this work, and while no date is given, it appears she was baptized for her deceased older sister, Lavina Robison, in the summer of 1843.[114] Lavina was the first wife of Orange Warner and had died eight years earlier.

Nauvoo Crisis

During the rest of 1843 and the first part of 1844, the crisis days of Nauvoo were fast approaching. Joseph's social, political, and economic policies were so varied from the pattens of the established society that many began to raise their voices with such vengeance that conditions within the community were starting to spin out of control. People both in and out of the Church were challenging him at every turn, and many sought his life. In addition, the old Missouri charges of treason and

---

114 "Nauvoo Index of Baptisms for the Dead 1840-1845." The individual references are on microfilm at the Family History Library, Salt Lake City, Utah.

attempted murder would not go away, bringing constant harassment and the threat of extradition.

Socially, Joseph had introduced the emotionally charged practice of plural marriage in 1841. "Polygamy, a criminal act under the 1833 Illinois Anti-bigamy Laws, was so unacceptable to the monogamous nineteenth-century Victorian society that Joseph could introduce it only in absolute secrecy."[115] Publicly, Joseph denied any such knowledge, while privately he had married at least a score of women and taught and encouraged his closest associates to do likewise. Only the most trusted friends were given this information and expected to practice it, and rumors abounded of an elaborate "spiritual wife" doctrine. John Bennett was one of the first to try and expose the Prophet, followed by many others who apostatized and continued the fight against his perceived duplicity. However, to Joseph, plural or celestial marriage constituted one of the highest and noblest ordinances of the gospel of the Father. Only those willing to live such a principle, like the ancient biblical prophets, would gain the highest benefits of heavenly glory. To the enemies of the Church, it represented adultery, harlotry, and ecclesiastical abuse at its worst. Of all the doctrines and principles introduced by Joseph Smith, none created a more divisive or controversial problem within the newly founded Church of Christ or American society in general.

Politically, the citizens of Hancock County were up in arms over the voting practices of the Saints. Their large numbers and bloc voting controlled the politics of the county, and they had substantial influence in state elections. By 1844, the Mormon population of Nauvoo and the adjoining area was about 15,000 with additional people moving in all the time.[116] Many were also from foreign countries, such as Canada and England. In addition, Joseph was preaching the concept of a theocratic "Kingdom of God" on earth. He had organized what was called the Council of Fifty, a secret religious/political group of the leading and most influential Brethren, whose responsibility was to assist in creating and legislating the Kingdom of God. This kingdom was not the Church, but a political kingdom set up in fulfillment of Daniel's prophecy that a stone cut out of the mountain would consume all the kingdoms of the earth (Daniel 2:31-45). This council stayed in existence until the late 1800s as the Brethren held to their belief that Christ would return and assume his rightful place to rule the world. From this council came many of the plans for the westward

---

115   Richard S. Van Wagoner, *Mormon Polygamy, A History* (Salt Lake City, Utah: Signature Books, 1986), 17.

116   Estimates of Nauvoo's population and surrounding area vary considerably from 12,000 to 20,000. The 20,000 figure is quoted frequently but appears to be somewhat exaggerated. See Janath Cannon, *Nauvoo Panorama* (Nauvoo Restoration Inc. 1991), 35.

migration, the establishment of the state of Deseret, and the shadow government of the Saints that existed during the territorial era. This council was also the basis of many of the accusations made against the Brethren and the Saints of treason, sedition, and a lack of loyalty to the United States government.[117] Joseph had himself ordained king and was claiming that the Saints would soon rule the world under Christ's direction. This gave rise to Joseph's announced candidacy for the presidency of the United States in January 1844.

Economically, Joseph had introduced in Ohio and Missouri the biblical principle of having all things in common. While this principle had been put on hold in Nauvoo, Joseph had entered into some substantial financial obligations to purchase property in and around Nauvoo, and the Iowa property spoken of earlier. Also, obligations were incurred in the construction of several large public works projects such as the temple and the Nauvoo House. These debts were further compounded by old claims from the rise and fall of Kirtland, Ohio, in the 1830s. Even though Joseph had filed for bankruptcy in April 1842, to try and alleviate his economic problems, objections were raised and he was never discharged from his financial obligations. Obstacles continued to arise and many creditors were actively pursuing Joseph by every legal means.

On top of all of these difficulties, add religious bigotry, intolerance, and jealously. It was also a period of time where states' rights prevailed and the federal government was not about to get involved in what was considered a local issue. The Jacksonian laissez-faire attitude predominated, leaving the states to settle their own internal affairs. Right and wrong was not so much what was written in the law, but what the majority of the people believed and wanted at the time. Minority interests were easily and often subjugated to the majority. This was graphically illustrated by the experience of Joseph Smith when he appealed to U.S. President Martin Van Buren in November 1839, for redress for the Saints for their losses when they were driven from Missouri. The retort that will always be remembered in Mormon folklore is, "Your cause is just, but I can do nothing for you."[118]

In the face of these prevailing attitudes and forces, charismatic Joseph stood in complete command of his people and was therefore a threat to the greater society. He was mayor of one of the largest cities in Illinois, chief justice of the city court system, prophet and president of the Church, and general of the local militia, the Nauvoo Legion. In short, Joseph had

---

117   Klaus J. Hansen, *Quest for Empire* (Lincoln, Nebraska: University of Nebraska Press, 1967).

118   Smith: *History of the Church*, 4:80.

violated a precious principle of the American republic. In a democratic society, he had done the unthinkable by merging church and state.

The culmination of all of these circumstances was the brutal murders of Joseph and his brother Hyrum on June 27, 1844, by a mob militia, although the brothers were under the protective custody of the governor. Obviously, the Saints were stunned and devastated. Joseph was supposed to have led them through the cataclysmic events preceding the return of Jesus Christ and the advent of the Millennium.

Thomas and Matilda were two of the thousands that passed by to pay their respects as the bodies of Joseph and Hyrum lay in state at the Nauvoo Mansion House.

Freemasonry

One of the early peculiarities of Mormonism was the introduction of Masonry in 1842. Historians have long debated what to express about this little understood secretive fraternity and its relationship to early Mormon thought and curious ceremonies.[119]

Masonry dates back several hundred years as an organization of skilled stone workers.[120] Over time it grew into a fraternal secret society fostering the brotherhood and spiritual growth of man. Many notables from George Washington, Benjamin Franklin, and Andrew Jackson to Mozart and Voltaire were Masons. However, by the 1820s and 1830s there began a backlash against Freemasonry because of the secret nature of the order, its ceremonies, and oaths. Many citizens felt that Masonry was repulsive to a free people by assuming titles and creating an aristocracy which was incompatible in a Christian democracy.

The first Masonic lodge in Nauvoo was organized March 15, 1842, with forty members.[121] Eventually the five Mormon lodges had 1,492 members,[122] three in Nauvoo, and two across the river in Montrose and Keokuk, Iowa.

---

119   I am indebted to Carol Gates Sorensen, Tucson, Arizona, for making this information available.

120   Based on comments by Joseph Smith and Heber C. Kimball, Mormon tradition dates Masonry back to the days of David and Solomon and identifies the temple ceremony in an apostate form. Joseph had specifically said, "Masonry had been taken from the Priesthood." See Stanley B. Kimball, "Heber C. Kimball and Family: The Nauvoo Years," *BYU Studies,* no. 4, Summer 1975, 15:459. Other writers on Freemasonry have also assumed the same idea, but there is little historical evidence one way or another.

121   Ibid., 457.

122   Ibid., 459.

The Masonic emblem contains many symbols of the Masonic order: The compass and the square at the top; the large G symbolizing the geometry of earth measurement; the all-seeing eye of God, the Bible, the beehive, and the hand clasp.

By October 1843 the membership had increased so dramatically, the Nauvoo lodge conceivably could have taken control over the Grand Lodge of Illinois. With this threat and because of other irregularities, the Grand Lodge withdrew its support, but Joseph Smith continued to add new members and advance the brethren through the various levels or degrees.[123]

Why Joseph Smith introduced this controversial order into an already troubled Mormon society and then quickly offended the Masons with his maverick Masonic activities is not fully understood. The introduction of Masonry also flew in the face of the admonishment of the Book of Mormon to avoid any kind of secret orders.[124]

Joseph may have been trying to win friends to protect him and Nauvoo after the difficult New York, Ohio, and Missouri periods. He may have been trying to teach the brethren the concepts of secrecy with the Masonic secret oaths and signs as he was introducing polygamy, the Anointed Quorum, and the Council of Fifty. "The secret of Masonry is to keep a secret" declared Smith on one occasion.[125] It may have been a situation where the Lord inspired Joseph to use the Masonic experience to give him an understanding of the basic format for the temple ceremony. Another reason may have been that Joseph was simply enamored of the perceived prominence and gentility of Masonry.

In the words of Mormon historian Richard Bushman, Joseph was intrigued by the Masonic rites and turned the materials to his own use:

> The Masonic elements that appeared in the temple endowment were embedded in a distinctive contest -- the Creation instead of the Temple of Solomon, exaltation rather than fraternity, God and Christ, not the Worshipful

123   D. Michael Quinn, *The Mormon Hierarchy, Origins of Power* (Salt Lake City, Utah: Signature Books, 1994), 130.

124   For example see Helaman 2:13-14 and Ether 8:21 (Book of Mormon of the Church of Jesus Christ of Latter-day Saints).

125   Quinn, *The Mormon Hierarchy, Origins of Power,* 131.

Master. Temple covenants bound people to God rather than to each other. At the end, the participants entered symbolically into the presence of God. . . . The aim of the endowment was not male fraternity but the exaltation of husbands and wives.[126]

After the exodus to Utah, Masonry among the Mormons was discontinued and it was several years before a Masonic lodge was organized in Utah. Considerable tension between the two organizations has existed over the years in large part over the death of Joseph Smith and the temple ceremony. The Mormons have felt that the Masons at Carthage failed to come to the aid of Joseph after he gave the Masonic distress sign. The Masons in turn have resented the similarities between their ceremonies and the Mormon temple ceremony. The similarities were close enough for Heber Kimball to quote Joseph as saying that Freemasonry "was taken from the preasthood but has become degen[e]rated. but menny things are perfect."[127]

Nevertheless, for whatever reason the order existed in Nauvoo, Thomas King made application to become a Mason on December 19, 1844. He was accepted two weeks later on January 2, 1845.[128] His experience as a Mason and what level he achieved is not known. But his experience as a missionary, a member of the Seventies presidency, membership in the Masonic lodge, and later the temple ceremony — all brought him closer to the core of Mormonism.

Nauvoo Temple

After the death of Joseph there was not much for the Mormon people to do except to pick up the pieces of their shattered lives, their abiding faith, and the Church they had sacrificed so much for and loved. However, a succession crisis loomed before the Church as no viable successor to Joseph had been made public prior to his death. During a special conference of the Saints in Nauvoo, Thomas and Matilda were among the many who experienced and attested to the transfiguration of Brigham Young to look and sound like Joseph Smith as he addressed the congregation. This was witness enough for the Church to recognize Brigham as Joseph's rightful heir. Matilda later described this event to her family as a very remarkable

---

126   Richard Lyman Bushman, *Joseph Smith Rough Stone Rolling* (New York: Alfred A. Knopf, 2005) 450-451.

127   *BYU Studies,* no. 4, Summer 1975, 15:457.

128   Mervin B. Hogan, "The Vital Statistics of Nauvoo Lodge, Exhibit A" LDS Church Historical Department Library.

spiritual manifestation.[129]

Under the new leadership of President Young, preparations were made to leave Nauvoo and move to the Rocky Mountains. Before the Kings left, however, the events of life and death would visit their family. On March 25, 1845, a second daughter, Matilda Emily, was born and appropriately named after her mother. Four months later, Thomas King Sr. passed away and is probably buried in Montrose near where he was living. He was seventy-four years of age; and Elizabeth, now approaching age seventy, would have to face the move west without her husband.

The final remaining obligation and responsibility that the Saints undertook before moving west was to finish the temple and receive their prom-

Thomas King's name is listed on the plaque at the Nauvoo Pioneer Memorial Cemetery honoring those who died before the great exodus.

ised endowments. "Let this house be built unto my name, that I may reveal mine ordinances therein unto my people; for I design to reveal unto my church, things which have been kept hid from before the foundation of the world, things that pertain to the dispensation of the fulness of times."[130]

In Joseph Smith's view a man could only be saved as fast as he is able to gain godly knowledge, and the endowment ceremony was a sacred gift of knowledge of man's progress from creation to his emergence into the presence of God.

Following the endowment, they were promised further priesthood blessings where husbands and wives could be joined together for not only this life, but for the life to come in the eternal order of God.

The cornerstone of the temple had been laid on April 6, 1841, and

---

129   Lillian King Hinckley, "History of Matilda Robison King," A Short Biographical Sketch, Utah State Historical Society, Salt Lake City, Utah.

130   *Doctrine and Covenants* 124:40-41.

The Nauvoo Temple took five years to build at a cost of a million dollars. Ordinance work began in December 1845, and continued round the clock before the Saints left Nauvoo. Thomas Rice and Matilda received their endowments on January 12, 1846. (*Church History in the Fulless of Times*, p. 242.)

construction continued for the next five years under a mandate from the Lord that they would be under condemnation if the temple was not finished.[131] The 50,000 square-foot building was 128 feet long, 88 feet wide, and 65 feet high, with the tower and spire reaching to 165 feet. The cost would approach a million dollars, a tremendous sum for the impoverished Saints.[132]

In order to have all qualified members endowed before leaving for the Great Basin, endowment ordinance work began in December 1845, and sessions at times were conducted round the clock until the latter part of January 1846. Entrance into the temple was for only those whose names were listed in the Book of the Law of the Lord, the master ledger of Temple contributors.[133] The contribution (tithing) required was "one-tenth of all anyone possessed at the commencement of the building, and one-tenth part of all his increase from that time until the completion of the same, whether it be money, or whatever he be blessed with."[134]

Thomas and Matilda were privileged to go through for their endowments January 12, 1846, and then they were sealed to each other on the 27th. Others of the King and Robison family also went through the temple, such as Thomas's brothers Rufus and Timothy and their wives and Elizabeth, widow of father Thomas.[135] The Kings and Robisons were only a few of the 5,200 people who participated in temple worship before the

---

131   *Doctrine & Covenants* 124:32.

132   *LDS Church Almanac (*Deseret News Press, 1985), 261.

133   Flanders, *Nauvoo, Kingdom on the Mississippi*, 201.

134   Smith, *History of the Church*, 4:473-4.

135   Church of Jesus Christ of Latter-day Saints, "Nauvoo Temple Endowment Register," located at the LDS Church Family History Library, Salt Lake City, Utah.

announced exodus.

Buoyed up and strengthened by a reaffirmation of commitment and dedication, Thomas and Matilda were now prepared to face a most challenging future. They had experienced several spiritual manifestations and had participated in missionary activity and solemn temple covenants. Their prophet-leader lay dead before them as a religious martyr. No one had done more than Joseph except Jesus Christ for the salvation of men.[136]

---

136 *Doctrine and Covenants* 135:3.

Exodus
(Leaving Nauvoo)

When ancient Israel left Egypt, they were promised they would receive the oracles and priesthood of their God. These divine gifts were to include sacred rites in a holy sanctuary and a property inheritance in the "promised land." They were to be free of servitude and could practice their religious beliefs. When modern Israel was driven out of Missouri and later Illinois, they were leaving the promised land and the center place of Zion to go into the wilderness. Left behind was their holy sanctuary, which they had worked and sacrificed so hard to build. Rather than going to a land where they could be free to worship their God and practice their religion, they would find a place where federal judges, U.S. marshals, and armies would suppress and hold them hostage. Hundreds of their leaders would be imprisoned and their economic, social, and political fabric would be uprooted and forcibly changed. Religious practices would be curtailed, and in a few short generations the focus and emphasis of their Church would be disrupted and significantly modified.

Just as ancient Israel looked with anticipation for their prophet-leader to take them out of Egyptian bondage, modern Israel is looking and hoping for their Savior to create their Kingdom of Heaven. In a historical context, Moses accomplished for ancient Israel what modern-day Israel's Redeemer has yet to perform.

The Saints began leaving Nauvoo in the winter of 1845-46, and by spring the exodus began in earnest. Thousands of people were on the westward trail struggling with rain, cold, and mud. Many were only

CHRONOLOGICAL EVENTS

Spring	1846	The King family leaves Nauvoo for the West.
Jul 17,	1846	One year old Matilda Emily King dies along the trail.
Fall	1846	The King family settles in Winter Quarters, Nebraska.
Mar 11,	1847	Volney King is born.
Spring	1847	The King family moves to Fremont County, Iowa, to prepare for the trek west.
Sep 13,	1847	Elizabeth King dies at Winter Quarters.
Aug 21,	1850	LeRoy King is born.
Jun 10,	1851	The King family leaves Council Bluffs for Salt Lake City.
Sep 23,	1851	The King family arrives in Salt Lake City.

partially prepared and left in haste. Wagons easily broke down, illness was prevalent, and death frequently visited their camps. The job of moving so many people was a herculean task even for the capable "Lion of the Lord," Brigham Young. But Brigham, like all great leaders, learned from his mistakes and quickly became equal to the task, and he was able to turn chaos into a well-planned and organized exodus where over the course of the next two decades tens of thousands of people would be transported to the Great Basin. By 1869 when the transcontinental railroad was completed at Promontory Point in northern Utah, some 60,000[137] people had emigrated to Utah in ships, wagons, handcarts, horseback and on foot. These people came not only from Nauvoo but from all parts of North America, including Canada, and from England, Europe, and the islands of the sea.

As pressure by their enemies mounted, the Saints began a feverish campaign in the fall of 1845 to prepare for a general exodus the following spring. The logistics of moving 12,000 people, the rich, the poor, the prepared, and the unprepared bordered on an impossible dream. Every possible shop or tool was employed in the construction of wagons with 2,000 of them completed by year end. There were also cattle, oxen, horses and other critical animals to be rounded up, and supplies and provision of every kind to be raised, purchased and assembled. Yet all of this activity needed to be balanced with the command by their God to finish first the construction of the temple. The promised endowments were to be given before leaving.

The timetable for leaving was set, but the location was another daunting problem. California, Oregon, the Great Basin all were under intense scrutiny and consideration, but no public announcement was forthcoming from Church leaders. In addition, the Mormons were not the only ones looking west. Between 1843 and 1846 thousands of other hopeful Americans turned their focus on California and Oregon, still part of Mexico and disputed territory with England. By 1847 the estimated number of people on the Overland Trail would reach 15,000, and the Saints would have to compete for trail routes and critical provisions. As their unfavorable reputation would proceed them, there would also be suspicion on the part of the local citizens all the way to the federal government as to their intentions and loyalties.

In February the first groups began to leave made up of Church leaders

---

137 Lamar C. Berrett, *Encyclopedia of Mormonism, 4 vols.,* Daniel H. Ludlow, Ed., (New York: Macmillan Publishing Company, 1992), 3:1255 places the count as high as 80,000, but most historians put the number closer to the 60,000. For example see S. Kent Brown, Donald Q. Cannon, and Richard H. Jackson, *Historical Atlas of Mormonism* (New York: Simon & Schuster,, 1994), 86.

and concerned citizens fearing they were being left behind. The vast majority of the Church members began leaving as temperatures moderated and roads began to dry out. The third group was the less fortunate who didn't have the means to leave and had to wait until the fall when wagons were sent back to pick them up.

Thomas and Matilda were the first part of the second group. Moving by wagon and walking across Iowa, they experienced all the hardships of any Saint: hunger, illness, physical pain, and death. When they had traveled from New York to Nauvoo, five short years earlier, a new life came into the world. This time they gave one up. Little Matilda Emily, just a year old, died of scarlet fever and was buried along the trail near a little place called Indian Town, located just a few miles east of Council Bluffs. Thomas took the boards out of the end of two wagons and made a small coffin and then wrapped the little body in a quilt and placed her in a deep grave. To prevent the body from being disturbed by coyotes, a brush fire was built on the grave to take away any human smell. As was so frequently the case, there was no time for mourning and sorrow, and the King family had to move on with the pain only a father and a mother can feel. Matilda remembers looking back the following night across the flat plains of Iowa and still being able to see the grave. It was all she could do to keep from running back.[138]

The long trek across Iowa lasted for 325 miles and probably took four to five weeks before they reached the banks of the Missouri River at what is now known as Council Bluffs. Within days thousands of covered wagons with some 10,000 Saints became jammed eastward into a six-mile stretch of prairie soon called by some as the Grand Encampment. To bring order out of what could possibly have become total chaos, Brigham Young and the other leaders of the Church began to make assignments to give organization and structure. Men were assigned to build fences, hunt, and repair tents and wagons. Women washed clothes, tended children, and prepared the meals. Older boys tended large herds of cattle, oxen, horses, mules, and sheep. And a community organization was put into effect with officers and ordinances. For example on a humorous note, an ordinance was passed that "if any dog [was] found worrying sheep, [it] may be shot — without trial."

To further complicate matters and at a most inopportune time, a desperate move was made by Brigham Young. To find needed financial aid to assist the Saints in their move to Utah, President Young had petitioned the federal government offering, among several things, to provide troops

138 Correspondence from Eliza Rosetta King Black Lythgoe, a granddaughter of Matilda King, to David S. King, July 8, 1952. A copy is in my possession.

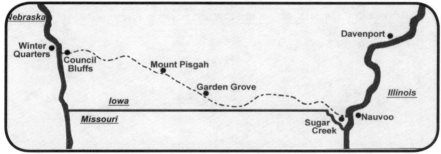

The three-hundred-mile trip across Iowa began in the spring of 1846. Thomas Rice King and his family were one of the first to leave for Winter Quarters.

for the war with Mexico. In response the call soon went out for 500 volunteers. They were to be known as the Mormon Battalion, and would be attached to Colonel Stephen W. Kearny's Army of the West. This move would bring needed cash into the coffers of the Church and individual families, but it would drain the Mormon camps of sorely needed manpower leaving many wives and families to fend for themselves in the coming winter. One of the families so effected was Matilda's sister Margaret, who was left without winter shelter or food for her young family.

Brigham Young also soon realized it would be impossible for anyone to continue westward until the following year and negotiations were entered into with various Indian tribes and government Indian agents to allow the Saints to temporarily occupy Indian lands on both sides of the Missouri River. The group would soon be broken up and dispersed into many settlements up and down the river. Arrangements for food, fuel, fiber, and shelter were desperately needed to prepare for the coming winter.

But, in the priority of things, food took precedence over shelter. During the weeks that followed while families were living in wagons and tents, nearly 2,000 tons of wild prairie grass was cut and stacked to feed the cattle, corals were built, and wells dug. Critical crops were planted for spring and summer harvest. Exploring parties were also sent out to find the most suitable locations for settlements; and in October; Winter Quarters, Nebraska, one of more than ninety camps was surveyed and laid out.

Both Thomas and his brother Timothy were traveling together along with Matilda's brother William Robison, and by the end of September they had joined a group under the leadership of a Major John Scott. Included in the group were fourteen families.

Part of the camp organization by Brigham Young was the creation of a 400-man militia force for the common defense of the people. There was

Settlements along the Missouri River. The King family moved to Franklin, Fremont County, Iowa, near present-day Hamburg in the spring of 1847 to prepare for the trek west. *(Historical Atlas of Mormonism, p. 75)*

still a concern about the temperament of the unpredictable Missourians to the south and the numerous Indians whose land the Mormons were camping on. The Omahas were known for their thievery, and there was always a possibility of a Sioux war party. As part of this military preparation was the organization of a sixty-man artillery unit with four cannons. Major Scott was given command with two captains, and Thomas was commissioned a lieutenant.[139] Additional security precautions were taken later by building a stockade around the settlement together with a blockhouse and rude fortifications.

Desperately in need of provisions Thomas and others of the Scott group contracted out to help build a mission in Bellevue, Nebraska, located fifteen miles south of Winter Quarters. In 1846 the Presbyterian Board of Missions in New York City sent the Reverend Edward McKinney and his wife to minister among the Omaha and Oto Indians. At Bellevue they employed the Mormons to help build the mission, a two-story fourteen-room cottonwood log building, thirty-six by eight feet. Thomas, Timothy, and others began work on September 30, but the stress of the trip and the coming of winter was starting to take its toll on emotions and attitudes. By the middle of October, dissension arose in the ranks and Norton Jacob claimed that "through the mean, undermining conduct of [James] McGaw, Thomas King & [John] Groesbeck," Brother John Scott and the remander of the company were discharged from the work by Revered McKiney.[140] However, King, Groesbeck and James Baldwin were retained to finish the work. What caused the dispute is not recorded, but it appears that part of the group was not carrying its load, and McKinney let them go and retained those he could count on to get the job done.

Due to this conflict, Thomas, Timothy, and several others withdrew from the group with Jacob claiming that these men were "influenced by a Spirit of covetousness and insubordination."[141] Perhaps "insubordination" meant that Thomas refused to accept the leadership of Scott and Norton. In any event, volatile emotions were running high.

As quickly as Winter Quarters was laid out, cabins and other crude shelters sprang up. The community was platted in forty-one blocks, three rows wide and of various sizes. Some blocks contained as many as twenty homes. Overall there were some 528 log homes, eighty-three sod houses, and many dugouts against the hill, yet many were still living in their

---

139 Ronald O. Barney, ed., *The Mormon Vanguard Brigade of 1847: Norton Jacob's Record* (Logan, Utah: Utah State University Press, 2005), 82, 87. While most of the officer positions went to men who had served in Nauvoo, there is no known record of Thomas belonging to the legion in Nauvoo. It was an Illinois state law that all able-bodied men between the ages of 18 and 45 belong to the state militia but Thomas lived in Iowa Territory. Researchers have identified about 1,200 members of the Legion out of a total between 3,000 to 4,000 members, but Thomas's name is not one of them. (My thanks to Donald Q. Cannon for this information.)

140 "Norton Jacob Autobiography," 43-44.

141 Barney, *The Mormon Vanguard Brigade,* 89

Winter Quarters was surveyed and laid out in traditional Mormon fashion. There were forty-one blocks with eight hundred and twenty lots. Also organized were twenty-three wards with the Thomas King family located in the Twenty-second Ward. Here they spent the winter of 1846-47. *(Winter Quarters Project Website)*

wagons and tents.[142]   The houses were generally built out of logs from 12 to 18 feet long.   Roofs were made out of split oak timber about 3 feet long and 6 inches wide and supported and kept in place by weights and poles. Other roofs were made of willows, straw, and earth, about a foot thick. Many cabins had no floors, and few had stoves.

Thomas and Timothy built their primitive cabins outside the stockade on the north end of Turkey Creek in the Twenty-second Ward. Joining this section with the main settlement to the south was a small bridge constructed across Turkey Creek. With the Kings in the Twenty-second Ward were mother Elizabeth and Matilda's sister, Margaret, and her four small children.[143] Margaret, alone and struggling, had seen her husband, Alva Phelps, march off with the Mormon Battalion in July.

With Thomas and Matilda through all of these experiences were many of their extended family members and close friends. Already mentioned were Timothy King, step-mother, Elizabeth, and sister, Margaret. Other Robison family members included William, Joseph, and Peter and their

---

142 Juanita Brooks, *John Doyle Lee: Zealot, Pioneer, Builder, Scapegoat* (Logan, Utah: Utah State University Press, 1992), 105.

143 Winter Quarters Project Website www.winterquarters.byu.edu.

families. The family of Orange Warner and his wife Delilah Robison stayed in Montrose for one more year to raise additional crops before moving west in the summer of 1847.

Noticeably absent from the group was Rufus King. Even though he had helped build and had gone through the temple for his endowments,[144] it appears he could not muster the faith and courage to move west. In 1848 he was in St. Louis; and in 1850 his wife, Elizabeth Fidelia Parker, died in Indiana. Whether Rufus made any attempt to come west is not known. There were many people who made an attempt and got as far as the settlements on the Missouri River, but for one reason or another turned around and went back to where they may have come from. For some it was the intimidating task of moving to Utah, others left over conflict and disagreement, while others simply gave up over health or a loss of faith. According to family records, Rufus was widowed and remarried twice after leaving the Saints.[145] The fact that, years later, the King family had Elizabeth Fidelia and her deceased children sealed to Thomas Rice is an indication that Elizabeth may have remained committed to the Church, regardless of the intentions of Rufus.

The official census of Winter Quarters during the fateful winter of 1846-47 was 3,558 people with hundreds emaciated with sickness.[146] It definitely was not a fun experience and the worst was yet to come as fall stretched into winter and the physical strength of the Saints gave out. The quick exodus from Nauvoo, the exhausting trek across Iowa, the endless spring storms, insufficient provisions, and poor diets, plus the unhealthy conditions of the riverbank environment sent over seven hundred people to their graves by the summer of 1847.[147]

Overall the condition of the Saints was deplorable. Located on the eastern side of Nebraska next to the Missouri River, Winter Quarters was only one, although the largest, of many makeshift camps that fateful winter. Another twenty-five hundred people were camped on Pottawattomie Indian lands on the east side of the Missouri River; an estimated seven hundred people were at Mount Pisgah, six hundred at Garden Grove, at least a thousand spread throughout other parts of Iowa, and five hundred

---

144 "Nauvoo Temple Endowment Register," Family History Library.

145   LDS Church Ancestral File identifies that Rufus married an Elizabeth Dodge on June 18, 1851, in South Milford, Lagrange, Indiana, and later to a Margaret Wagoner on February 11, 1866, in Unionville, Putnam, Missouri. Rufus's first wife, Elizabeth Parker, died June 2, 1850.

146 Brooks, *John Doyle Lee*, 105.

147 Richard E. Bennett, *Mormons at the Missouri: Winter Quarters, 1846-1852* (Norman, Oklahoma: University of Oklahoma Press, 1987), 280-292.

Winter Quarters **painting by Gregory Sievers. Thomas King's home would have been to the left of the painting, just over Turkey Creek.**

in the Mormon Battalion on their way to California. In addition to the Saints camped in Iowa Territory, there were another three thousand or more scattered down the Mississippi River towns, including St. Louis, where the Mormon population swelled to nearly fifteen hundred.[148]

For the Brethren, it was a huge responsibility and a management nightmare. They themselves were sick and had their own families to care for, not to mention the affairs of the Church and the thousands scattered so far and wide. But the Saints did the best they could by trading with people in the settlements in Iowa and even into Missouri. Some were able to find work; and with their earnings, together with the wages of the members of the Mormon Battalion, they obtained many lifesaving provisions. Church meetings were held twice a week, and celebrations and dancing were frequently held to lift the morale and spirits of the people. All the while, preparations were made to launch the first companies of pioneers toward the Salt Lake Valley the following spring.

To add to this uncomfortable situation for the King family, Matilda was pregnant. And the following March, their fifth son, Volney, was born. But again as life would come into the world, life would leave. The first to go was Alva Phelps, Matilda's brother-in-law, and a member of the Mormon Battalion. He died in September 1846 and was the first member of the battalion to die on the trail. Two months later, Matilda's

148 Ibid., 320.

brother, William died of Cholera, and the following April Matilda's sister, Delilah, died shortly after child birth in Montrose. In September 1847, Elizabeth, the seventy-year-old widow of Father King, died at Winter Quarters. William, Elizabeth and Delilah are three of hundreds of people buried at Winter Quarters where a monument stands today as a testimony to the faith and devotion of a persecuted people. In the span of just a few months Thomas and Matilda alone experienced five difficult deaths: a daughter, a brother-in-law, a brother, a sister, and a stepmother.

A glimpse of the suffering of these people ap-

Memorial at Winter Quarters, Nebraska dedicated to the many who lost their lives while attempting to move to the Rocky Mountains. Included in this memorial is the name of Elizabeth King.

pears in a letter written by Matilda's twenty-seven-year-old sister, Margaret, outlining her feelings on losing her husband. The letter graphically describes her destitute condition and Alva's departure in mid-July 1846:

> We were traveling when the call came for him to leave us. It was midnight when we were awakened from our slumbers with the painful news that we were to be left homeless, without a protector. I was very ill at the time, my children all small, my babe also extremely sick; but the call was pressing; there was no time for any provision to be made for wife or children; no time for tears; regret was unavailing. He started in the morning. I watched him from my wagon-bed till his loved form was lost in the distance; it was my last sight of him.

Margaret then goes on to identify her feelings when news reached her of Alva's death.

> Two months from the day of his enlistment, the sad news of my bereavement arrived. This blow entirely prostrated me. But I had just embarked upon my sea of troubles; winter found me bed-ridden, destitute, in a wretched hovel

which was built upon a hill-side; the season was one of constant rain; the situation of the hovel and its openness, gave me free access to piercing winds, and the water flowed over the dirt floor, converting it into mud two or three inches deep; no wood but what my little ones picked up around the fences, so green it filled the room with smoke; the rain dropping and wetting the bed which I was powerless to leave; no relative to cheer or comfort me a stranger away from all who ever loved me; my neighbors could do but little, their own troubles and destitution engrossing their time; my little daughter of seven my only help; no eye to witness my sufferings but the pitying one of God -- He did not desert me.

Spring brought some alleviation from my sufferings, yet one pan of meal was my all, my earthly store of provisions. I found sale for the leaders of my team. The long, dreary winter had passed, and although it was months before health and comparative comfort were my portion, still I thanked the Lord this was the darkest part of my life.[149]

In analyzing the deplorable conditions of the Saints at this time, many historians consider this period as one of the most under-researched areas of Mormon history and feel that, when all the facts come out it will go down as perhaps one of the darkest times in our history. It is difficult to understand how good men could be accused of "covetousness and insubordination," or how Margaret Robison Phelps would have to live in a hovel with three inches of mud as a floor, all without the help and support from nearby family members. Perhaps Margaret's letter gives a clue when she said that "my neighbors could do but little, their own troubles and destitution engrossing their time." The terrible conditions of economic poverty, debilitating sickness, and general privation were so widespread that one person was not even able to help another in spite of the best of intentions or relationship. Over 11 percent of the population in Winter Quarters died the first year.

In the history of the Overland Trail this number, as a percentage, pales against the 50 percent loss of life with the Donner party of 1846 where forty people died, and the 25 percent loss of life in the Willie and Martin handcart disaster ten years later when 265 people died. But in painful numbers alone, the 723 people who died along the Iowa trail and in Winter Quarters in the winter and spring of 1847 overshadows by far what the Saints had experienced to date.

Hamburg, Iowa

Even though the difficult winter was behind them, Thomas was in no condition to make an attempt to move on with vanguard companies

---

149 Daniel Tyler, *A Concise History of the Mormon Battalion in the Mexican War, 1846-1848* (Glorieta, New Mexico: The Rio Grande Press, Inc., 1881), 129-130.

heading for the Salt Lake Valley. Economic resources were exhausted and in March Matilda had delivered another son. To support the family, Thomas and family moved approximately fifty miles south to Fremont County, Iowa, near the modern community of Hamburg in the corner of the Iowa-Missouri-Nebraska border.[150] At this time there was only a handful of local settlers scattered from farm to farm; and as the Mormons spread out, the Hamburg area was the southern farthest point. Some family records have Thomas moving into northern Missouri, but this may have come from the fact that the border between the two states was still in dispute. Brother Timothy stayed in Winter Quarters keeping stepmother Elizabeth with him until her death in September. Also, staying in Winter Quarters was Margaret who remarried a year later in February 1848. Joining Thomas was his friend Orange Warner; and as there is no record of the Kings or Warners owning land, it appears they simply became squatters until they could move west.

The King farm was located somewhere near the banks of the Nishnabotna River.[151] Here Thomas farmed, primarily raising corn, and worked for the next four years to accumulate the necessary provisions and equipment. Referring to all the corn they raised, John Robison, as a fourteen year-old boy, may have expressed some of the feelings of the family at this time when he lightheartedly stated that he "was tired of having to plant corn, harvest corn, carry corn, and eat corn. If we could just settle some place where corn would not grow." [152]

---

150   In a journal entry by William King he records on October 5, 1881 that during a trip to Nebraska that he and Culbert stopped at Hamburg and visited there old home which was located four miles north of town.. See "William Rice King Journal," July 28, 1880, to January 6, 1882. The original is in the possession of David S. King, Kensington, Maryland. This is the only known journal of William. All his diaries were destroyed by fire while they were stored in a barn in Fillmore. This journal and a journal of William's wife, Lucy, were discovered several years ago by a Ralph Bennett while tearing down an old building in Bountiful, Utah. The journals had been buried in one of the walls of the building. In 1995, Ralph Bennett's wife, Flora, gave them to David King. A copy is in my possession.

151   The 1850 U.S. census confirms his location in Fremont County, Iowa, and both he and Orange Warner are together. They could have made trips to Missouri to obtain supplies and sell their crops. In a small autobiography by William King, he says they "moved down on the Nishnabotna fifty miles below Florence." Thomas Edwin in his autobiography says, "In the Spring of 1847 we moved down to the Nishnabotna, near Hamburg, Iowa." (*See The Daily Journal of the Kingston United Order 1877-1883,* by Volney King, LDS Church Historical Department Archives. An abbreviated typed copy by Max Sudweeks, Kingston, Utah is at the Utah State Historical Society.)

152   Carol Reed Flake, "Of Pioneers and Prophets," a personal history in my possession.

It appears that to further assist the family Thomas went to Missouri later in the summer to assist with the wheat harvest, receiving his pay in much-needed wheat. The following year he entered into a contract with a Thomas Tootle to build a "hewed-log store-house" in Austin, a small settlement just a short distance north of Hamburg. Thomas was to provide all the materials and have it built within a year for the sum of $105. It was not much of a return, but Thomas was desperate and labor was cheap.

> Witnesseth, that I, the said King, agree to furnish all the materials and built a hewed-log store-house 20 by 26 feet large, one story high, with shingle roof, a good jointed floor, two doors, two windows with shutters; counter on one side, and end shelving on two sides and one end, at the direction of the said Tootle six drawers under the base shelf of one side; to be ceiled overhead with good seasoned plank, or will be lathed and plastered, the house to be white-painted out and inside with lime and sand, the corners to be sawed down, the logs for the above building to face, when hewed, not less than 12 inches. Said building is to be finished complete for use, of good materials, and to be done in a good and workmanlike manner, by the tenth day of April next. For which the said Tootle is to pay said King one hundred and five dollars.
> Given under our hand this 8 th March, 1848.[153]
>
> Thomas R. King.
> Thomas E. Tootle.

This building subsequently passed into the hands of another person before becoming the county court-house.

By 1848 a few early residents of the Hamburg area began to object to the LDS presence in the region raising many of the traditional allegations against the Mormons. In October 1848, a public meeting, for political purposes was held. During the progress of the meeting a paper was drawn up and signed, petitioning the legislature to organize a county in southwestern Iowa, with the belief that it could be successfully controlled by the Gentiles. By 1849 the final organization of the county occurred as the boundary disputes with Missouri were settled.

Regardless of any opposition from the local settlers, it appears that Thomas and the other few Mormon families were not hindered in finding employment or fertile fields to plant their crops. It was a time for addressing the economic needs of the family. As outlined by biblical writ, "it was a time to sow." Other issues including education of the children would become secondary; and while maintaining their commitment to their Church and God, for four years they were out of the loop of Church activity and affairs. Most Mormon settlements were serviced by a circuit rider-type branch president, but the Hamburg area was beyond the reach

---

153 *History of Fremont County, Iowa: A History of the County, Its Cities, Towns, Etc.* (Des Moines: Iowa Historical Company, 1881), 377.

of most activities. Thomas would have been out of touch with the controversies swirling around in Winter Quarters and Kanesville over the issues of First Presidency reorganization, polygamy, or the scores of people defecting and returning to the East. Perhaps they did prosper with the surge of gold seekers who traveled through Kanesville in 1849-51 and drove up the price of commodities to unheard-of levels. The price of corn shot up from $.20 to $3.00 a bushel.[154]

While Thomas and family may have been out of the primary loop of Church activity, they did attempt to stay in touch with basic Church news. Established in February 1849, the *Frontier Guardian* newspaper was published in Kanesville (Council Bluffs) and edited by Apostle Orson Hyde for the benefit of the Saints in Iowa. This bi-weekly newsletter included information on both the national and local level. It included sermons, conference reports, news from Salt Lake, trail conditions, and Indian threats. As one paying an annual subscription of $1, Thomas's name appears on the list of subscribers.[155]

For the King family, the winter of 1848-49 in western Iowa will always be remembered as one of the worst in memory. With an exceptionally heavy snow fall in the upper Missouri, the spring brought unprecedented flooding. Together with the warm rains of spring, "the accumulating water reached the lower Missouri [and] the circumjacent country was submerged, dwellings and out-buildings were carried away, farms disappeared beneath its waters, the channel changed, the river's course became somewhat different, but higher and higher still the water rose, until the month of August, when they [it] began slowly to subside."[156] As Thomas and family were close to the banks of the Nishnabotna River which flowed directly into the Missouri, they must have been frightfully affected in some measure. No King family record mentions this experience, but it must have been a serious impediment in living conditions and getting ready to move west.

In spite of any impediments, Thomas was determined to produce the resources necessary to make as comfortable a journey to Utah as possible and to provide a stake for a good start once there. For a family the size of the Kings, the basic recommended provisions included nearly 4,000 pounds of food and clothing. This would include 2,000 pounds of flour, 200 pounds of sugar, 50 pounds of salt, 20 pounds of dried apples, and 2 bushel of beans. Besides these items they also were to take tents, farming

---

154 Bennett, *Mormons at the Missouri, 1846-1852,* 223.

155 *Frontier Guardian* Newspaper, March 7, 1851, LDS Church Historical Department Archives.

156 *History of Fremont County, Iowa,* 369.

and mechanical tools, a half dozen muskets or rifles, nails, cooking and eating utensils, and 30 pounds of iron and steel. In addition, they were to bring three or four milk cows, a couple of beef cattle, and sheep if they could find them.[157]

All of these provisions were to be carried in three wagons with a bed about ten feet long, four feet wide, and two feet high. Caulking sealed the bed for river crossings; and a waterproof canvas, held by five or six hickory bows, covered the rectangular box. The large wooden wheels with iron-plated tires were set with smaller wheels in the front for maneuverability, and the load was pulled by mules or oxen. Before leaving, Matilda would give birth on August 21, 1850, to her last child, whom they named LeRoy.

The Trek to Salt Lake City

Finally in the spring of 1851 the nine-member family was ready. Thomas was a robust thirty-eight years old, Matilda forty, William seventeen, Culbert fifteen, John Robison nearly fourteen, Thomas Edwin twelve, Delilah ten, Volney four, and LeRoy nearly one. The oldest boys helped drive the wagons, and everyone had to help with the stock. Overall this must have been an experience that would have caused any young man or woman to grow up in a hurry and take on critical responsibility.

They assembled with several other families and wagons the first part of June, near Council Bluffs (Kanesville), Iowa, where they joined Easton Kelsey's company. They were then further organized into two groups of fifty with Luman Shurtliff[158] as captain over their group.[159]

---

157   *LDS Church Almanac,* (Salt Lake City, Utah: Deseret News Press, 1997-1998), 114.

158   In several King family histories and in the book, *Pioneers and Prominent Men of Utah,* by Frank Esshom, (Salt Lake City: Western Epics, Inc., 1966), 980, Vincent Shurtliff is given as the captain of Thomas's group. The records of the LDS Church Historical Department, have no record of Vincent Shurtliff as a trail captain in 1851, only Luman A. Shurtliff. (See Melvin L. Bashore and Linda L. Haslam, *Mormon Pioneer Companies Crossing the Plains 1847-1868: Narratives, Guide to Sources in Utah Libraries and Archives,* LDS Historical Department Library, 1990, 3rd Revised Edition.) When the Shurtliff Company arrived, Luman writes in his journal that his cousin, Vincent Shurtliff, came out to meet him on his way to England to serve a mission. (See The *Journal of Luman Andros Shurtliff,* LDS Church Historical Department Library, 58.) Vincent Shurtliff served as a trail captain in July 1853. See Daughters of Utah Pioneers (DUP), *Mormon Emigration 1840-1869* (Salt Lake City, Utah: Utah Printing Company, 1963), 260.)

159   *Biographical Sketch of the Life of Luman Andros Shurtliff, 1807-1864, 400.* This sketch is taken from his personal journal written during his lifetime and is located in the LDS Church Historical Department Library.

The King family began the long march to Utah in June 1851, arriving in Salt Lake three months later. The large dots represent the 300 mile detour the King family took up and around the Elkhorn River.

Subsequently they were subdivided into smaller groups of ten. Apostle Orson Hyde was the Church's presiding officer in Pottawattomie County and in charge of emigration, and Thomas and his family were part of 150 people in Kelsey's Company of 100 wagons.[160] Unfortunately a complete roster of the members of this company was not maintained or has been lost, so it is not possible to determine who may have traveled with the Kings. From a partial list the only other known family member in the same company was Orange Warner, who had married two of the Robison sisters, but they both had died and Orange's third wife was Mary E. Tyler. One account refers to the possibility of Peter Robison, Margaret Robison Phelps, and Cornelia Warner being included in their company.[161] Inasmuch as many of these people were sent to Fillmore by Brigham Young, it could be speculated that many of the original settlers of Fillmore were found in the Kelsey company.[162] However, from the surviving records we know only the names of 117 people, and out of this known list only the King and the Warner family went to Fillmore.

Church records are also incomplete about how many people emigrated to Utah in 1851. Thousands had made the trek during the gold rush years of 1849 and 1850, yet a significantly large number of some eight thousand Saints still resided in Iowa and Missouri. Extant records indicate that 1851 was a somewhat meager year for emigration before the push in 1852 to have all the Saints emigrate as rapidly as possible. One estimate put the 1851 emigration at about 5,000 people.[163] This appears to be a rather high

---

160 Bashore and Haslam, *Pioneer Companies that Crossed the Plains 1847-1868.*

161 See Dwight L. King, *The Two Volneys: Volney King 1847-1926 and Volney Emery King 1878-1962* (Privately published, January 1993), 38. The book refers to two sisters and a brother of Matilda. According to Carol Gates Sorensen, Tucson, Arizona, Cornelia was a daughter of Orange Warner.

162 See Appendix 3 for a list of the original settlers of Fillmore.

163 Daughters of Utah Pioneers, *Mormon Emigration 1840-1869* (Salt Lake City,

estimate considering that only about 550 to 600 wagons can be identified from most records as coming west. At four to five people per wagon, the number of people would have been between 2,200 and 3,000.

Recognizing the open window for travel, most of the people who traveled left Council Bluffs during the months of May and June, placing hundreds of wagons on the trail within close proximity of each other. Water and feed for the animals was essential, and the Mormon trail followed the Platt and Sweetwater rivers through Nebraska and Wyoming before going over the mountain passes into Salt Lake. Prairie grass was abundant along the trail, but the most imposing obstacle was traversing the continental divide. South Pass with an elevation of 7,085 feet was discovered in 1812 and became the major passage for most westbound travelers. While the terrain out of Kanesville and across Nebraska was fairly even, its upward slope rose from an elevation of under 1,000 feet above sea level to over 4,800 feet by the time the pioneers arrived at Fort Laramie. From Laramie to South Pass was another 3,000 in elevation before the final ascent over the 7,245 foot summit coming into Salt Lake. Characteristically, along the trail were numerous small rivers and streams to ford, ranging in width of two to three feet to more than fifty yards with depth ranging from a few inches to three to four feet. The Mormons also established ferries on major rivers such as the North Platt at Casper and the Green, and it would take several days just to ferry one wagon train across

Mormon companies were known for their organization and discipline. Each company was organized by wagons into 100s then 50s then 10s with a captain responsible for each group. Travel was by the sun as people were up at 5:00 in the morning. By 7:00 prayers were to be offered, food prepared and eaten, and teams fed. There were rules for noon and evening stops and by 9:00 in the evening everyone was to be at rest. No travel was permitted on Sunday, giving everyone, including their beasts of burden, a day of rest.

As soon as Thomas's company was organized, they were ferried across the Missouri River and on June 10 they started westward for the Elkhorn River. Normally the Elkhorn was a fordable river at a width of fifty yards and a depth of about three feet. However, from the first day they met to organize themselves into companies, the weather turned inclement and the rain fell in torrents. The flooding in the spring of 1851 was of a similar character to that to 1849. For seven days the rain fell continuously until streams and rivers reached a high-water mark that has since never been reached.[164] On instructions from President Hyde, the group turned north

---

Utah: Utah Printing Company, 1963), 258-259.

164   *History of Fremont County, Iowa,* 369.

Overland Journey painting by William H. Jackson. (Courtesy Utah State Historical Society.)

and traveled up the Elkhorn to "head the Horn" as they called it.[165] The river just thirty miles west from Winter Quarters could not be forded by wagon.

President Hyde thought they could lessen the risk of high water and do better by taking a more north-westerly route to Fort Laramie rather than the traditional route which dipped southward, but the travel was very slow as the rain continued to fall. In the words of Luman Shurtliff's journal, the thunder shook the earth and two brethren were even knocked down with lightning while standing by a stove.[166]

Water seemed to be everywhere. One evening they camped on a hill side, and by morning the water was running down the hill with such force that it was running under their wagons and washing away frying pans, plates, and even chains lying lengthwise. After ten days they tried to build a bridge across one of the forks of the Elkhorn by dropping trees across the river, but by the next morning all their efforts had washed away.[167] One can only imagine four adventuresome teenage boys driving wagons and herding cattle in a forceful rain pelting them in the face, wearing soaked clothes day and night. Sleeping, working, and trying to get something to eat along the way would have been most difficult. Inside the cold and bouncing wagons was an anxious mother with a crying baby, not a year old, and a small four-year-old boy, bored yet afraid of the thunder and lighting. The only assistance was from a ten-year-old girl who herself was terrified and wondering how to cope with the arduous circumstances. At the head was a tired father trying to give comfort and encouragement to keep things together, yet himself suffering from the same gruelling conditions.

Their problems were further complicated when a group of armed brethren rode into camp with instructions for them to return to their base camp. A difficulty had arisen between the Indians and the Mormons, and

---

165 *Biographical Sketch of the Life of Luman Andros Shurtliff, 1807-1864,* 401.

166 Ibid., 402.

167 Ibid., 403.

President Hyde feared for their safety. The brethren were to serve as an armed escort to ensure their protection. After some discussion, the group decided to return, although it appears there were some who disagreed with the decision and wanted to move on.[168]   They had been on the trail for several days, and they were anxious to keep going. To return would delay them even further, and companies moving out after the first of July stood the possibility of hitting cold weather and even snow through the mountain passes of Wyoming and Utah.

The wagon train arrived back to their starting place on June 27th. Evidently the difficulty with Indians was now settled, and they could move on, although all their problems with the Indians were not over as they would soon find out. For two days they restocked their supplies and prepared to once again continue their journey. Although, the weather now appeared to have moderated and their travel was much easier, the rivers were still swollen, and they again set a course north westward following the divide between the Missouri and the Elkhorn rivers for a distance of nearly two hundred miles. This time they were behind President Hyde's company which had left the previous day.

After traveling several more days they came to the Elkhorn, which by now they were able to cross, but problems with the Indians plagued them across Nebraska. While the Indians were not necessarily as hostile as they would become a decade later and an outright assault was unlikely, the pioneer company was still under continuous watch. Whenever possible the Indians would steal horses, cattle, or anything else they could get their hands on. They would also come into camp begging for food. As William and Culbert helped drive the three wagons along with their father, responsibility for tending the cattle fell to John and Thomas Edwin. In preparation for the trip, Thomas Rice had also brought along more cattle and horses than was customary or required; and only because of his large and industrious family were they able to take care of them. Even then it was not without difficulty. William was shot in the knee with an arrow on one occasion, and John was chased and nearly caught by two Indians while he was tending the horses only a quarter mile from camp.[169]   One experience occurred that must have proved embarrassing to President Hyde, whose company was just ahead of them. Without much warning, about 300 Indians rode into their camp and robbed them of more than $700 worth of provisions, clothing, arms, and equipment.[170]

---

168   Ibid., 404.

169 M. Lane Warner, *Grass Valley 1873-1976: A History of Antimony and Her People* (Salt Lake City, Utah: American Press, 1976), 114.

170   Andrew Jenson, "A Church Emigration," *The Contributor*, 13, 1892:351.

As the Kings continued their journey, the route proved to be about 300 miles longer than anticipated[171] and far more inhospitable than the main trail south of them near the Platte River. They had to cross many streams; and to do so at times they had to unload part of the wagons to lighten the burden for the oxen to pull. Other times they were forced to go through quicksand, completely fatiguing their animals. On occasion they even had to dismantle some of the wagons to use the wagon beds for makeshift bridges over the quicksand.[172] If it wasn't the sand at the bottom of the river beds, it was the sand dunes with wind blowing sheets of sand in their face as the wagon train wound its way around hundreds of dunes from five to fifteen feet high.[173] Frequently there would be the typical Nebraska sudden and violent thunderstorms that would create a soggy trail and a general nuisance in camping. Then there was the hot July sun beating down on them as they slowly moved along at eight to twenty miles a day. Perhaps the question could be asked, What would it have been like to have been the last wagon in the line of march? With all the dust and dirt and fear of Indian troubles, it would not have been easy.

From time to time, it was necessary to stop for a couple of days to rest the cattle, mend the harnesses, and repair the wagons. Frequently axles and wheels would break, wagon tongues would split, and camp equipment would fall into a state of disrepair. Pressure would also mount on the animals, and on occasion they would be spooked by the wagon behind them and stampede, overturning the wagon and scattering the contents over the prairie.

The cattle were always a concern and given priority care. They not only were a source of livelihood but were the means to pull the wagons. To lose one through sickness, exhaustion, theft, or stampede was always a great loss to the whole camp. Guards were posted each night, and most nights the cattle would slumber without incident. On other nights, for no reason the cattle would become frightened and stampede. For example, one night:

> as the guard was sitting at their fires in the gatway [gateway] singing one of the songs of Zion, when quick as thought, all the cattle was on the jump and burst threw the gateways, and away they went and ran several miles before the best

---

171   Thomas Edwin King claims a 300 mile detour. (See a short autobiographical sketch on Edwin in *The Daily Journal of the Kingston United Order.*) Andrew Jenson's *Contributor* article, claims they traveled nearly two hundred miles in a northwesterly direction before turning directly westward. This would have put the mileage detour closer to 400 miles.

172   *Biographical Sketch of the Life of Luman Andros Shurtliff, 1807-1864*, 412-413.

173   Ibid., 415.

Chimney Rock, located in western Nebraska, was considered the halfway point of their westward trek. *Painting by William H. Jackson.* (Courtesy Utah State Historical Society.)

horses could get ahead of them. After the men and boys and some of the women had labored several hours, the cattle were again safe in the correll where they were verry [very] content untill [until] near daylight when they made a rush to the North side of the correll [corral] and over the wagons they went, breaking three wheels and one axel besides smashing the bows, cover, and broke down another at the end of it.[174]

Fortunately no one was hurt, but several cattle were injured and one had to be left behind.

Besides the disagreeable weather, animals, and terrain, the pressures of travel and life under these most circumstances must have produced their share of personal disagreements and patchwork relationships. There were exhausted men falling asleep on guard duty and quarrels over firewood. One young man was horsewhipped by an older gentleman. In all, Captain Shurtliff must have been a very judicious and compassionate leader to keep it all together.

After considerable effort, the group turned south; and by the end of July, they finally linked up with the main Mormon trail near Fort Kearny, midway across Nebraska.[175] From the few records available, there appears to have been a sigh of relief when this juncture was reached. By 1851 the Mormon trail as well as the trail on the south side of the Platte were well-marked and well-traveled roads, and the Mormons were only one of many groups traveling to California, Oregon, and other points west. There were also military patrols along the way to protect the travelers as best they could from marauding bands of Indians.

Their struggles were certainly not over, but the going was much easier; and the farther west they traveled, the more moderate the weather became

---

174   Ibid., 418.

175   "Thomas Edwin King, A Short Autobiographical Sketch."

Fort Laramie was first established in 1834 as the area's first permanent trading post. Later it became a military installation. Painting by William H. Jackson. (Courtesy Utah State Historical Society.)

both in temperature and rainfall. One problem they soon had to contend with was the lack of grass. Because of the heavily traveled trail and the large numbers of buffalo they now encountered, the grass for their cattle became more sparse. Nevertheless their wagon train moved on. Soon they begin to encounter many of the notable landmarks along the trail such as Chimney Rock, a famous pillar of rock rising out of the flat lands of western Nebraska that could be seen for days. This rock formation was also celebrated as the halfway point of their trip.

Fort Laramie, the first major outpost, was reached the middle of August. Here they could make further repairs and even trade some of their fatigued animals for fresh stock. From Laramie the trail became more rugged and mountainous as the wagon train now turned northwesterly and moved through what is now Casper, and then southwesterly to Independence Rock. Here they passed during late August. Perhaps Thomas King and his family stopped to carve their names in the rock as so many of the pioneers would do to celebrate their westward trek. Graffiti does not appear to be a modern phenomenon.

It is natural for writers to focus many times on the difficulties along the trail, but there were also the happy times. There were the social events among the women, children's games along the way, evening entertainment, and teenage men and women's gamesmanship and flirting as they eyed each other. Times were difficult, but people are still people; and social conditions will always prevail as people move out of a survival mode. While camp discipline was always maintained, there would always be

Salt Lake City in 1851 as viewed by Thomas and Matilda as they entered the valley at the end of their journey from Council Bluffs. It was not much to look at for those from the green hills and mountains of New York. (Courtesy Utah State Historical Society.)

irritating items — not a disaster, but items such as the wagon ahead traveling slower than yours, or dust coming up from the wagon wheels, always making sure one is walking with the wind and not against it. Then there is fetching and drinking the water out of a muddy river or dealing with sanitation issues without trees to hide behind.

With September now upon them, days and nights were beginning to cool. Some evening temperatures even approached freezing. From Independence Rock they would soon pass Devil's Gate and historic Martin's Cove, not found in the annals of Mormon history for five more years, where the Martin and Willie handcart companies tragically lost so many people in early winter storms. The continental divide was reached as they traveled over the 7,100-foot-high South Pass on down to Fort Bridger, another major point of interest. This was reached early in September. From there they traveled on to the difficult and treacherous mountain passes of western Wyoming and northern Utah, following the road of the earlier pioneers. First there was Echo Canyon and then up and over Big and Little Mountains. Finally, on September 23, the company emerged from Emigration Canyon east of Great Salt Lake City to end a hundred and five day epic journey covering more than thirteen hundred miles.[176] It was nice to know that their effort and sacrifice did not go unnoticed. In a letter to

---

176   Not knowing for sure how far they may have traveled during the nineteen-day false start, they may have traveled close to 1,600 miles. The measured mileage between Winter Quarters and Salt Lake is 1,031 miles plus the detour of 300 to 400 miles.

Parley P. Pratt, President Young acknowledged that those emigrating the year of 1851 had experienced general prosperity and little sickness or loss compared with previous years.[177]

It would be difficult to understand such a journey and the privations endured without actually experiencing and living the event hour by hour, day by day, and month by month. This was no modern day camp-out or sideshow. It was real-life human drama, unfolding moment by moment. As the laborious struggle increased, their faith in the divine expanded proportionately. Only with a faith in their God and devotion to a higher principle could such a feat be accomplished. However, as one test was passed, another loomed on the horizon. New homes were yet to be built, and farms and communities were to be carved out of the wilderness, not once, but twice more.

177   DUP, *Mormon Emigration 1840-1869*, 259.

Joshua

(Settling Fillmore)

F or bringing the Mormon people to Utah, Brigham Young is frequently referred to as the American Moses.[178] Perhaps to his credit and reputation he might also be referred to as a Joshua. Moses, Joshua's mentor and advocate, was not permitted by the Lord to lead the children of Israel into the promised land, and the responsibility fell to this warrior-prophet. Just as Joshua had to conquer the armies of the Canaanites and Amorites before partitioning the land among the people, Brigham Young led the conquest of the Great Basin, a conquest against drought, flooding, hoards of crickets and grasshoppers, and the local aborigines or Indians. Hundreds of settlements were established, and an empire was carved out into what became known as the Territory of Utah.

Joshua established a free people in a land to be their own. However,

---

178 See Leonard J. Arrington, *Brigham Young: American Moses* (Urbana and Chicago, Illinois: University of Illinois Press, 1986).

CHRONOLOGICAL EVENTS

Oct 31,	1851	Thomas King and his family arrive to help settle the new city of Fillmore, Utah.
Nov	1851	Thomas appointed counselor to Anson Call, presiding elder.
Mar 20,	1852	LeRoy King, one and a half years old, passes away.
Aug	1852	Thomas elected county recorder.
Dec 16,	1852	Thomas appointed probate judge for Millard County. Serves for nine years in between his mission to England.
May 7,	1855	Thomas joins the Consecration movement with $2,535 in assets.
Apr 6,	1856	Thomas called to England on his second mission.
Jun	1858	Thomas arrives home from mission.
Jan	1859	Thomas elected Fillmore City Alderman.
Dec	1859	Thomas elected to the Territorial Legislature.
	1860	Thomas elected Millard County notary public.
	1862	Thomas re-elected to the Territorial Legislature.
Jan	1867	Thomas elected to the Fillmore City Library Board.
Mar 9,	1869	Thomas called to the first Millard Stake High Council.
Oct	1869	Thomas and Matilda called on a five-month visiting mission to Michigan, New York, and Pennsylvania.
Apr 15,	1874	Thomas joins the second United Order at Fillmore.
	1876	Thomas called by Brigham Young to establish a United Order in Circle Valley.

Israel later became a conquered people, their religious traditions compromised and their temple destroyed. Brigham Young, leading a group of latter-day Israelites and likewise possessing a unique religious experience, also had his work compromised through surrender and intervention.

The King family as part of modern-day Israel participated in this conquest and surrender. After they arrived in the Salt Lake Valley, they were assigned, together with some thirty other families, to settle Pauvan or as the Indians called it Pahvant Valley, 150 miles south of Salt Lake. Included in this group were the Orange Warner family and probably some of the members of Thomas's pioneer company who were anxious to establish new homes. Absent, but who would later join the Kings, was Timothy King who arrived a year later and Joseph Robison, Matilda's brother, who didn't arrive until 1854.

While their was excitement for a new home, for many, the thought of traveling another 200 miles was a punishing if not challenging decision. They had just traveled 1,300 miles, the season was late, and winter would soon be upon them without proper shelter for the women and children. Animals and equipment were worn out, and Fillmore would have to be built from the ground up without any outside support. Salt Creek (Nephi) would be their closest neighbors, sixty miles away. But the will of the Lord was the will of the people.

Brigham Young, governor of the Territory of Utah, had determined to relocate the territorial government to a more central location than Salt Lake. When the State of Deseret was first organized in March 1849, the proposed boundaries embraced practically all of present Utah, Nevada, and Arizona and portions of Oregon, Wyoming, Colorado, New Mexico, Idaho, and California, including the ports of San Pedro and San Diego. The Mormon leaders envisioned controlling this vast region by means of colonization and from their headquarters in Utah. Geographically, the Fillmore location was part of the Pahvant Valley and deemed a more suitable site for a more centralized state capital.[179]

The Pahvant Valley had been the site of an extensive investigation, and President Young had sent several exploring parties to determine the feasibility of settlement. As early as 1849, hundreds of wagons full of gold seekers had traveled through the area, establishing the roadway as a main artery to southern California. So impressed was Brigham Young with the potential of the valley that he wrote to an experienced colonizer, Anson Call, to determine a spot for a community and then raise fifty families to settle it. Thomas and others so selected were to be the founding citizens

---

179 Eugene Campbell, "Early Colonization Patterns," *Utah's History*, Richard D. Poll, General Editor, (Logan, Utah: Utah State University Press, 1989), 140.

of this important community.

Thomas, his family, and the rest of the group (nearly one hundred adult men, women, and older children) set out for Fillmore October 18, 1851. The additional hundred and fifty mile passage was a continuation of the wagon and foot travel they had been experiencing for three and a half months. A second group comprising many Church leaders under the direction of Brigham Young led the way to help identify the spot for the proposed statehouse.

The actual name for their new city and county was des-

Brigham Young was governor of Utah Territory from 1850 to 1858 and president of the Church for thirty years. He passed away August 29, 1877. (Courtesy Utah State Historical Society.)

ignated after the president of the United States, Millard Fillmore, perhaps an appropriate name to evidence loyalty to the federal institution and to honor the president who appointed Brigham Young Territorial Governor.

By this time of the year, winter was fast approaching and temperatures began to drop. On Sunday, October 26, the thermometer at 6:00 a.m. registered only 14 degrees,[180] and by the time they reached Round Valley near present day Scipio, snow began to fall. The wagon train then had to make the steep accent up Scipio Pass before enjoying the gradual descent in the valley that would be their home for the next twenty-eight years. At the end of the month they arrived on the banks of Chalk Creek, a stream with a swift current about fourteen feet wide and a foot deep.

The fertile valley had an abundant supply of sandstone and limestone for building purposes, and they were in close proximity to the mountain canyons for needed timber. With no time to spare, the settlers began to survey the city and farming lands and to build a fort near what was known as State House Square. The west wall of the fort ran north along Main Street beginning at Center Street for about two blocks, and the south wall ran east just past what is now First East. Along these two walls, most of the homes were constructed with the center of the fort used for gardens, livestock corrals, and a few common buildings, including a mail station

---

180 Day and Ekins, *Milestones of Millard: 100 Years of History of Millard County* (n.p.: Daughters of Utah Pioneers, Art City Publishing Co., 1951), 5.

and church. The fort was nearly square except on the east side, where the brow of a ridge dropped off quite sharply and sloped down into the old creek bed some distance away. Originally, the fortification encompassed about five and one quarter acres, but over time enlarged to some thirty-six acres. Along this ridge at the east end of the fort, a waterway was built for conducting water into the fort.[181] As the houses were built on the outside lines of the fort, it was their intention to fill in the space between each home with pickets so as to form a complete stockade. However, they found the ground so dry, hard, and rocky it was impossible to fill the space in with pickets so they simply built their homes in close order. Later an eight-to ten-foot-high adobe, mud, and stone wall supported on a rock foundation was constructed with a large entrance consisting of two heavy doors built on a cross beam, opening from the inside. Most people stayed in the fort for almost ten years before it was safe enough to venture out and build homes on city lots.[182]

Before Brigham Young and his party returned to Salt Lake, the new community was organized with Anson Call appointed probate judge, Indian agent, and presiding elder. Call came to Utah in 1848 and built a home in Bountiful, Utah, where he also served as bishop. In a special session of the legislature in 1851, he was appointed probate judge with instructions to organize Millard County. His mission to Fillmore ended March 5, 1854, when he returned home to his family in Davis County.[183]

In addition to Anson's appointment, Thomas King and his brother-in-law, Peter Robison, were named counselors, and Noah W. Bartholomew was selected bishop. The duties between Call and Bartholomew are not totally clear. It has been argued that Call was acting as a Stake President, but no stake was organized and there was only one ward. It appears that

---

181 A description of the fort is taken from Old Fillmore Fort brochure by Jeff Lindren and funded by the Utah Humanities Council and Fillmore City as part of the Fillmore Sesquicentennial Celebration (2001).

182 Joleen Ashman Robison, *Almon Robison: Utah Pioneer, Man of Mystique and Tragedy* (Lawrence, Kansas: Richard A. Robison, 1995), 93. In a letter to the Salt Lake *Deseret News* by Anson Call under date of March 27, 1853, he states: "I would say that some few of the brethren have left the Fort and encamped on their city lots, and many more are preparing to build on their lots the present season." Quoted in Duane D. Call, "Anson Call and His Contributions Toward Latter-day Saint Colonization" (M.A. thesis, Brigham Young University, 1956), 97-98. Anson Call, recorded in his journal, "In consequence of the Indian war we tore down our houses and buildings of every description that was outside the fort, spent our time during the fall and winter (1853) fortifying ourselves in connection with almost every settlement in the mountains." (The Life and Record of Anson Call, 49, LDS Church Historical Department Library.)

183 Call, "Anson Call and His Contributions Toward Latter-day Saint Colonization," 42, 52.

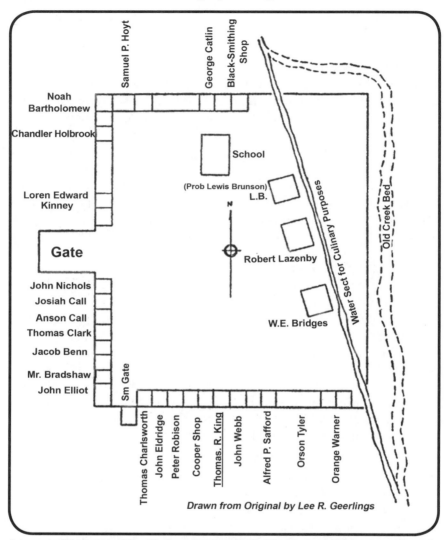

A layout of the original Fort Pahvant, about 1852. The Thomas King cabin is located on the south side. (*Utah Humanities Review*, 23.) See Appendix 3 for a more detailed listing of the early settlers of Fillmore.

Call and his counselors were more to ensure the temporal welfare and protection of the group while Bartholomew was to take care of the ecclesiastical responsibilities.[184]

As the urgency of providing shelter before the fast approaching winter a competition developed to see who would complete the first cabin. It is said that Thomas with his teenage boys won the contest, but Orange

184 Ibid., 93.

Anson Call, an established leader, was called by Brigham Young to organize Millard County. Thomas served as his counselor until March 5, 1854, when Anson was released as presiding elder and returned to his home in Bountiful. (Courtesy Utah State Historical Society.)

Warner and family also claimed the distinction. Many others soon followed as Anson Call reported at the end of December to the *Deseret News* that about thirty homes and a schoolhouse had been erected.[185] A few families were not as fortunate and had to live throughout the winter in their wagons.

These first log homes were primitive with dirt floors and roofs and were built from the soft cottonwood trees that lined the creek. Time did not permit them to build a road to the canyons for the better pine trees.

Thomas first built his home on the south end of the fort; but when the fort was enlarged in about 1855, he built a new home in the expanded section on the west side. To support their families, each man was given as much land as he could fence and cultivate.

A later report identified, "We have made a road into the canyon with the expense of a hundred-and-fifty-day work, where we find pine and fir quite plenty, timber necessary for building purposes. Our stock is doing well; we did not get here in time to cut hay."[186]

Fortunately, the weather during their first winter moderated and temperatures were above normal. During this early activity, the citizens received frequent visits from Chief Kanosh and his tribesmen and, despite their cultural differences, soon developed a friendly relationship. Kanosh could speak English; and while he could not always control everyone in his tribe, he wanted peace with the white man and to learn his ways. Several groups of Spaniards also frequented the area.[187]

The growth of this tiny village appears rather rapid. In January of 1852, several new people arrived and took their place in the budding community. Throughout the year and into the next, additional families were

---

185 Anson Call to the *Deseret News*, dated December 22, 1851 and published February 21, 1852, Salt Lake City, Utah.

186 Ibid.

187 Ibid.

welcomed, including several members of the famed Mormon Battalion. By October conference in 1853, Bishop Bartholomew reported the population of Fillmore at 304 people.[188]

Identifying the importance of education to these people, the first public building erected by these new settlers was a schoolhouse. The little school soon had fifty students, and a dozen additional homes had private schools. For unknown reasons the Robisons and Kings elected to home-school their children.[189] It may have been an economic issue, or perhaps Matilda had been schooling her family during the years they were in Iowa and wanted to continue the established pattern.

Fillmore City plaque marking the southwest corner of Fort Pahvant located at the corner of Center and Main Streets. Erected August 3. 1935.

As soon as the first signs of spring began to appear in 1852, the energetic Thomas and Josiah Call began to establish the first industry in the community. They petitioned and received approval in April from the Millard County Court to construct a grist mill and two saw mills.

The first death in Fillmore was little LeRoy King. LeRoy had endured the trip across the plains and the first year of settlement but died of scarlet fever in March 1852, only a few months after arriving in Fillmore. This now left Thomas and Matilda with five sons and one daughter who would grow into adulthood.

The first crop of grain in the valley was harvested in the fall of 1852 and exceeded all expectations. Without the benefit of any specialized equipment, the harvest was by cradle (scythe) and hand-raked, and bound in bundles by hand, and then threshed under the hoofs of horses. Apostle Ezra T. Benson reported to Salt Lake that Fillmore had threshed 8,000

188 Day and Ekins, *Milestones of Millard: 100 Years of History of Millard County,* 9.

189 Edward Leo Lyman and Linda King Newell, *A History of Millard County* (n.p.: Utah State Historical Society, Millard County Commission, 1999), 49.

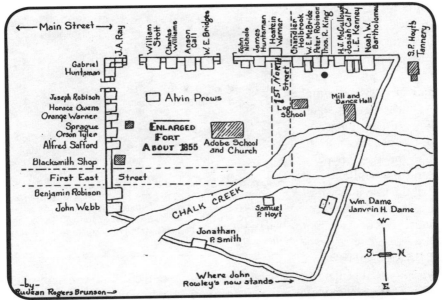

A map of the enlarged Fort Pahvant, about 1855. The Thomas King home is now located on the west side toward the north end. It should be noted that the King's next-door neighbor was Levi Hamilton McCullough, not H. J. McCullough. *(Milestones of Millard, p. 5.)*

bushels of wheat and that other grains, including corn and oats, were stacked and ready to be threshed.[190] This production created a surplus of over 2,000 bushels of grain that were shipped to needier settlements.[191]

The wheat was washed and cleaned and then at first, ground in coffee grinders to produce a small amount of flour. Corn was boiled in lye water or water and wood ashes to soften the hulls so they could be removed. A sort of hominy was then made from the kernels. It was a lot of work to produce so little food, but these destitute citizens of Fillmore were grateful and enjoyed what they could harvest. Later in March of 1853, the first threshing machine, called a chaff piler, was brought into the valley; and in May Noah Bartholomew completed a grist (flour) mill.[192] This enterprise must have been the one Thomas and Josiah Call had received earlier approval for and then turned it over to Noah.

The citizens of Fillmore continued to enjoy a bountiful and prosperous harvest that exceeded their immediate needs for the next three years. Much has been written about the crickets in the Salt Lake Valley, but in

---

190 Ibid., 57.

191 Sadie Rogers, *"History of Fillmore,"* Utah State Historical Department, Salt Lake City, Utah.

192 Day and Ekins, *Milestones of Millard: 100 Years of History of Millard County,* 11.

Fillmore the devastation was by grasshoppers and worms. The grasshoppers first made their appearance in 1855 and came in such hordes that they ruined most of the crops. Again, in 1856 the grasshoppers came; and while fewer than the previous year, they were still sufficient to do considerable damage. The worms also made their first ap-

Log homes were generally the length of a tree or from 12 to 18 feet long and wide. This would provide for about 144 square feet to 324 square feet of living space, not much larger than a regular size living room in a modern home.

pearance that year and destroyed most of the potato crop and vegetable gardens. The year 1855 also was the start of a two-year drought in Utah; and Chalk Creek, by June, was no more than a trickle. Farmers could only helplessly watch as their crops shriveled up and died.

Lifestyle

Early pioneer life for the King family and their neighbors in Fillmore was built around survival and completing tasks to produce food and fiber. While their lives may have appeared routine and predictable, perhaps it was no more so than any society at this juncture in fulfilling basic human needs. Individual and group creativity built a family and community spirit unique to that era, possibly lost to a more contemporary society. Lifestyles were simple, and a special closeness to nature and the land were always evident in their living. These people did not have much money, and their economy was built on bartering, borrowing, and sharing. There were few retail establishments from which to buy. Everything needed had to be grown, processed, or built with their own hands and ingenuity.

One pleasant advantage the citizens of Fillmore enjoyed more than many Utah settlers was the trade executed with many California-bound wagon trains. Many gold-seekers were willing to trade just about anything in the way of clothing, equipment, and utensils for food and fresh animals to cross the Nevada desert. As mining activity developed in Nevada, other economic advantages became available. Produce and other supplies could be carried in wagons and sold to the miners at a nice profit.

**The old adobe meeting house in Fillmore, built in 1854.
(Courtesy Utah Territorial Statehouse.)**

The failure of Fillmore to achieve its dream of becoming the capitol and the political and economic hub of the state proved to be a disappointment. The federal government funded the construction of only a small part of the overall proposed building; and with the Utah Territory carved up into adjoining states, interest in Fillmore began to wane. Salt Lake was becoming too well established, and after one session of the legislature in 1855, Fillmore was forgotten. The beautiful statehouse, however, became a blessing for the citizens of Fillmore as no other community could boast such a large community, religious, and social center.

Domestic responsibilities within the home were generally defined by the day of the week. Monday was wash day. Tuesday was for ironing the clothes. Wednesday was for making soap and churning butter. Sewing and mending occurred on Thursday. Candles were made on Friday. Fridays were also a day for corn husking, fruit drying, and some socializing. Saturdays were spent getting ready for Sunday by scrubbing floors, cleaning carpets, scouring kettles, polishing shoes, and baking. Sunday was a day of worship and church attendance.

For washing, water had to be carried from a cistern or ditch. It was then heated in large brass kettles that stood on irons or hung from an iron rail out in the open. The clothes were scrubbed on homemade wooden washboards, and the white clothes were boiled in brass kettles, rinsed, blued, and hung out to dry. Before the ironing could be completed, the heavy irons were first heated on a wood stove, and then as they would cool they were put back on the stove to heat and be replaced by a hot one. Soap was made from scraps of fat mixed with lye made from hardwood ashes. These ingredients were boiled together, cooled, and cut into bars. Candles were made from beef or sheep fat. It was melted and poured into molds, wicks were inserted, and the candles were then left to harden.

The stagecoach made two stops a day, one from the north and one from the south at Fillmore and Cove Fort (Painting by Leavitt Christensen, Kanosh, Utah).

The culinary water supply for these settlers came from the frequently muddy Chalk Creek. The dirt and debris first had to be filtered and settled out, and then the water was placed in rock and charcoal cisterns. Each day the cisterns were flushed out with fresh water from the ditches, and the animals were not allowed out until all the cisterns of the community had been cleaned. The cisterns also provided a cool place for the storage of milk and butter. In addition, the families worked out a system to provide ice year around. A small pond was filled with water during the coldest part of the year. After a layer of ice had formed, the pond was flooded for another layer. When the ice reached a certain thickness, the men would saw it into large blocks and then stored in an ice house, covered with sawdust for insulation against the heat of the warmer months of the year.

In Fillmore recreational activities and differing lifestyles were not always an option, although what they had was enjoyed. Brigham Young always encouraged the people to throw off the cares of life through wholesome amusement and activity; and after a hard day's work, a few minutes would be spent in telling stories, singing songs, and square dancing. At this time round dancing such as the waltz was considered immodest and suggestive by the Brethren, especially Brigham Young. However, as the years passed, President Young began to relax his attitude toward round dancing, and two or three such dances were permitted during an evening.

Special events such as the Fourth of July and weddings were celebrated with great merriment, activity, and on occasion, feasting. Later as facilities were available in the form of the schoolhouse and statehouse, plays and musical groups regularly performed. In all of these activities, the King family heartily participated.

Indians

Not unlike the first King and Rice ancestors to this country, Thomas, upon arriving in Fillmore, had to deal with the Native Americans and the dramatic societal differences that often led to conflict. Although the Pahvant Indians who occupied the valley appeared cordial under the leadership of their chief, Kanosh, many other bands of Indians of unknown temperament often moved through the area. For their protection and safety, Brigham Young always counseled the Saints to "fort up" and take adequate defensive precautions.

Kanosh was a young, strong, and peace-loving Indian who was chief of about six hundred Utes. They were a simple people with a meager culture and living conditions. They used deer skins for robes and coverings, wove baskets from willows, and through a process of tanning made deer skins into a soft pliable leather for moccasins. Their dwellings, called wickiups, were made of a few wooden poles used as a frame for a covering of animal skins. Weapons consisted of crude bows and arrows and other ordinary items. Their religion was as simple as their lifestyle. They believed in a great and good spirit, whom they called Shenobe. Everything good or evil came from Shenobe as rewards or punishments. Thus, prosperity was a result of their good behavior. Drought and other tribulations came through offending Shenobe in some manner, and they could blame only themselves for their afflictions. Their government also followed this same modest pattern. Sometimes the chief was chosen by his strength and ability to lead. At other times the title was passed down from father to son.[193]

Conflicts between the settlers and the Indians were inevitable as the Mormons were no different than their European progenitors who colonized the New World. Their desire was to acquire and control as much land and as many natural resources as possible; and in the arid Great Basin, productive land was at a premium for farming and cattle grazing. With farming came the need for irrigation, and streams and rivers were soon dammed and diverted. Unfortunately the same land and water claimed by these new settlers was also needed by the Indians to support their hunting and rudimentary food-producing lifestyle. One Utah historian writes:

> The Indians soon realized that the Mormons had come to stay, and that they were not going to stay in one place. It was the good fortune of the first settlers that the Great Salt Lake Valley was a neutral zone between Ute, Gosiute, and Shoshone territory; a salt source for everyone, it was not hotly contested. This was not true of the area around Utah Lake, which had been an Indian gathering

---

193 Ibid., 141.

place "since time immemorial," as the legal documents say. As the Mormons moved south, the early friendship with Utes ruptured.[194]

Besides the cultural and social differences and conflicts over land and water, a well-established Indian slave trade also produced strife and controversy. The more aggressive Utes would steal or barter children from the weaker tribes such as the Paiutes and trade them to the Spaniards for horses, guns, and ammunition. This practice had gone on for generations, if not for more than 200 years, to supply the conquistadors with labor in

Chief Kanosh, a peace-loving Indian, was chief of about 600 followers. (Courtesy Utah State Historical Society.)

their gold and silver mines. Governor Young refused to recognize the legitimacy of this practice in the territory now under his jurisdiction and moved to eliminate it. However, not to be denied a source of recognizable wealth, the Indians then threatened to kill the captive children if the Mormons did not purchase them. In response, territorial laws were soon changed to allow Mormon families to buy and adopt these children.[195] This may have eased tensions to some degree, but the issue of slavery continued to be a festering ulcer between the whites and the Indians for several years.

Brigham Young's public policy toward the Indians was a recognition of their degraded and ignorant condition. However, irrespective of their circumstances, it was far more economical and less expensive to feed and clothe them than to fight them.[196] Friendly relations were always extended to them, and his goal was to transform the Indians into self-supporting communities. When this failed he was more supportive of the segregated reservation policy   which removed the Indians from areas of potential Mormon settlement.

---

194 S. Lyman Tyler, "The Indians in the Territory," *Utah's History*, Richard D. Poll, General Editor, (Logan, Utah: Utah State University Press, 1989), 358.

195 Ibid., 360.

196 Ibid., 359.

Mormon Corridor
The State of Deseret

Salt Lake City
Provo
Nephi
Parowan Fillmore
Cedar City St. George
Las Vegas
Cajon Pass
San Bernardino
San Pedro
Los Angeles
San Diego

The route through southern Utah and across Nevada into southern California was known as the Mormon Corridor. This corridor road included Fillmore. The large outline represents the proposed state of Deseret, comprising more land than present-day Texas. (Courtesy Utah State Historical Society.)

The Mormons also identified the Indians as a branch of Israel, a "chosen people." The Book of Mormon held out great promise for these people, and the Mormons made every effort to send missionaries to convert them, not only to their way of life but to their religious doctrines. Noted converts included Chiefs Black Hawk, Walker, and Kanosh, but the cultural differences were too significant to expect or hope for a dramatic or immediate lifestyle change.

As the white man's aggressive and often contradictory policies became more explicit and visible, most Indians were left destitute without means of traditional support. It was always a troublesome problem to keep Indian men from stealing cattle and horses, and for the Indian women to go through Fillmore and later the town of Kanosh with gunny or flour sacks begging for food. Many times the settlers felt the Indians made a general nuisance of themselves, and they were often considered a mean, unpredictable, and loathsome people.

One of the first serious incidents with the Indians in Fillmore occurred December 29, 1852[197] during the Christmas season. An Indian by the name of Watershub had been employed by the King family to chop wood and became dissatisfied with his pay.[198] Either wanting more money or

197 Emiline Hoyt Diary, 1806-1893, LDS Church History Department Archives, Salt Lake City, Utah.

198 Another account of this incident states that Watershub wanted "bread" and Matilda kept insisting she had "no bread." Perhaps he wanted to eat before he chopped the wood. Chief Kanosh's opinion of Watershub was he "was a heap good warrior but a no good Indian." (See "Mother Stood Tall," by Rosa Vida Black, an unpublished manuscript,

**Painting by William W. Majors, of Fort Pahvant in the early 1850s, looking west.
(Courtesy Utah State Historical Society)**

food he confronted Matilda and tried to follow her into her home. To prevent him from entering the frightened Matilda quickly slammed the door
in his face, but in the heat of the excitement, Watershub ran to a window
and thrust his knife through the glass at Matilda. Peter Robison, Matilda's
brother heard the commotion from an adjoining room and rushed out. In
the ensuing struggle Watershub stabbed him between the ribs. Another
Indian close by tried to pull a gun; but before he could shoot, he was
subdued by a group who had quickly gathered. Kanosh begged the men
to settle the affair peacefully, and it was agreed that Watershub should
be imprisoned in the blacksmith shop until the outcome of Peter's wound
could be determined.

Watershub was able to escape but was quickly recaptured, chained,
and guarded until an agreement could be reached. Fortunately Peter did
recover and a council was held between Kanosh and his men and the settlers. It was decided that Watershub would give the wounded man ten
day's work and then receive twenty lashes to be administered by one of his
own tribe. When the sentence was carried out, it was reported that many
of the whites turned pale before the flogging was completed.[199]

Overall friction between the settlers and the Indians continued to

a copy is in my possession, 63-64.) See also Lyman and Newell, *A History of Millard
County*, 61-62.

199 Day and Ekins, *Milestones of Millard: 100 Years of History of Millard County,* 8.

escalate until June 1853, when the first major confrontation occurred in what became known as the Walker War. Chief Walker was a bold and hot-tempered Ute who became a bitter enemy of the whites. As he watched the pioneer encroachments and interferences in the lives of the Indians, he fostered among the Indians hatred and malice toward the settlers. He would make long trips to California, stealing horses along the way. By so doing, he became very wealthy and powerful throughout Utah and with some of the tribes in Idaho and Nevada. He also tried, without success, to persuade Kanosh to join with him in making war on the people of Millard County.

The few clashes that did occur were mostly with the settlements over the mountains east of Fillmore and could hardly be classified as a war, but the Fillmore settlers took no chances and withdrew behind their fortifications. They were required to farm and tend their cattle with adequate guards and sentinels. Thomas was in charge of a company of men selected to move the stock to a safer place west of Salt Lake City until the conflict was resolved.

> The one major clash involving the residents of Fillmore occurred in October 1853. Captain John Gunnison and his party of government topographical engineers surveying a possible railroad route across Utah were all killed by Indians near Sevier Lake. The massacre was in revenge for the killing of an Indian by a wagon train en route to California. The unfortunate task of communicating the tragedy to officials in Salt Lake fell to four Fillmore express riders. Two of the four were nineteen-year-old William King and seventeen-year-old Culbert King, a major assignment for any young man. When they left Fillmore, there were some who wondered if they would complete the trip alive.[200] Anson Call also reports in his journal that Walker's Indians undertook to intercept the express riders in Juab Valley, but they were able to out-distance the Indians.[201]

The conflict was largely over by the end of October, with a formal treaty signed March 30 of the following year. Chief Walker was pacified with a gift of sixteen head of oxen, some clothing, and ammunition. Overall, during the hostilities fewer than twenty whites and an unknown number of Indians were killed along the Mormon corridor.[202]

The next and last major hostility with the Indians came in 1865-68. Again, the Indians struck out at what they considered the injustices against them. Led by Chief Black Hawk, the raids began across the mountain

---

200 Volney King, "Millard County, 1851-1875," *Utah Humanities Review*, no. 3, July, 1947, University of Utah, Salt Lake City, Utah, 1:147.

201 The Life and Record of Anson Call, 47, LDS Church Historical Department Library.

202 Tyler, *Utah's History*, p. 361.

northeast of Fill-
more in Sanpete
County. While the
conflict occurred
mostly in Sanpete
and Juab Coun-
ties, the threat was
always evident in
Fillmore, and sev-
eral of the Kings
served in the mi-
litia guarding the
communities and
cattle. About fifty
Mormon settlers
were killed, and

The cabin Chief Kanosh and his wife Sally occupied. Culbert King helped construct it adjacent to his own home in the town of Kanosh, Utah. (Courtesy Leavitt Christensen, Kanosh, Utah.)

several southern Utah villages were abandoned during the conflict. Indian casualties in all probability exceeded those of the settlers.[203]

At the early age of seventeen, Culbert King learned the Indian language and, on many occasions, acted as an interpreter. After peace was
established, he was determined to win the friendship of the Indians; and
by speaking their language, he could call them by name. As a result, on
June 28, 1875, he baptized eighty-five Indians; and he and Chief Kanosh
became good friends.[204] Later when Kanosh married Sally, the adopted
Indian daughter of Brigham Young, in the LDS Endowment House in Salt
Lake, Clara Young gave Sally a fine black silk dress to wear and Kanosh
was presented with a black suit by Culbert King. Culbert also provided
a building lot for the chief and helped build a house, where he and Sally
lived.

However, all of the Indians were not on the same friendly terms with
Culbert, and on one occasion an Indian by the name of Mustache was
caught and put in jail for some offense. He blamed Culbert for his imprisonment and swore revenge. Soon after when Culbert was out after a load
of wood, he heard a voice distinctly tell him to drop to the ground. He did
so and immediately a bullet whizzed passed him and lodged in the nearby
tree. Culbert raised his head in time to see Mustache dart into the underbrush and disappear. Later Mustache was caught and reprimanded by
Chief Kanosh, who drove him from the tribe. Interestingly enough, Mustache was told that the bullet went through Culbert, the "White Bishop,"

---

203 Ibid., p. 365.

204 Jenson, *Church Chronology*, 94.

but did not kill him.[205]

Another experience with Indians involved Culbert's daughter, Clarinda. As a young girl she had a sweet and friendly smile and became a favorite with the Indians. When she was three years old, one young Indian lad said she was the prettiest girl around and when she grew up he wanted to marry her. Culbert, thinking it was a joke, went along with the conversation and agreed to the proposition, then quickly forgot about the matter. Years later when Clarinda turned sixteen, the man returned with many beautiful decorated ponies and blankets to claim his prospective new bride. Although Culbert remembered the conversation and tried to explain it away, the young Indian became very angry; and members of Culbert's family later described the confrontation as a frightening and difficult experience for all.[206]

Because the Indians were such a nuisance and at times almost barbaric, the story is told that Esther King, Culbert's wife, kept a small pearl-handled revolver near her at all times. Many a night when she was home alone with the children, she would put the children to bed and then wait up all night watching for any sign of Indians. The children would remember on several occasions how she would slip to the shelf where the gun lay and put it in her pocket and quietly return to whatever she was doing. When this would happen, the children knew Indians were approaching.

One day at the ranch when Esther was home alone with the children, a group of Indians came toward the house. She met them at the gate and told them to stop. When they demanded food and a number of other items her family needed, she told them to leave. As the Indians kept advancing she took out her revolver, took aim and hit a small rock some distance away. She then took aim at the Indians. The leader of the group quickly acknowledged: "Squaw heap good shot," and with several steps backwards, left the ranch.[207]

One summer when the family had moved into the mountains above Kanosh for the season to graze the cattle, living nearby was an old Indian friend who would help them around the ranch and tell them about the activities of the other Indians. One morning in the early part of August he came rushing into the house and said "You Big Chief Squaw (Esther

205 Angie Ross Buchanan, "A Life Sketch of Culbert King — My Grandfather," December 5, 1937. A copy is in my possession.

206 Esther B. Mathews, "History of Esther Clarinda King Black," *Levi Hamilton McCullough Family History Book*, 1974, 1:296-297.

207 Mary King Stenquist, a granddaughter, "History of Eliza Esther McCullough King." This history was written for the Daughters of Utah Pioneers and a copy is in my possession.

Fillmore, looking east, in about 1856 as captured by this painting. Note the fort in the background and the statehouse standing alone at the right. (Jules Remy published this engraving in his book, *Journey to the Great Salt Lake, 1861*, Courtesy Utah State Historical Society.)

was always called that by the Indians) must leave at once. The Indians are on the war path!" The family quickly gathered what few belongings they could and started for Kanosh. When darkness overtook them, they were able to spend the night with another family that lived about ten miles from town. Early the next morning, both families arrived safely in town. About a week later the Indian friend came to town with what cattle he could gather up and reported that the night Esther and her family had left, the Indians had come planing to scalp and massacre the whole family. The Indians were surprised and angry to find the family gone, and quickly destroyed the ranch house and everything they could before driving off the cattle. When the King family friend refused to tell the Indians where the family had gone, he was badly beaten and left to die.[208]

During the Black Hawk war in 1867, Brigham Young directed that a fort was to be built at Cove Creek just thirty-five miles south of Fillmore. In his instructions to Ira Hinckley, whom President Young called to supervise construction, he identified the object of the fort: to afford protection from Indians to the "Telegraph and Mail stations and to travelers who are almost constantly on the road. Also to furnish feed and protection from bad weather to this latter class."[209]

208 Mathews, "History of Esther Clarinda King Black," 1:296-299.

209 Ira Nathaniel Hinckley Diary March 1857 to June 1858, LDS Church History

Apparently Thomas King owned some of the land to be used and was asked by President Young to help build the fort, but the cost of the project turned out to be far greater than Thomas anticipated. In a letter to Brigham dated July 8, 1857, he explains:

Cove Fort, located thirty-five miles south of Fillmore, was built in 1867 for additional protection against the Indians. (Paintings by Leavitt Christensen, Kanosh, Utah.)

When you were here you asked me if I would help build a fort at Cove Creek, or sell my interest there to you, to which I replied I would help build the fort. I did not then think it would cost so much. I thought that two thousand dollars, or at most Twenty five hundred dollars would cover the expenses. One fifth of that I could accomplish, but to build one fifth of the present contemplated fort would take more than I am worth. I am willing to do what I can -- say four or five hundred dollars, but if it is expected of me to build one fifth of the whole fort, I would rather draw off entirely.[210]

President Young's response was a simple "just get the job done and we will settle later:"

You can do what you can to help build the fort, and we can settle about that afterwards. You will be at liberty to live in the Fort, and to enjoy such advantages as will attend its erection.[211]

The fort was built with thick heavy stone walls eighteen feet high and four feet thick at the ground tapering to a width of thirty-two inches at the top. The front gate was fourteen feet square so that covered wagons could easily be admitted. There was also a smaller gate at the rear with both gates having an inner construction that was filled with sand. This

---

Department Archives.

210 Thomas Rice King to Brigham Young, July 8, 1857, Incoming Correspondence, Brigham Young Office Folder, LDS Church Historical Department Archives.

211 Brigham Young to Thomas Rice King, July 9, 1867, Letterpress Copybook, Brigham Young Office Files, Selected Collections, LDS Church Historical Department Archives.

The interior of Cove Fort. (Painting by Leavitt Christensen, Kanosh, Utah.)

provided a safety feature from possible fire caused by burning arrows and would also prevent enemy bullets from penetrating the gate. Inside they built twelve rooms to accommodate families who occupied the fort, every room having a fireplace. Portholes between each chimney were also installed for those inside to keep watch for any hostile activity on the outside and to fire on any potential enemy.

Several King family members also became involved with the fort. John Robison helped in the construction and at one time was put in charge of the guards. Volney was the clerk and bookkeeper during construction and became the telegrapher. Whether Thomas and Matilda ever lived there as residents as spelled out in President Young's letter is not known, although on occasion they did spend time at the fort.

On just such an occasion, the men had left the women and children alone and gone to the canyon for wood. The Indians had not bothered the people for some time, so the gates were left unbolted. Sure enough, after the men had departed, several war-painted and fierce-looking Indians stalked through the gate. The frightened women quickly picked up their children and hurried to Matilda's room, only to have the Indians follow. They banged loudly on the door and as usual demanded food. Not daring to refuse, the women gathered the Indians at the table and quickly set before them what food they had available. As the Indians quickly downed the food, one of them who appeared to be the leader, motioned to Matilda and grunted, "You sing now."

At first Matilda hesitated. With the fright she felt, she was sure she could never control her voice. But with a second, gruffer request, the other sisters, fearing for their own and their children's safety pleaded with her, "Please, Sister King, sing for them." Not knowing what else to do she started to sing the first song that came to her mind, hardly realizing that it was "Oh, Stop and Tell Me, Red Man, Who You Are," a Latter-day Saint hymn by W. W. Phelps. The words of the song describe the fallen condition of the Indians who once was pleasant Ephraim, and their promised gospel blessings.

After the first verse she stopped, but the Indians, who had stopped eating to listen, seemed intense and interested and demanded more. The women were looking at her in open astonishment. When she had sung the entire hymn, the Indians, to the utter amazement and relief of the women, quietly arose and filed silently out of the room and then the fort. "Why, Sister King," the women exclaimed, as they gathered around her. "We didn't know you knew the Indian language."

Matilda couldn't imagine what they meant and quickly told them she didn't know their language. Unaware of what she had done, Matilda had sung the entire song in the Indian language and it seemed that the Indians had understood every word. She had possessed the gift of tongues that day, and it appeared that the words of the song went straight to the hearts of the Indians.[212]

This was not the first such an experience with Indians. Several years earlier in Montrose, she was crossing the river to Nauvoo; and on board the river boat with her was a band of Indians. Matilda recounts that the

"Oh, Stop and Tell Me, Red Man, Who You Are"

Oh, stop and tell me, Red Man,
Who are you, why you roam,
And how you get your living;
Have you no God, no home?
With stature straight and portly,
And decked in native pride,
With feathers, paints and brooches,
He willingly replied.

I once was pleasant Ephraim,
When Jacob for me prayed;
But oh, how blessings vanish,
When man from God has strayed!
Before your nation knew us,
Some thousand moons ago,
Our fathers fell in darkness
And wandered to and fro.

And long, they've lived by hunting,
Instead of work and arts,
And so our race has dwindled
To idle Indian hearts.
Yet hope within us lingers,
As if the Spirit spoke,
He'll come for your redemption,
And break your gentile yoke.

And all your captive brothers,
From every clime shall come,
And quit their savage customs,
To live with God at home.
Then joy will fill your bosoms,
And blessings crown our days,
To live in pure religion,
And sing our maker's praise.

---

212   This story may be embellished to some degree. It is hard to believe that Matilda did not know at least some of the Indian language, having lived around the Indians for several years. This story was first published in the "Cove Creek Gazette," no. 1, Spring 1975, 1:4. It appears the story was written by Irene Rowan, Provo, Utah, in January 1959.

Spirit of the Lord rested upon her and she sang to them in their native tongue. She sang about the Book of Mormon and she records that the Indians "rejoiced exceedingly."[213]

John Robison was also a good friend to the Indians and he was affectionately known as "Kinky John." He had a compassion and understanding for them, and in return they trusted him and would come to him for help when in trouble. John also learned their language, and he would often act as an interpreter. He would give them food and lend them horses when needed even though the general consensus was that he was making a big mistake. To his credit and the credit of his Indian friends, he never lost a horse he lent to an Indian. On one occasion a young Indian boy, by the name of Enoch, had been accused of stealing a horse. When Enoch came to John for help, John replaced the missing horse, and Enoch stayed on and worked at John's ranch for many years. John saw in Enoch a remarkable affinity for horses and an ability to work with and tame even the wildest of the herd.[214]

The Utah Militia

During the early years of settlement of the Utah Territory, the responsibility for providing protection against the Indians fell to the local militia, or Nauvoo Legion as it was called. Federal troops were not stationed in Utah until 1858 and even then did not participate in the Black Hawk War of 1865-68. The militia was organized in Utah in March 1852 with Daniel H. Wells in charge as lieutenant general. It was simply made up of citizen soldiers who would come and go as the need arose or when their particular community was threatened. The territory was also divided into military districts mainly along county lines, and annual musters were held. Rank was somewhat fluid; discipline, training, and tactics were based on circumstances and in no way compared to the federal army. It continued in existence until 1870, reaching peak strength during the Black Hawk War with 12,000 men, involving infantry, cavalry, artillery, engineers, and ordnance.

Mormon Battalion members with their prior military training and experience were given many of the primary positions. For example in the Pauvan district comprising Millard County, Levi McCullough was selected as district commander with the rank of major. Levi was the father-

213 Kingston, Utah Relief Society Minutes, Kingston Ward, Panguitch Stake V1 Relief Society Minute Book 1878-1898, September 5, 1878, LDS Church Historical Department Archives.

214 Warner, *Grass Valley,* 116.

in-law of Culbert King.

For the Walker War, William and Culbert served as express riders, and Culbert served for a short period of time as a private and a second lieutenant. Thomas also served in some capacity, as the records show that he was court-martialed September 4, 1852, for some unknown offense. Culbert was also court-martialed August 19, 1853, for refusing to stand extra guard duty.[215] Because the militia was made up of citizen soldiers, discipline at times was casual, and it appears that people were court-martialed for many different offenses. Fines of $5 to $20 were usually the penalty, and the money was turned over to the public treasury.

During the Black Hawk War, William, John, and Volney served on a ten-day campaign, June 10 to June 20, 1866. They were privates in James C. Owens' Company. (Owen was an early settler of Fillmore and the town marshall.) The operation against the Indians was prompted by an Indian raid on one of the neighboring towns (probably Scipio) in Round Valley. The Indians had killed one man and a boy, had stolen some 300 head of cattle, and had made their way up the canyon to Round Valley Lake.[216] An interesting account of their campaign is as follows:

> The forenoon of the day we left was cloudy and threatening, and along about three o'clock the rain began pouring down in a steady torrent. We waited in Thomas R. King's barn until the entire party was ready. Our provisions of bread and dried beef were carefully wrapped in a blanket or quilt and tied to the back of our saddles. Our eating utensils consisted of either a hunting or pocket knife. More attention was paid to firearms than to useless luxuries.
>
> There were about forty men and we were under the command of Captain James C. Owens. Our march began at a slow canter, and as the horses warmed up the pace was increased to a fast gallop, then there would be intervals of walking to rest the animals. Every art known was applied by those practiced horsemen to conserve the strength of our faithful brutes.
>
> The rain continued its steady downpour. While ascending the Round Valley divide, which was a few miles southwest of the original raid, we noticed a phenomena none of us had ever seen before — on the top of each ear of every horse, there seemed to be a tiny light that rose and fell with the movement of their heads and amid the blackness of the storm those tiny lights were the only visible objects.
>
> When we were within a couple of miles of the village in Round Valley (Scipio) we were suddenly stopped by an obstacle worse than a band of hostile red men. The rain had washed out the dam at the lake and a raging torrent of water fifteen feet wide and ten to twelve feet deep, with vertical banks, lay directly before us. It was still raining and dismally dark. A hasty consultation was held to determine whether we should turn back and cross the stream near

215 "Territorial Militia Service Records," Utah State Archives and Records Service, Salt Lake City, Utah.

216 Volney King Affidavit, "Volney King Papers," Utah State Historical Society..

the village, or take chances on swimming. We were fully soaked and more water was a matter of pure indifference. The detour would consume valuable time, and the Indians had about a twenty-four-hour start, however they were handicapped by having to drive the stolen cattle.

In the darkness we could barely distinguish the swiftly moving current and shadowy forms of the men and their horses. Captain Owens weighed considerably more than two-hundred pounds. He instructed his men to go slowly. They had come to the brink of the torrent and by intuition the horses shied away from the raging water. They knew the men expected them to plunge into the stream. Owens went first. His animal completely disappeared -- only the head and shoulders of the Captain were above the water.

The intelligence of those mountain bred horses was acute, the one ridden by the Captain by some inexplicable faculty, found a cow trail on the opposite bank of the flood and carried his rider to safety. It was fortunate for some of us that the Captain had instructed each man to loosen his lariat, and thus be prepared to rescue any of his comrades that might meet with an accident. One after another we ventured into the stream. Some were successful in making the crossing without accident, but others were compelled to abandon their horses and swim to shore as best they could. Some were swept down stream but were able to make a landing further down on the opposite bank. Some had to be rescued by men throwing out ropes to pull them in. Danger was at last behind us and the Indians still miles ahead of us.

We stopped and relieved the horses of their trappings and permitted them to graze while each rider spread his blanket, and as wet as "drowned-out rats" and still managed to get to sleep.

We didn't rest long -- in less than an hour we were aroused. A hasty repast of well-soaked bread and dried beef was eaten then we were on the trail again before the sun appeared over the eastern horizon.[217]

The story continues, but the Indians eventually got away. The militia was under orders not to pursue the Indians north beyond the Sevier River; however, as they approached the river, a small fire fight broke out in which casualties were inflicted upon the Indians.

Culbert was a major in the 4th Battalion Cavalry and Infantry.[218] He also served for a period of time in the Captain Henry Standwich Company. During one of the skirmishes he was wounded in the right hand and leg[219] and for his services received a government land patent.[220] How large

217 See Joleen Ashman Robison, 99-100. Material was published in "The Millard County Progress Newspaper" and is quoted by Ms. Ashman without date. The date is confirmed, however, from the writings of Volney King under date of June 10. (See "Twenty-five Years in Millard County," by Volney King, 37-38.)

218 "Territorial Militia Service Records," Series 86195, Utah State Historical Society.

219 Angie Ross Buchanan, "A Life Sketch of Culbert King - My Grandfather," a copy is in my possession.

220 "A short autobiography of Culbert King" from *The Daily Journal of Kingston*

a land grant he received has not been determined. For his service, Volney received a government pension in December 1913 of twenty-five dollars until his death.[221]

The Consecration Movement

The Mormon economic cooperative movement first began February 9, 1831, by revelation to Joseph Smith.[222] Briefly, "the law was a prescription for transforming the highly individualistic order of Jacksonian America into a system characterized by economic equality, socialization of surplus incomes, freedom of enterprise and group economic self-sufficiency."[223] The order was based on the principle "that the earth is the Lord's and the fullness thereof,"[224] and "if ye are not equal in all things ye are not mine."[225]

The Saints began a process of economic cooperation, isolationism, and self-sufficiency in Ohio and Missouri that would have significant and lasting consequences. Later in Utah, based on this theoretical blueprint Church-sponsored industries, irrigation, transportation, and construction companies, co-ops, and boards of trade were all established with varying degrees of success to help develop the Mormon community.

The settlement of the territory was an economic challenge for both the people and the institutional church. Crop yields were marginal, jobs were scarce, business and industry were hampered by competition from eastern firms (especially after the completion of the railroad in 1869) and the Church incurred heavy expenditures for settlement, emigration, and the construction of temples and other religious edifices.

Under this financial strain to meet their expenditures and to restrain capital from flowing out of the territory, the Church in 1855 begin to implement what is commonly called the Law of Consecration. Individuals were required to consecrate, or deed over, their property and resources to the Church and receive back a stewardship. The amount of stewardship would be based on the needs and the abilities of the individual. The third

---

United Order.

221 Dwight L. King, *The Two Volneys, Volney King 1847-1926 and Volney Emery King 1878-1962*, p. 93.

222 *Doctrine and Covenants*, Section 42.

223 Leonard J. Arrington, Feramorz Y. Fox, and Dean L. May, *Building the City of God: Community & Cooperation Among the Mormons* (Deseret Book Company, Salt Lake City, 1976) 15.

224 Psalm 24:1 (Holy Bible).

225 Doctrine and Covenants 78:6.

step was the periodic transfer to the bishop of the surpluses generated from the operation of the stewardship.

Fillmore was one of the first communities asked to begin this practice; and in January 1855, the first deed was completed. Most residents had little to consecrate. However, included in the number transferring their property were Thomas, his son Culbert, his brother Timothy, and Matilda's brothers, Joseph and Peter Robison. Based on

Largest Contributors to the Consecration Movement in Fillmore and Total Amount Contributed	
Samuel Hoyt	$11,887.94
Jacob Croft	4,582.00
John Kay	3,308.69
Thomas R. King	2,535.00
Noah Bartholomew	2,529.00
Joseph Robison	2,413.25
Other Contributors	
Culbert King	520.00
Timothy King	245.00
Total Amount	$76,301.94

the early records, Thomas had the fourth largest amount in Fillmore to contribute. The highest amount contributed was $11,887.94 from Samuel Hoyt and the smallest amount was $33.00. The average amount for the eighty-two participants was $930.50, not a lot of assets even for that day.[226] The poverty of the average person is evident as most only had a modest home in the fort worth from $50 to $350, a few acres of land worth from $1 to $3 per acre, household furniture, and farming utensils worth from $50 to $100, and perhaps a horse or two, a cow, and a wagon.

In Hoyt's consecration, it appears that the primary reason for such a large amount was his position with Brigham Young. He was President Young's agent to supply provisions to the workers on the Statehouse and many of the items so listed were for this purpose. Samuel was also an enterprising young man with a tannery and a nice home.

The following is a copy of the document transferring all of Thomas's property to the Church under date of May 7, 1855.

Be it known by these presents that I Tho. R. King of Fillmore City in the County of Millard Territory of Utah For and in consideration of the good will

---

226 This is taken from "The Early Records of Fillmore Beginning in 1855," found in the Territorial Statehouse Museum, Fillmore, Utah.

Assets Contributed by Thomas R. King to the Fillmore Consecration Movement

Real Property:

- One house in Fillmore Fort:	$250
- Forty acres of land on lot one, block two, Range south @ $3 per acre:	120
- Seventeen acres of farming land on the north half of lot eight, block two, range three @ $3 per acre:	51
- Thirty acres of land on lot three, block two, Range three, Chalk Creek sink survey @ $1 per acre:	30
- Lot two and five, block forty seven @ $50 a lot:	100
- Lot one, block thirty two and lot four, block fifteen Fillmore city survey @ $25 per lot:	50
- One fourth interest in sawmill:	300

Livestock and Animals:

- Four horses @ $60 per head:	240
- One yoke of cattle:	80
- Eight cows @ $30 per head:	240
- Six two year old cows @ $25 a head:	150
- Eight yearlings @ $10 a head:	80
- Eight calves @ $5 per head:	40
- Three hogs @ $25 per head:	75
- Twenty hens @ .25 per hen:	5

Other Personal Property:

- Household furniture:	200
- Two wagons @ $50:	100
- Farming utensils:	100
- One hundred bushels of wheat @ $2 per bushel:	200
- Three hundred pounds of pork @ .25 per lb.:	75
- Cash and receivables:	50

Total   **$2,535**

which I have to the Church of Jesus Christ of Latter-day Saints give and convey
unto Brigham Young Trustee in Trust for said Church his Successors in office
and assigns all claims to and ownership of the following described property
to Wit: (The format has been changed from the original to make the text more
readable.)[227]

One of Thomas's responsibilities, as probate judge, was that of transferring all the property to the Church. Thomas was also responsible for
helping enlarge the farming land by constructing a canal to the sink. The
sink farms were so-called due to their location. At this time before the
water of Chalk Creek was fully utilized for irrigation, the excess water
ran north and west of Fillmore for about six miles and then sank into the
ground.

All produce was stored in a common storehouse, and from this storehouse each family was supplied as needed.

In practice, the Church never did actually take ownership of the property; and within a few months, due to several external as well as internal
problems, the consecration movement came to an end. Some have tried to
equate this movement with living the United Order, but this would come
later. Consecration is a part of living the Order, but without the institutional structure.

The reasons for the demise of the consecration movement could be
summarized within a couple of comments. Most notable was the fact
that the people technically did not own their land and, in the eyes of the
government, were squatters on the public domain. A federal land office in
Utah was not established until 1869 so any serious effort to live this principle could not be done until land titles could be perfected. Any attempt
by the Church to take title to the land would have been met with considerable opposition by Congress.

The advent of the Utah War was also a deterrent, which occupied the
attention of the Church leadership and drained off critical resources to
support the defense of the territory. A final factor was the lack of support
by the general membership. In Millard County, with an estimated population of 600 people within 120 families, mostly in Fillmore, 83 people
transferred property to the Church, or the equivalent of about 70 percent,
obviously not a full participation by the populace. Throughout Utah the
ratio was less than half.[228] "The movement for the observance of the principle of consecration in the 1850s proved to be a symbolic gesture — faith
and the willingness of the Saints too literally to lay all they possessed

---

227 Ibid.

228 Arrington, Fox, and May, *Building The City Of God,* 66.

upon the altar."[229] For the Kings and Robisons, that is just what they did. When the movement broke up, the economic loss was considerable, not to mention the emotional and spiritual disappointment.

Second Missionary Journey

Thomas was again called as a missionary on April 6, 1856, this time to the British Mission. Several years earlier, England, except for Canada, had the distinction of being the first foreign mission of the Church. Led by Apostles Heber C. Kimball and Orson Hyde, the mission was launched in July 1837, and then again in April 1840 under the direction of Brigham Young. Together with a majority of the apostles, President Young and his brethren experienced almost legendary success. From their work, some three thousand converts emigrated to Nauvoo between 1840 and 1844 to bolster and vitalize the Church at its darkest moments.[230] It was now Thomas's opportunity to return to the land of his forefathers and continue the work of earlier missionaries.

Traveling back over the trail that he had journeyed on five years earlier, Thomas left Salt Lake on April 22 in company of Peter Robison and thirty-six other brethren, including Porter Rockwell. The noted Rockwell was assigned to travel with the missionaries to assist them in any way.[231]

Thomas left with two horses, one to ride and another to carry his belongings. They camped out along the way until the first of June when they reached Atchison, Kansas. Here they sold their horses in exchange for provisions and fare to St. Louis and then to New York City. On their way and before setting sail on July 5, Thomas and Peter stopped and visited King and Robison relatives in the Onondaga, New York area. They probably included Thomas's brother, Volney.

Thomas and Peter arrived in England August 7, three and a half months after leaving Fillmore;[232] and they were two of forty-two British missionaries serving in 1856, and two of only twenty-one during the following

---

229 Ibid., 78.

230 Richard L. Evans, *A Century of Mormonism in Great Britain* (Publishers Press, Salt Lake City, Utah, 1937), 245.

231 Journal History of the Church of Jesus Christ of Latter-day Saints (chronological scrapbook of typed entries and newspaper clippings, 1830-presnt) June 8, 1856. The above account is taken from the diary of James Ure, camp clerk. LDS Church Historical Department Archives.

232 "Manuscript History of the British Mission," LDS Church Historical Department Library, August 7, 1856.

year.[233] Thomas was first assigned by Mission president and Apostle Orson Pratt to labor in London.

During his mission Thomas was filled with the zeal and spirit of the work and enjoyed his experiences. In a letter to the *Millennial Star* written on November 21, 1856, he describes his feelings and his attitude toward those who opposed the work:

> I feel first-rate in my labours, and rejoice in my mission. The Saints in my field of labour enjoy the Spirit of God, and the gifts of the Gospel are manifested in

After arriving in Liverpool, Thomas was first assigned to labor in London. In January 1857 he was placed in charge of the missionary work in the counties of Nottingham, Leicester, and Derby.

the congregations of the Saints. The heathen may rage, and the people imagine vain things, and many rise up to oppose us, but they only manifest their folly and ignorance in so doing.[234]

He then goes on to defend the principle of plural marriage and points out the folly of the so-called enlightened age. From the efforts of all the British missionaries, more than 5,350 baptisms were experienced during 1856-57.

In January, 1857 he was assigned to take the pastoral charge or leadership of the three-county area of Nottingham, Leicester, and Derby in central England.[235] However, this experience was soon cut short by the Utah War. Out of necessity for the defense of the territory and a concern for their families, all the missionaries wherever they were serving were called

---

233 Evans, *A Century of Mormonism in Great Britain,* 245.

234 "The Latter-day Saints Millennial Star," (Saturday, December 13, 1856) 18:796-7, LDS Church Historical Department Library, Salt Lake City, Utah.

235 Letter of Appointment, January 1, 1857 and signed by Orson Pratt. Original in the LDS Church Historical Department Archives. Actual date of appointment was November 29, 1857. (See "Manuscript History of the British Mission.")

ELDER'S CERTIFICATE.

To all Persons to whom this Letter shall Come:---

THIS CERTIFIES that the bearer, Elder _Tho. R. King_ is in full faith and fellowship with the CHURCH OF JESUS CHRIST OF LATTER DAY SAINTS, and by the General Authorities of said Church, has been duly appointed a MISSION to _Europe_ to PREACH THE GOSPEL, and administer in all the ordinances thereof pertaining to his office.

And we invite all men to give heed to his teachings, and counsels as a man of GOD, sent to open to them the door of life and salvation—and assist him in his travels, in whatsoever things he may need.

And we pray GOD the ETERNAL FATHER to bless Elder _King_ and all who receive him, and minister to his comfort, with the blessings of heaven and earth, for time and for all eternity, in the name of JESUS CHRIST: Amen.

Signed at Great Salt Lake City, TERRITORY OF UTAH, _April 10th_ 185 _6_, in behalf of said Church.

Brigham Young
Heber C Kimball } FIRST PRESIDENCY.
J M Grant

**Thomas served a mission to England from April 1856 to the summer of 1858
(Courtesy LDS Church Historical Department)**

home. Thomas, with several other missionaries, sailed from Liverpool January 21, 1858, and arrived in New York seven weeks later on March 11. The trip from Liverpool to New York was on the 1,168-ton clipper ship *Underwriter*. This ship was about twice the length and width of the ship of his forefathers, Thomas King and Edmund Rice. During Thomas's trip home the *Underwriter* encountered a couple of severe Atlantic storms that shredded the sails. Waves poured over the ship's deck, and beds and baggage were soon soaking wet as water tumbled through the hatches into the lower decks.

It was customary for all Mormon emigration ships to be organized with a presidency to give direction and leadership for on board activities. Thomas was chosen as one of the counselors to Henry Harriman.

From New York they traveled to St. Louis (probably by rail) and then from St. Louis by boat up the Missouri River to Florence (now Omaha), Nebraska. Here they were outfitted with wagons, and teams for the trek home.

The company of 112 people was made up mostly of returning missionaries from England and other parts of the U.S. The group finally moved out on May 3. During the trip home they had to use all caution, for as soon as they were in the United States, they had to be careful not to let on that they were Mormons. With the pending war against the Saints, sentiments were at a flash point. In some parts of the country "government officials were enlisting men to go to Utah, offering $30 a month including a bounty of beauty and booty on their arrival in Utah."[236] In traveling past military installations, movement was carried on at night or at a distance.

For Thomas the trip home from Florence must have been filled with some nostalgia as it was a repeat of his trip only seven years earlier. The heavy rain, the cold nights, stampeding cattle, fatigue, long days, and short nights would bring back many memories. This time however, the travel was in all haste, even traveling after dark on many days, and traveling as many as thirty-eight miles in a day to get ahead of Johnston's Army. They were successful in that Thomas and the others arrived in Provo three days prior to Johnston's march through Salt Lake.

They arrived in Provo on June 23 almost five months to the day from leaving England. Here they reported their mission to President Young, and then Thomas immediately left for Fillmore.

Rumors were also rampant and anxiety grew among the citizens of Utah as it was hard to sort out fact from fiction. One eastern newspaper even reported that the first battle had been fought with government troops incurring over 600 causalities, 550 of them dead. Colonel Johnston was also listed among the wounded. The Mormons had allegedly driven off 800 head of U.S. cattle.[237]

---

236 Smith, *History of the Church*, June 23, 1858. The above entry is taken from the diary of Thomas Bullock, camp clerk.

237 James Lovett Bunting Diary (1857-1877), L. Tom Perry Special Collections and Manuscripts, Harold B. Lee Library, Brigham Young University.

The Utah War

The antagonistic attitudes and religious bigotry that had plagued the Saints from its earlier days in New York would not go away, regardless of their attempts to pacify their neighbors, isolationism, and pleas to be left alone. But by their very religious nature the Mormons were different. They viewed the world as a wicked enemy; and by implementing social, economic, and political programs that flew in the face of the larger society around them, the Mormons opened themselves up to persecution and intervention. The more they sought peace and the freedom to live their religion, the more the forces of persecution were mounted against them.

At first it was the local neighbors, then local and state governments, and now the full weight of the federal government was upon them claiming that they were guilty of revolt and sedition. With orders from President James Buchanan, 2,500 troops left Fort Leavenworth July 18, 1857, together with another 2,500 civilian wagon masters, teamsters, and camp followers. Their purpose was to put down the so-called Mormon rebellion against the laws and authority of the United States. Brigham Young was to be deposed as governor, and a new governor installed. Later another 3,018 military personnel were added to the line of march, bringing the total troop strength to more than five thousand infantry and mounted calvary.[238]

Besides the primary expeditionary force coming from the East, preparations were also made by the government to advance troops from the south, possibly up the Colorado River. Thus, the Saints from a practical standpoint were surrounded. The troops from the south could be used to mount a full-scale attack against the smaller settlements in southern Utah, including Fillmore, or simply could be used for hit-and-run warfare.

To counter this invasion, a citizens' army of approximately 5,000 men was quickly assembled under the leadership of President/General Daniel H. Wells.[239] Martial law was declared, and the mountain canyons fortified. To slow Johnston's advance, Major Lot Smith and a handful of forty-four men were sent out to meet the advancing army, burn their supply trains, and steal their cattle. While their objectives were clear and with the advantage of defending their homeland in a terrain they knew, it is doubtful whether the Mormons could have successfully held off the federal troops

---

238 Leonard J. Arrington, *Great Basin Kingdom: Economic History of the Latter-day Saints, 1830-1900* (Lincoln, Nebraska: University of Nebraska Press, 1958), 171,79.

239 Donald R. Moorman and Gene A. Sessions, *Camp Floyd and the Mormons: The Utah War* (Salt Lake City, Utah: University of Utah Press, 1992), 21. Besides the commander of the Nauvoo Legion, Daniel Wells was a member of the LDS Church's First Presidency.

General Albert Sydney Johnston (1803-1862) was in charge of the federal troops who were sent to Utah. He would later distinguish himself as an outstanding officer for the confederacy during the Civil war. (Courtesy Utah State Historical Society.)

for a lengthy period of time. But time was what they needed to encourage some type of peace negotiation to take place and to wait for public opinion to turn against President Buchanan for such an expensive expedition.

In the event the invasion was not called off, Brigham Young believed there were several oases in the southwestern desert to which the Saints could flee and find a safe haven. These places of safety were protected by the security of a harsh desert. Full preparations were made to move large groups of people at a moment's notice. President Young's policy was clear. He would invoke the "Sebastopol" or scorched-earth policy if the Mormon militia failed to halt the advance of U.S. troops. The only problem with this tactic, however, was that the western desert of Utah and most of Nevada had not been fully explored and there were no known places which could support a large population of at least 40,000 people.[240] Painfully aware of such a problem and perhaps a little naive, President Young in February 1858 called for an exploring party to be sent out to try and find the envisioned sanctuaries.

Two groups were organized for what became known as the White Mountain Expedition. The name originally was given by the Indians to a mystical white mountain west of Fillmore near the Utah-Nevada border; however, by the late 1850s "White Mountain" came to mean the entire desert region west of Utah's southern settlements.

Of the two groups, one was led by George W. Bean from Utah County and the other by William H. Dame from Cedar City. In a letter to Bishop Lewis Brunson of Fillmore, President Young stated in part:

> It is our intention to send out some old men and boys to the white and last mountains to the west of the settlements and find places where we can raise grain and hide up our families and stock in case of necessity. It is our wish to

---

240 Clifford L. Stott, *Search for Sanctuary: Brigham Young and the White Mountain Expedition* (Salt Lake City, Utah: University of Utah Press, 1984), 49.

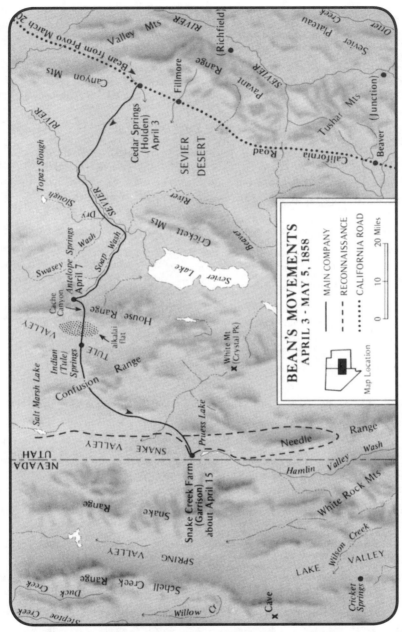

John King participated in the White Mountain Expedition to the desert of western Utah and eastern Nevada. The expedition was charged with the responsibility of looking for possible settlement sites in case the Mormons had to flee during the Utah War. (Stott, *Search for Sanctuary,* 66.)

have the brethren go prepared with teams, seeds of various kinds and farming utensils so as to have grain raised at these places the present season . . . . You will also select a few young and middle aged to go as explorers to pass about after having made a location to find other suitable places and report back.[241]

Orange Warner, 1805-81, Thomas King's good friend and Matilda's brother-in-law. (Courtesy, Utah Territorial Statehouse).

Fillmore's contribution to this exploration party was sixteen men under the direction of Thomas King's old friend Orange Warner. Included in the group was twenty-year-old John King. These men started out the first part of April to join with George Bean at Cedar Springs near Holden. En route they encountered a severe snow storm. Volney King's history of Millard County tells how the tempest hit them with such fury for three days that many were fearful of losing their lives. It was only because of Warner's leadership and perseverance that they were able to survive.[242]

After linking up with Bean, the group now totaled 104 men with more than forty teams and wagons. For the next several weeks they, together with the sixty-man group under William Dame, wandered back and forth across the desert, charting and mapping the area. However, for all their efforts they were unsuccessful in finding a place of refuge and John returned home on May 5.

Through the efforts of a good friend of the Mormons, Colonel Thomas L. Kane, a peaceful conclusion to the conflict was brought about, and presidential appointee Governor Albert Cummings was allowed to assume his post. The disappointed federal army marched through Salt Lake City without incident and was required to move on and establish its camp at what became known as Fairfield in west Utah County. All the brethren were required to make a pledge of loyalty to the United States and were

241 Ibid.

242 Volney King, *Twenty-Five Years in Millard County,* 26.

granted a presidential pardon.

The aftermath and effects of the invasion on the citizens of Fillmore were significant. The war hysteria produced anxiety and fear about a possible invasion from the south, and people from the north were everywhere. The streets of Fillmore were clogged with people and wagons having nowhere to go.[243]

The logistics of an evacuation from the north was a tremendous burden on every settlement in the south, and Bishop Brunson was told by President Young to expect families to stop for a season in Millard County. President Young further suggested they be settled at Cedar Springs, the sink of Chalk Meadows, and Corn Creek. Brunson was instructed to plant an assortment of specific crops from the sink of the Beaver River to the mouth of the canyon.[244]

Equipment including the *Deseret News* press was also hauled in from Salt Lake for storage in the basement of the Territorial Statehouse; and for a short time between May and September, the *Deseret News* was published in Fillmore.

Another casualty of the Utah War was the demise of the previously announced Consecration Movement. Its failure was a hardship on all its members, including the problem of how to re-divide many of the assets, an obstacle with which the Kings would become more familiar with in the next few years. Through all of this, the impact on the King family was significant. Thomas was traveling home from England, William was en route from his mission in Hawaii, and John was away on the White Mountain Expedition. This left Culbert to take care of his family, and Edwin and Volney to take care of their mother and sister.

Continuing Activities

During the twenty-eight years Thomas and his family lived in Fillmore, he not only supported and participated in all aspects of Church activity, but he also became a spirited community leader. His first appointment was in May 1852 when he was appointed clerk of the Second Judicial District Court when it was held in Fillmore. It was an honor, but an expensive one as he was required to post a $2,000 bond. Both his friend, Orange Warner and Bishop Noah Bartholomew signed as

---

243 Leavitt Christensen, *Birth of Kanosh,* 7. This book was produced at the request of Terry Higgs, mayor of Kanosh, Utah, and is part of the Utah Centennial celebration of 1996.

244 Stott, *Search for Sanctuary,* 62.

Thomas served over nine years as probate judge for Millard County.
(Courtesy LDS Church Historical Department)

sureties. His first election to public office came a short time later in August 1852, when he was elected county recorder.[245] Four months later he was appointed probate judge for Millard County by a joint session of the territorial legislature and served until his mission in 1856.[246] He was again appointed in January 1863,[247] and served until he resigned in February

---

245 "Secretary of State Election Papers," Series 00364 and 00364, Utah State Archives and Records Service, Salt Lake City, Utah.

246 Journal History of the Church, December 16, 1852.

247 Ibid., January 13, 1863. Also see "Utah Legislative Journals: 1851-1869," Utah State Archives and Records Service. One unresolved issue is that Thomas performed the weddings of his sons: John (and his wife Helen Matilda Webb) in September 1860, William (and his wife Josephine Henry) in January 1861, and Edwin (and his wife Rebecca Henry) in April 1862 — all in Fillmore. If Thomas was not appointed probate judge until 1863 and was not an ecclesiastical officer, by what authority did he perform these marriages? Perhaps he was given special permission as a former judge, and at times he was called upon to fill in when the sitting probate judge was ill. (See the short biographical information on John R. King and Edwin King in "The Daily Journal of Kingston United Order.") John indicates that at his marriage, "My father [officiated] as he did at the marriage of each of our family, excepting the youngest." Edwin states he was united in matrimony "by my father."

1869.[248] For this position Thomas was required to increase his bond to $10,000. This time Orange Warner and Peter Robison signed as sureties.

One grandson wrote of his grandfather:

> He had a legal knowledge of the laws of the land and was considered just
> the one for that position. Everybody respected him for his honesty and his
> fairness; in the community at large his word was never doubted, his honesty
> never questioned.[249]

Thomas also drew up the ordinances of the city of Fillmore and was the law adviser in public affairs.

The position of probate judge in early Millard County was more than a judicial officer. It was a dual position as a judicial officer and head of the county court, or what would be called today a county commission. The county court or commission was comprised of the three selectmen, the sheriff, and a clerk, with the probate judge as presiding officer, and had jurisdiction over such things as roads, schools, timber, mill sites, and the distribution of water. In judicial matters, the court presided over both criminal and civil proceedings. In a young and growing rural area where state and federal power were a long way off, the powers of a court became far greater than those of current day county officers.

In developing their community, the court was very much involved in seeing that roads and bridges were built, schools established, and justice and community standards maintained. They approved water and timber rights in the various and adjoining canyons for economic purposes such as the establishment of grist and saw mills. These were usually conditioned on the proprietor's building and maintaining a good wagon road which also in many cases became a private toll road; however, the court set the rates on tolls. Depending on whether a wagon was pulled by one, two, or three span of horses or yoke of oxen, the rate was usually set at $.25 to $.50 per wagon load of timber being hauled out   The court established grazing rights for cattle, watched over irrigation rights, surveyed and al-located land, and certified elections within the county.

The traditional aspects of establishing and appraising the county's tax base and setting tax rates was a big part of the job. The rate to begin with was set at 1/4 percent of the assessed value of a person's property, but as some societal things never change, the rate by 1866 was up to 1/2 percent

---

248 Ibid., February 1869.

249 [W. F. Olson], "The Life of Thomas Rice King," 1, Utah State Historical Society, Salt Lake City, Utah. No specific author is given, but the typewritten article is in the W. F. (William Francis) Olson collection along with several other histories written by Mr. Olson.

with a larger tax base. In 1853 they determined that the county tax could be paid in wheat at two dollars per bushel or lumber at four dollars per hundred. In 1854, the county spent only $208.75, but by 1866 a ten-fold increase had occurred as approved expenditures amounted to $2,717.75. This would put their tax base at about $550,000.

Most of the bills presented to the court for services rendered were from fifty cents to $5.00, some larger and were for a wide range of items. Peter Huntsman was paid $50 for an ox he purchased from the county that belonged to another person. John Cooper was allowed $4 for halter chains used by the county. Two men were given $2 for acting as judge and clerk at the election in Meadow. The clerk of the court was reimbursed $12 for stationery. Culbert King was presented with fifty cents for stationery. Allen Russell was allowed $12.00 for locating and letting the job of building a bridge over Chalk Creek. Peter Huntsman was given $5.00 for guarding a prisoner for two days, and R. W. McBride was compensated $19 for furnishing meals for the grand jury and for boarding and guarding a prisoner. In September 1868, $100 was approved to construct a jail in one of the cellars of the Statehouse.

The court met in various locations: the schoolhouse, the Statehouse or in one of their homes. To begin with, they only met three or four times a year for a couple of hours in the evening, but as the demands grew they met more often and during the day. For his services Thomas was paid a stipend of $4 to $12, usually based on a daily rate of about $2.50 a day.

The job was not always easy, and with extended family in the community, it presented some difficult decisions. A petition from Culbert King requesting the right and privilege of water rights on Corn Creek for a mill and running any sort of machinery was approved, but the petition from Peter Robison and Isaac Riddle asking for water rights on the same river were declined. Edwin King presented a bill for surveying for $75.00, yet the court approved only $55.00. Other bills were sent back requesting additional information, and social issues such as refusing a liquor licence were also dealt with.[250]

The records of Thomas presiding as judge in a criminal or civil dispute are few. As the county was still being established, cases were limited to estate and property settlements and a few divorce cases. Records are not available covering his second term as judge.

The only session of the territorial legislature held in the Territorial Statehouse in Fillmore was the forty-day session of 1855-56. Dignitaries in attendance included territorial officers from Governor Young on down,

---

250 The above information is taken from the "Millard County Minute Books," Family History Library film # 26,135, and "Millard County Court Minutes," Family History Library film #482,035, pt. 2.

including the Supreme Court justices John R. Kinney, George P. Stiles, and the infamous William W. Drummond. Thomas, as probate judge, was accorded the freedom of the floor of the general assembly.

Drummond was known for his aggressive attacks on the Mormon institution and his scandalous lifestyle, but an interesting note in the Fillmore Court minute book states that the grand jury with Thomas King as judge indicted on January 9, 1856, Drummond and his black servant, Cato, for assault with the intent to murder. It is not known how much of Drummond's reputation preceded him before he arrived in Fillmore; but in any event, a Mormon merchant living in Fillmore by the name of Levi Abraham knew of Drummond's past, and while the legislature was in session, began to spread the word. Drummond took offense and sent Cato to assault Abraham, but in the ensuing struggle Abraham got the best of Cato. The following morning Abraham appeared on Main Street well armed and verbally challenged Drummond's actions. A crowd of spectators all watched the proceedings, but no one dared to interfere. Finally, Abraham swore out a complaint against the judge, and Drummond was arrested. Drummond immediately appealed to the governor and legislature who quickly passed a law limiting the jurisdiction of the probate court. Drummond was released but then filed his own action against Abraham who in turn was acquitted by the jury. Soon after, Judge Drummond left the territory, and his letters to the president of the United States were responsible in a large measure for Johnston's army coming to Utah the following year.

Before his second appointment, Thomas did serve as an attorney. In March 1859, he represented Mary Sutton in a divorce case against her husband for adultery, and in August of the same year he defended Peter Boyer who was charged with assault and battery with intent to commit murder. This latter one appears to be Thomas's first big case, and he was successful in gaining a verdict of innocent.

Thomas was elected Fillmore City alderman in January 1859, as Millard County notary public in 1860,[251] and to the Fillmore City Library board in January 1867. His most influential position was his election to represent Millard County in the territorial legislature in Salt Lake. He served from December 1859 to January 1860 and was appointed to the Committee on Counties, and Public Domain, and School Lands. In 1862 he was again elected and served on the revenue and elections committees.[252]

In addition to the above, he served on many committees and councils

---

251 "Utah Legislative Journals: 1851-1869," Utah State Archives and Records Service.

252 Journal History of the Church, April 14, 1862.

for various civic and church functions. Whenever memorials, petitions, or resolutions were needed for public and political purposes, Thomas always participated and was at the forefront of activity. Many times he was called upon to deliver addresses or make public speeches at notable events such as July 24th celebrations and mass meetings.

Another important function performed by Thomas was that of post-master. The mail service was one of the major sources of information about the outside world and was very important to the people. Anson Call was the first postmaster until June 10, 1854, when Thomas took over the responsibility until January 3, 1866.[253]

Dates are not available, but Thomas also operated a hotel. The size of the hotel is not known; but based on the value of his property when the Kings left Fillmore,[254] it was probably an extension to his home where sleeping rooms were offered to travelers. It was probably a modern-day bed and breakfast with dinner if needed. Matilda especially enjoyed entertaining President Young and other Church officials traveling between St. George and Salt Lake.

One description of their home was from Elizabeth Kane, wife of Thomas L. Kane, a friend of the Mormon people and peace broker during the Utah War. In 1872-73 the Kanes visited "Polygamous" Utah; and during their trip south to St. George, the fastidious Elizabeth recorded her impressions of people and places including their visit in Fillmore and their overnight stay with the Kings.

The home was built out of red brick or sandstone to which "the wooden eaves and other trimmings adhered but did not belong." The interior description was less flattering as the parlor was roughly plastered and only whitewashed. There was broken glass in the window pane and the house impressed Elizabeth as being dirty. The parlor was in keeping with the exterior of the house and heated almost to suffocation by a large sheet-iron stove. Elizabeth found the bedroom cold and the basins both empty and dirty. The lounge (sofa) was badly stuffed with straw. Decorations included the "usual photos" of Brigham Young, George A. Smith, Heber C. Kimball, and Daniel H. Wells were hanging on the walls, and a center table had a large "Yankee type" Bible and a pictorial family register and photographic album from William King serving as a missionary in the Sandwich (Hawaiian) Islands.

Elizabeth's description of Thomas was that he was gray-haired with red eyelids, but she found Matilda less impressive and looking rather large and untidy. "She sat with us a few moments, lamenting that her children

---

253 National Archives, Washington, D.C.

254 See Appendix 4.

Matilda Robison King created this beautiful quilt that is done by applique. It is not known if the pattern, called "Washington Plume" is her original design or a popular one of the day. It is an example of artistry in color (red and green) and layout and the work of an excellent seamstress. The quilt is on display at the Utah Territorial Statehouse in Fillmore, Utah (See *Quilts & Women of the Mormon Migrations* by Mary Bywater Cross, 76-77).

were all married and gone; lamenting the trouble of housekeeping unaided; and by inference lamenting the trouble of entertaining me. I consoled with her most sincerely, regretting her latest trouble perhaps even more than she did."

In the evening Culbert and a small group of Indians called to pay their respects and to meet the Kanes, causing a complete turn-around in the feelings of Mrs. Kane towards Matilda. "She rose a hundred per cent in my opinion."

When Culbert entered the room with "a quintette of Indians, emboldened by his presence," Matilda soon called them to supper. "I looked helplessly at her. She said a few words in their dialect, which made them at once squat down again, huddling their blankets around them, with a pleasanter look on their dark faces than they had yet worn." Matilda explained that these strangers came first, and "I have cooked enough for them; but your meal is on the fire cooking now, and I will call you as soon as it is ready."

Elizabeth goes on to describe that she expected the Indians to be served, perhaps, scraps at the kitchen door, but Culbert explained: "Mother will serve them just as she does you, and [will] give them a place at the table. And so she did. I saw her placing clean plates, knives, and forks for them, and waiting behind their chairs, while they ate with perfect propriety."

The rest of the evening was spent visiting with Kanosh and several Indians with an appeal to Thomas Kane for government help, and assistance in dealing with dishonest Indian agents.[255]

A more flattering commentary by a grandson described Thomas and Matilda's house as a large brick home surrounded by a neat little picket fence atop a rock wall with lawns and flowers. For its day it was considered a "home of outstanding and comfort and beauty" with lawns and flowers. It included a large barn and a granary with fenced fields.[256]

Besides his holdings in Fillmore, Thomas bought his brother's property in Meadow. Timothy and his family had first settled in Fillmore prior to 1855, and then in 1858 he moved to Meadow. A year later Thomas purchased Timothy's farm and dairy operation, and Timothy moved to Beaver. He later moved back to Fillmore where he died in 1867. Thomas also had a dairy operation east of Fillmore in a mountain area called Three Creeks. Perhaps he merged the two operations together as Meadow was a struggling community at the time.

An intriguing side note is found in the Fillmore Ward Records under the date of November 12, 1868. It reported that the Relief Society was organized with Matilda King and Mary Ann McBride called as counselors, "but were not set apart because they were not living the Word of Wisdom." Family tradition acknowledges that Matilda smoked a corncob pipe most of her life and would drink coffee from time to time if she felt ill. The action of the Fillmore Ward is a little surprising as the observance of the Word of Wisdom was still somewhat fluid in the Church and compliance was not always noted except where taken to an excess.

---

255 This information on the Kane's visit is put together from two sources: "The handwritten St. George travel diary of Elizabeth Kane dated between November 19, 1872 to March 9, 1873, "A Gentile Account of Life in Utah's Dixie 1872-73;" and "Twelve Mormon Homes Visited in Succession on a Journey through Utah to Arizona," by Elizabeth Wood Kane, Published by the Tanner Trust Fund, University of Utah Library, Salt Lake City, Utah, 63-67. Both items are required to put the entire story together and are found in the L. Tom Perry Special Collections and Manuscripts, Harold B. Lee Library, Brigham Young University. A special thanks to Lowell "Ben" Bennion for bringing this reference to my attention.

256 [W. F. Olson], "The Life of Thomas Rice King," 2, Edmund Thomas Olson Collection, Utah Historical Society, Salt Lake City, Utah.

The Struggle for Economic Independence

With the trans-continental railroad advancing toward completion, a host of new problems was about to challenge President Young's desire for economic independence. While the railroad would expedite the immigration process, it was also destined to flood the Mormon community with imported goods, jump-start the mining industry, and bring in a non-Mormon population, all of which President Young wanted to inoculate the Saints against. While the mining industry was a natural comparative advantage for Utah and potentially could raise the living standard of the citizens, it was not the economic foundation the Church president envisioned.

Temporal self-sufficiency and cooperative living were the hallmarks of Young's perception, and he began to espouse the idea of organizing co-op stores among the vast Mormon settlements. The parent company was ZCMI (Zion's Cooperative Mercantile Institution) in Salt Lake. Formally organized on May 1, 1869, its purpose was to encourage economic trafficking and home industry among the Saints rather than becoming dependent on the Gentile merchants who imported eastern goods at perceived inflated prices into the basin, thus exporting needed capital and allowing profiteering at the expense of the Saints.

The severity of this economic imbalance is all too visual in the numbers for the years 1872 and 1873, the two years for which this information is available. In 1872 the territory imported $12,400,000 in goods, most of which was manufactured merchandise, while exporting only $2,800,000. In 1873 the figures improved slightly by importing $11,900,000 with exports improving to $4,900,000.[257] To President Young this was most discouraging as these resources could be better spent building the Salt Lake and St. George temples, meeting the cost of church immigration, and providing Church related public works projects.

The only way of fixing this problem and preventing the constant depletion of capital resources was to (1) to encourage the exploitation of the territory's natural resources such as minerals, coal, and lumber; (2) to dramatically increase agricultural production; (3) to establish manufacturing facilities to produce the products needed locally; (4) to band together in co-ops fostering new industries, economic trafficking between Mormons, and creating better and more stable prices for agriculture products.

As mentioned above, the first was socially and religiously unacceptable;

---

257 Bentham Fabian, "Statistics concerning the Territory of Utah, Years 1872-3" (Stevens & Company, Salt Lake City, Utah, 1874), 11-13, L. Tom Perry Special Collections and Manuscripts, Harold B. Lee Library, Brigham Young University.

the second was most difficult due to the climate in Utah mixed with the recurring appearance of the voracious grasshoppers and crickets. The next two had possibilities, although to compete with the eastern establishment for manufactured products with their skilled and trained workforce operating in up-to-date plants was going to be most demanding.

The most successful enterprise of the Mormon cooperative movement was the merchant activity of ZCMI, but other co-ops were also encouraged. In Fillmore a sheep co-op was organized in November and in March the following year a cattle co-op was organized to improve the breeding and raising of horses and cattle.

In June 1868, Thomas had established in June 1868, a successful mercantile store. He had also built a small brick building near the southwest corner of the old fort; and when a mass meeting was held in Fillmore to organize a branch of ZCMI, the proposition was to bring willing Mormon merchants into the fold. Thomas, always prepared to follow Church counsel, wrapped his operation into the co-op movement. ZCMI purchased his inventory, rented his store building, and retained Thomas as an assistant clerk to help run the store at a 5 percent commission.[258] To raise the necessary capital, a 175 shares in the co-op were sold within the community at twenty-five dollars per share for a total capitalization of $4,375.[259] Bishop (and soon to be stake president) Thomas Callister, was appointed president of the co-op and Thomas was elected one of five directors with Levi McCullough treasurer. To increase the size of the operation Thomas and Francis Lyman, another director, were authorized to purchase $3,000 of additional inventory in Salt Lake.[260] From this it could be surmised that Thomas and Gabriel Huntsman, another Fillmore merchant, were paid approximately $1,375 for their inventory and business interest, less any organizational expenses and necessary working capital. Initially, this would have initially made Thomas one of the larger shareholders, but from the dividend records Thomas appears with only a minor interest.

---

258 Volney King Diaries, 1873-1925, 48. Part of these diaries are located at the University of Utah Special Collections Library and part are found at the Utah State Historical Society. A transcribed copy is located at the Utah State Historical Society and has been used for my purposes. Many entries are by date and many are summarized and cover a period of time. A page number is cited in all cases, and if a specific date is given it also is cited.

259 Ibid., Volney King is not always clear in his writings. At first he mentions that the inventories of both T. R. King and G. Huntsman were purchased by the Co-op, and it is Thomas who rents the building to the Co-op. Later he says that Huntsman is running a competing operation across the street. It is possible King and Huntsman were partners until after the Co-op is set up and then Huntsman opened a competing store.

260 Volney King, *Utah Humanities Review,* 393.

Organized at this time by Apostle George A. Smith and others, was a School of the Prophets, an extension of the school first organized in Kirtland in 1833. It was restricted to faithful holders of the priesthood who were also community leaders. Not a school in the ordinary sense, it represented an assembly of men in which theology, church government, and problems of the Church and community were discussed and appropriate plans for action were made. The school might also be considered a sort of economic planning conference and in many ways became a means of carrying out the economic programs of the Council of Fifty.[261]

The initial enrollment included 122 brethren.[262] While there are no surviving records of this chapter, it seems reasonable that Thomas and at least two of his sons, William and Culbert, were included in the school. Also, at this special conference, the Millard Stake was organized with Thomas Callister as president. Members of the high council included Thomas, his son William, and his brother-in-law Joseph Robison. Culbert King was sustained as bishop of Kanosh.[263]

Evidently, at this time, food supplies were still not plentiful in this small community, and the settlers continued to experience periods of crop failure and food shortages. Eighteen years had now passed since the first settlers had arrived in Fillmore, but Volney King reports in his journal that a fast meeting was held in April 1869, with speakers noting the scarcity of breadstuffs and encouraging sharing with those who were destitute.

Shortly after the organization of the ZCMI co-op, Thomas and Matilda were called on a joint short-term mission. In October 1869, after all their children were married except Volney, they were asked to go to Pennsylvania, New York, and Michigan to serve what was called a "Visiting Mission." Traveling with them were Joseph Robison, Matilda's brother; and his wife Martha. The purpose of this mission was to visit with family and former friends to see if they could interest them in the Church and to gather genealogical information. The following is taken from a letter written by Thomas to his son William who was on a mission in Hawaii:

> We arrived here at James Bennie's [Matilda and Joseph's brother-in-law, married to their sister Susan] in Michigan on the 10th and found the folks well and pleased to see us but do not want to hear anything about Mormonism. Your ma was wonderfully disappointed in the looks of your Aunt Susan, can't believe that she is her sister, has altered so much and then her ideas are so foreign to the

---

261 Klaus J. Hansen, *Quest for Empire,* (University of Nebraska Press, Lincoln, Nebraska, 1967), 143-145.

262 *Journal History of the Church,* March 9, 1869.

263 Ibid.

Thomas and Matilda on their mission in the Eastern States in 1870 *(The Henrys and the Kings).*

principles of truth. Sends her love to Aunt Margaret, would like so much to see her.[264]

Another excerpt from a letter written from Onondaga, New York, to William in Hawaii, dated December 20, 1869:

I am sure that Gt. Aunt Matilda gathered what genealogical information she could while we was there. I am very grateful to her for the genealogical work she started and the record she left for us to build on.[265]

It is not known to whom Thomas may be referring. The only known person of that generation is Matilda Collier Guinal, Matilda's grandmother, not a great aunt.

Overall the success of this mission until March 1870, would probably be measured more in the genealogical research performed and maintaining family ties, than in converts. There is no record of anyone joining the Church because of their labors; however, there are extensive family records that have been preserved, and there was considerable temple work performed as soon as the St. George and Manti temples were completed.[266]

While in Gilead, Michigan, where Thomas served his first mission, he received word that Henry McCullough, son of Levi H. McCullough and Culbert's brother-in-law, was also in Michigan visiting with family on his

264 Lucretia Lyman Ranney, "The American Ancestry of Joseph Robison and His Wife Lucretia Hancock." A copy is in the LDS Church Family History Library, Salt Lake City, Utah.

265 Ibid.

266 No specific genealogical records from their mission have been discovered by the author, but Lucretia Ranney in her book on the Robison family (1958) claims to have used considerable material from Matilda's records. It is evident that Volney King in his "Genealogy of the King Family By Thomas Rice King Utah Territory," an unpublished manuscript also records much of the King family information. The original King manuscript is in the possession of Forrest King, Gilbert, Arizona. A copy is in my possession and the LDS Church Historical Department Archives.

Holiness to the Lord.

TO ALL PERSONS TO WHOM THIS LETTER SHALL COME:---

This Certifies that the bearer, Elder *Thomas R. King*
is in full faith and fellowship with the Church of Jesus Christ of Latter-
Day Saints, *and by the General Authorities of said Church, has been
duly appointed to a* mission to *the United States N.A. to* Preach
the Gospel, *and administer in all the ordinances thereof pertaining
to his office.*

*And we invite all men to give heed to his Teachings and
Counsels as a man of GOD, sent to open to them the door of Life
and Salvation—and assist him in his travels, in whatsoever things
he may need.*

*And we pray GOD, THE ETERNAL FATHER, to bless
Elder* King *and all who receive him, and
minister to his comfort, with the blessings of heaven and earth, for
time and for all eternity, in the name of JESUS CHRIST: Amen.*

SIGNED AT SALT LAKE CITY, TERRITORY OF UTAH,
October 29 1869, in behalf of said Church.

Brigham Young
Geo. A. Smith   } FIRST PRESIDENCY.
Daniel H. Wells

**Thomas and Matilda served a five-month "visiting mission" during the winter of
1869-1870 to Pennsylvania, New York, and Michigan (Courtesy LDS Church Historical Department).**

way home from his mission to England. Henry was without train fare and
Thomas sent $10 to help him get home.

Although the cooperative movement was moving forward, it did not
fulfill the indomitable President Young's ideal, and the cooperative movement was only the stepping stone to a more perfect society — that he

called the Order of Enoch,[267] a socialistic movement of having all things in common including all resources and means of production. However, to make the transition from philosophy to reality required a human sacrifice of immense proportion as it played itself out on the religious, economic, and social stage of life.

Spurred on by the national Panic of 1873 and the depression that followed,[268] Brigham Young realized that the regional economy of Utah was out of his hands and had become integrated into the national landscape. His goal of having the Saints economically independent with no poor or rich, was being throttled by the spreading mining, railroading, and manufacturing industries, and the growing disparity of financial wealth. To combat these developments he began to experiment with Mormon economic institutions that went beyond the earlier pronouncements of simple consecration. This time the purpose was to insulate the communities from the spreading paralysis of unemployment, bank failure, and economic depredation by encouraging an independence with home and local industry.

Contrary to twenty-first century popular perceptions, the brethren did not have a master plan of what an ideal order should look like, and several types or variations of orders were experimented with starting in the fall of 1873. One of the best-known was what has been called the Brigham City plan, built around a community-owned industry or industries with the intent of strengthening and reinforcing existing cooperative arrangements. The local people were encouraged to buy stock, and dividends were paid out in kind or script rather than cash. Profits were invested back into the business creating a higher probability of success.

A second type of order was a modification of the first for Church units, such as wards and stakes in larger cities. Here a particular industry could be fostered and focus could be given to items such as manufacturing of soap or hats that were normally imported into the territory.

A third type was patterned after the order in St. George. Here the people consecrated all their economic property to the order and received differential wages and dividends depending on their labor and property

---

267 The Law of Consecration and Stewardship announced by Joseph Smith became known by various names: the Lord's Law, the Order of Enoch, the United Order, and the Order of Stewardship. (See Doctrine and Covenants 78, 82, 92, 96, 104.)

268 The ensuing depression lasted six years, one of the longest downturns in the U.S. economy. Unfortunately, there is little statistical information available to draw a conclusion as to the results of Brigham Young's economic policies and the over-all effect on the financial well being of the people. It was a difficult time for everyone, and it appears that, as a whole, if the people benefited it was more from the sharing of the economic resources of those who had it, like Thomas King, with those who did not.

contributed.

The fourth type was built around a communal or large family organization; and was perhaps an idea generated by Sidney Rigdon's "The Family" program of the early 1830s in Kirtland, Ohio.[269]

Because of a higher degree of unemployment, the southern Utah communities were the first to be set up by President Young beginning with St. George on February 28, 1874.[270] Six weeks later, Young arrived in Fillmore to do the same, and on April 12, 1874, the first steps were taken to fold the previously set-up mercantile and cattle co-ops into the St. George pattern of Orders. The following officers were elected:[271]

President:	Thomas Callister, Stake President	
First Vice President	Edward Partridge, Bishop,	
Second Vice President	Thomas R. King	
Treasurer	William King	
Secretary	Thomas C. Callister	
Directors	Ira N. Hinckley	Benjamin Robison
	Chandler Holbrook	Culbert King, Bishop
	William Stott	David Stevens
	David Thompson	Pratt Lyman
	Joseph V. Robison, Mayor	

All the farming was to be under one head, but in Fillmore as the land under cultivation was in different locations several superintendents were selected.[272] Thomas was appointed superintendent of Old Field and Sink

---

269 Rigdon was a former member of the First Presidency and confidant of Joseph Smith. Prior to his conversion to Mormonism in 1831 he was a zealous Cambellite preacher in northern Ohio who believed in the imminent return of Jesus Christ. In preparation for this second coming, Sidney advocated communal living and set up what became known as "The Family" organization in the Kirtland area. There were many similar groups in the country; and according to his biographer, Richard S. Van Wagoner, Rigdon was profoundly affected by Robert Owen, a wealthy Scottish reformer and industrialist, who advocated a system of "family commonwealths." (Richard Van Wagoner, *Sidney Rigdon A Portrait of Religious Excess*, Salt Lake City, Utah: Signature Books, 1994, 49-50.)

270 All together, about 150 United Orders were organized throughout northern Arizona, southern Nevada, and Utah. Approximately half of these orders lasted no more than one year (*Great Basin Kingdom,* 329, 331).

271 Edward Partridge Journal April 15, 1874. A copy is in the L. Tom Perry Special Collections and Manuscripts, Harold B. Lee Library, Brigham Young University. I am indebted to Lowell "Ben" Bennion, for bring this valuable reference to my attention.

272 Volney King, *Utah Humanities Review,* 399-400.

farms, and William was one of two superintendents of cattle.[273] Just how much property was placed in the order is not known. If Fillmore followed the pattern of other orders, the people were selective in the property they consecrated, and this may have been more of an emblematic gesture as a search of the land records of Millard County shows no property deeds to the United Order.

> President Young preached to the people about the value of living up to the Order, and told them the motto was "Perfect Obedience to the priesthood, industry and rigid economy." Each person (who) joined the United Order had to pass a test on the following qualities: temperamental qualities, social and domestic faculties and reasoning faculties."[274]

Additional comments provided both a carrot and a stick approach in encouraging the people to live the order, they would either apostatize or become the richest people on earth.

> The President spoke more plain and powerful in relation to the Order than he had done anywhere south of here. Said the Saints must receive it more or they would apostatize. We have gone just as far as we could in our present course and the Lord requires us now to unite ourselves together in the Holy Order of Enoch, which if we do we will be blessed and become the richest people on the whole earth.[275]

On another occasion and place, Brigham identified his basic economic philosophy when he emphasized that labor was the source of all wealth.

> If men would but cooperate intelligently in the use of land and water, he [Brigham Young] maintained, they could start barehanded and soon acquire an abundance of possessions. It was of little consequence whether men entering the United Order subscribed their property so long as they fully dedicated their time and talents to the development of the new system.[276]

While it is recorded that most of the people accepted the formation of

---

273 Day and Ekins, *Milestones of Millard: 100 Years of History of Millard County,* 35.

274 Ibid.

275 Edward Partridge Journal, April 15, 1874

276 Arrington, Fox, and May, *Building the City of God,* 267. Perhaps President Young was trying to make a point to motivate the Saints to work harder, or he overly simplified his approach to the struggling members. Most economists would agree that labor alone is only one of three basic components of wealth (the production of goods and services). The three ingredients are labor, land, and capital. Labor would include the elements of skills and technology, land includes natural resources, and capital includes the equipment to produce economic goods.

the order, there was considerable opposition. For example, George Mason complained:

> The Order was calculated to expand the intellect of the few only while the many not being required to rely upon themselves but someone else to manage everything and tell them what to do would have no brain work and consequently would not develop their brains and hence would become mere machines to do the bidding of others.[277]

The people of Fillmore had the fundamental trappings of a United Order with a co-op store, sheep and horse herds, and cooperative farming; but within a year, the order met the same fate as the consecration movement sixteen years earlier. In the words of Volney King, "The result of that united movement was no more satisfactory to the people of Millard County than of other counties that engaged in the United Order movement through the Territory."[278]

People began to think it was not the Order of Enoch but simply another cooperative movement and they wanted little to do with it. Arguments soon broke out between the haves and the have-nots (an old story). Under the plan as organized, those who contributed the most in assets and labor had the most votes and received the larger dividends, but to the have-nots this was not in keeping with the spirit of equality in all things. They wanted those who had the means to contribute their resources without compensation and to have only have one vote like everyone else.

Those with the means were not willing to do this. They felt that men who have the ability to make the money are those best qualified to manage the resources, more so than those who never had anything and never had more than their basic "subsistence and a very poor one at that."[279]

Even Brigham Young was perhaps becoming discouraged. In February 1875 as the Fillmore order was collapsing (as they were throughout the territory) President Young and George A. Smith arrived in Fillmore. The disappointment of what they didn't say was recorded by the ever obedient Partridge:

> They do not give us anything more about the Order and to me it seems they are studiously avoid[ing] the subject ... and instead of getting encouragment as they anticipated, and instead of being just right as they were so sure, they begin to think they are just wrong, and instead of knowing all about the UO they say

---

277 George Mason quoted in Edward Partridge Journal, June 4, 1874.

278 Volney King, "Utah Humanities Review," 400.

279 Edward Partridge Journal, September 11, 1874.

they don't know anything about it. So much for getting enthusiastic.[280]

With the demise of the order, several members of the community began to consider a community industry similar to the Brigham City plan,
and the proposal was made to buy the tannery building owned by the
Robisons and manufacture boots, shoes, harnesses. Thomas King was one
of three men selected to determine the feasibility of this proposal. They
soon reported back that it would take about $6,000 to $7,000 to set up the
operation; but within a few weeks, they could come up with only $2,750
in pledges,[281] not enough to continue. The proposal was abandoned.

The mercantile branch of ZCMI seemed to have done better over the
early years and did pay some dividends before it went out of business. In
1870 it paid out $1,183 to 107 people or about a 25 percent return on in-
vestment.[282] In 1871 the dividend increased to $4,700 to 282 stockholders
with Thomas receiving $19.63 and the other King brothers collectively
receiving $108.73. Edwin was the heaviest investor, receiving half of this
amount.[283] The following year there were 311 investors; but as economic
events deteriorated, so did the fortunes of the store. By March 1874 Edward Partridge resigned as superintendent, and Thomas agreed to take it
over for a 4.5 percent commission on sales with Volney actually running
the day-to-day operation. The co-op was in debt $5,000 and receivables
amounted to eight to ten thousand dollars. Thomas continued until the
following year when he resigned, but continued as one of the directors.
The capital stock was discounted by 25 percent, and a year later the stock
was discounted 50 percent.[284]

All in all, it doesn't appear to be a good time to be living in Fillmore.
In 1876 President Young, a few months before death, made one last push
to create order out of the United Orders. He proposed to take the Saints
to a new level. As a result, this would not be the last time Thomas and
the King family would be asked to live religious economic principles for
gospel purposes. More was to come later as the strife and contentions of
Fillmore began to have its effect on the family.

A King grandson, William F. Olson, claimed that some of the people

---

280 Ibid., February 16, 1875.

281 Ibid., January 17, 1876,

282 In a letter from Thomas Rice King to William King, June 12, 1870, Thomas indicates that the dividend was 37 1/2 per cent after tithing payable in wool and sheep. The
apparent discrepancy is probably due to the method of calculation.

283 Fillmore Account Book (A ledger book of the co-op store), L. Tom Perry Special
Collections and Manuscripts, Harold B. Lee Library, Brigham Young University.

284 Edward Partridge Journal, March 14, 1874, May 24, 1875, May 15, 1876.

of Fillmore were starting to feel the Kings controlled too much of the region. They alleged that the family had secured all the prime land and owned nearly all the best cattle and horses. There was no chance for the rest of the people who had come to Utah to secure such resources.

An analysis of this claim may have had some credence. In a letter from Thomas Callister to Brigham Young dated March 19, 1868, Callister specifically mentions "the Kings and Robisons" as the wealthy brethren of Fillmore.[285] Thomas ran the store and had been the probate judge, William was the constable and country selectman, Edwin was the county surveyor, and Culbert was the bishop of Kanosh. Furthermore, the Kings operated the hotel, ran the school, and were involved in the operation at Cove Fort. John's cattle and horse herds were some of the best. When you add to this the community interests of the King in-laws, the Robisons and Warners, most everything was out of reach for non-relatives. Joseph Robison was mayor from 1863 to 1867 followed by Joseph V. Robison who became mayor until 1875, except for a two-year absence when he went on a mission. Peter Robison founded and had the town Petersburg named after him. The Kings had also married into the families of Thomas Callister, bishop and later stake president, and of Ira Hinckley, builder of Cove Fort and later mayor and stake president.[286]

Olson claimed that the people told Brigham Young that if the Kings did not move, there would be nothing left in Millard County worth owning that was not already controlled or owned by the Kings, and Brigham realized that jealous feelings and dissatisfactions on the part of the complainers had to be adjusted in some manner. Even some of the leading brethren were starting to champion the cause of those who complained. At a critical conference, as recorded by Olson, the stage was set by Apostle Snow (He does not specify whether this apostle was Lorenzo or Erastus). Turning to Thomas King, who was seated on the stand, Snow began talking about all working for the common good. Then he said:

> "Even Brother King dug a ditch for the purpose of taking out the waters of Chalk Creek for his own use and not for the good of all, so I am told."
> "I did not!" spoke Thomas sharply, "I bore the expense of the ditch and gave all who were entitled to the water the privilege of using it."
> "Keep to your text Brother Snow, never mind about the water," said President Young.[287]

---

285 Thomas Callister to Brigham Young, March 19, 1868, Incoming Correspondence, Brigham Young Office Folder, LDS Church Historical Department Archives.

286 See also King, *The Two Volneys*, 14.

287 Edmund Thomas (Olson), "Dan and His Violin," 219-220. This book is a 229-page typescript. The book is written in many respects as a novel and while based on historical

According to Olson these comments by Snow rankled Thomas right to the core. Taking water from his townsmen was a serious accusation, and to have his integrity attacked in public by one of the leading apostles must have hurt deeply. Now the thunderbolt came as President Young announced a call for Thomas and his family to go to Circleville in Piute County to build a whole new community on United Order principles. A call from the prophet was a call from the Lord for Thomas and Matilda; and while hurt and devastated, they were determined to obey the mind and will of God. While their devotion to the Church was supreme and never a murmur was heard from them, the test proved insurmountable to other members of the family. Olson goes on to say:

> When Grandfather King was called to this mission he was 70 years old and suffering from heart disease and he died on that God-forsaken flat to which Brigham Young had called him. Had Brigham taken him out and had him shot it would have been an act of charity, but at that age to send him away to that Godforsaken country at the request of jealous church members in old Fillmore was a shame.[288]

Mr. Olson made this assessment several decades after the fact and his account appears to have some noted flaws. Thomas was sixty-three, not seventy, and there are no conferences of record in Fillmore in 1875-76 attended by both Brigham Young and either Lorenzo or Erastus Snow. Also, the Olsons by this time had basically disengaged from the LDS Church, and their viewpoint may be embellished or dramatized to some extent by time and distance.

While this story of the Kings being forced out of Fillmore cannot be specifically corroborated, all the ingredients and stated conditions by Olson are in place. Edward Partridge's diary speakers of considerable quarreling among the people and a lot of horse and cattle stealing. The economic value of the region was pretty well spent with only limited possibilities for the future. Cattle, sheep, and horses had been imported to the point that the grazing land had become denuded, and under current

---

fact, appears to be embellished to some extent with some poetic license. The prospectus also lists the author as Edmund Thomas, although it appears to be Edmund Thomas Olson and there is no date of authorship, although it is apparent it was written in the early 1940s. See the Edmund Thomas Olson Collection, Utah State Historical Society.

288 W. F. Olson, "John Robison King," 5. This is an article in the Thomas Edmund Olson collection at the Utah State Historical Society. The letters and articles of W. F. Olson and the writings of Edmund Thomas Olson are all undated except one letter which is dated July 26, 1950, when they both were eighty-one and eighty-six respectively. It is apparent that Mr. Olson wrote several of his article in the 1940s. Several details in Mr. Olson's letters, such as dates, are in error.

conditions, no more land could be cultivated or improved. Partridge described the country as fit only for "wild horses and Texas cattle."[289] Fruit production with apples and peaches had possibilities, but scarce water resources made a viable crop difficult.

In the political arena there was a fight in 1875 over the reelection of Joseph V. Robison as mayor. According to Partridge, the opposition obtained the "votes of all the rowdies and hoodlums, gentiles and apostates, those pretending to be Latter-day Saints."[290] After the August election and as soon as the votes were counted showing Robison had won, he resigned because of all the ill feelings.

This fact suggests the possibility that Olson's earlier comments may have more to do with the Robisons than the Kings. The Robisons and the Kings were in-laws, and Joseph, a nephew to Thomas and Matilda, had far more wealth than Thomas, as did Joseph's younger brother, Almon. In a ranking of financial assets as reported in the 1870 federal census for Fillmore, Thomas was only twelfth, with Edwin and Volney quite a ways down the list, but significantly above the median wealth level. The two Robison brothers accounted for 11 percent of the city's wealth. This is significant, but would it have been enough to raise the hackles of the people? Hard to tell.

A partial financial breakdown from the census is as follows:[291]

Joseph V. Robison	$17,600
Noel Bartholomew	16,010
Chandler Holbrook	16,000
Almon Robison	10,000
Gilbert Webb	9,500
Thomas Callister	8,100
Amasa Lyman	7,000
Thomas King	6,175
Edwin King	1,500
Volney King	1,425
Median Wealth	500

289 Edward Partridge Journal, June 15, 1874.

290 Ibid., August 2, 1875.

291 While the first few numbers look impressive, especially compared to the median wealth of the community, it must be remembered that most of the people were living in acute poverty. Compared to today's dollars, $500 is worth about $8,000 with half of the people living at or below this level. Thomas King's wealth would be worth about $100,000.

The quarreling and dissatisfaction of the people also extended to their religious affiliation. In the 1880 census, of the total population of 987, more than 25 percent of the people had become disaffected in some manner from the Church.[292] Church courts were frequent and included the excommunication of Noah Bartholomew, Fillmore's first bishop, and Fillmore resident Amasa Lyman, one of the Church's twelve apostles. The Godbeite movement, a group of prominent Utah businessmen in opposition to President Young's economic policies, also became well established in Fillmore and influenced considerable hostility. Volney in a letter to William speaks of how "the spirit of apostasy runs rife amongst our unstable confederates be that as it may. Every fellow will have to be for himself for the devil is for all, he ain't dead."[293]

As to the water issue, in 1875 water was a scarce commodity, and there was considerable infighting over allocations, it was considered the most pressing problem by the citizens.[294] To help minimize this obstacle a small reservoir was being built and several of the men were building ditches to help distribute the anticipated run off.

Never-the-less, due to these conditions, by 1875, several of the King brothers begin looking for a new venue in which to carry on their cattle and farming operations. Both Edwin and John had already decided to relocate in Grass Valley, located in Piute and Garfield counties; and for whatever reason, perhaps it was time for the larger King family to move on.

---

292 This information was provided by Lowell "Ben" Bennion, March 15, 2007. In the 1880 census there were notations made behind peoples names identifying them as (D) for disfellowshiped, (AM) apostate Mormon, (G) Gentile, or (I) Infidel.

293 Volney King to William King, Volney King papers, Utah State Historical Society, August 7, 1870.

294 Edward Partridge Journal. See August 11, 1875, November 21, 1875, and December 23, 1875 for specific references.

First Kings

(The Next Generation)

At the time of the move to Circle Valley, each of the King children had become well established in his or her own right.[295] They had pulled together as a family, enduring the hardships and poverty of the trip west and carving out homes in the barren frontier of Fillmore. In one way or another, they had all helped build both community and church and had proven their abilities and character. Now a new frontier lay before them that would challenge their family solidarity and faith in their Church.

Chronological Events

May	1854	William leaves for his mission to Hawaii.
Feb 5,	1855	Culbert married to Esther Eliza McCullough.
	1858	John participates in the White Mountain Expedition.
Jun 2,	1858	William returns from Hawaii.
Sep 23,	1860	John married to Helen Maria Webb.
Prob	1860	William elected as Millard County Constable.
Jan 20,	1861	William married to Josephine Henry.
Dec 14,	1861	Delilah married to George Daniel Olson.
Apr 29,	1862	Edwin married to Rebecca Jane Murray.
Prob	1863	Edwin elected Millard County Surveyor. He serves for twelve years.
Oct 10,	1864	Culbert married polygamously to Elizabeth Ann Callister.
Spring	1867	Culbert moves to Kanosh.
Feb 12,	1868	Josephine passes away.
Aug	1868	William seriously wounded by a gunman.
Mar 9,	1869	Culbert appointed bishop of the Kanosh Ward. He serves for nine years.
Mar 26,	1869	William ordained a high priest and set apart as a member of the first Millard Stake High Council.
Nov 29,	1869	William married to Mary Ann Henry.
Dec 17,	1869	William and Mary Ann leave on William's second mission to Hawaii.
May 15,	1871	Volney married to Carlie Eliza Lyman (Div).
Jul	1873	William and Mary Ann return from Hawaii.
Oct	1873	Volney called to England on a mission.
Nov	1873	Volney returns from England.

---

295 See Appendix 4 for a map of Fillmore City and part of the property the King family owned before they moved to Circle Valley.

William Rice King

William, the oldest of the King sons, was an ambitious young man of many talents: farmer, blacksmith, carpenter, and home builder. In a large measure, his education was self-taught; and as a young man, he soon demonstrated his leadership talents. While still in his teens he carried the United States mail to Cedar City and St. George on horseback. It was a feat requiring considerable physical and mental stamina, involving all kinds of weather and the most trying conditions. On one occasion he rode more than twenty-eight miles in frozen clothes.[296]

William Rice King, 1834-92, was the oldest of the King children. He served three missions to Hawaii, the last one as mission president. He was married to two plural wives. *(The Henrys and the Kings)*

At the age of twenty, he became the first of the King sons to be called on a proselyting mission, his destination the Sandwich (Hawaiian) Islands. This would be the first of three missions he would serve to the Polynesian people. He was ordained a Seventy in April 1854 and left in May, probably at a time when a pioneer family and an emerging community still needed all the manpower they could muster. Due to a lack of money, William had to first work his way to Los Angeles and then by boat to San Francisco. Here he worked an additional three months to earn passage to the islands, finally sailing on November 13.[297]

His arrival in Honolulu was only four years after the first missionaries had been sent to Hawaii, and the language and cultural hurdles still remained almost insurmountable. On top of this were the prejudices directed at the Mormons and perpetuated by the Protestant and Catholic clergy who had arrived many years before and Christianized most of the people.

---

296 Lillian King Hinckley, a daughter, "William King." A copy is in the Utah State Historical Society.

297 "Historical Records and Minutes of the Sandwich Islands Mission," LDS Church Historical Department Archives.

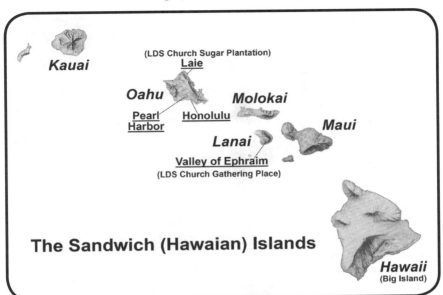

The Sandwich (Hawaian) Islands

Kauai

(LDS Church Sugar Plantation)
Laie

Oahu

Molokai

Pearl Harbor Honolulu

Maui

Lanai

Valley of Ephraim
(LDS Church Gathering Place)

Hawaii
(Big Island)

William served three missions, or a total of nine years, to Hawaii, the third as Mission President. A gathering place on the island of Lanai was established in 1854, but later changed in 1865 to the north end of the main island of Oahu. The new gathering place was known as Laie where a large sugar plantation and sugar mill were established. William's years of service were from January 1854 to June 1858, December 1870 to July 1873, and October 1886 to the spring of 1890.

Other hardships included the destitute condition of the Polynesians themselves; and with the missionaries traveling without purse or scrip, they also experienced severe economic privation. One of the biggest obstacles, however, was the moral condition of the Hawaiians. Their cultural view on morality was significantly more liberal than the view of the Latter-day Saints, and it was a struggle for the missionaries to try and reverse such an inherent cultural pattern.

When William arrived in late 1854, the Hawaiians had just experienced a severe outbreak of smallpox during which thousands had died, including many members of the Church. In spite of these misfortunes, a gospel beachhead had been established. Membership exceeded 3,000 people,[298] the Book of Mormon had been translated into the Hawaiian language, and a gathering place had been established on the small island of Lanai, called the Valley of Ephraim. This was in keeping with the spirit of "the gathering," a place where the Hawaiian Saints could gather rather than asking them to move to Utah. A large acreage was acquired in the

298 R. Lanier Britsch, *Moramona: The Mormons in Hawaii* (Laie, Hawaii: The Institute for Polynesian Studies, 1989), 35.

valley of Palawai; and while conditions were hopeful, the success of the enterprise was marginal to fair at best. The lack of water and cultural work ethic, together with a general lack of interest on the part of the people, greatly hindered the project.

William was one of thirty-one foreign missionaries; and by the July 1855 conference, membership had grown to 4,650 people.[299] However, dark clouds of apostasy hung over the islands, and by June 1856 the momentum began to change and membership began to decline. Reports of renunciation of the gospel came from nearly all areas of the mission, and the missionaries became more discouraged as time went on. The following year, several new missionaries arrived to try and reverse the trend, including one of the founding missionaries, Henry Bigler. When he arrived in September he recorded in his journal that while attending church in Honolulu he felt that "everything [was] dead or dieing."[300] To his dismay he found that elders were working as hired labor simply to sustain themselves.[301] Under these conditions and with the impending war in Utah with Johnston's Army, the mission was closed in December 1857. The missionaries were to return home as soon as affairs could be settled and arrangements made for travel. With the missionaries gone, membership plummeted; and by October 1858, there were only 632 members.[302] It was truly a dark time for the gospel in the Sandwich Islands.

William returned to Fillmore on June 2, 1858, just before his father returned from England and Johnston's Army moved through Salt Lake. The ordeal of his trip home are best described in a biography of a fellow missionary and future president of the Church, Joseph F. Smith, who traveled with William:

> To travel steerage as the missionaries had to do in journeying to the Hawaiian Islands in 1854, was bad enough, and the smell of the ship almost more than they could endure, but the homeward journey in the hold of the vessel was even worse. In that day sanitary conditions were poor and there was no refrigeration or ice on board as a means to preserve foods.[303]

William's experiences in Hawaii would have a lasting impression on his life and create a special love for the Hawaiian people. More was to come.

---

299 Ibid., 44.

300 Ibid., 46.

301 Ibid..

302 Ibid., 49.

303 Joseph Fielding Smith, Life of Joseph F. Smith (Salt Lake City, Utah: Deseret News Press, 1938), 187.

Josephine Henry, 1844-68, was the first wife of William King. She died seven years after their marriage.

Shortly after his return William acquired an interest in law enforcement and was elected constable for Millard County. This interest may have had some impact on the life of his oldest son, William H. King, who later became a noted lawyer and U.S. Senator.

At the age of twenty-seven, Will, as he was called, married a young lady whose parents had moved to Fillmore to work on the construction of the State-house. Sixteen-year-old Josephine Henry was the daughter of Andrew and Margaret Creighton Henry, and she and Will were married January 20, 1861, by Will's father. From their short marriage came four children: William Henry, Lillian, Josephine, and Samuel. Unfortunately, Josephine died seven years later at the tender age of twenty-four. She had just given birth to Samuel the month before, and her death must have been a tragic experience for William. He was now faced with taking care of a small family, the oldest only five years old and the youngest a new baby. However, as was customary in those days, the extended family took an active part in caring for the children, especially Matilda King and Margaret Henry, the two grandmothers.

In August 1868 came another experience for William that just about orphaned his children. While acting as constable, he was severely wounded trying to take an outlaw into custody. A crime had taken place just outside of Holden. A couple of emigrants from Montana traveling south were accosted and robbed of all their money; and from the description provided by the victims, the perpetrator was recognized as one of the local citizens, Willis Bartholomew. Willis was the son of Noah Willis Bartholomew. Bishop Bartholomew was also the uncle of Eliza Esther McCullough, Culbert King's wife. This was not Willis's first offense as he was wanted for cattle rustling and other depredations that required the attention of the law.

The Endowment House was built in 1855 on the northwest corner of Temple Square in Salt Lake City and used by the Saints for many years for endowments and sealings until temples could be constructed. Here all of the King children received their endowments and had most of their marriages solemnized. (Courtesy Utah State Historical Society.)

William, suspecting that Willis was making nocturnal visits to his father's home, placed a lookout on the residence. Sure enough when Willis showed up, William moved in to make the arrest. A gunfight ensued, and William was struck by two bullets, one in the shin, breaking both bones.[304] As Willis made a dash on his horse into the street, Volney, who was at the gate standing watch, pulled the trigger twice but his gun did not discharge; and Willis escaped, supposedly never to be heard from again.[305]

As there were no doctors in Fillmore, Will was taken across the street to his parent's home, where Matilda cared for him, but his condition worsened. Fearing for his life and not knowing what to do, Matilda retired to her parlor, weeping and praying for the Lord's help. The story is told by her granddaughter, Lillian King Hinckley, that as Matilda got up from her knees a knock came at the door. She opened it, and a man stood in the doorway asking for lodging. He said he was an army doctor passing through the state.[306] Matilda knew it was an immediate answer to her prayers as the doctor was able to give the much-needed medical attention for William's life to be saved, although his leg did give him much pain

---

304 Edmund Thomas Olson in his book, "Dan and His Violin," 206, says that William received two wounds with one bullet splintering a leg bone. A daughter of William King, Lillian King Hinckley in her history of "William King," reports that William was badly wounded by a gunshot breaking both bones in his leg.

305 "Dan and His Violin," 206.

306 Lillian King Hinckley, "William King," a copy is in my possession.

Mary Ann Henry, 1854 - 1943, was a cousin to Josephine Henry, and the second wife of William King. She accompanied him to Hawaii on his second mission.

over the years and proved to be a contributing factor to his later death.[307] Needless to say, this event caused lingering ill feelings between the Kings and the Bartholomews.

During the first stake conference in March 1869 for the newly formed Millard Stake, William was ordained a high priest and set apart as a member of the first stake high council with his father.[308] However, this assignment was soon cut short. The following October he was called on his second mission to the Sandwich Islands. He was counseled by Brigham Young to find another wife and take her with him. As a result, William married Mary Ann Henry, a cousin to Josephine on November 29, 1869. They made immediate preparations to leave for Hawaii. Mary Ann was only fifteen at the time and William thirty-five. The four children from Josephine were again left with the King and Henry grandparents. It appear from the 1870 census that William Henry, Lillian, and Josephine stayed with Thomas and Matilda and Samuel, the youngest, lived with the Henrys. Samuel's association with the Henrys is further evidenced in one article which reads in part:

> Mr. King's mother died at his birth, and he was then reared and educated by his mother's parents, who were both people of strong character, well educated, and of the usual Irish brilliancy and temperament. Mr. King, as well as his brother, Senator William H. King, are both indebted to their grandparents, and particularly to their grandmother, for their education, and today they give her the principal credit for their education and position in life.[309]

307 *William King: A Short Autobiography* in "The Daily Journal of the Kingston United Order."

308 The stake was organized March 10, 1869; however, from William King's brief autobiography in "The Daily Journal of the Kingston United Order," William indicates he was called to the high council and ordained a high priest on March 26.

309 *History of Utah since Statehood,* 3:369 (No author given, found in the Orem, Utah City Library.)

Will and Mary Ann left December 17 by rail for San Francisco, and then sailed on the 24,[310] no doubt under much more favorable circumstances than William's first mission. The mission had been reopened in 1864 under the most trying of conditions. Joseph F. Smith, the new mission president, recorded that he could see no evidence that the gospel had "benefitted the Hawaiians one iota."[311] Brigham Young in a letter to President Smith expressed his sentiments by indicating how disturbed he was by the "unfaithfulness of the natives and wanted to see some indication of repentance before he committed more Church resources, either missionary time or money. He repeatedly stated that he felt the Church was under no obligation to the Hawaiian people until they repented and showed they were worth the trouble."[312]

During a mission conference in October, 1864, only two hundred Saints could be accounted for, but they manifested a strong spirit of determination; and from this humble beginning, the gospel began to move forth once again. A new gathering place was located on six thousand acres of land on the north side of the island of Oahu. The plantation was called Laie, and the principal crop became sugar cane.[313] The Church also established a large factory for processing sugar.

When William and Mary Ann arrived in late 1869, William was asked to take charge of the sugar plantation. Mary Ann soon became occupied with a family by giving birth to two children: Harvey William and Margaret. Because of Will and Mary Ann's activity and involvement with the people, their affection for the Polynesians continued to grow throughout their mission, and they dearly loved the people. When he and Mary Ann returned to Fillmore, they were permitted to bring with them two young men, a fourteen-year-old-native Hawaiian named Kahana and a white boy named Charles E. Rowen, whose parents were good friends with William. Charles was only twelve at the time but worked as a cattle herder until he could afford his own herd. Later he married Delilah King, the daughter of Culbert. Their son, Charles N. Rowen, later went on to become the president of the Garfield Stake and president of the Texas Mission.

William and his family returned to Fillmore at the end of July 1873. He and Mary Ann looked upon Kahana and Charles as their own and raised them in their home. At a later time William even brought back with him a young native girl named Cleo as a wife for Kahana. They

---

310   "Historical Records and Minutes of the Sandwich Islands Mission," LDS Church Historical Department Archives.

311   Britsch, *Moramona, The Mormons in Hawaii*, 61.

312   Ibid., 62.

313   Ibid., 62-73.

had several children, but eventually returned to their native island.[314]

For the next three and a half years, William and Mary Ann established themselves in Fillmore in a small adobe house. When the decision was made to move to Kingston, it was hard for the family to leave, but the desire to follow the brethren prevailed, and William and his family prepared to make the move.

Culbert King

When the call came to move to Circle Valley, Culbert, while not the oldest, had been married the longest of any of his siblings. At forty-one years

Culbert King, 1836-1909, was the husband of three plural wives and spent six months in prison. He was a bishop for twenty-six years and a stake patriarch for another nine years.

of age, he had settled his two families in Kanosh, a short distance southeast of Fillmore. He had married Eliza Esther McCullough in February 1855, and they had eleven children, eight of them living at the time of the move to Kingston.

Esther, as she was called, was the daughter of Levi Hamilton and Clarinda Altania Bartholomew McCullough. Levi was an early convert to the Church in Michigan; and when the Saints were driven out of Nauvoo and were on the trail west, he volunteered as a member of the Mormon Battalion. He made the trip to San Diego and then to Salt Lake as the Saints were first arriving in 1847. However, by the time he made it back to Winter Quarters in December of that same year after a most difficult trip, he found that his wife and their youngest child had died. Levi picked up Esther and her older sister and younger brother and came west four and a half years later. They settled in Fillmore with the Kings. Clarinda was the sister of Noah W. Bartholomew.

---

314   Until about 1875, the Hawaiian government made it nearly impossible for Hawaiian citizens to leave the islands to go to another country. Afterward the laws were modified to some extent, but still emigration was strongly discouraged until 1898 when Hawaii became a territory of the United States. See Dennis H. Atkin, *A History of Iosepa, The Utah Polynesian Colony (*M.A. thesis, Brigham Young University, August 1958), 29-32.

Eliza Esther McCullough, 1837-98, was the first wife of Culbert King. Her father was a member of the Mormon Battalion.

Esther was a small lady with black hair and deep blue eyes, who possessed great courage and determination. One day Esther and her son, Volney, were home alone when two men rode up and told them that one of their best riding horses was in a quicksand hole some distance from the house. Unable to free the horse, they were going for help. Esther knew something had to be done fast, so she asked Volney to grab a pole from the fence. She did the same and started for the hole. When they arrived at the spot, the horse was already half submerged in the wet sand. It is not known how they did it, but by pushing the poles somehow under the horse, they gradually helped it to solid ground. When the two men returned with assistance, the horse was exhausted but safely lying on the edge of the quicksand. The men could not believe that a tiny woman and a small boy had done what they themselves could not do.[315]

After their marriage, Culbert and Esther lived in Fillmore for about ten years and then moved to Petersburg,[316] located about fourteen miles south of Fillmore. Here they settled in a small, two-room brick home. Believing plural marriage was a divine principle, Culbert married his second wife, Elizabeth Ann Callister, on October 10, 1864. Elizabeth was the daughter of Thomas Callister and his second wife, Helen Mar Clark Callister. Bishop Callister had served as bishop of the Salt Lake City Seventeenth Ward until his move to Fillmore in 1861 where he became the bishop of the Fillmore Ward. Later he was called as the first stake president of the Millard Stake.

Before moving to Petersburg, Culbert made two trips to California.

---

315 Mina King W. Oldham and Mary King Stenquist, his daughters, "History of Volney Henry King," *McCullough Family History Book,* 353.

316 Petersburg was named after Peter Robison, Matilda's brother. It had previously been called Corn Creek, and today it is known as Hatton.

The first was with Esther and his small family of two children. He and Esther left in November 1859, to visit Esther's sister, Julia Bemis, who had moved to San Bernardino five years earlier. Visits in those days were no weekend excursions, as they didn't return until

This bishop's storehouse was built next to Culbert King's home while he was the bishop of the Kanosh Ward.

five months later in April 1860. Culbert's second visit was three years later when he went to pick up supplies for the people of Fillmore. He was gone from January to April 1863, returning in time to take care of the spring planting.

While in Petersburg, Culbert was appointed presiding officer until his move to Kanosh in the spring of 1867, where he was appointed bishop March 9, 1869. He served in that capacity for nine years, the first two years without counselors.[317] The story is told that when the time came to choose a bishop for the new town, President Brigham Young and Apostle Erastus Snow contacted Bishop Callister, Culbert King's father-in-law, and asked him who among the men in Corn Creek would make a good bishop. Callister replied, "There's a young man down there that's the best hand I ever saw to break a pair of mules," to which President Young declared: "That's the man for bishop."[318]

Kanosh, or Upper Corn Creek as it was initially called, was first settled in 1867 when Brigham Young counseled the settlers in Petersburg to move about three miles southeast up the creek to conserve water and to avoid early frost. The area was also suitable for raising fruit. Living in the area was Chief Kanosh and his small band of Indians. In honor of the chief, the town was so named.

In Kanosh, Culbert built a small but comfortable adobe home on Center Street. Besides the regular amenities of a pioneer farm, Culbert had

---

317 Leavitt Christensen, *Birth of Kanosh*, 42, 170.

318 Day and Ekins, *Milestones of Millard: 100 Years of History of Millard County*, 11, 356.

Elizabeth Ann Callister, 1848-1901, was the second wife and first plural wife of Culbert King. She was the daughter of Thomas Callister, Millard Stake President.

a sizable dairy operation and a large fruit orchard. His apples became widely distributed throughout the area and as far away as Nevada. He was also the postmaster of Kanosh for a short period of time.

A frequent visitor to the King home was President Young, who from time to time traveled to St. George to stay in his winter home and to check on the construction of the temple. One family story told is how Esther, looking out of the window and seeing his black carriage and spirited team of horses approaching, exclaimed, "My land! Here comes President Young, and I am cooking pork."[319] Brigham could never eat pork so she hurried about and prepared something else. Other times when they knew in advance of his coming, the children would dress in their best attire and go out to meet the caravan with songs. President Young never failed to greet each child individually and sometimes would take them on his knee and talk to them, encouraging them to live right and to strive for high ideals. His favorite supper was a large bowl of bread and milk, but he loved cream best of all. To Esther this was rather odd, as she would spend hours cooking chickens, pies, and other special foods which the other members of the party thoroughly enjoyed. At times the President would take his shoes off and warm his feet by the fire while he told many delightful stories.

By December 1871, Brigham Young was under intense pressure from the federal government to appear in court and answer charges against him for polygamy. As he was returning from St. George, his party was caught in a severe snow storm between Beaver and Cove Fort. At Cove Fort, Culbert and five others from Millard County brought in fresh horses to

---

319   Melba Utahna Riddle Gottfredson, her granddaughter, "History of Delilah King Rowan," *McCullough Family History Book,* 326-327.

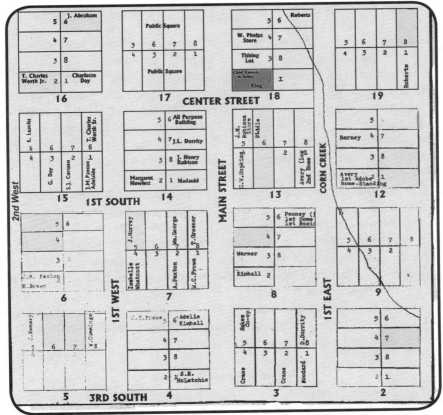

Culbert King's home in Kanosh was located on the east corner of lot 2 on Main Street. Here he lived for over ten years. (See *Birth of Kanosh*, 238-239)

break a road through the snow.[320]

Among the memories of Fillmore and Kanosh were the recollections of children born and children who died. Esther gave birth to eleven children before moving to Kingston, but sadly she and Culbert also buried three of them. The first was eight-year-old Ida Roseltha. Prior to her ninth birthday Ida was playing dress-up when her mother was away caring for a sick neighbor. While adorning herself in a long hoop skirt, she reached up on the mantle over the fireplace for a pin. From the open hearth her skirt caught on fire, and the flames spread rapidly. An older sister, Clarinda, was preparing the noon meal for the children in an adjoining room, and when she heard the screams she rushed in and did what she could to extinguish the fire with a pan of milk. Help was summoned but Ida Roseltha

---

320 B. H. Roberts, *A Comprehensive History of the Church,* 6 vols. (Provo, Utah: Brigham Young University Press, 1965), 5:403.

was so overcome by smoke, and her burns were so severe that she soon died on April 24, 1869.[321]

Their second child to die prematurely was Elda Hamilton who, due to an illness, expired the first of November 1873, only three months old.

The third to pass away was two-year-old Parley, again a tragic experience for the family. In July 1877 Parley was home alone with his mother and sister Matilda. When he came up missing, Esther immediately sensed something was wrong and asked Matilda to get the pitchfork and feel around in the open well. As she suspected Parley was just below the surface of the water and Esther and Matilda had to fish the little body out by hooking the tines of the pitchfork under his clothes.[322]

From Culbert's plural marriage to Elizabeth, five children were born before the Kingston move: Thomas Callister, Caroline, Elizabeth Ann, Collins Hyde, and John. What the living arrangements were between the two families is not known. It appears that Elizabeth and her family had a separate home in Kanosh, but no record can be found of a second piece of property. The building lots in Kanosh were an acre and a quarter. Culbert's home was on the southeast corner of his lot, and Chief Kanosh was located on the northwest corner. Culbert may have had a second home on the southwest corner.[323] This would leave the inner northeast corner for out buildings, a garden, and an orchard.

John Robison King

John was known for his many talents and abilities, including his humor and playing the fiddle. It was even "rumored" he could sing when prevailed upon. One nephew commented that when Uncles William, Culbert, Volney, or Edwin came to town "there was nothing which created any excitement. But when Uncle JOHN came to town in Fillmore everybody came to our home to see him. He was a free lance. His friends was everybody, regardless of their profession or business."[324] It was also claimed that no man possessed a more charitable heart than John.

Of his many abilities, his building activities stood at the top, and he had one of the finest brick homes in Fillmore. But, more importantly, John unselfishly helped build the community, including a school, homes for

---

321 Velma Black Burns, her daughter, "History of Matilda Emily King Black," *McCullough Family History Book*, 310-311.

322 Ibid., 311.

323 Based on an interview between Larry King and Leavitt Christensen, August 30, 1995, author of the book, *The Birth of Kanosh*.

324 W. F. Olson, "John Robison King," 11.

the needy, and the fort at Cove Creek.

Whatever John did, it was always the best, and he was known to have one of the finest cattle and horse operations in the area. It was no secret that John loved horses. He raised draft horses, race horses, and range horses, and no one was ever allowed to abuse a horse in his presence. His horses were mainly sold to the military, and the government buyers made annual trips to obtain his fine breed. Those not purchased by the army were called "scrubs" and John would trade these horses to the Navajos for blankets. In Salt Lake he would in turn trade these blankets for furniture, cloth, silk, ribbons, and lace. He would also bring back books for his

John Robison King, 1837-99, was a successful rancher and businessman. His outgoing and humorous personality attracted many friends.

family, and his family had the first organ in the valley after they moved to Grass Valley.

The passion of John's life was horse racing, and all during his life he had two or three horses just for that purpose. People from all over the area would come to witness his horse races, and many a race was against the Indian ponies. He would also race his horses in other communities throughout Utah, Colorado, and Nevada.

John and Helen Maria Webb, a young lady of only fifteen, were married September 23, 1860 — a significant day for Helen as it was her birthday. John often joked and embarrassed Helen by telling the story that "the only reason he married her was because she owned a fine milk cow, then soon as they were married, 'blamed if she didn't give the cow to her dad.'"[325]

After living at Meadow Creek and Cove Fort for a short period of time, John and Helen returned to Fillmore in time for their first child to

---

325 Irene King Read, "Sense and Nonsense: My Life Story," 1. A copy is in my possession.

Helen Maria Webb, 1845-1904, married John on her fifteenth birthday.

be born, the first of seven, before they moved to Antimony. Their family was made up of five girls and two boys, with one dying prematurely. Clara Adelia lived only one day after birth.

When the call came to participate in a new United Order, it was no surprise that John refused. He was considered by some to be the "black sheep" of the family,[326] although he had been endowed in the temple at age twenty, ordained a seventy a few months later, and sealed in the temple at age thirty. He flatly refused to go on a mission, saying that he had a family to care for, and his family came first. He did not believe in polygamy, and he would not attend church nor have anything to do with it. But in other ways John's commitment was significant. He always paid his tithing, and as one daughter remembers it, every tenth and the best load of hay and all eggs gathered on Sunday went to the Church.[327] He always supported the families of his brothers while they served missions and made long trips to California to aid the returning missionaries across the desert. As mentioned earlier, John also participated in the White Mountain Expedition, an exploring expedition into the western desert of Utah and Nevada in 1858.

After considerable pressure and persuasion from his family, John finally succumbed and joined the order. Of course, all that he had in cattle, horses, and an eighty-five-cow dairy herd now became the property of the order.

Thomas Edwin King

Thomas Edwin might be considered the least known of the King brothers, yet his level of contribution to church, family, and community

326 Rosa Vida Black, "Mother Stood Tall: Writings and History of Our Mother Eliza Rosetta King Black Lythgoe," 73, 75. A copy is in my possession.

327 Read, "Sense and Nonsense, My Life Story," 83.

is significant. His recovery from brain fever as a child in Zarahemla was remarkable; and while he was basically healed, it appears the effects and consequences of the illness lingered for several more years. As his health improved, he was able to participate more and more in the

Edwin helped work on the St. George Temple, which was dedicated January 1, 1877, and became a significant temple in the lives of the King family. (Courtesy of the Utah State Historical Society.)

responsibilities of his father's farm. But schooling and receiving an education appeared to be his first love, and he speaks of it frequently in his short autobiographical sketch. He attended school each winter for three months at a time; and at the age of twenty, he attended the city academy during the winter months in Salt Lake for two years. He studied algebra, bookkeeping, and surveying. Afterward he came back to Fillmore and taught school.

At age eighteen, Edwin was ordained an elder and received his endowments. The following year in 1858 he was ordained a seventy. Later during the spring and summer of 1860, he was asked to take a four-yoke ox team to Florence, Nebraska, to help the emigrating Saints who needed assistance.

While teaching school in Fillmore, Edwin was assisted by a talented and beautiful young lady by the name of Rebecca Jane Murray. Rebecca was the cousin of Josephine and Mary Ann Henry, wives of William King, and the daughter of Rebecca Henry Murray who was sealed in the temple to Thomas Rice King. The professional relationship between Rebecca and Edwin quickly turned romantic, and they were married April 29, 1862. Edwin had just turned twenty-three, and Rebecca was almost twenty-one. From their marriage came seven children, five girls and two boys. But as was the case so frequently in those days, two of the children died the same day they were born.

Edwin built for his family a brick home in Fillmore with an orchard

Thomas Edwin King, 1839-1923, was the educated, faithful, and stately looking brother.

Rebecca Jane Murray, 1841-78, was the educated school teacher-wife of Edwin.

and all the amenities of the day. Rebecca was a gifted writer and loved to write articles and poetry, many of which were published in the *Woman's Exponent,* the forerunner to the LDS Church's *Relief Society Magazine.* She also wrote papers for the "Athenian," a literary organization in Fillmore. It is interesting that all of their five children, who lived to adulthood taught school at some point in time, a tribute to the emphasis and skills of their parents to instill a love for an education in each of their children.

Soon after his marriage Edwin decided to put his surveying skills to work. He campaigned for and won the county surveyor's job. He held this position for the next twelve years and surveyed such towns as Kanosh, Holden, and Oak City. He was even asked to do surveying jobs outside the area such as in Arizona, for Anson Call, who had moved to Arizona. While surveying near the Colorado River, he surveyed a spot for the landing of the steamer *Explorer,* the first ship ever to sail that far up the Colorado River.

In addition to his surveying responsibilities, Edwin did some co-op farming with his father in 1871; took a contract to deliver ten herds of stock to Pioche, Nevada, in 1872; and then worked with Volney to provide logs and to haul some 500,000 feet of lumber for a saw mill in 1873. Edwin also worked on the St. George Temple during the winter of 1874-75. He hauled timber with teams provided by his family and was supported by the people of the Fillmore Ward.

Like his older brother Culbert, Edwin also entered into the patriarchal order of marriage by taking a second wife. He married Isabella El-isha Savage January 16, 1878, in the St. George Temple. Isabella, eighteen, was the daughter of David Leonard

Isabella Elisha Savage 1859-1927, the plural wife of Thomas Edwin King was affectionately known by the family as Aunt Izzy.

and Mary Ward Savage. Edwin, at thirty-eight, was twenty years her senior. However, the polygamist arrangement was short-lived when Rebecca died on September 8, 1878. She had just given birth to Clifford Carol less than a month earlier and died of typhoid fever due to her weakened condition. Like his brother, William, Edwin lost a wife to problems associated with childbirth, and his second wife, as a young girl, was faced with raising a ready-made family, an enormous responsibility for a young lady still in her teens. Yet Isabella didn't take long to integrate within the family and became affectionately known as Aunt Izzy.

Delilah King

Delilah, the only surviving daughter of the Thomas King family, was considered intelligent and the "flower of the flock." She was ambitious and became what is commonly known in modern-day circles as a "Super Mom." She raised a large and talented family; was active in the LDS Church, held many leadership positions, was active in the political arena, and by profession was a school teacher.

A few years after the founding of Fillmore, a talented young musician by the name of Daniel Olson came to the city, and he and Delilah were

Delilah Cornelia King, 1841-1907, was the only surviving daughter of Thomas and Matilda. She was a highly competent and educated Church and community leader.

married December 14, 1861, at the Statehouse by her father. He was twenty-seven years old at the time, and Delilah was twenty.

Daniel was from Hostevkyoh, Denmark, and was a convert to the Mormon Church. He had joined the Church under some very adverse conditions and very much against the will of his parents and two sisters, but he was determined to come to America and be with the Saints. He worked as a carpenter until he had saved enough money to pay his passage in 1854. He then left home in the middle of the night without the luxury of even being able to say good-bye to his family.

In Salt Lake he continued in the furniture-making business and was active in music as an accomplished violinist. He was also skilled on several wind instruments. Prior to coming to America he had received many musical honors; and because of his musical talents, he conducted an orchestra in the old Salt Lake Social Hall and at the opening of the Salt Lake Theatre on March 8, 1862.

Delilah and Dan first met at the old Social Hall in 1859. Her father had been elected to the territorial legislature from Millard County, and Delilah accompanied him to Salt Lake to attend school. Besides falling in love, Delilah gained an excellent education with instructors like Apostle Orson Pratt who tutored her in mathematics.

The story is told by her family that when she returned home from Salt Lake and announced her desire to marry a Danish musician, her distressed parents called an emergency family council. For some reason, the thoughts of Delilah marrying a fiddler didn't appeal to the King family. It was felt that she deserved better, such as a high Church or government official. In due course they finally invited Daniel to Fillmore, and they were even more surprised to find a man much smaller than themselves, who averaged six feet in height. In addition Thomas and Matilda were also quite robust in stature and weighed close to 200 pounds.[328] Besides, Dan was no cowboy or farmer, but a musician and furniture maker who spoke with a strange Scandinavian accent. Wanting to be fair, Thomas asked him to play but Dan refused until he could have some fellow musicians come down from Salt Lake and play with him. A dance was agreed upon.

On the appointed night, he and his friends were an immediate hit with the townspeople, playing all kinds of music including waltzes, polkas, and rounds. No one had heard such music, and the townspeople knew for sure they wanted Dan to stay. But the Kings were still not so sure.

George Daniel Olson, 1835-93, was the very talented husband of Delilah.

In June 1861, Dan appealed to his prospective father-in-law to lay the matter before Brigham Young. Apparently President Young, like Moses of old, customarily addressed many of the individual, domestic, social, and economic issues of the Saints. (Where was Jethro?)

Brigham first acknowledged that he didn't know much about Brother Olson, but had heard that he associated and was employed by the Gentiles playing in the drinking and gambling saloons of that society. He then goes on to say:

> Of late I hear that he is inclined to pursue a more commendable course, evincing a disposition to occupy his time and energies more steadily in some laudable avocation for a livelihood, which course it is to be hoped he will continue and improve in, that he may be useful in society and honor the course in which we are engaged.[329]

President Young's personal bias maybe coming through a little as he

---

328 W. F. Olson, "The Life of Thomas Rice King," 1.

329 Brigham Young to Thomas Rice King, July 6, 1861, Letterpress Copybook, Brigham Young Office Files, Selected Collections, LDS Church Historical Department Archives.

The Social Hall was dedicated January 1853, in Salt Lake City as a place in which dramas, musicals, dances, and other social gatherings were held. Here Delilah and Dan Olson met in 1859. Dan also demonstrated his musical skills on many an evening in this building. (Courtesy Utah State Historical Society.)

did not think highly of violins and dancing. A participant would not be held in high esteem as a contributor to society.

Having said what he did, his practical approach to life finally came through.

> He wishes to marry your daughter, and desired me to recommend him to you, but when it comes to that I can only inform you of my practice in such cases; when my daughters wish to marry I permit them to exercise their own choice, for they are certainly the parties most concerned, simply giving them such cousel upon the point as my judgement may at that time dicate.[330]

After this response in July and an additional five months, to allow Dan to grow on them, Delilah's parents and one brother finally gave their marital blessing. Of course, that one brother was John, who felt Delilah should be free to make up her own mind. This decision on John's part also created a special relationship for years to come between Delilah's and John's families. John and Dan became kindred spirits as John's humor and native intelligence created a lasting relationship.

Some relatives still thought it was a mistake, but Thomas's generous character prevailed as he presented Lila, as she was called, with a wedding present of eighty acres of land and a small cabin on the creek, an ideal

330 Ibid.

The first Territorial Capitol, Fillmore, Utah, was built between 1851 and 1855. The building was also used for many social events in Fillmore, and here the Dan Olson family played for many community activities and dances. (Courtesy Utah State Historical Society.)

location for Dan to locate a small saw mill for his cabinet-making business. In due time the cabin was fixed up, and Dan later built an addition for his shop. The brothers came through with additional gifts of cattle, horses, and other farm animals. In the back of the home was a large cottonwood tree; and many an evening, Dan and Lila could heard playing the violin and guitar.

After their marriage on December 14, 1861 they returned to Salt Lake for a short period of time, where their first child was born. By the time the move to Kingston was planned, Delilah had a family of six children: four boys (George, Thomas Edmund, William Francis, and Culbert Levy) and two girls (Mary Evelyn and Bertha Matilda). Delilah was also involved as a counselor in the ward Relief Society, teaching school, and participating in drama and musical groups in the community. It was not uncommon to have the Dan Olson family play for activities and dances on Friday nights, holidays, and special occasions such as the 4th and 24th of July. In most cases these events were held in the Statehouse.

The building was constructed of red sandstone and is 60' x 40'. Each of the three floors has 2,400 square feet with the upper floor assembly area ideal for dances and other activities. Original plans called for the building to have four wings connected by a Moorish domed building in the middle. Only the south wing was ever finished.

Fillmore was fortunate to have such a fine building for all occasions which complemented the talents and abilities of the Olson family. Originally built as the territorial capitol, it was never really used as such. As much of Utah Territory was carved up and given to other states, Fillmore no longer was the center of the region, and the building was turned over to the city and county for their use. Even before ownership changed hands, this stately building quickly became the community and entertainment center for Fillmore and Millard County. Dances, receptions, parties, and celebrations were all held and enjoyed in this unique place of stature and dignity.

Delilah's and Dan's decision not to go to Circleville was a disappointment to Father King. He had hoped to have his entire family join with him, but Dan could not accept the United Order concept and Delilah was counseled by Church authorities in Salt Lake to stay with her husband and share her talents with the people of Fillmore.[331] The relationship between the families continued, however, and there are many recorded instances of visits back and forth between the brothers and the sister.

Volney King

Volney King was the youngest of the King brothers and only thirty years old when the family was asked to move to Circle Valley. Like Edwin and Delilah, Volney was able to obtain a formal education and afterwards taught school at Kanosh. He was also selected by President Callister, at the request of Brigham Young, to learn telegraphy. He then worked for a period of time as the telegrapher at Cove Fort.

Volney will always be best known for chronicling the day-by-day events of his era. In the possession of the Utah State History Society and the University of Utah are sixteen books varying in size and shape, spanning the years from 1873 to 1925, and looking as if they had been carried over many miles of travel in saddle bags or pants pockets. He also wrote a history of Millard County and kept the records of the United Order from February 1876 to May 22, 1883. Recently discovered is an extensive record book by Volney profiling the extended King family's genealogy and evidence of collaboration with George Oscar King of Corry, Pennsylvania (See footnote #35).

---

331   A letter signed by W. F. Olson. A typescript of the letter is available at the Utah State Historical Society.

As the younger brother, Volney many times helped his brothers take care of their horses, cattle, and logging operations. As a boy he received a severe injury from a horse belonging to his brother, John.

Volney King, 1847-1925, was the writer, diarist, and genealogist of the King family. (Courtesy Territorial Statehouse.)

> I had taken it up thinking to break it to ride. I jumped on it, but instead of it running and jumping as I supposed it would, it plunged into the air and fell backward upon me rendering me insensible, inflicting an injury in my back that I will carry with me to the grave.[332]

On another occasion, he records that a "wild horse I was riding threw its self on me injuring my right side."[333]

Volney also helped as a teamster in 1868 to go to Laramie, Wyoming, to help transport the emigrating Saints. The railroad had not been completed to Ogden, and wagon trains were still sent out each year to pick up the Saints coming in by rail. The three-month journey was about 1,500 miles round trip, and Volney claimed it was a pleasant one except for the wagons breaking down from time to time.

Volney's first marriage was an unfortunate experience resulting in considerable disappointment. In May 1871 he married Carlie Eliza Lyman, daughter of former Apostle Amasa M. Lyman and half-sister to Apostle Francis M. Lyman.[334] However, the marriage lasted only a few days. Quoting from Volney's journal:

> We attended the Theatre [theater] a couple of times and took a short ride upon the cars, bought a few things to keep house with, then returned home. The day we returned home I found Carlie was dissatisfied, at what I knew not. I asked her reasons. She said nothing. A few days more and she had rejected

---

332 Volney King Diaries, 1-2.

333 Ibid, 2.

334 Apostle Amasa Lyman was excommunicated from the LDS Church in 1870 for apostasy and died in Fillmore in February 1877. His son, Francis M. Lyman, became an apostle October 27, 1880.

the house I had prepared for her. Said she would rather stay with her mother and not resume the responsibility of a wife and of keeping house. So went my passion, and pride fled at the appearance of dissatisfaction without reason or forethought. A bill of divorse [divorce] was the consequence.[335]

Before obtaining the divorce, Volney sent a letter to Brigham Young asking for his advice. His response in part is interesting and perhaps not what Volney expected. Brigham's insight into the nature of women is also rather unorthodox.

> My impression after reading your letter is, that you do not treat your wife as you ought to do. If this is so, you should try to remedy it and create in her a better feeling towards yourself. Woman's nature craves affection, she must have Man's love and society, or she cannot be thoroughly happy, and nothing will disappoint her more than to be denied this. Treat her lovingly, take her to your bosom, give her every privilege a wife ought to have, and when you have done this, and maternity begins you will find that her feelings will not be then as you say they are now. ***You say your wife complains you are too fast with her, my opinion is, she means you are too slow.***[336] (Bold italic by author)

As no reason was given by Carlie, only speculation can be made as to why she would terminate the marriage. Perhaps she was experiencing considerable emotional stress because of her father being dropped from the Quorum of the Twelve Apostles and excommunicated a few months earlier. Also, her first love had returned home early from a mission only to be excommunicated. Less than a year later her marriage to Volney and living in Fillmore, her family's hometown, may have just been too much to face. Carlie eventually married President Thomas Callister as a plural wife and died almost three years later after giving birth to her first child.

Later a mission call was in the offing, and in October 1873, Volney was set apart by President Young and commenced his journey to England. It was a special time for Volney as Thomas accompanied Volney to Salt Lake for his setting apart and departure. He served a year, but due to a lung problem, was released early. During his mission, he met an attractive young lady by the name of Eliza Syrett. She and her brother Ephraim came home with Volney; and a week after returning to Salt Lake, he and Eliza were married on November 9, 1874. Volney was twenty-seven at the time and Eliza was eighteen. They were the parents of one child when they moved to Circle Valley.

The adjustment to pioneer life was difficult for Eliza, but she soon

---

335   Volney King Diaries, 2.

336   Brigham Young to Volney King, June 13, 1871, Letter Press Copy Book, Brigham Young Office Files, Selected Collections, LDS Church Historical Department Archives.

adapted to the rigorous western lifestyle. She had never
before made bread, cared for
milk, seen an Indian, danced,
or ridden a horse. Her English
words were always a source
for a good laugh, and when
William King was a Senator,
he would tease her about how
the Americans whipped the
English and made fun of her
saying "weel" for wheel, and
"weet" for wheat. In return
she would always come back
with how the Americans always talked through their nos-
es.[337]

**Eliza Syrett, 1856-1938, was the classy Eng-
lish bride of Volney. (Courtesy Territorial
Statehouse.)**

Volney was also the ped-
dler of the family and evidently very successful. He would
load up his wagon or wagons with cheese, butter, apples, and oats, and
drive to the settlements and mining camps of eastern Nevada. His bar-
gaining skills were excellent, and at times he even sold at a profit some of
his horses and wagons. These trips, which lasted for three to four weeks,
were an excellent source of cash, but also were filled with loneliness, tem-
peramental horses, and unfavorable weather.

On his first trip in November 1877 he sold:

800	lbs of butter	@	$.315	=	$252.00
250	lbs of cheese	@	$.175	=	43.75
800	lbs of apples	@	$.050	=	40.00
	Total				$335.75

The following year he was able to increase his load and, with higher
prices, he increased his earnings to $600.[338]

MOST KING FAMILY RECORDS center around events and activities,

337 Black, "Mother Stood Tall," 66.

338 Volney King Diaries, 59-60.

but a series of letters written in 1870[339] to William by his family while he and Mary Ann were in Hawaii on William's second mission reveal what they were thinking about in everyday life. It is a one-year snapshot into their social relations, their economic and personal challenges, and their moods and feelings.

The letters, for the most part, are well written and identify a literate and expressive family. The penmanship of Delilah and Culbert[340] is some of the best, although punctuation in many cases is missing, even periods at the end of sentences. Warm affection is evident and the family misses their son and brother. Excellent feelings are expressed in the slang of the day "first rate," and negative items or feelings are expressed as "dull."

Positive memories of times past are reflected upon by Delilah "as though we are living in a new era and the past a dream." This reflection also brought up remembrances of past hardships William had to endure on his first mission to Hawaii and "I do hope that for your comfort and those with you that time & civilization has not been idle with those people with whom you are again associated, that peace and plenty may surround you and success crown your labors."

Volney was quick to pick up on William's discouragement in one of his letters. "I was as ever glad to hear from you though the tone of your letter did not express much cheerfulness. I suppose it was on account of parting with some of the homebound missionaries therefore I hope that this uncheerfullnes will pass away in due time. I know that it is a dull prospect that surrounds you, we shall all hope for a brighter day."

Sickness and accidents were always a concern and it appears that Matilda had several sick spells during the year. When William and Mary Ann were sailing to Hawaii, they suffered considerable seasickness and were quite miserable the whole trip. While they were gone, his four children by Josephine were cared for by the grandmothers and, from time to

339 The following letters are found in the Volney King papers, Utah State Historical Society. In the quotes I have left the spelling intact, but have added necessary punctuation to make for better reading.   Volney King to William King, January 30, 1870; Delilah King Olson to William King, February 19, 1870; Thomas Rice King to William King, April 24, 1870; Volney King to William King, June 5, 1870; Thomas Rice King to William King, June 12, 1870; John R. King to William King, June 25, 1870; Thomas R. King to William King, July 24, 1870; Volney King to William King, August 7, 1870; Delilah King Olson to William King, August 14, 1870; Volney King to William King, September 18, 1870; Volney King to William King, November 6, 1870; Margaret Henry (Mother to Josephine) to William King, November 22, 1870.

340 No letters from Culbert to William have been found, but in other letters and written items, Culbert's penmanship and writing skill exceed those of his school teacher brother, Volney, and sister, Delilah. For an example, see Culbert King to Volney King, July 12, 1909. A copy is in my possession.

time, other family members. In many of the letters William and Mary Ann are assured of the well being of the children. One son, two-year-old Samuel, tripped and fell into a pot of boiling water resulting in painful burns to his arms. In April Thomas reported that Lillian and Josephine had been sick with colds but were doing quite well. Willie and Lillian were going to school and "are getting along fine." In another letter Delilah says, "We are all well and enjoying ourselves firstrate. You would think the children were [first rate] if you could see them now chasing each other across the room. Jossie [four year old Josephine] is well and hearty [and] has been all winter, but her hair has nearly all fallen out. It is commenced growing again."

Economically, both Delilah and Thomas complained about the lack of money in the community and Thomas reports that "business is verry dull." At first there was some discouragement with the ZCMI cooperative store as there was little prospect that the value of their stock would improve. Afterwards in June Thomas reports a 37 1/2 per cent dividend payable in wool and sheep. He expresses disappointment in the store and feels it could have done better if those in management had purchased more wheat. He had strongly encouraged them to do so a year ago; but when he and Matilda had left on their mission, management stopped buying. The price of wheat had increased to $2.00, so the store would have done far better to have followed his advice.

Later in August Delilah is also more optimistic in reporting that business is becoming better and "the store (ZCMI) is doing [a] good business. We have a copperative Butchership which is a great benefit."

During the year grasshoppers were a blight and "are doing a great damage to crops." All the crops at the sink farm and in Round Valley had been destroyed. Later in the season, in August, Delilah identified the problem with the grasshoppers is being compounded by a severe drought. "This is the dryest season we have had, no rain and water is low and crops that have been saved from the grasshoppers are dying for want of water."

In February, John had moved to Cove Creek and bought a large ten year old American stallion, the color of Thomas's horse, Franklin. The purpose of the horse must have been for breeding as Thomas, Edwin, and Volney all bought shares.

While William was gone, his business affairs were in the hands of several family members. Volney is collecting the rent on William's home and in January collected $13 in currency and $10.25 in wheat, and then jokes that if William could not read his writing to get a lawyer to decipher it. No further mention is made of rent and perhaps it is paid annually, but by September Volney is buying more land at $1.25 an acre and asks

William if he would like to buy any. Volney had purchased forty acres payable next June, Thomas had purchased twenty acres and Edwin eighty acres.

John is taking care of William's cattle and horses, and he struggles to get a good price for the cows. He has to sell some for only $30 when a year ago they were selling for $50 or more. There was a glut of cows on the market with few buyers, and many of William's cows had not been rounded up. Evidently, when William left, much of his livestock was still in the mountains or out on the range, and John said that he is still looking for them, "but there is a good many that I have not seen this year. I am on the lookout all the time." John and Thomas also speak of putting some of William's livestock in the community co-op, and Thomas indicates that everyone in the family has put "something in except John and Dan." The depressed prices are also having an effect on John's business as it appears that he is getting about what he owes. Thomas reported that "John has delivered up the horses he has to herd but the pay he will be able to get will not amount to as much as he has paid out, and he owes considerably yet still he is coming out better than I was afraid he would."

The problems with a lack of money are also extended into their social life and disposition. Delilah complains in the middle of February that dancing has pretty well been "ruled out this winter. We have had only two balls in the state house since New years. The young folks are so engaged in school they have no time and money so scarce it impossible to get up a party. It is very dull this winter. There is no trade or money to do nothing."

Politically, the Cullom Bill, then under consideration by the Federal government, was very much a concern of the family as it enhanced the government's ability to prosecute polygamy cases. If passed it would completely disfranchise the Mormon populace from voting and holding public office, and it would strengthened the powers of the territorial government to appoint judicial officers and sheriffs who were non Mormon. A women's rally was held in Salt Lake protesting the bill, both Volney and Thomas expressed their concern; and Thomas reports, that if the bill is passed, "our government is nearly ripened in iniquity consequently her destruction is near. The way the Lord will bring it about we poor mortals are not able to understand."

Another item of interest was the conviction of Andrew Henry, Josephine Henry's father, for selling liquor without a licence. He was charged with two offences costing him $90 plus court costs. Delilah reports that it was "pretty hard with the old folks. A great many sympatize with them and others think it just."   Dan and Delilah are excited about adding on to their home, and Dan's work in his shop is growing. In May Delilah delivers "a fine large boy" to add "to her little flock," and is also first counselor in the Relief Society. Volney claims that she has to do most of the work because the president is not able to get around. In August, Volney expresses considerable regret about the excommunication from the Church of John Kelly, Noah Bartholomew and his wife, and other prominent citizens of the community due to their views and involvement with the Godbeites who have become very active.[341] Delilah adds "There are a great many affected this way but are afraid to come out yet."

No doubt this type of correspondence continued until William and Mary Ann returned three years later, but unfortunately the rest has all been lost.

---

341 Besides coming out in open opposition to Brigham Young's economic and business policies, the Godbeites were also involved in a type of spiritualism with séances. The movement lasted for a few years before dying out.

Leviticus

(The Order of Enoch)

At the age of 63, Thomas must have felt that he would live the remainder of his life in Fillmore. Besides, he had been asked to leave his home twice before for gospel's sake. He was a community leader and well established with a comfortable brick home, orchard, cattle, and farm. His family was grown and established with their own families. Yet life is always full of uncertainties, and his was no exception. Another move was in the making.

The Fillmore United Order experiment had been a difficult disappointment, and it could be argued that the Brigham City and the St. George plans for a United Order were not true orders under the decree of having all things in common but rather an extension of the cooperative movement that had been incorporated in the late 1860s.

This now leads to the fourth type of order that President Young believed most closely fit the economic ideal of heaven, a plan to be built around a communal or a large family organization. In economic terms it was to be a command or managed economy paralleling the theocratic

---

Chronological Events

Fall	1876	Thomas King proposes to his family the move to Circle Valley to establish a United Order.
Dec 30,	1876	First official meeting of the order.
Feb	1877	The order begins to purchase property in Circle Valley and families begin moving.
May 1,	1877	Articles of Incorporation for the United Order of Circleville. Thomas King elected President.
Sep 8,	1878	Rebecca Jane Murray King dies.
Dec 19,	1878	William takes a second wife, Lucy Maranda White, and Culbert takes a third wife, Sarah Elizabeth Pratt.
Feb 3,	1879	Thomas passes away, just short of his sixty-sixth birthday.
Feb 22	1879	William elected president of the Kingston Order after considerable disagreement.
	1880	Cracks began to appear in the unity of the order.
	1883	The decision is made to abolish the order.
May 22,	1883	The last entry of minutes is made in the order's journal.

aspects of Church government and built around socialistic rather than market principles   All members were to consecrate their real and personal property, share more or less equally in the common production of the order, and live as a well-regulated family, and eat in a central dining hall. All economic decisions of production and distribution were to be determined at the top by the board and officers. As there was no specific detailed plan or handbook, local leaders were encouraged to improvise where needed and to adjust to local circumstances. The best known communities following this plan were Orderville (Kane County), Price (Washington County), and Springdale (Washington, County), Utah; Bunkerville, Nevada; and Sunset and St. Joseph, Arizona.

Regardless of previous disappointments, Thomas was still caught up in the perceived potential of economic oneness and was encouraged by President Young to take his family and everyone else who would join with them, and move to Circle Valley in Piute County. Here they were to go all the way with a full communal system.

How could Thomas refuse the advice of his Church leader? He truly believed in the principle. In the words of his son, Volney, "His whole heart was in the matter and his self elongation and determination by the help of the Lord was sufficient to accomplish it."[342] The Preamble of the Articles of Agreement governing the proposed United Order in Kingston mirrored his commitment:

> And whereas we are taught by the Apostle that we as a people cannot advance any farther in the things of the Kingdom of God only by entering into the United Order. And whereas we are told by Jesus Christ, our Savior, that unless we become one we are none of His."[343]

Circle Valley is located about fifty miles south of Richfield on U.S. Highway 89. Circleville and Junction are now the main towns in this small valley measuring about twenty-seven miles long and six miles wide at its widest point. Dividing the valley about equally, east and west, is the south fork of the meandering Sevier River. In contrast to today's view of a green and beautiful area, in the nineteenth century it was windy, dry, and desolate with alkalitic soil, covered with greasewood, sagebrush, and rabbit brush. Many people felt that the word "sevier" better described the condition of the valley more appropriately than the river. However, directly to the east are the timber-rich 12,000-foot Pavant Mountains.

The valley was first settled by Mormon pioneers in the early to middle 1860s, but they were soon met with discouragement and despair. The

---

342 Volney King, "The Daily Journal of the Kingston United Order," February 1876.

343 Ibid., May 1, 1877.

wind never seemed to stop blowing; and when they turned the water onto the parched fields, the light and porous ground, filled with gopher and prairie dog holes, absorbed the water only to discharge it through another hole, washing away newly planted seedlings. Circleville and Marysvale became the principal settlements and Piute County was officially formed in 1865. When the Black Hawk war erupted the following year, these settlements were evacuated.

At the conclusion of the costly Indian war, interest in the valley was rekindled; and by the late 1860s, a few scattered farms began to emerge. In the late 1860s, gold, silver, and lead were discovered in and around the northern end of the valley, and by 1873 Marysvale became a well established boom town. By the time the King families arrived, Marysvale and the surrounding area had several hundred people, Circleville, just across the river west of Kingston, a handful.

Located less than twenty miles east of Circle Valley through a small canyon and along the east fork of the Sevier River is Grass Valley. Bordered by current Burrville on the north and Antimony on the south, this valley was so named because of the lush vegetation found when the area was first explored in 1873. It is said that when the first explorers came into the valley the grass was so tall in places it would rub against the bellies of the horses.

In the fall of 1876, discussions within the extended King family led them to consider President Young's advice. A risky proposition in light of the track record for previous orders, the Kingston Order would tax to the limit the ambition, imagination, and work ethic of the family in organizing and executing such a large project. In the end, whether the order proved to be a success or a failure is left to the judgement of the individual student or reader. However the experiment is viewed, the individual accomplishments, growth, and experience must be recognized and honored regardless of the end result of the order

William, Culbert, Edwin, and Volney all agreed to the proposal. Regrettably, Delilah and Dan declined and remained in Fillmore. She wanted to join and felt it was a call from the Lord, but Dan resisted saying, "NO NO, I came down to Fillmore and left my profession in Salt Lake City at the call of the Church authorities, but I absolutely refuse to go down into that wild country or go through again the sacrifices which we have passed through."[344] This was reported to Salt Lake, and word came back from Church leaders that Delilah should remain as an instructor in the schools and stay active in the Church in Fillmore. This counsel came as a great relief as she was torn between her husband and her father and the call that had come to her father through the Prophet.[345]

---

344 W. F. Olson, "John Robison King," 4.

345 Ibid.

At first, John also refused to join the order; but under heavy pressure from his father and brothers, he finally agreed to unite. How much later is not known. John was already living in Grass Valley, and while all the brothers became officers or directors in the order, John didn't become a director until towards the end of the order on May 13, 1882. It appears that he participated but remained aloof from most activities.

Preliminary discussions within the family must have been going on for several months before the final decision was made and specific plans formulated to create a new community, nor did all members of the order join or leave to go to Circle Valley at the same time. The first official meeting was December 30, 1876, in Fillmore at Thomas's home. Attending were Thomas, William, Culbert, Edwin and Volney King together with David Savage, John Wilcox, and Mortimer Warner.[346]

In this meeting they conducted their initial business and then agreed to meet in Circle Valley, on May 1, the following spring to install a permanent organization. To demonstrate their commitment and enthusiasm for the venture, the Kings over the next two years contributed 70 percent to 75 percent of the investment capital.[347] One report has Thomas himself stepping forward and agreeing to put in all of his resources amounting to $20,000.[348] However, according to an analysis of the property and other family assets in Fillmore, from the 1870 federal census and the Millard County land records, this figure does not appear realistic, except by the combined King family. Other contributors of any consequence based on 1870 assets were:

Joel White	1,300
Mortimer Warner	1,250
John Wilcox	500
Susan Black	400
James Huff	300
James Knight	300
David Savage	300

Records are incomplete for determining other contributors but they appear to be few.

---

346 David Savage came to Utah in 1847 and after three years moved to Lehi, later to Holden, Cedar Fort, Paris, (Idaho), Hiram, Goshen and then back to Holden, just a few miles from Fillmore. He had been a freighter and mail carrier between San Bernardino and Salt Lake. Mortimer Warner was the son of Thomas's good friend Orange Warner. No background information is available for John Wilcox.

347 This estimate is based on the 1870 federal census, Millard County property records, and Volney King's Diary. No information is available for William who was in Hawaii in 1870 on his mission, and the records of John's livestock holdings are unclear.

348 Phil Robinson, *Sinners and Saints,* (Boston: Roberts Brother, 1883), 212.

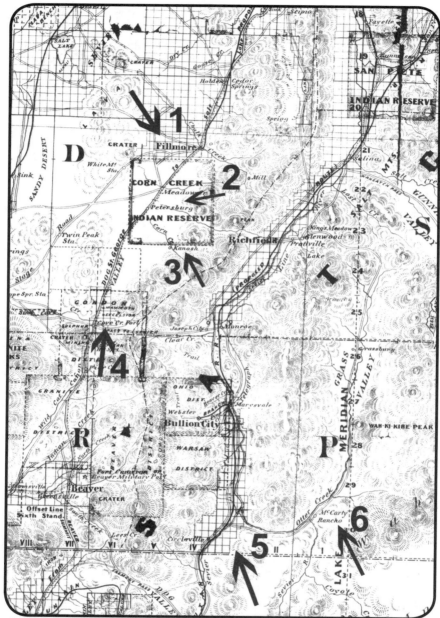

The above is a section taken from a 1878 map at the time of the move to Circleville. Cities like Kingston, Antimony and Junction did not exist at this time. Item #1 is Fillmore, #2 is Petersburg, #3 is Kanosh, #4 is Cove Fort, #5 is where Kingston was first located, and #6 is where Antimony was settled. The 100 mile trip from Fillmore to Kingston in 1877 with all their provisions would take over a week. (Courtesy of the Utah State Historical Department.)

For these people, it was a time of religious fervor and rejoicing. To build a new community on the economic, social, and millennialistic principles of the gospel of Christ would create conditions to bring about the return of their Savior.

The basic underpinnings and philosophy of this communal society were described by President Young on numerous occasions and in explicit terms. According to historians Leonard J. Arrington, Feramorz Y. Fox, and Dean L. May:

> The model was the "well regulated family," an institution characterized by sharing of resources according to need, contributions of labor according to ability, and a concern for the welfare of others in the group that transcended selfishness and promoted harmony and unity. The physical environment of an ideal Order would be similar to that of a family as well, with a common kitchen serving both as a symbol of equality in consumption and labor and as a hearth, the center of the family social and spiritual life. Private apartment houses or rooms would accommodate the members for sleeping and more personal aspects of their lives, but the social experiences of Order members were to take place in the community environment rather than within the nuclear family.[349]

Land and Water

In the later part of the 1800s land and water issues were both simple and complex. In 1869 the federal government implemented the Homestead Act in Utah, and it was necessary for the citizens of the territory to firm up their property claims that had been issued to them under arrangements of the territorial legislature. As existing property lines did not always match up with the federal survey, several adjustments had to be made, but for the most part important issues had been worked out.

In going forward, each person wanting to take up land needed to file under the Homestead Act's provisions requiring them to improve their land for five years. One hundred sixty acres could be acquired in this manner, or a person could simply buy the land outright for $1.25 an acre. During the five-year period, there were always potential claim jumpers who could challenge a claim; and sometimes people would settle on land thinking it was theirs only to discover that after improvements were made, another person had filed a previous claim. This became a sticky problem two years later when the order built its new grist mill in Kingston. It took some time for William to resolve the problem.[350]

No water came with this homestead land; but until 1880, people could

---

349 Arrington, Fox, and May, *Building The City Of God*, 203.

350 I am grateful to Max Sudweeks, Kingston, Utah for providing this information.

A microfilmed copy of a handwritten page from the original agreement, covering Articles 15-18. Although mostly unreadable, it does give a representation of the hand-writing. (Courtesy LDS Church Historical Department.)

file claims with a locally appointed water master on a first-come-first-served basis. While these were not definitive claims, water masters under Church direction, could take considerable liberties during periods of drought to be judicious, the claims did have legal standing. In 1880 a territorial law required all previous claims to be formalized with the county selectmen, and broken down between primary and secondary rights. Grazing land for livestock was usually on government land available for use without formality or restrictions.

It is under these arrangements that the Kings began to move into Circle and Grass valleys. The first to express an interest in the area was John, who began herding cattle in Grass Valley in the summer of 1875. A year later he purchased the homestead rights to the John Guiser ranch. Edwin, Volney, and a few other men soon followed buying property and planting crops.

To set up the order, it was determined that a large tract of land was needed for farming, and the Kings soon began negotiations for 1,760 acres in Circle Valley that was "a good tract of land with plenty of water privileges ... that was for sale by a few transients (non Mormons)."[351] While it is claimed these people had it for sale, they didn't actually own the land but had filed a homestead claim and were willing to sell their claim to the Kings. Land records are not complete enough to analyze all the transactions, but it appears they purchased these claims for most of their land and then members of the order filed homestead claims on other properties. For example, they paid a Mr. Heister $250 for a quarter section of pasture land, a Mr. Brewer $300 for another quarter section, a Mr. Girioux $250 for his 160 acres, and a Mr. Burns and Henry Griffen $400 each for their respective 160 acres. In most cases horses and cattle were used as currency to complete the transaction. On one parcel, a couple of gentlemen later returned and claimed a prior right, and it took another $200 in cattle to buy them off.

The Kingston canal, built by the order, soon provided vital water, but in November 1880 William:

> In behalf of the company known as the "United Order of Kingston" complied with the new law by filing a claim "to be entitled as primary right appurtenant to the law named in ... petition to water from the South Fork of the Sevier River and Tributaries taken out on the east side of said stream to the amount and reasonable necessity for domestic purposes and water of stock and the irrigation of 440 acres of farm land of a sand and clay nature..."[352]

After acquisition, it could be argued that the property remained in the name of the claimant and not the United Order for the basic reason that fee simple title was not available until after the required five years.

During the course of the next few years, additional property was filed on by the King brothers and other members of the order in both valleys. According to an entry in the "Daily Journal" by Volney, $217.50 was sent to the land office "to pay for the Geo[rge] H Dockstader land which

351 Volney King, "The Daily Journal of the Kingston United Order," February 19, 1876.

352 Piute County Land Records, Junction, Utah, Book 1:463.

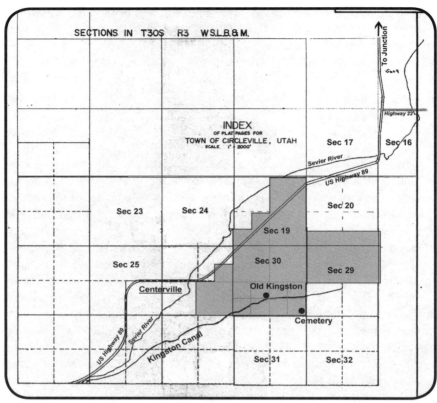

The shaded area in the above map represents a composite of information about where the order was located; however, no land records are available to verify exact location. The map gives the approximate location of the community, canal, and land they occupied. Each section represents one square mile. (Information from Volney King's "Daily Journal," and Max Sudweeks, Kingston, Utah.)

includes a portion of our north Ranche."[353]

The Move to Kingston

In February, 1877, William, Edwin, and Volney all moved into Circle Valley; and as soon as weather permitted, they planted about thirty acres of wheat and ten acres of oats. Volney describes the adverse conditions under which they worked with the statement, "We were all working with diligence putting in our crops under quite discouraging circumstances as we had no ruffness for horse feed. Picking for the horses was very poor but I managed to go to Elsinore and get some grain for feed and seed

353 Volney King, "The Daily Journal of the Kingston United Order," August 22, 1882.

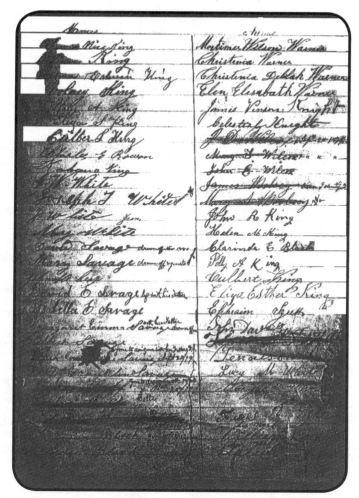

One of the signature pages from the original agreement with some computer touch up. Note the signatures of Thomas Rice King, William King, Thomas Edwin King, Volney King, John R. King, and Culbert King. Names were crossed out when the people moved from the order. (Courtesy LDS Church Historical Department.)

which was a very cold trip and I suffered with cold considerable."[354]

Again describing the traveling conditions in those days, Volney writes about his trip back to Fillmore. Leaving the others behind, he started for Fillmore on March 30. By the time he reached Marysvale, it had started to snow and the storm began raging in earnest. At the canyon, the snow was piling up fast to within three feet, and his horses soon become exhausted.

354 Volney King Diaries, p. 53. Besides the Kingston United Order Journal, Volney maintained his personal diaries located at the J. Willard Marriott Library Special Collections, University of Utah. A typescript copy can be found at the Utah State Historical Society.

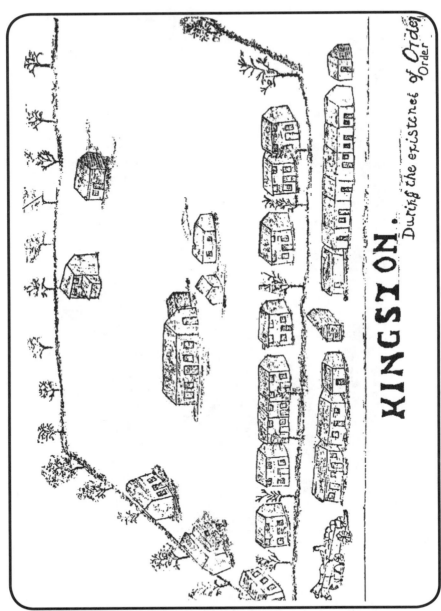

This drawing of Kingston by Volney King shows the outer row of log cabins and the inner row of homes, with the dining hall and kitchen in the center. (Volney King Papers, Utah State Historical Society.)

There was nothing he could do but camp for the evening. He tramped the snow down for the horses, put grain out for them, and then without a fire crawled into what bedding he had under his wagon cover. All through the night the storm "raged and roared like the sea in a storm," and because of his own exhaustion, his legs began to cramp. All in all, Volney wondered if he would even survive.

The next day Volney again continued his desperate journey and at times he would have to get out to find the ruts in the road before he could move on. The snow soon became deeper than the height of the wagon bed preventing any further travel, but finally, in company with some other travelers he discovered on the road, he was able to cut down a tree and drag it through the snow to break a trail. He didn't arrive in Kanosh until three days later, and then continued on to Fillmore arriving on April 4. Needless to say his family was very concerned about his safety.[355]

Joining with the Kings were such families as the Blacks, Knights, Mineers, Savages, Warners, Whites, and Wilcoxes. The initial population of Kingston numbered twelve families with sixty people. Later as other families joined, the apex of the order, with nearly two hundred people, was reached in 1879.[356] Each person played an important part in the success of the enterprise with needed skills and talents: James Huff was a skilled mechanic and blacksmith, Reuben Syrett was a shoemaker from England, Henry Edward (Old Ned) Desaules was a skilled carpenter and furniture maker from Switzerland, Robert Forrester was an expert gardener, George Dockstader was a tailor, and Andrew Mineer was a master musician and band leader. Several of the women from Sweden, Denmark, and Holland operated hand looms. "Old Ned," as he was affectionately called, had a library consisting of several hundred books, all made up of history and classics, "no shoddy fiction." He would make these books available to anyone who would read and take care of them. Thankful Harmon became the leader of the choir and taught, with just a tuning fork, the members of the group to sing in four-part harmony.

The Kingston Order's Articles of Incorporation[357] signed by all adult members, including some older children, transferred all personal and real property of each individual to the company with the president acting as

---

355 Ibid., 55.

356 It is difficult to register an exact number as Volney reported numbers only once a year. In Appendix 6 an attempt has been made by the author to identify most of the people belonging to the order at one time or another.

357 See Appendix 5 for a copy of the "Articles of Incorporation for the United Order of Circleville." The original articles are found at the LDS Church Historical Department Archives.

trustee-in-trust. All remuneration was fixed by the board of directors, and each person agreed to live an economical and frugal lifestyle. No person was to "seek to obtain that which is above another."[358]

In addition, the agreement provided for the usual agricultural, manufacturing, and commercial pursuits, as well as setting lofty goals for a total society. It also provided for the establishment and the maintaining of colleges, seminaries, churches, libraries, and other charitable or scientific associations.

As was the custom and by direction of Apostle John Taylor, members of the order were re-baptized as members of the Kingston Order. This was a practice dating back to when the pioneers first came into the Salt Lake Valley to demonstrate a re-commitment as Saints and for a remission of sins.

> Having authority given me of Jesus Christ I baptize you for the remission of your sins, the renewal of your covenants, and the observance of the rules of the holy United Order, in the name of the Father and of the Son and of the Holy Ghost.[359]

Thomas was appointed president of the order; and in his honor, the town they built was named Kingston. William King was appointed bishop with Joel White and James Huff as counselors.[360] Later Culbert, was appointed one of his counselors. Most of the accounts of the order have come from the personal diaries of Volney and William King, Ella Vilate King Christian, Henry Desaules, and Teancum Pratt.[361]

The entire operation was located in four areas. Just across the Sevier River east of Circleville, the order purchased 1,760 acres for farming and gardening, and on a ten-acre block the Kings built their community. This is located about five miles southwest of present-day Kingston. Here they built their homes, school, dining hall, kitchen, store, carpenter shop, and blacksmith shop. To supply needed water for irrigation, they built the Kingston Canal, which runs south of their property for more than three miles. This was a quite an engineering feat for their day with only horse power to dig, and scrape and manpower to push a shovel. The canal is still in use today.

---

358 "Articles of Incorporation for the United Order of Circleville." See Appendix 5, Art 9.

359 Arrington, Fox, and May, *Building The City Of God*, 154.

360 "Kingston, Utah Manuscript History," LDS Church Historical Department Archives.

361 Ella was the sixteen year-old (in 1880) daughter of Thomas Edwin King. Henry Desaules was a Swiss bachelor convert to the Church, Teancum Pratt was the brother-in-law of Culbert King, all members of the order.

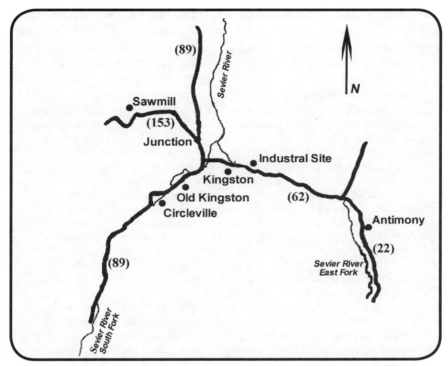

A road map of the Kingston area. The distance between Old Kingston and the sawmill is about 10 miles, and the distance between Old Kingston and Antimony is about 15 miles.

The second area was located up City Creek Canyon about six miles northwest of the present-day city of Junction (so named because this is where both the south and east forks of the Sevier River converge). The selected site was ideal for a saw mill with good timber and plenty of water power to drive the mill thus providing needed lumber for homes and other buildings.

The third area was about fifteen miles east through Kingston Canyon and along the east fork of the Sevier. Here in Grass Valley they built their dairy and cattle operation with horned cattle, sheep, and horses. Later the town of Coyote (now Antimony) was established.

The last area was just a half mile northeast of present-day Kingston. Here along the east fork of the Sevier was their industrial site where they would build a flour mill, tannery, and woolen mill.

As in many cases, when moving, the pioneers would relocate in the cold winter months after harvesting or before planting. The move to Kingston was no exception, and by November 1876, the realization of their plans for the 100-mile exodus began in earnest. The trail would take them south to

Cove Fort and then east over the mountain to what is now the small community of Sevier. At this juncture the trail would again turn south along present day Highway 89 to Circle Valley. The move must have taken eight to ten days to complete. Mrs. Christian describes the move as follows:

> When we consider the means of transportation then it was a tedious and long route, driving pigs, sheep, horses and cattle over trails with no food to give them excepting that which could be procured by the roadside. Fifteen miles was a big day's journey. The roads, up hill and down, were a problem. They often had to unload half of the load, take it to the top of the hill and go back for the rest. This was repeated time and time again as we made the journey. So you can easily see that women and children did considerable walking.
>
> Tents were pitched at night where mothers and their little ones slept, but many of us slept on the bare ground under the starlit sky. I remember one morning as I was picking up my bedding after a sound and pleasant nights sleep, there was a tarantula curled up enjoying the warmth of my body. At another time it was a rattlesnake. But neither had harmed me and they seemed to say "I thank you for sharing your bed with me." Did I kill them? How could I, they had not harmed me, why should I harm them?
>
> In those days the flood waters were not under control by reservoirs, dams, or irrigation ditches. It was floods in the springtime and drought in the autumn. Rafts were made to convey some of the things across, but the most difficult problem was getting the sheep over, they just stubbornly refused to enter that torrent of water. Finally father (Edwin) got an idea Every band of Sheep has a leader, get that one over and the others will follow. So he tied a rope around this sheep's neck, then jumped on his horse and lunged into the water. The horse, swam across dragging the sheep with him. When the other sheep saw their leader going they all followed and soon all were safely across. Such were some of the obstacles to be overcome in making the move.[362]

After the first groups begin arriving in the spring of 1877, the first and most important matters of business were the clearing of land for crops, digging a well, and the construction of homes. At first these crude homes were log cabins with dirt floors and roofs and the community well was more of a cistern to hold water. At first they had to haul their water from the river until the canal was finished. William and Edwin started working on the sawmill in February 1877 and by August it was completed with a capacity of 1,800 board feet of inch thick lumber in a sixteen-hour day. The flume, pen stock, water wheel, and all parts of the framework of the mill were made out of wood, even wooden pegs for nails. The only iron used in the mill was for the saw, ax, crowbar, and hammer.

Soon thereafter the Kings started to move their families. Volney was the first, and then in April, William moved his family as well as Father

---

362 Handwritten letter by Ella V. Christian to Donald Whittaker, September 20, 1946. A copy is in my possession.

Type of log cabin with clay-covered roof built by the United Order. (Courtesy Max Sudweeks, Kingston, Utah.)

King, as Thomas was now called. Culbert did not arrive until November when he brought over Esther and Elizabeth and their families. Matilda arrived in April 1878, when her new home was finished, and Edwin's family arrived after the death of Rebecca Jane in September. John's family had already moved over earlier and was living in Grass Valley. No doubt the lengthy time (almost two years) to move everyone was due to simple logistics on both the front and back sides. It took considerable time to build homes and establish crops, and families were not brought over from Millard County until they could be housed and cared for.

Furthermore, orchards, gardens, and grain crops were still being raised in Millard County, and the Kings would go back from time to time to harvest these crops to supplement the Kingston production. Millard County homes and other assets had to be liquidated, some for whatever they would bring. For example, during 1878 Thomas sold his home and hotel for $2,000 less a mortgage given by the buyer for $1,350, and both John and Edwin received $1,000 for their properties. Volney was not able to sell his property until August 1879 and for only $225. William didn't do much better. His land didn't sell until January 1885 and for only $300. William had a five-acre parcel of land that didn't sell until after his death.[363]

Community Lifestyle

The order was set up with houses all built alike regardless of family size, and arranged in two rows in the style of a fort. The outer row consisted of log cabins, and homes in the inner row were built out of lumber from the sawmill. By the end of their first fiscal year, they had built their first fifteen homes, six log and nine frame, and had completed a schoolhouse, blacksmithy, and carpenter and shoe shops.

---

363 See Appendix 4 for more details.

From the operations in Grass Valley, large quantities of butter and cheese were made for their own use and to exchange for needed products outside of the order. The annual report of the order which was published in the Salt Lake *Deseret News* by letter from Thomas King gives a limited account of the first year's economic production and consumption:

Consumed		Produced
33,937	pounds of flour	
10,697	pounds of beef	
2,491	pounds of pork	
197	bushels of potatoes	
2,223	pounds of butter	3,000
372	pounds of cheese	1,000
201	dozens of eggs	
232	pounds of dried fruit.	

In addition to the above, the order produced 1,800 pounds of wool, 300 yards of cloth, 50 colts, and 300 calves. It also purchased a labor-and time-saving threshing machine. The surplus cheese and butter were sold or bartered as a cash crop. The amount of flour produced was taken from their equivalent wheat production and could also be used to barter for other needed items.

The capital stock of the order increased to $27,041.20, with a good part of the $7,041 increase coming from the King brothers. The population had also increased to 157 people in 27 families.

To reinforce their early optimism, Thomas finishes his report by stating that the general health of the community is good, and "the prospects before them encouraging in every way."[364]

While the enthusiasm of Thomas is commendable, a break-down of the numbers presents a more realistic picture of this struggling community. Assuming an average number of teenagers and adults in residence for the full year as seventy-eight, the per person consumption might be considered adequate, but the diet somewhat marginal. It would amount to only about 1.19 pounds of flour, .46 pounds of meat, and less than half a pound of potatoes per day. It is true their diet would be supplemented with vegetables and cheese; but to curtail sickness, the amount of available fruit would be questionable.

In December 1878 Volney gives a description of their meals after the completion of the large dinning hall. He says that breakfast was a warm meal, dinner was a cold lunch, and supper was usually bread, mush, and milk. Bread was both yeast and salt rising; biscuits were made with both

---

364 *Salt Lake Deseret News,* June 26, 1878, 333.

yeast and soda; potatoes were boiled, baked, mashed, and fixed in soup; and their beef and pork was boiled, fried, or baked. They would have hash, butter, and cheese; and cakes and pies were served at least once a week.

A description by another member of the order gives a few more details.

> The menus were simple with little variation, except meat. For breakfast; potatoes, bacon and eggs, milk and fruit (when they could get it), mostly wild berries and dried apples. In the summer they had breakfast at six o'clock. For dinner: boiled beef and vegetable soup was a favorite, pork or mutton, sometimes fish from the Sevier River, potatoes and gravy, vegetables of all kinds, dry beans and hominy, simple puddings, sometimes pie or cookies. For supper: corn meal mush and milk, no sugar, minute pudding was a rare treat, (flour mush served with cinnamon, sugar and cream.[365]

Several months earlier, Ned Desaules, complained of the food. While it certainly would not be fair to compare unsophisticated Kingston to French cuisine, there is a basis to his complaint.

> I was quite sick on New Year's Day. I almost thought that I would die. I had both a shivering fever and after that a hot fever, and then a great bodily exhaustion. I could not eat anything for four days. But the goodness of the Lord raised me, and I am doing a little better day to day. The cause of my sickness is the poor quality of food that we have here. The cows have dried up, and we have no more milk. These Americans do not know how to cook – they are like savages, or worse, as to preparing meat. They also eat pork mixed with beef, which makes me suffer because I am like the Jews in respect to pork, and eating a little of it by mistake makes me immediately ill.[366]

Difficulties with food is again mentioned by Desaules in July 1879 before the new crops were harvested.

> Our company grows steadily, two families came last week, and we must feed all of them. Our granary is empty and we must economize in order to buy wheat, and we have so many other expenses as well. . . We have neither corn nor fruit here, except for a few mountain currents that grow along the river. Our peas are only half up, and I don't think we will have green peas before the middle of August. Our only crops are wheat, oats, hops, potatoes, carrots, and beets. Our wheat won't ripen before next month, and we have already lost much of it, the wind having cut and blighted more than a hundred acres so that we

---

365 Kate Carter, *Heart Throbs of the West* (Salt Lake City, Utah: Daughters of Utah Pioneers, 1939), 1:63. This account was related by Mary T. Wilcox.

366 "Henri Edward Desaules diary 1833-1904," January 16, 1878, LDS Church Historical Department Archives.

The four-mile Kingston canal, which was built by the Kingston Order in early 1879. The canal was about three feet wide and two feet deep.

will have to buy the greater part of our grain for next year.[367]

The first mention of school for the children was made on February 5, 1879, when 60 scholars were enrolled. The following November 1879, forty students attended with sixty-three students enrolling in the second term on February 9, 1880, but the number dropped to twenty-five when school begin in November 1881. No mention is made after this later date, but it can be assumed that the education of the young people continued. Both Volney and Edwin took an active part in promoting general education and teaching basic subjects. Prior to the inauguration of the Kingston school, home schooling could have been held in many homes depending on parental motivation and ability.

Everyday life at Kingston was very hard even for the most rugged of people. The 6,000 foot elevation brought seasonal early and late frost, and during the coldest months temperatures would vacillate in single digits above and below zero and on several occasions reaching as low as 20 below. To supply fuel for the drafty cabins and homes, three and four loads of wood had to be hauled in nearly every day and frequently as many as five to six loads were required. It is assumed that most of it came from their sawmill where dried wooden tailings were available from their summer sawing, but nevertheless a twenty-mile round trip. In contrast, during the summer months the breezy winds from the north and the south frequently kick up dust storms, blanketing the valley.

For the next fiscal year, building activity reached a new level with the completion of thirty-one more 450 square foot homes and fifteen log dwellings. A 576 square foot school house was built, perhaps larger than the first one, and in November their 1,568 square foot communal dining

367 Ibid., July 20, 1879.

hall and 450 square foot kitchen were finished.[368] It wasn't until the next year in March 1879 that, after considerable work, the irrigation canal was finished and began furnishing needed water.

The dining hall and kitchen were located behind the homes, and all the members of the order ate together as one family. The women were organized into seven sets of six women to take turns in the kitchen, each responsible for one day of the week. The one exception to this organized pattern was mothers with small children who were excused from all kitchen duties. To aid in the duties were two to three men who worked as bakers and helped with washing dishes, building fires, carrying wood, and running errands.

The kitchen was set up with two large cooking stoves with an adjoining room for baking bread and cakes, and roasting meat. Again according to Mrs. Christian:

> This bakery was another homemade affair; in it was built a large oven made of brick and divided into three compartments; 1st the place where the fire was built, 2nd the oven, and 3rd the flue which carried off the smoke. Steel or iron slides or small doors separated each compartment. These two slides were back when the fire was first built and the blaze allowed to circulate throughout the oven. When the oven was properly heated, all smoking embers were taken out of the first compartment and thrown into the third one where the smoke could escape; the hot coals could be shoveled back into the first if more heat was needed; then the iron slides were drawn to close these two open spaces; so as to hold a uniform heat in the oven. [369]

Mrs. Christian further claimed that 100 loaves of bread could be adequately baked in the oven at any given time, and their "meats were roasted perfectly in this oven; also puddings, pies and cakes."

One anecdote told by Mary Wilcox claims that when "a meal was late the cooks hoped Uncle Volney King would be called upon to pray; when it when it was all ready and might get cold, they hoped Uncle Volney would not be called on to pray."[370]

This organization and method of food preparation and serving would last for only two years before it reverted back to individual homes.

Recreational activities at Kingston included many of the traditional pioneer amusements. On Saturday afternoons were sports and games, picnic parties, and dances. Often Father King would be seen lying or sitting on the ground, directing some kind of pastime or contest. A ball

---

368 Volney King, "The Daily Journal of the Kingston United Order," May 1, 1879.

369 Warner, *Grass Valley*, 10-11.

370 Heart Throbs of the West, 1:63.

game, "six sticks", "hoist the gate high as the sky", and "let the troops pass by" were some of the favorites. If the weather would not permit outdoor exercises, games and plays were held in the homes. After the woolen factory was completed, the equipment in the factory was often pushed aside for dances and special activities. Weekly dances were held either on Monday or Friday night, and dancing was permitted until 10:00 p.m., except for holidays or special occasions when dancing was permitted until midnight. Strict rules were usually enforced with a prohibition against alcoholic beverages, tobacco in any form, or swearing. The local citizens were not allowed to go to other dances, but outsiders could attend their dances if they would agree to obey the rules.

President King's attitude was to encourage this activity for proper mental development of youth, and he felt that they would respond more readily to the religious activities of the Church if they had a balance of activities.

Special occasions were marked by commensurate activities. For example, their first Christmas was "celebrated with a zest." There was a picnic party held at the Warner home followed by a dance. Music was provided by James Huff, John Whetton and Cyrus Earl; however, the day was marred when the McDonough's house across the river caught fire, destroying all their possessions.[371]

On Christmas Day 1880 Volney records that "Santa Claus took a slight glance at us last evening" and this morning a few guns were fired. They also played ball and some of the boys went deer hunting. The ranch folks from Grass valley all came over and the daughter of John and Helen King, Helen Matilda, was married to William Hardy, William King performing the ceremony at the home of Matilda King. There was then a party for the young people and one for the adults that evening including a dance. The dance was interspersed with songs and dialogues.[372]

On July 24, 1882, the Olson family came over and provided the music for the evening dance that lasted into "the late hour." Besides the dance the day was filled with program and celebration and the citizens all marched to the mill in a procession with a grand marshal.[373]

Church services were held each Sunday and throughout the week. Sunday school began at 10:00 a.m. and then regular services started at 2:00 p.m. and again in the evening at 7:00. The first Thursday morning was reserved for the traditional fast meeting and frequently there was a

---

371 Volney King, "The Daily Journal of the Kingston United Order," December 25, 1878.

372 Ibid., December 25, 1880.

373 Ibid., July 24, 1882.

priesthood meeting on Thursday evenings. Various religious topics were discussed such as the Godhead and apostasy. The Relief Society for women and the Mutual Improvement Association (M.I.A.) for both the youth and adults were organized on December 16, 1877. During the late fall and winter months M.I.A was held on Saturday evenings and on occasion Relief Society was held on Thursday evenings.

The meeting of the sisters in Relief Society provides additional insight into the feelings of the people. While they met monthly for the bearing of testimonies and receiving counsel from the Bishopric, in the winter months they met weekly for work meetings.

At first the sisters expressed much gratitude for their membership in the order and how they felt they were directed by the Lord to join. Sister [Mary Ann] McDonough said "she was much pleased with the united order."[374] Susan Black commented that "she had wished very much to join the united order, had made it a subject of prayer and was led to come to Kingston. She had thanked the lord every day since for the privilege of living in the holy order."[375] Sister [Brita Catherine] Peterson felt grateful to be in the order and had even left her husband to join, but "wished to do right."[376] Sister Nielson "felt well in the society and also in the united order, was never satisfied outside of it for she knew it was the command of God for he has said except ye are one ye are none of mine."[377] Mary Wilcox remarked, "I have taken a great interest in the order ever since I came here and I feel as much interested in it today as I ever did. I know it is a commandment of God and I never intend to settle down outside of the order. It is my desire to do right and keep the commandments of god and do my duty where ever my lot may be cast."[378] Sister Susan [Black] Savage commented that they came to Kingston "to get rid of their old traditions."[379]

On May 1, 1878, Matilda bore fervent testimony of how "pleased she was with the Relief Society and had belonged for 30 years beginning in Nauvoo. She remembered well the martyrdom of Joseph and Hyrum Smith. She was truly happy to be with us here in the united order and hoped we would take the onward march ~~and to onward~~ to perfection." Matilda goes on to say that "some are loath to deprive themselves of the

---

374 "Kingston Relief Society Minute book 1878-1898," January 1878, 5, LDS Church Historical Department Archives.

375 Ibid.

376 Ibid., May 1, 1878, 20.

377 Ibid., May 1, 1878, 20.

378 Ibid., September 18, 1879, 68.

379 Ibid., 74.

luctourous of life but she rejoiced in it."[380] In a later testimony she spoke
of going back to Jackson County, and said the only "way we would ever
get back there was by carrying out the principles of the united order."[381]

Other points of interest stressed by the sisters were to teach and raise
their children in a proper manner. "Plural mariage was true and from
god and was for our exaltation." As sisters they felt the need to overcome
pride and vanity and the fashions of the day and live in accordance with
the principles of the gospel.

When the Kings first made the move to Kingston, it was known that
Thomas had a weak heart. For nearly two years all his energy, with a
passion, had been directed towards building a new community. The expended effort was now beginning to take its toll, and Thomas fell ill on
January 14, 1879. His condition worsened and by January 26 the family
gathered to pay their last respects. Volney describes Thomas's suffering
as intense, and he began to give instructions on his burial and disposition
of personal items. His commitment to the order was manifested in his
expressions of love for the people and encouragement to continue. There
were to be no underhanded games and everything was to be above board.
Righteousness would effect the right. In turn he wished to be remembered
by all his friends and felt that he did not have any enemies.

He then commenced to counsel specific individuals. He encouraged
Dan Olson to stick to his religion and he would come out all right. He also
gave encouragement and instruction to Mary Ann and Eliza King. John
had a good heart and was to be humored. Patience was to be exercised
toward him.

Two days later, Thomas reaffirmed his belief in the order and counseled his family "that he or she who would not believe in the principles of
the United Order would not believe a person would rise from the dead."[382]
The relationship between the united order and the resurrection is not clear,
but perhaps Thomas was trying to identify a level or degree of faith needed
to participate in the saving principles of the gospel.

Thomas continued to suffer and lingered until February 3, when he finally passed away, a month short of his 66th birthday. The funeral services
were held in the public hall, and speakers included, interestingly enough,
two of the brethren who would later challenge the Kings for leadership of
the order, David Savage and Joel White. Appropriately, Thomas was buried
in the little cemetery in old Kingston, the community he had founded.

380 Ibid., May 1, 1878.

381 Ibid., June 6, 1878.

382 Volney King, "The Daily Journal of the Kingston United Order," January 28,
1870.

Among the letters and expressions of condolences is a letter to William King from future Apostle Francis M. Lyman, dated February 14, 1879. The Lymans were early settlers of Fillmore and good friends of the Kings. Apostle Lyman was the Church authority who later counseled the Kings to abandon the United Order.

Apostle Francis Marion Lyman, 1840 - 1916, was a good friend of the Kings. He was ordained an apostle October 27, 1880. (Courtesy Utah State Historical Society.)

> I visited with Brother King last Fall. I must acknowledge the hand of the Lord in my little tour to Kingston. I was thirty days from Tooele all the way round and it was the happiest thirty days of my life. My heart is sorrowful for those who remain, but I am so full of joy for your fathers condition. He was as true as steel and never knew what it was to flinch. His reward is sure and his crown will shine with eternal increasing splendor. Oh may his mantle of wisdom, intelligence and integrity fall on his sons and all his posterity to turn them from the fiery assaults of an enemy of righteousness. Now that father passed around the corner ahead of you, the sons should subject themselves more surly [sic]to the will and service of God that they may have the comforter to guide them in matters temporal and spiritual . . . I think about your father frequently and thought of me among his friends and I am quite sure he did not think of me oftener than I thought of him. Our spirits were always like kindred spirits.[383]

Following the reading of this letter to the assembled order members, a resolution was adopted which said in part:

> We the people of Kingston and members of the United Order in meeting assembled feeling the loss of our most beloved and esteemed president Thomas R. King do unitedly tender a tribute of respect to the memory of the departed who was an instrument in the hands of God put forth as a leader to establish the principle of union whereof we are all made equal partakers of its benefits and privileges do sincerely tender a tribute of most profound respect to this most blessed, good, and great man...[384]

Individual comments from some of the sisters included Susan [Black]

---

383 Ibid.

384 Ibid., February 22, 1879.

The west side of the grist or flour mill. (Courtesy Max Sudweeks, Kingston, Utah.)

Savage, "Our late trouble had thrown a gloom over the place but the Lord giveth and the Lord taketh. Perhaps our beloved president could do more good behind the vale."[385] Mary Wilcox "felt sorrowful and depressed in spirit on account of our recent trouble in looseing our beloved president. We had truly been called to part with a great and noble man."[386]

In the same meeting William was elected president, thus holding the leadership role in both ecclesiastical and temporal affairs of the order; but during the meeting the warm feelings of unity began to break down. A few opposed William and it was recorded that some people stood neutral, far from the normal unanimous votes of confidence.

This lack of unity would plague his presidency until the order broke up four years later. Within six months a small group of dissidents got together and formed a new group with John D. Wilcox as president, Hans S. Jensen as vice president, John T. Wetton as treasurer, and Peter Nielson as secretary together with a small board.[387] It cannot be determined to what extent they carried their dissent, but many of them soon left and went to Arizona.[388]

Further problems with their cattle occurred the following April when it

---

385 "Kingston Relief Society Minute book 1878-1898," February 6, 1879, 51.

386 Ibid., 53.

387 Volney King Diaries, 89, September 14, 1879.

388 Ibid.

was reported that 200 head of cattle had died, 150 of them were cows, and their hay was about gone. Besides starvation and freezing temperatures, disease also played a part in the loss.[389] With their cattle starving, is again an indication that production of hay was not keeping up with demand.

In spite of these setbacks, the May 1880 board meeting of the order was filled with enthusiasm as the hall was well decorated. Before the meeting four people were baptized, and eight people were rebaptized. The population had increased to 177 souls, and a grist mill had been finished in January. The old grist mill at Junction no longer could satisfy their needs so the order undertook to build its own. Besides grinding their member's wheat, the order had earned an additional 150 bushels in just three months from grinding the wheat of outsiders.[390]

In addition to the mill, they had built a home at the mill site, a two-room storehouse for dispensing various forms of merchandise, and an 800 square foot carpenter shop for making furniture. Unfortunately, this apparent success did not last; by the following year, the May 1881 report marks a significant loss of members, now totaling only 114 people.[391] Besides this loss in members, a shift in location began to occur. With the construction of the grist mill, the fourth area or the industrial site, of the Kingston Order was established. Following the completion of the mill, a tannery for leather products was built in October. These new enterprises now started a gradual migration of families from old Kingston to the industrial site.

The last business enterprise in their little industrial center was a woolen factory. It was a second-hand mill purchased in Lagrange, Michigan, from proceeds from the sale of cattle. William, John, and several other members of the order drove a large herd of 450 head of cattle 1,183 miles, by their own calculation, to Pawnee City, Nebraska.[392]

An interesting account of the cattle drive is found in the journal of William King. Rather than ship the cattle by rail, the Kings elected to conduct a traditional cattle drive. William drove the chuck wagon, cooked the meals, and took care of the camp business along the way. John King together with Charles Rowan, and Jesse Tyler took care of the cattle. They left May 28, 1881, after cutting a deal with George Hazel to deliver to Pawnee City, Nebraska 300 head of three-year-old steers at $20 a head, and 200 head of two-year-old steers at $17 a head.[393]

---

389 Volney King, "The Daily Journal of the Kingston United Order," April 30, 1880.

390 Ibid., May 1, 1880.

391 Ibid, April 30, 1881.

392 "William Rice King Journal,"

393 "William Rice Journal," March 23 1881

The south side of the woolen mill or factory as it was called. (Courtesy Utah State Historical Society.)

The trip took them through central Utah to Nephi, then eastward up Salt Creek Canyon, and then north into Wyoming. They took a course across the Mormon trail through central Wyoming and on across Nebraska. William describes in detail how when they would lose a few head of cattle, they would have to go back until they could find them. On one occasion the cattle stampeded, and many times cattle became lame. To help the cattle heal, they would have to pry apart the hoofs with ropes and pour in hot grease. Or they would administer tobacco to a sick horse. For additional food supplies, they would shoot deer and antelope or catch fish. They would also purchase supplies along the way and on one occasion they bought some mellons. William goes on to write that "I never enjoyed so much eating mellons" that they were able to purchase when they reached the Platte River.

At their destination they delivered 439 head of cattle for approximately $8,250 in cash, part of which was paid to other cattle owners who added to the Kingston herd. It appears that most of it was paid to a Mr. Forsha for $1,483,[394] leaving the Kings with about $6,500. William and John also sold their horses and rented a team to go over the river to visit their old home near Hamburg. Later they caught a train to Chicago, where they were able to visit some of the Robison family. In Lagrange they purchased the mill for $2,000, and in Chicago they bought additional equipment needed by

394 Ibid, October 27, 1881.

the order. Transportation home for William and John was by train, arriving October 24, 1881, but it appears the other men rode their horses back to Kingston from Pawnee City.[395]

The mill was set up by the following February and had about 300 spindles, two sets of carding machines, and dyeing

The remains of the raceway bringing the water into the mill from the east side.

vats. From the factory were made cloth for dresses and men's clothes, sheets, blankets, and yarn.

Before the mill was built carding, spinning, and weaving were done by hand. Each home had its hand cards for preparing the wool for spinning and also a spinning wheel. Several women from Denmark, Sweden, and Holland wove rag carpets, plain flannels, and cloth for men's suits.

The reason for the decision to purchase the mill is not clear, but it may have been an attempt to diversify operations away from such a large dependence on agriculture products. With the grist mill, tannery, and woolen factory, a secondary source of income could be generated. The Brethren were also encouraging the construction of woolen mills as a means towards greater industrialization within the territory.[396] However, the woolen mill required a certain degree of skilled labor and a favorable supply of wool the order or surrounding area could not provide, and it functioned for just a few short years.

Another challenge to William's leadership was Sylvester Earl, a rather

---

395 "William Rice King Journal."

396 In a statistical report on the Territory of Utah for the years 1872-3 prepared probably for the territorial government, it identifies segments of the Utah economy that could be improved. It specifically mentions that Utah has an economic advantage in raising sheep, and "Among *Manufacturing* industries, a very important one is that of Woolen Goods, which go hand in hand with that of Wool growing. There is no reason why all the wool produced in the Territory should not be woven into cloth" for the benefit of the local people. (Stevens & Co., "Statistics: Territory of Utah for the Years 1872-23," Salt Lake City, Utah, 1874,14-14. A copy is available in the L. Tom Perry Special Collections, Brigham Young University.) Thus, several woolen factories were established in the territory including Kingston, Beaver, and Orderville.

cantankerous teenager who had a brother and two sisters in the order. In late October 1881, Sylvester in concert with two other men, stole 337 head of sheep belonging to the order. They then sold the stolen property to James Whittaker, a successful farmer and rancher in Circleville. When the loss was discovered by the Kings an investigation was launched and 133 of the missing sheep were believed to have been found in Whittaker's herd. A writ of replevin was obtained directing the sheriff to take possession of the sheep in question, but in the process an explosive confrontation ensued. Volney claims that "a spirit of murder [was] manifest, but the Lord gave us wisdom sufficient not to ignite it."[397]

On the scheduled day of the trial, several men of the order testified before Justice of the Peace James Wiley of Circleville that they could recognize their sheep by their appearance and countenance, which was not a very strong argument; and the decision of the court went against them. Not only did they loose their sheep, but to rub salt in the wounds the judge charged the Kings $65.00 in court costs and $100 to Whittaker for damages.[398]

This event also raises the question whether the Kings were properly marking their sheep for identification. Cattle are usually branded with a hot iron to distinguish ownership, but sheep are branded with paint. In a court of law "appearance and countenance" can not be counted on as strong evidence of ownership.

When William paid the check to Whittaker for damages he called the award an "unjust decision of Justice Wyley." [399] Unfortunately, this was not the first encounter with Wiley and Whitakker. A year earlier when Wiley and Whittaker were employed as arbitrators to help settle a dispute with Joel White when White left the order, Volney wrote that Whittaker and Wylie were "two bitter enemies to the U.O. & apostates of the church."[400] Mr. Wiley, several months later, was also caught deliberately tearing down a section of pasture fence belonging to the order

---

397 Volney King Diaries, 167, November 15, 1881.

398 "William Rice Journal," November 24, 1881

399 Ibid., December 9, 1881.

400 Volney King, "The Daily Journal of the Kingston United Order," September 17, 1880. In fairness to Wylie and Whittaker, Volney's and Williams's remarks appear to have been made in the fog of emotional disappointment and loss. The use of the term "apostate," even today within Mormon circles, is considered the lowest level or form of a person's commitment and character. The case presented by the Kings before Justice Wyley was weak and Whittaker's prominence and economic success has already been noted. It is hard to believe that he was a thief, although there must have been some question in his mind where 300 sheep may have come from. Regardless of these events the Kings and Whittaker will continue to do business together.

and Volney reported that he "takes up against [us] at law & where ever he can."[401]

Sylvester Earl in a book he wrote sixty-three years later, recorded that he had the "pleasure in seeing the Kings brought low with sorrow."

> The sheep were the product of the peoples hard work; the Kings of the Kingdom we[r]e not the owners of the sheep, virtually speaking, and further fact that those who had produced the sheep would never realize so much as one red penny from them, justified the conclusion that the sheep were not owned by anybody; hence, I did not steal them. They were just as much mine as they were the Kings. Consequently, I had harmed no man, and did a favor to another neighbor.[402]

Earl's justification is interesting and involves the historical economic struggle between labor and capital, and how people view ownership. Does ownership come from expended labor or from people willing to risk assets and resources? The socialist would lean in favor of labor while the capitalist would favor invested capital. This perhaps is the basis of the argument and feelings of being cheated when people would leave the order, expecting in settlement more than they received.

Regardless of setbacks the enthusiasm of the Kings to promote the gospel of equality was not confined to their sermons in Kingston. In 1879 during one of his trips back to Fillmore, Volney was invited to speak in a Church meeting in the Statehouse. He talked for 30 minutes on the United Order and how it was necessary to accept the order and live in such a community to be perfected.

His remarks did not go unnoticed, nor were they appreciated. Perhaps they were even considered a little arrogant. President Callister promptly responded to his talk by saying "he was not prepared to live among perfect people. Since men were not constituted alike, they do not see alike. He thought that if the Lord was not satisfied with his lifestyle, he would jostle him into line; otherwise, he would herd him along just as he was going."[403]

After the meeting Volney's temperament also came through as he got

---

401 Volney King, "The Daily Journal of the Kingston United Order," September 13, 1882.

402 Sylvester Earl, *My Life's Philosophy: Religious-Politico and Otherwise,* (n.p.) 27-32, L. Tom Perry Special Collections and Manuscripts, Brigham Young University. In Mr. Earl's writings he identifies the date of this incident as early October 1879, making for two sheep stealing events, but this entry was made over six decades after the incident occurred. There is no evidence of two sheep stealing events. The two other men involved were James Marshall from Panguitch and who had ties to Butch Cassidy, and Earl's brother-in-law, Ormus Nay. Both Nay and Earl went on to further escapades and became train robbers in 1883. My thanks to Ardus Parshall for providing this information.

403 King, *The Two Volneys,* 26. Either the date or the name of the president is in error. President Callister was released in 1877 and replaced by President Ira Hinckley.

Lucy Maranda White, 1860-1938, was the plural wife of William King and the daughter of Joel White. She accompanied William to Hawaii on his third mission.

into an argument with a brother about whether the United Order was a way of life acceptable to all members regardless of Church pronouncements.

Plural marriage, as identified by their sermons, was also a major item of consideration. Culbert, who already had two wives when he entered the order, took a third wife, Sarah Elizabeth Pratt, the daughter of Apostle Parley P. and Sarah Houston Pratt. William King took a second wife, Lucy Maranda White, the daughter of Joel and Frances Ann Thomas White. Both marriages were solemnized December 19, 1878, in the St. George Temple.[404]

Frequent visitors also made their way to Kingston for observation and examination, and this small community soon became known as one of the more successful orders. Included in this entourage were most of the leading brethren, who preached dramatic and moving sermons on a variety of subjects, not the least of which included plural marriage and the importance of living in the United Order. During one July 24th celebration, Apostle Wilford Woodruff spoke on the return of the Savior and prophesied that Christ would return to the earth within 30 years. On November 23, 1881, President John Taylor and Apostles Wilford Woodruff and Franklin Richards visited and attracted the largest group ever assembled in Kingston. On another occasion, Brigham

---

404 Many family records have Culbert and Sarah getting married civilly in November 1878 and later sealed in the St. George Temple on December 19, 1878. No specific date in November has been found. In The "Daily Journal of the Kingston United Order," Volney states that he and Culbert left on October 25, 1878, to go west to "market goods of the United Order." It appears that Culbert did not return until November 20, 1878, when Volney states that Culbert returned with Elizabeth and family from Kanosh. If he went west and then spent some time with Elizabeth, it would mean he must have married Sarah between November 20 and the end of the month. In Volney's above writings there is only an entry for December 5: "Culbert and others go to St. George." Another record without an author identified, gives the date of marriage as September 19, 1878. This may be a correct date, but there has been no way to verify it. (See Stella Day, *Builders of Early Millard,* Daughters of Utah Pioneers, n.p.: Arts City Publishing Company, 1979, 419.) December 19, 1878 is most likely the correct marriage date.

Young, Jr. cautioned the order to stay out of debt. He also said those who participated in the United Order would receive more temporal blessings than those outside the institution.

Non-church visitors who made their way to Kingston included Phil Robinson of London, England. Mr. Robinson traveled to Utah in 1882 and toured and wrote about the Mormon empire. While the tone of his book is from an outsider's point of view and for a non-Mormon audience, he appears to have written a fairly balanced composition. After arriving in Kingston he relates his impressions as follows:

Sarah Elizabeth Pratt, 1856-1891, was the plural wife of Culbert King and daughter of Apostle Parley P. Pratt. (See *Autobiography of Parley P. Pratt*, 345+.)

Among the social experiments of Mormonism, the family communism of Kings of Kingston deserve a special notice, for, though in my opinion it is a failure, both financially and socially, the scheme is probably one of the most curious attempts at solving a great social problem that was ever made.

Kingston is the hamlet of fifteen wooden cottages and a stockyard which has been planted in the center of the most desolate plains in all the Utah Territory - a very Jehunam of a plain. Piute County, in which it is situated, is as a rule, a most forbidding section of country, and the Kingston "Valley" is perhaps the dreariest spot in it. The mountains stern and sterile, ring it in completely, but on the south-east is a great canyon which might be the very mouth of the cavern in which the gods used to keep their winds, for a persistent, malignant wind is perpetually sweeping through it on to the plain below, and the soil being light and sandy, the people live for part of the year in a ceaseless dust-storm. One year [in 1879] they sowed 300 acres with wheat, and the wind simply blew the crop away. That which it could not displace, it kept rubbed down close to the ground by a perpetual passage of sand. They planted an orchard, but some gooseberry bushes are the only remaining vestiges of the plantation and even these happen to be on the side of a solid fence. They also set out trees to shade their homes, but the wind worked the saplings round and round in their holes, so that they could not take root. It can be easily imagined, therefore, that without a tree, without a green thing except the reach of meadow land at the foot of the hills, the Kingston, plain, with its forlorn fifteen tenements looks for most of the year, desolation itself. That anyone would ever have settled there is a mystery to all; that he should have remained, there is a simple absurdity, a very jumbo of a folly. Yet here, after five years of the most dismal experiences, I found some twenty households in occupation.[405]

Mr. Robinson continues his description in stinging terms:

> . . . it is significant of errors in the past that after five years of almost superhuman toil they should find themselves no better off materially than when they started. Nor, socially, has the experiment hitherto been a success, for Kingston is, in my opinion beyond comparison and lowest in the scale of all Mormon settlements that I have seen. It is poverty stricken in appearance; its houses outside and inside testify, in unmended windows and falling plaster, to the absence of that good order which characterizes so many other villages. The furniture of the rooms and the quality of the food on the tables are poorer than elsewhere, and altogether it is only too evident that this family communism has dragged all down alike to the level of the poorest and the laziest of its advocates, rather than raised all up to the level of the best off and the hardest working. The good men have sunk, the others have not risen, and if it were not so pathetic the Kingston phenomenon would be exasperating.

While these comments of Mr. Robinson are colorful, they are also brutally and painfully honest. While anyone associated with the order or their descendants want to look at it in the positive and encouraging aspects of faithfulness and sacrifice, the order also depicts the dark side of human nature. The noble ideal of lifting the economically disadvantaged should never be forgotten within any society, yet an incentive must be given on both sides. As the order was set up, there was no incentive for the rich except the principle of sharing and helping others, as there was everything to lose and nothing to gain. For the poor, there was every incentive to join as they had nothing to lose and everything to gain. Kingston exemplified this pattern in that many people who joined were so poor, they had to have order members go out and bring them to the settlement. They had little or nothing to add and many times their poverty extended to their economic skills and abilities. Without the incentive to pull themselves up, the social and economic level would eventually and naturally gravitate to the lowest common denominator.

In contrast, Mr. Robinson's comments about living conditions, during his subsequent visit to Orderville, were much more complimentary and congenial.

---

405 Robinson, *Sinners and Saints*, 208-9.

Organization and Management

The management of the order followed a familiar structure of a board with elected officers of president, two vice presidents, secretary, and treasurer. Superintendents were then chosen to oversee a specific operation such as the tannery or dairy production. In many of the orders, the president was also the ecclesiastical bishop; but at Kingston,

A general store was built about 50 yards east of the woolen mill. It is the only building still standing after the fire of 1970, which destroyed the factory, mill, and several other buildings. Still stenciled on the walls inside are prices such as: oats 1.20 per CWT, wheat taken 75 cents per Bu., eggs taken 10 cents per doz., and butter taken 20 cents per lb.

Thomas King was elected president and William was appointed bishop. It wasn't until after William was elected president that both offices were filled by the same man, as in other orders.

In 1877 Joel W. White, Sr. and William King were elected first and second vice presidents, Edwin King was elected secretary, and Mortimer W. Warner treasurer. Directors chosen were James Huff, David Savage, and George Black. William and Edwin were also appointed superintendents of the farm. Besides William, the bishopric included Joel White and James Huff as counselors.

The following year in 1878, Culbert was added to the four-member board which then appointed William King superintendent of the farm with Joel W. White, Sr. as his assistant. Culbert was appointed superintendent of stock, his son Culbert Levi as his assistant. Thomas Edwin was appointed superintendent of the lumber trade, and James Huff superintendant of the buildings with David Savage as his assistant. Mortimer W. Warner was appointed superintendent of the sheep herd.

The third year of operation reflects several changes brought on by the death of Thomas. William becomes both president and bishop. John D. Wilcox replaced Mortimer Warner as treasurer, and Mortimer was elected to the board in place of Culbert. Niels Nielsen was added as a fifth member of the board.

The organization of the order continued to follow this same pattern through May 1883, although, as the members began to leave, the King brothers became even more involved. Volney became treasurer in 1881, and John finally joined in the leadership of the order by becoming a director in 1882. By 1882 the Kings were the superintendents of all operations except for the farm, which was held by Horatio Morrill.

Within this organization work assignments were made by the officers based on needs and skills. Primary duties centered around plowing, planting, irrigating, and fencing. They also spent a lot time hauling wood, making trips to the grist mill for flour, hauling lumber, delivering bark to the tannery, and milking cows for their daily supply of milk. In Grass Valley there was herding cattle and sheep, shearing sheep, milking cows, and making butter and cheese. The traditional sty of pigs was maintained, and supplementary products such as molasses and preserves were acquired through barter in communities such as Marysvale. Much of their fruit (apples) was brought in from Fillmore. The primary crops of the order were oats and hay for the animals and wheat, potatoes, turnips with some beans and peas for human consumption. In addition, the shoe and carpenter shops were kept busy and additional men were assigned to help Reuben Syrett and Ned Desaules. The women were kept busy with raising the children and in assisting with the production of food and fiber.

The order also took on somewhat of a militaristic atmosphere. Kahana King would blow through a large seashell from his native land of Hawaii at 6:00 a.m. to wake everyone, then again for meals, and at 9:30 p.m. for evening prayer in the dining hall. Limitations were also placed on people leaving to visit with friends and family.

Frequent irritations were broken wagon wheels, lost cattle and horses, and animals breaking into fields. Once they even found some horses that had been lost for a couple of years, and they numbered their sheep periodically to account for all of them.

In the "Daily Journal of Kingston," Volney gives an example of his day's labor as one of the superintendents. While it is doubtful that this is a typical day, it does shed light on many different items.

> I arose at 5 A.M. & Fed oxen & horses hay. Then took a borken wagon
> tong out of the wagon & fitted another in. Then helped August Peterson milk
> 17 or 18 cows. Then hitched up some steers & hauled swill for the hogs. Then
> fixed a yoke & put it together & yoked up the steers & Horatio Morrill & I went
> after wheat & when we came back from the field I corraled 4 head of stock that
> were among the shocks of grain & then took a yoke of oxen & helped move
> Mary Fuel over to Ephraim Syretts late residence making two trips & when I
> had put the oxen the 2nd horn had blown for dinner after which I helped Bro

Springthorpe to a stove out of the new store house then went to the store & got some things for Sr Savage then returned & lifted Eliza out of bed into her chair. Then went to the yard to send the teams off after grain & found two men missing & I had to find them to supply this place. Then I pitched my load off on a very high stack & topped it out & hitched up the 2 yoke of steers & went for another load of wheat & returned just sundown & then hauled swill again for Bro Davis and when I had put up the team the 2nd horn had blown for supper but the cows were not milked so I milked four of them & took to the hall & got my supper which many there were

Kingston, Utah

From time to time there has existed some confusion as to which community is being referred to when the name Kingston is mentioned. The current town of Kingston is not the Kingston originally built by the order. This is old Kingston, which no longer exists, located about 3.5 miles southwest of the present-day Kingston.

unable to do as they were depending on milk for supper. I then returned to the yard & finished milking 18 cows. Part of them had layed out over night. When I had taken the milk to the house I returned home & washed my face & combed my hair for the first time today. While I was milking a Mutual Improvement Association was called of which I was secretary but I could not attend. After reading some letters to Edwin King I visited Bro White who had come home from thrasing grain & counciled with him about a number of things. I retire at 10 A[P].M. aftr writing in my diary & the U.O. Journal.[406]

Perhaps the most noticeable item in Volney's comments is about his wife Eliza who is very sick and has to be helped out of bed and into a chair, yet no further mention is made of helping her. He takes time to read letters to Edwin and to counsel with Brother White. Perhaps after Volney lifted her out of bed, the older children could take over.

As Kingston and Grass Valley were so closely allied, people frequently went back and forth for a variety of purposes including hauling meat and dairy products. When the central dining hall was discontinued the first part of December 1880, the treasurer assumed the responsibility of giving out weekly rations to each family. In their bookkeeping they kept a record of labor performed at the predetermined fixed rate. This was offset by a record of consumed products and produce. At the end of the year, those with a credit balance consecrated their surplus to the order as additional paid-in capital and those with a debit balance were forgiven their debt.

Management Problems

The Kingston Order survived longer than most United Orders, but

406 Volney King, "The Daily Journal of the Kingston United Order," October 16, 1880.

cracks in group unity begin to appear as the order's limitations and the frailties of people began to surface. The death of Thomas was a contributing factor to its demise. Perhaps the King brothers didn't have the same passion or the leadership skills as their father, although from a historical standpoint, the economic and social life of the order was limited. The first major issue was the family concept of eating in a common dining hall. Several individual families had moved east to Grass Valley to support the cattle and horse operation. With the construction of the grist mill, tannery, and woolen mill, many families moved to the industrial site, while others simply wanted to control their own food preparation and eat in their own homes. With differing tastes, appetites, ways of management, and size and ages of families, food distribution became troublesome. The last meal in the large dining hall was on December 1, 1880.

In a type and shadow of earlier Rice and King generations, many younger people by 1881 were becoming restless and wanted to leave to work for wages outside the order. The values and perspective of the young people began to be much different than their parents, and they were feeling held back, wanting greater opportunity than the order could provide. One story that gives some insight into the problem is told by Ella Christian, then sixteen:

> Once there was an epidemic of colds going around and the women were unable to work in the mills. I went to the Bishop and asked if I could have enough cloth for a dress if I spun and wove it. He said "yes." When I had enough woven for a dress, I took it to the store and had it checked up. Everyone was suppose to share alike, so a record was kept of all supplies that each received. When I handed the cloth over to the clerk for inspection, a woman standing nearby objected, claiming that she needed the cloth more than I did. She began telling how destitute her children were - her tears and lamentations won and she got the cloth. Again, I wove another piece, only to have to give it up to another woman who, also, was skillful in making pleas. The third time I wove my dress pattern, I took it home and notified the clerk that I had the cloth. I have my photograph with that dress on, and I'm proud of it.[407]

Another major crack was the privatization of the dairy herd. In May 1882, it was decided to divide up the milk cows and give one to each family for their own purpose and responsibility.

All of these problems, however, appeared after the death of Father King, which set the stage for disagreement and division. Unfortunately he died only two years after the order had been set up, and his death led to rivalry and discontent over succession. Some wanted William King,

---

407 Kate B. Carter, *Treasures of Pioneer History* (Salt Lake City, Utah: Daughters of Utah Pioneers, 4:171.

and others wanted Joel White. Joel was William's father-in-law by his plural wife Lucy, and was three years his senior. He was one of the founding members of the order, a shoemaker from Salt Lake, and was elected first vice president. Perhaps he thought he outranked William who was second vice president, but who had received the endorsement of his father before his passing and had the support of his brothers. William won out, and much jealousy and displeasure followed. The Kings were considered a forceful and strong-willed people, and by some were referred to as the "Kings of the Kingdom."[408] Joel stayed with the order for two more years before withdrawing. No settlement is recorded.

Another dissident was Teancum Pratt, brother to Sarah Pratt King, wife of Culbert King. Teancum records in his journal after the death of Father King:

> During this time, I felt quite quiet and undisturbed I think thinking about how I would be perfectly satisfied when the voice of the people would be given on Election day and abide by majority choice. But when the Bishop and the Board of Directors took the case by the forelock and had the Presidential office filled by a man whom I have no confidence and that without the proper consulting the people's will. It was the last straw upon the camels load and I am already making arrangements to leave the company willing to let time decide whether my coarse is right or is that of something otherwise.[409]

There may be some reason to believe that the feeling was not widespread as Teancum admits that "I am the only one so far that has proceeded to the extent of leaving the company for that reason."[410]

---

408 Irene Elder, "The Kingston Story," *Richfield Reaper*, July 7, 1877.

409 This entry is dated January 23, 1879. Teancum pursues his feelings further in another entry dated March 11, 1879, "On account of my dissatisfaction and the proceedings of the Kingston Company I am now free from it. The cause for this step I will briefly note down. The form of government in the companies that are formed in various places in the Church at the present time that is those companies that are called the United Order is Republican and the peoples voices are given generally once a year to elect the officers. By this means, any cause of dissatisfaction in an officer is subjected to the public voice. This and many other of the actions and customs that form the essential elements of Republicanism are dear to every freedom loving heart. The Kingston company are gradually becoming dirt and are losing the elements of freedom owing to the power so zealously sought after and so ridgedly held or retained by William King, a man of small parts who assumes to much of authority and control of man's agency being supported by his brethren of his father's house because he is the oldest and the favorite of his parents. The principle of charity was carried to such an extent after the death of Father King that it nearly made a great disruption, but I am the only one so far that has proceeded to the extent of leaving the company for that reason." ("Teancum Pratt Diary 1851-1900," LDS Church Historical Department Archives.)

410 "Teancum Pratt Diary 1851-1900," March 11, 1879.

Whether directed toward the Kings or not, there was considerable dissatisfaction within the community. On another occasion, Volney King records that a special meeting was held to help iron out difficulties between Brother Huff and Brother Pratt. After some discussion, adjustments were made.[411]

Shortly after the organization of the Relief Society, the warm and congenial feelings of the sisters began to break apart as early as July 1878. Matilda begged:

> Oh my sisters I beseech of you to lay aside all bickering and fault finding and I beseech of you to be faithful, be true to each other and try to build each other up and be kind and if we see any thing [w]rong in a sister go to her in love and kindness and talk to her and show her the folly of her ways and all will be right.[412]

Later in November Matilda again rose to express her feelings.

> She thought there was not as much peace and union of late as she would like to see. There was much talking and backbiting. She had had her feelings hurt. There was a great deal said about her and she felt very bad. She had come here to walk in the ways of the Lord and she had tried very hard to do this.[413]

It appears that many of these ill feelings were smoothed over for the time being.

By the 1880s the sisters continued to meet, but there were no longer comments about how glad they were to be in the order. Soon the meetings became more sporadic with attendance falling to single digits. One sister, Betsey Franks, commented that "she had been to orderville she thought things were better there than here but she did not feel to leave here to go there for they said we should have to go through the trials before we can enjoy the blessings. Everyone [at Orderville] seemed to [be] filled with love and joy."[414] Earlier, Susan Black resigned as Relief Society president due to ill feelings.

As the cracks deepened, the membership of the order began to drop precipitously, from a high of 177 members in May 1880, to 114 by May 1881. No census numbers are recorded after that date; but by the time the order officially broke up, the count must have easily dropped well below seventy-five to eighty people. With this decline, homes were becoming vacant, and there soon became a lack of people to work the mill. There is

411 Volney King, "The Daily Journal of the Kingston United Order.," July 4, 1878.

412 "Kingston Relief Society Minute book 1878-1898." July 4, 1878.

413 Ibid., November 7, 1878, 42.

414 Ibid., June 11, 1880, 75.

even evidence that people were leaving the order and then coming back the next day and working as employees. Economically they could command a higher wage as employees than the order could pay its members.

As more and more people were leaving the order homes and buildings were soon being dismantled and moved from Old Kingston to the industrial site, where more and more people were working. Symbolizing these problem to some extent, the Church in a state conference in Panguitch in March 1881 called nine Kingston families to help settle St. John's, Arizona. It is curious to know the circumstances of this call from the Church.[415] These families had already given notice they were leaving the Kingston Order, and they now were being asked to move to a new community. It may have the been the Church's way of trying of alleviate a difficult situation. The Church was creating settlements in Arizona and the call would enhance both areas. St. Johns would be getting needed settlers and it would possibly help defuse some of the tension in Kingston.

Many of these people problems, however, could be summarized in the comments of one family member. William Henry King, the seventeen year-old son of William and later a U.S. Senator, withdrew from the order July 31, 1879. Seeing the operation as a young man, he took a strong dislike to the system. On several occasions, he commented to his family that the underlying reason for the disintegration of the order was the lack of personal responsibility. In a communal society, a collective responsibility becomes no one's responsibility, and disagreements arose because of people's failure to accept accountability. Whenever there was a tough job to be done, such as going out in bad weather to rescue some strays, everyone would leave it to someone else, and the job would never get done.[416]

This is confirmed as early as March 3, 1881, in a private conversation between Apostles John Henry Smith and Francis M. Lyman with William King. While conducting a conference in Kingston, the apostles commented that "the Order would not last at least but a short time — that all of the united orders that now existed their desolation was only a matter of time." They went on to further say that anything that "aimed a blow at the individuality of man could not stand." William concurred by expressing his own feeling that "man should not lay aside his individuality but come to the front and exercise his right and privilege to govern & control."[417]

---

415 Ardis Parshall, an independent historian, believes there is evidence that the call for these people to go to Arizona was at the King's request.

416 Conversation between the author and David S. King, son of William Henry King, August 25, 1995. The experiences that William had in the order helped shape his conservative political attitude.

417 *William Rice King Journal,* March 3, 1881.

It was a trying time for all. At one time members had called it the happiest time of their lives, but now disappointment and bitter feelings prevailed. By agreement a withdrawing member could receive back what he had put into the order, but there was little money to compensate those leaving. Yet sometimes people received property of even greater value. In February 1881, Joseph Chambers received a yoke of young matched oxen and a steer in return for a harness and some wheat he had originally given to the order. Others were upset over small matters such as, upon leaving, that they didn't receive a ration of butter or dried apples. Settlements also included wagons, cattle and horses. John Springthorpe settled for a mare worth $60; and Joseph Nay agreed to take three unbroken horses, an old harness, a cow, and yearling. Others received much less, like Joel White, Jr. who took two pigs as his settlement. Many others simply withdrew and some, in the words of Volney, were "dropped for uninterestedness, grumbling and fault finding."[418]

The amount of these settlements also reflects a more deep-seated problem; most other issues were only symptomatic. When the order was established, initial capital was $20,000; and within a year it had increased to over $27,000, mostly from the Kings. It peaked in 1879 at $27,741, and then dropped to $24,144 in 1880 with 177 members. In comparison the order in Orderville, Utah started with $21,550 and 150 members, and in five years grew to 700 members[419] with a capitalization of $70,000.[420] After five years of operation, the Orderville per person capital contribution was $100 with no large donors to skew the numbers. In Kingston after three years it was $136, but if the initial contribution of the Kings are discounted, this figure drops dramatically. While there may be other factors to consider, it appears that a higher percentage of the people coming into Kingston had little or nothing to contribute in terms of assets and once in the order consumed more than they produced.

Under this heavy burden, tempers began to flare. When David Savage (Edwin's father-in-law) tried to withdraw, a settlement could not be reached. An arbitrator was selected to try and resolve the dispute. When the decision went against Savage, he became abusive and slanderous against William.[421] On another occasion a Ward Teachers trial was held to settle a dispute between two members.[422] And, again, when some stray

---

418 Volney King Diaries, February 15, 1881.

419 Leonard J. Arrington, *Great Basin Kingdom*, 334.

420 Leonard J. Arrington, *Orderville, Utah: A pioneer Mormon Experiment in Economic Organization,* Utah State Agricultural College, no. 2, March 1954, 2:15.

421 *William Rice King Journal,* October 23, 1880.

422 Ibid. The Church has bishop's courts and high council courts. A Ward Teachers

stock belonging to Marvin Dalton was found in the grain field and held for damages, Dalton became angry, called Volney a liar, and swore at him. Dalton tried to hit Volney, and the fight was on. Dalton was subdued and beaten.[423]

In 1882 Ned Desaules, a meticulous writer who seemed to complain constantly to Bishop King about one thing or another, records in his journal:

> I had a quarrel with Volney King, he refusing to let me have stamps. I went to Bishop King who had him pay me. I am satisfied that Volney is an [line crossed out]. Unless he mends his way he shall never be loved. Most dislike him. Few if any like him. This week was spent mostly home idling away the time. I am discouraged because I do not feel fairly treated and I want to have a house of my own at the mills, but they do not seem willing to let me have it. I do not know whether I shall stay or not. I would rather go away to another place where there could be more people and a warmer climate where I could at least have a garden of my own and raise fruits of all kinds that could be raised even a watermelon to ripen. Besides I don't like to always be treated with disrespect. I have lived here so long that I am like the man the Savior spoke of who could not be a prophet in his own country. Besides the United Order is all degenerated into a company of very few members who have little love and affection for one another. It is true I have been guilty of ingrading a good deal of selfishness in and for myself. But I had that — I feel so lonesome with so few pleasures and seemly no friends at least none that could comprehend — with me in my lonesome feelings. It doesn't matter, I must be patient and wait a little longer.[424]

Another entry refers to a misunderstanding over tearing down and moving a house lived in by John Davis. Without finding out the reasons why until later, Desaules records: "A wrong was committed today by Bishop William King and his brother Edwin. . . . Shame on them! May the Lord of Heaven give them as they have done. Amen."[425]

The social struggle of people getting along is not only illustrated by these comments, but in comparing them to the comments recorded by Desaules in Richfield before he joined the Kingston Order.

> Last Wednesday, three of the brethren from our company and I made a trip to see the country fifty miles south of here along the valley of la haute Sevier (in English, Upper Sevier), also called Pi-Ute Valley. We found a pretty little place that greatly pleased us, and there was a small company of families who have joined together for their spiritual and temporal well-being. We were pleased

court must have been a more informal way of trying to settle disputes.

423 Ibid., 39-40.

424 "Desaules diary 1833-1904," April 18, 1882, to December 31, 1882, LDS Church Historical Department Archives.

425 Ibid.

with them, and we have decided to join them. I expect to go there in eight or ten days at the most. I feel that it is the will of the Lord that I go there, where we can find the true principles of the United Order. The Order in Richfield wasn't perfect and therefore fell. Our United Order family wasn't perfect, so we will separate to join other people more to our taste.[426]

The remaining people continued to struggle until, under advice of Apostle Francis M. Lyman in 1883, the decision was made to abandon the Order.[427] The Church leaders realized the hard reality that the outside world was coming in upon them, and they could no long operate in a vacuum. The United Order program for the last time was to be phased out throughout the territory. Of the scores set up during the 1870s, most did not last more than a year, with only a few lasting into the 1880s. Kingston was one of the last surviving orders.

Not only were times changing in the social and economic climate of the territory; but also with the death of Brigham Young in August 1877, John Taylor took over the leadership of the Church. It was common knowledge that President Taylor and other Church leaders did not always agree in many respects with Brigham Young's economic program.[428] President Taylor was more of an advocate of individual freedom and did not approve of the "big family" concept. On one occasion he went to the heart of the matter when he said, "The greatest embarrassment that we have to contend with at the present time is not in knowing what to do, but knowing how to do it."[429]

Final Resolution

As the order broke up, many people moved back across the river, homesteading and building a new community which now bears the name of Kingston. Other people moved to or stayed in Antimony or simply moved away. In 1970 a brush fire raged out of control and burned all of the remaining buildings and homes at the industrial site except for a small general store.

While many positive things were accomplished during the operation of the order, to shut one down was a major task resulting in compromised feelings and emotions. Dividing up the assets fairly was next to impossible. Generally the ones who put the most in were the ones who lost the most.

---

426 Ibid, September 30, 1877.

427 Irene Elder, "The Kingston Story," *Cove Creek Gazette,* Vol, #1, Spring 1975

428 Arrington, Fox, and May, *Building The City Of God,* 311.

429 Ibid.

The minutes of the order were no longer maintained after May 22, 1883; however, as it took time to create the order, it took time to unravel and settle all accounts. During early May 1883 the brothers moved the management of the assets of the order to a cooperative system, and Volney set the stage with some determination by stating that "if there was any dividing it was to be divided equal among the heads of family." However, it wasn't until February of the following year that the brothers and their mother were able to make a final accounting of their capital stock. For two days, February 25 and 26, William, Edwin, Culbert, and Volney met at Culbert's Antimony home to determine the value of their capital stock and came up with $26,136.63[430] to be divided as follows:

John	$ 6,165.37	23.33 %
Edwin	5,163.78	19.83
William	4,794.91	18.41
Culbert	4,313.26	16.56
Volney	3,062.97	11.75
Matilda	2,636.34	10.17
	$26,136.63	100.00 %

Noticeably absent from the meeting was John, and it appears that a breaking point had now been reached. For months thereafter Volney does not mention John in his diary. The following June, he curtly recorded, "We went to John's to try and get some horses, but didn't get any." The following day, "I was up to Johns this p.m." with no explanation for the visit as was usual in his previous record. In November, after Volney claimed some horses, Culbert and his son, Thomas, were "incensed" as there was still an indebtedness to John and Matilda.

In spite of these figures, it is difficult to give a complete and accurate accounting. The account books recording individual consecrations to the order have not been found, but there are three known reports of assets from journal entries. Volney's last financial record on May 1, 1880, lists the capital stock of the order at $24,144.88.[431] Ned Desaules reported in July 1879 that the order had 1,000 head of cattle, 1,000 sheep, 400 horses, and an $800 gristmill.[432] With the addition of the land and grist mill, it would put the value of the assets over $40,000. Phil Robinson in his earlier assessment in 1882 concurs with the $40,000 figure and lists cattle

---

430 Quoted in King, *The Two Volneys,* 51-2. Taken from Volney King Diaries, February 26, 1884.

431 Volney King, "The Daily Journal of the Kingston United Order," May 1, 1880.

432 "Desaules diary 1833-1904," July 20, 1879.

and sheep at $10,000, horses at $12,000, the woolen factory, grist mill and land.[433]

To get to the above settlement figure for the Kings is a bit of a stretch. These figures would not account for any indebtedness against the assets as evidenced by Desaules who reported that the King "brothers sold all their sheep for cash to pay all their debts." At most this would have amounted to only about $2,500 to $3,000. Later William gave Volney $1,500 "to pay indebtedness in Grass Valley" which may or may not have been part of the above proceeds.

Another critical variable in Volney's accounting system appears to be how an inventory of property and livestock was maintained. There was no provision for any value that might be added to assets, such as growth or loss in the cattle, sheep, and horse herds. It appears that the only adjustments made at the end of each year were for individual consumption rubbed against production, and for people coming or leaving the order. In addition, it may have been that the people holding on to the end of the order's life cycle were those who had made a more significant investment generating a material payout in the end. The people who bailed out early may have been those who had contributed little to the order.

The cattle herds remained together until the following October, when the sheep were sold at a depressed price of $2.25 a head, together with some cattle. The horses and cows were then divided. In the final distribution, it is not known for sure which King brother got what; but from all indications, besides a share of the cattle and horses, John and Culbert received their ranches and homes at Grass Valley.[434] Volney received his home and forty acres at Wilmont, Edwin possibly the tannery and sawmill and some Kingston property, William the woolen factory and Kingston property, and Matilda a home in Kingston, although there is some evidence that she lived with Edwin until her death. The grist mill was sold to James Whittaker.[435]

However, after all is said and done, based on the diary entries of Volney identifying the livestock he and his mother received, plus the Garfield County tax assessors reports for 1885 and 1886, it is evident that the true extent of assets the Kings received was substantially less than the reported $26,000; it could have been less than half. For example, John reports only twenty horses and fifteen head of cattle for the 1884 tax assessment with total value of assets of only $1,140 compared to his share in

---

433 Robinson, *Sinners and Saints,* 212.

434 See Appendix 9 for a map of Antimony and its early settlers.

435 While Irene Elder gives much of this information, I have tried to reconstruct the disposition of the property from bits and pieces from many sources and references.

the settlement of $6,165.37. Even after few years of rebuilding their herds, the brothers never got back to the settlement numbers.[436]

While disagreements were eventually overcome and families again associated together, the emotional effect of the order's activities on John was immeasurable, and he carried the scars of disappointment and feelings of betrayal to his grave. He was the major supplier of assets to the order, and he felt he had received but a small part in return.

No doubt the King family sacrificed extensively through the whole ordeal; and after seven years, they came out of the order with much less than when they had joined. Furthermore the value and usability of many of the assets could be in question. While the idea and concept of having all things in common may have been based on a correct theory, the implementation of those assumptions in the real world needed some refinement and a better understanding of economic principles and human nature.

---

436 See Volney King Diaries, 250-1, October 21 to 31, 1884, and the Garfield County Tax Assessors Rolls 1884-89, Panguitch, Utah. While the tax rolls appear to be hard evidence and it's what I have used to draw my conclusions. I also wonder about the validity of these numbers. While the economic loss to the Kings was substantial and recorded in family lore, there is a serious gap between the records of Volney and the county and I wonder if all the livestock was counted by the county. During the summer months the Kings took most of their livestock for grazing to the "King ranch" several miles in the mountains southeast of Antimony. If the assessor didn't take the time to locate these animals that were scattered for miles over the mountains, they would never be included in the assessment.

Second Kings

(The Next Generation Continued)

After the break up of the order, Matilda stayed in Kingston for a period of time and then later moved to Antimony. She survived for another ten years, passing away on February 19, 1894. Rather than Matilda being buried in Kingston with Thomas, Thomas's body was exhumed and moved to Antimony where both he and Matilda were buried on February 21, 1894.

Chronological Events

Sep 23,	1883	Culbert appointed Bishop of the Marion Ward in Antimony.
Mar	1884	Edwin leaves for a mission to Michigan, Indiana, and Illinois.
Dec	1885	Edwin returns from his mission.
Oct 18,	1886	William called on a third mission to Hawaii.
May 7,	1887	William appointed mission president in Hawaii.
Spring	1890	William returned from Hawaii.
Nov 1,	1890	William named president of the Iosepa (Polynesian) settlement in Tooele County.
Nov 23,	1891	Sarah passes away.
Feb 17,	1892	William died at the age of fifty-seven from causes incident to the gun shot wound of 1868.
May 8,	1893	Daniel passes away.
Feb 19,	1894	Matilda dies at the age of eighty-two.
Jun 11,	1898	Eliza Esther passes away.
Jul 24,	1899	John dies at the age of sixty-one.
Aug 20,	1900	Culbert released as bishop.
Pb	1900	Culbert sustained as patriarch of the Panguitch Stake.
Dec 26,	1901	Elizabeth passes away.
Sep 20,	1904	Helen passes away.
Jan 5,	1907	Delilah dies at the age of sixty-five.
Jun 3,	1908	Culbert marries Lydia Ann Webb
Oct 26,	1909	Culbert dies at the age of seventy-three.
Oct 9,	1912	Lydia Ann passes away.
Jan 19,	1923	Edwin dies at the age of eighty-three.
Jan 30,	1925	Volney dies at the age of seventy-seven.
Jan 2,	1927	Isabella passes away.
Jan 18,	1938	Eliza passes away.
Oct 23,	1938	Lucy is hit by a car and killed.
Apr 15,	1943	Mary Ann passes away.

William Rice King

When the order broke up, William stayed in Kingston and took possession of the woolen mill. He continued to serve as bishop of the Kingston Ward for another three years until he was called for the third time to the Sandwich Islands. It is interesting to note that, even though William was called on a mission, he was not released as bishop. Rufus Allen, his counselor, served as the presiding officer until March 29, 1887, when he was formally sustained as bishop.

William King (left) and Apostle Joseph F. Smith (right) who appointed William president of the Hawaiian Mission April 1887. (*The Henrys and the Kings.*)

William was set apart for his mission October 18, 1886, and the following spring on May 7, 1887, he was appointed mission president.[437] This time he took Lucy, his plural wife, with him; however, she was not able to leave at the same time as William, and she didn't arrive in Honolulu until June 10, 1887. She was also set apart as a missionary and served as president of the Relief Society.[438]

During William's tenure, the mission continued to be a serious challenge. Church membership continued to drift downward, although the missionary force increased a small amount. From available figures, in 1879, there were 4,408 members with only eleven missionaries. By 1890 the membership had shrunk by 289 members to 4,119 and the number of missionaries had increased slightly to seventeen.[439]

William served until November 1889, returning home in the spring of 1890. When he and Lucy returned, they brought with them some thirty Polynesians, to live in Utah. The Church had established in 1889 a Polynesian colony in Skull Valley, Tooele County. It was named Iosepa, "Jo-

---

437 "Historical records and minutes of the Sandwich Islands Mission."

438 Ibid.

439 Britsch, *Moramona, The Mormons in Hawaii*, p. 88. A few figures on membership and missionaries are available, but it appears the missionary force reached a peak of ninety-nine in 1877 and dropped to only eleven in 1879.

Hawaiian missionaries at a conference in Laie, Oahu, 1887. President King is the fourth man from the right. To his right is his wife Lucy. (Courtesy LDS Church Historical Department.)

seph" in Hawaiian, in honor of President Joseph F. Smith, who befriended the Polynesian people.

Iosepa served as a gathering place for the Polynesians, and at its height 228 people occupied the colony. The project continued for twenty-eight years before coming to an end. Eventually all but one family returned to the islands.[440]

On November 1, 1890, William was asked by the Church to take over the leadership of Iosepa and carry on his service to the Polynesian people. During his fifteen-month term, he was instrumental in helping the people acquire some additional land and inaugurated the first project of buying and fattening cattle.

Unfortunately William died prematurely while in office on February 17, 1892, just short of his fifty-eighth birthday. The cause of death was related to the wound he had received in his leg twenty-three years earlier. His leg had never entirely healed, requiring that the bone be scraped from time to time. He was operated on for the last time just before his death, and he died from the effects of the morphine. His burial was in Fillmore next to his first wife, Josephine.

One daughter, Lillian King Hinckley, wrote of her father:

> Father was an energetic, indefatigable worker, never resting or taking rest
> or giving his body any degree of relaxation, being so conscientious to duty. . . .

---

440 Atkin, *A History of Iosepa, The Utah Polynesian Colony,* 87.

Church plantation and sugar mill at Laie, Oahu in 1887. President King is the man on the horse at the right. (Courtesy LDS Church Historical Department.)

[He] was a man of courage, faith, and endurance. He was self sacrificing to a fault, with never a harsh word or criticism uttered. He gave his life and all that he had to his Church with never a regret, saying always, "The Lord will take care of my family."

He was a good speaker, familiar with his Bible and the Gospel teachings. . . . He was six feet in height and his average weight was one hundred ninety-five pounds. He had brown hair and blue eyes. He was good-looking, quiet, likeable, and very strong physically. He was a good foot-racer in his youth.[441]

After William's passing, Mary Ann lived another fifty-one years. She died April 15, 1943, a month short of her eighty-ninth birthday. After moving to Kingston, she and William had had five more children, for a total of seven. With the four born from Josephine, William had eleven children, plus the two adopted children he brought from Hawaii.

Lucy married Nephi Wood in 1895 and moved to Brigham City. She was widowed a second time when Nephi died in 1924.[442] No children are reported in her obituary from either marriage, except a stepson belonging to Nephi from his first marriage. She was killed when hit by a car on her way to church October 23, 1938.[443]

441 Lillian King Hinckley, "William King.+"

442 Salt Lake City, Utah *Deseret News* obituary, April 24, 1924.

443 Ogden, Utah *Standard Examiner* obituary, October 24, 1938.

Culbert King

After the dissolution of the order, Culbert simply stayed in Coyote where Elizabeth was already living. Esther who had been living in Kingston also moved to Coyote, but it appears Sarah and her family stayed in Kingston. In 1873 when Brigham Young had called for the exploration of Grass Valley, one of the explorers recorded: "We were just going to camp for the night, when we saw an old coyote with three young ones. We gave chase and caught the little ones, cut their ears and tails off short, tied a paper collar around one's neck and turned them loose"[444] — hence the name given to the settlement when two of the explorers returned to colonize the area. This name remained until June 1921, when the community officially became known as Antimony. At present, Coyote is practically a forgotten name, except for a few old-timers who say with pride they were born or raised in "Coyote."

The name Antimony came from the discovery of a tin-white substance, crystalline in appearance, called stibnite or antimony. The metal has few uses by itself, but as an alloy it can be used for hardening other metals such as lead. It can also be used as a compound in some medicines and explosives. The discovery of antimony in Coyote Canyon about eight miles southeast of the present town was first made in the early 1880s. [445]

In Antimony Culbert continued his ranching and farming operation, breeding cattle, managing a small dairy herd,[446] and maintaining an excellent herd of horses.[447] From the dairy, his family made butter and cheese, selling their products each year in Richfield.

In September 1883, as the order was coming to an end, the Wilmont Branch in Coyote was reorganized into the Marion Ward.[448] Culbert was named the first bishop, and served for seventeen years until August 20, 1900.[449] Upon his release, he was ordained a patriarch for the Panguitch Stake,[450] a position he held until his death on October 26, 1909, at age

---

444 Warner, *Grass Valley*, p. 3.

445 Ibid., p. 20

446 Mina King W. Oldham and Mary King Stenquist, "History of Volney Henry King," 352.

447 See Stella Day, *Builders of Early Millard*, 419.

448 The ward was named after Francis Marion Lyman, the visiting apostle (See Warner, *Grass Valley,* 21).

449 Andrew Jenson, *Supplement to Church Chronology,* 5. It is interesting to note that Culbert Levi King succeeded his father as bishop.

450 Salt Lake City, Utah *Deseret News* obituary, November 16, 1909, 7.

Culbert King and his family in the middle 1880s. Front row: Julia, Culbert, Alonzo, Esther, and Volney. Back row: William, Clarinda, Culbert Levi, Matilda, and Delilah.

seventy-three. As a tribute to his long service, his chair remained on the stand in the Antimony Ward meetinghouse for many years.[451]

One point of interesting trivia not commonly known is that at this time bishops, stake presidents, and patriarchs received compensation for their service. Bishops received eight percent of the collected tithing from their ward members while stake presidents got two percent of the tithing in their stake.[452] Stake patriarchs could charge recipients one dollar per blessing.[453] This would not amount to a lot of money for Culbert in the small town of Antimony and with only about 15 to 17 percent of the Church paying some tithing,[454] it would supplement his income to some degree. For example in 1886 there were forty-seven tithe payers who paid $1,142.14 and Culbert received $114.21, or 10 percent; but in the two previous years he received only $56.90 and $29.81 or about 4.6 percent of the amount collected. Evidently everything was not accounted for on a year to year basis as it is today. This doesn't sound like a lot of money, but a hundred dollars then would be worth about $2,000 in 2006 dollars. His responsibilities would be more than just collecting the money and sending it on to stake. At this time each ward had a tithing house and most tithing was paid in livestock and produce. These establishments, in the smaller

---

451 Warner, *Grass Valley*, 109.

452 D. Michael Quinn, "LDS Church Finances from the 1830's to the 1990's," *Sunstone,* no. 2, June 1996, 19:21.

453 Ibid.

454 Ibid., 20.

towns, became the local mercantile store that would buy, sell, and trade commodities with the local citizens. Before being remitting to Church headquarters, livestock would also have to be housed and cared for in adjoining corrals and barns. All of these duties would be taken care of by the bishop.

The records are interesting as they reflect the many items in which people would pay their tithing in butter, eggs, meat, vegetables, and grains; from time to time people would also perform labor. Because many of the items in kind were perishable, the records give an accounting of shrinkage and remittance to the stake headquarters in Panguitch was made periodically.

Evidently bishops were not required to pay tithing on their tithing earnings as Culbert only paid $23.15 and Esther $12.20 in 1884, and in 1885 Culbert paid the same amount as paid to him from tithing. As a comparison, John paid $59.75 in 1884 and $30.56 in 1886; Volney paid $72.92 in 1884, $52.02 in 1885, and $63.16 in 1886.[455] In Kingston, Bishop William King received $152.97 from tithing in 1882, $69.31 in 1885, and $117.53 in 1886.[456]

Culbert was a large man, and his hair and beard became snowy white with age. He had a pleasant personality and loved everyone he met. He was a great storyteller, and one of his favorites was how two young men chose a wife. The first watched to see if the young lady scraped the dough pan clean and didn't waste any flour. Another liked three sisters very much but didn't know which one to choose as his wife. He placed a broom flat on the floor in front of the door. The first and second girls just stepped over it, but the third girl bent, picked it up, and stood it in its place. This was the girl who became his bride.[457]

After moving to Coyote and while Culbert was serving as bishop, Esther served for twelve years as the first Relief Society president. It must have been a very busy household with both a bishop and Relief Society president in the same home. Besides service to her family and community, Esther, at the age of fifty-four, also raised the three youngest children of Sarah, who died prematurely at age thirty-five in November, 1891. The children were Orson age twelve, LaRene age eight, and Heber age five months.

---

455 All of the above information on tithing is taken from the Antimony Tithing Records, Garfield Stake 1883-1925, LDS Church Historical Department Archives.

456 Kingston Ward, Panguitch Stake 1879-1940 records, LDS Church Historical Department Archives.

457 Angie Ross Buchanan, "A Life Sketch of Culbert King - My Grandfather." A copy is in my possession.

Antimony Primary Association in the 1890s. Bishop Culbert King and his wife Elizabeth are standing at the left. (Courtesy Robert Hahne, Orem, Utah.)

During this time Esther made two additional trips to California to visit her sister Julia. The first of these two trips was in December of 1882 with her daughters, seventeen-year-old Delilah and fifteen-year-old Julia Frances, and her son, thirteen-year-old Volney. They also took along a big black dog, Gus, as a watch dog. He really proved his worth when they encountered some hostile Indians and troublesome white men along the way. When they were camped in Washington County in southern Utah, they were joined by Charlie Rowan and William Black, who rode their horses alongside the wagon. Many hardships were experienced crossing the desert, especially beyond Las Vegas. Water had to be hauled in barrels strapped on the sides of the wagon, and from time to time it was so full of alkali it had to be treated with vinegar to kill the taste before any attempt could be made to drink it. The trip must have also fostered a romantic relationship with Delilah and Charlie, as they were married two years later.

It took twenty-one days to make the trip. They had planned to arrive in time for Christmas, but their horses became so weak they didn't arrive until a few days after. It was truly a joyful reunion as the sisters, Esther and Julia, hadn't seen each other for twenty-three years. They stayed until the following May and went to parties, dances, church, and sight-seeing trips. They also enjoyed the California climate where tomatoes, grapes, oranges, and lemons grew freely, and everything was so green against the snow-capped mountains. They arrived back home in Kingston just in time to help make the move from Kingston to Coyote.[458]

Esther's second trip was in 1897. She had become quite ill, and her

---

458 Melba Utahna Riddle Gottfredson, her granddaughter, "History of Delilah King Rowen," *McCullough Family History Book,* 335-336.

family decided she should go to California to see if a better climate would be of any help. The records do not indicate how she traveled; but perhaps this time because of illness, she was able to take the train. She soon became restless, however, and decided to return home, where she died six months later on June 11, 1898.[459]

Culbert and his remaining wife, Elizabeth, continued to live together until her death three years later. Culbert was now alone except for a couple of teenage children. Six and a half years later and a year before his death, he married a fourth wife, Lydia Ann Webb, a sister to Helen Maria, the wife of John Robison. Lydia had been married twice before and had lived a rather difficult life. She had given birth to ten children, and eight of them had died early, a couple of them quite tragically. She was living in Antimony, and her marriage to Culbert was in the Manti Temple. She died three years after Culbert in 1912.

A touching letter from Culbert to his brother Volney just before Culbert died gives an account of his physical suffering from dropsy and his nostalgic feelings for the past. The letter is dated July 12, 1909, and while dictated by Culbert, it was written by Culbert's daughter LaRene. It was prompted by some questions from Volney, who was living in Cowley, Wyoming, asking for Culbert's recollection of the history of Fillmore.

> Your letter of June 2 was received and read with mingled emotion of joy and pain — joy at the remembrances of by gone days and pain to think that we cannot renew the pleasant associations of the past, except by writing to each other and recalling the past.
>
> As you say, I would certainly enjoy a visit with you but my health is very bad at present, the main disease that is bothering me now is the dropsy, am unable to sleep nights on account of shortness of breath and feel very poorly at the best, but am trying to make the best of things accept whatever comes with as much patience as I can.[460]

Dropsy, or edema, occurs when the heart muscle weakens due to factors such as prolonged high blood pressure or hardening of the coronary arteries which supply the blood to the heart muscle. The lungs not being properly supplied with blood results in a shortness of breath and an accumulation of fluid in the body.

Culbert died just three months later.

---

459 Alice King Gulbransen, a daughter, "History of Alonzo King," A short biographical sketch, *McCullough Family History Book,* 409-410.

460 Culbert King to Volney King, July 12, 1909, Volney King papers, Utah State Historical Society.

John Robison King

John and his family continued to live in Coyote after the order break-up. His first home was a log cabin with a dirt roof and floor, and the floor was kept sprinkled with water and swept until it was packed hard. To the delight of the kids, there was a sturdy post in the center of the room to help support the roof; and the children ran around it and swung on it until it was worn smooth. There were two bunks built in one end, and the cooking and eating were done at the other end. As a daily experience, this would be a laborious challenges by modern-day standards for a family of eight children, especially in the winter months. Later John purchased a ranch with a better home from a Mr. Forrest, before building a two-story log home with a separate kitchen.

After the order broke up, many people reported that John was never the same. The disappointment and bitterness of being strongly encouraged to join the order and then to have it fail was troubling and discouraging. It was also hard for him to accept the communal lifestyle, and one story illustrates the basis of these bitter feelings. When John and his wife were taking care of the cattle in Grass Valley, they sent their children, Frank, Lydia, Roy, and Irene to Kingston to go to school. They were supposed to be accepted and cared for as members of a family. After a period of time, Jack Tyler, who was like an older brother to the children, went to Kingston with a load of wheat for the grist mill. Anxious to see the children, he went at once to find them but became incensed at what he found. They had been put into a little one-room cabin to shift for themselves, and were hungry and neglected. He immediately bundled them up and took them back home to their shocked and angry parents.[461]

John left the order believing he had been stripped of much of his property and that the lion's share had gone to the more "faithful brothers,"[462] many of whom had put little or nothing into it. Understandably, there may be a basis for these feelings. While he did come out of the order with the largest share — 23.3 percent of the remaining assets — it appears he also contributed the largest share to begin with. His holdings in horses and cattle at Fillmore and Grass Valley were substantial, and the fact that Volney had helped him with his ranching is an indication that Volney was more of hired hand than owner of assets. Volney also had only been home from his mission for a short time, and there is evidence that John had helped to support him while he was in England. Edwin had worked for wages as the county surveyor but did own some property in Fillmore. William had

---

461 Warner, *Grass Valley*, 116.

462 Ibid., 116.

worked as constable and had been away on his missions to Hawaii, again with possible support from John. Culbert was well established in Kanosh with a farming and ranching operation, and family tradition speaks of his losses when leaving the order. Thomas and Matilda had a dairy herd at Meadow, the hotel, and other farming interests.

From this summary, it appears that William, Edwin, and Volney may have come out with more than their share. Culbert may have come out with a proportionate share to what he had first contributed or a little less. Matilda received her equal share or perhaps, as their mother, a widow's portion to insure her economic well-being in her later years. Obviously, this problem was enlarged by trying to divide up such things as the saw mill or woolen mill. If William and Edwin were to come out with some-thing, it would have been impossible to give them a third or a fourth of a mill. The fact that Edwin got the tannery and William the woolen mill may have been what enhanced their share.

While John had been considered a wealthy and respected man during his life, by the time he died he was a destitute alcoholic. It was said that, of all the King brothers, John was the only one that could tell the difference between good and bad whisky.

His alcoholism also led to fights, and in January 1885, he was nearly beaten to death in a fight with a liquor salesman. His condition also led to much heartache within his home, and on many occasions Helen would go over to her bishop/brother-in-law's home, pleading with Culbert to do something with his brother. In addition, John's passion for horse racing created an interest in gambling, and it was common for him to win or lose $400 to $500 in a race.

John was also a man of true grit. One time when he was visiting in Fillmore, he had a growth on his forehead; and before returning home, he wanted to have it taken out. The only doctor available was somewhat questionable, but in any event, as John sat in Delilah's front room, the doctor took hold of the growth and hooked it out, roots and all. The story is told that several male spectators present marveled at John's endurance, and each had something to help deaden the pain. John was soon hilari-ously drunk with a bloody bandage on his head.[463]

A niece reported another story about John and his mother:

> I wish my father was Uncle John. He could come to [Matilda's] house and before she had time to scold him for some escapade he would tell some funny joke and [Matilda], in spite of herself, would smile, then laugh and say "O, John, You are hopeless."[464]

---

463 Read, "Sense and Nonsense, My Life Story," 20.

464 Black, "Mother Stood Tall," 73.

John King in 1857, age 20. (Courtesy Territorial Statehouse.)

Another story about John that gives an insight into his character is from his daughter, Irene.

> [John] was a great horse trader, but an honest one. He never tried to cheat anyone. He had a real showy horse, a high stepper, one of the prancing kind, but after an hour riding he [the horse] was all in — a regular old plug. When he was fresh, it took the entire family to corral him, and almost as many to bridle him. A friend of [John's] came from another town, saw this fancy horse and wanted to buy him. John didn't want to sell the horse to him and told him, "Jake, you don't want this horse; he's no good. He's got three very bad faults." But Jake wouldn't listen. He was determined to have him. After a lot of bickering, Jake owned the horse. He then said, Well, John, now the horse is mine, I'll let you tell me his three faults."

> "Well," John said, "he's a son-of-a-gun to bridle. He's hard as hell to catch - and he isn't worth a tinkers dam after you catch him."[465]

One additional story told about John:

> On one of his trips he passed a house where a group of young boys and girls were having some fun out in the yard. The boys began shouting silly things at John, such as, "Hey, Mister, your wheels are going around." He drove to the

---

465 Read, "Sense and Nonsense, My Life Story," 82-83. Editor,s note: I wonder if this is what John really said.

John King, Helen Maria, and family in 1890. Back row: Forrest, Lydia, Roy, and Matilda. Front row: Irene, John, Helen, and Frank. Kneeling in front: Elma.

corner where he could turn around, drove back, stopped his wagon and said, "Say, if you fellows would keep your mouths shut people going by wouldn't know you were crazy."[466]

On another occasion John and his three brothers, Culbert, Volney, and Edwin, were called to Fillmore to Delilah's home, where their mother was seriously ill. Edwin had lost the sight in one eye, and when they stopped at night to rest the horses, as well as themselves, John said, "Well, Edwin you go take care of the horses and we will go to sleep. You have but one eye, so it will only take you half as long (to sleep) as it does us."[467]

The *Deseret News* reported that John died on July 24, 1899, at the age of sixty-three. He was found dead under a shed at the rear of Taylor's saloon in Richfield, where he had been drinking the night before.[468] The account given by one daughter adds significantly to the story. She reported that when John went to Richfield for supplies for the haying operation, he put his team up for the night and then spread his quilts out in the shade and laid down. Someone told the bartender in a saloon nearby that there was a sick man who seemed to have plenty of money across the street at the

466 Read, "Sense and Nonsense, My Life Story," 81.

467 Ibid., 82.

468 Salt Lake City, Utah *Deseret News* obituary, July 25, 1899. John's age would have been sixty-one.

barn. The next day John was discovered dead and the money gone. An autopsy showed he had died of poisoned whiskey. Everyone suspected the bartender, but there was no way of proving it.[469]

This was certainly an unfortunate situation for a man so capable and well-liked by all. Many people said he was his own and only enemy, and all remembered his humor. Nieces and nephews all enjoyed and always wanted to go to Uncle John's home, and "Kinky John" as the Indians called him was always held in high esteem. His generosity and support of the extended King family was significant and perhaps not fully appreciated during his lifetime.

Helen's life continued for five more years until she contracted cancer. She was kept alive with morphine pills to try to ease the pain, but when it got so bad, nothing would work. On one occasion one of her children was complaining about her condition, saying "There isn't a just God. If there was he wouldn't let you suffer so — you who have never done anything but good. If I had a hold of him I'd choke him!" A horrified family stood by as Helen responded: "The dear God knows who to put suffering on. He knows I'll bear it patiently."[470]

Her funeral was on September 23, 1904, the same day as her fifty-ninth birthday and what would have been her forty-second wedding anniversary.

Thomas Edwin King

Thomas Edwin also remained in Kingston, and it appears that he took possession of the tannery for a short period of time. He built another brick home for his family, which included a store and post office. He had been appointed postmaster in 1877, and he held the office for eighteen years[471] while raising a family of six children to maturity.

Soon after the order broke up, Edwin was called on a mission. He served for twenty-one months, leaving in March 1884 and returning in December 1885. His field of labor was the southwestern part of Michigan, northern Indiana, and eastern Illinois, criss-crossing back and forth continually looking for places to speak and people who would listen to his message.[472] Schoolhouses seemed to be a favorite place to preach, and many a night he and his companion were required to sleep on the hard

---

469 Read, "Sense and Nonsense, My Life Story," 81.

470 Ibid., 103.

471 Taken from the records of the National Archives in Washington D.C., submitted by Robert K. Whittaker and compiled by Dortha Davenport, Junction, Utah.

472 "Missionary Journal of Thomas Edwin King." A typed copy is in my possession.

The Edwin King home at 188 South 100 East, Kingston. At the left was a room and an outside window for the post office. My thanks to Max Sudweeks of Kingston for identifying this home.

benches of the school. As they traveled without purse or scrip, they were always beholden to the courtesy of the people for sustenance and a place to lodge. Polygamy seemed the biggest obstacle in preaching the gospel, as many people were always ready and willing to issue a challenge. Following polygamy, difficult questions were continually raised about the Mountain Meadows Massacre.

After Edwin's first year he was put in charge of the Indiana conference. He became responsible for several missionaries and reported to the mission president on their activities.[473] Edwin always maintained a positive attitude throughout his mission and bore his testimony with fervor and conviction.

As he traveled to his mission, he was overwhelmed by the development of the country through Missouri and across the Mississippi River. It had been just thirty-eight short years since he and his family had made their epic journey, and the territory had gone from a wilderness frontier to a well-developed area with a large bridge, a half-mile long, spanning the Mississippi River. The iron bridge had three large arches under which steamboats could pass and a road on top for wagons and footmen. He

473 Ibid.

Mountain Meadows Massacre

In the late summer of 1857 when Johnston's Army was advancing on Utah, the Fancher wagon train from Arkansas was came through the Utah territory bound for California. Attached to the train was a group called the Missouri Wild Cats, and together the group number some 140 men, women, and children.

There is some questionable evidence the Fancher members tried to provoke some of the local citizens along the way, but mainly wanted to purchase needed food supplies before crossing the Nevada desert.

With the U.S. army bearing down on Utah on orders from President James Buchanan to put down a perceived Mormon rebellion, the feelings of war hysteria were very much evident among the Mormon people. Remembering their suffering and expulsion from Missouri and Illinois at the hands of the state militia, Governor Brigham Young declared martial law. One of the provisions of the law was that no supplies were to be sold to anyone travelling through the territory. In the midst of this hysteria, news also reached Utah that Parley Pratt, admired and loved apostle, had been assassinated in Arkansas.

By the time the wagon train reached a spot called Mountain Meadows just a few miles southwest of Cedar City, a tinder box was set to explode as an attack was planned by some of the local citizens.

Whether a person wants to blame the fear and hysteria that surrounded the advance of an invading army, retribution for the death of Parley Pratt, left-over vestiges of the Reformation movement of the prior year, devastating economic conditions in the territory, poor communications, or all of the above, the attack nevertheless was carried out by Mormon men with limited cooperation from their Indian allies.

On September 11, 1857, 120 people were killed resulting in the worst depredation of any group along the Overland Trail. Only eighteen young children were spared and taken to the Mormon communities and adopted by various families. As a result, the massacre became a source of great bitterness toward the Church even to current day, not to mention an embarrassment and difficult situation for the missionaries to explain.

speaks of it as a great piece of engineering.[474] What a difference from when he and his family left Montrose in a small covered wagon.

After his mission, Edwin continued as postmaster in Kingston until October 1894. Shortly after his return, Edwin also had an unfortunate experience. While working outside, he got a foxtail (weed) in his eye. It became infected, and he finally had to go to Salt Lake and have his eye removed. Undaunted by this experience, he continued to serve his community and Church; and when he turned sixty-five, he and Isabella went to St. George and served a two-year mission working in the St. George Temple. Following his temple assignment, he served in a bishopric for a short time between March 1914, and August 1915. Later, Edwin also

---

474 Ibid.

Edwin King's home in Junction at 235 North Main Street. Edwin is at the right and Isabella in the middle. (Courtesy Dortha Davenport, Junction, Utah.)

helped operate a small store in Junction with his son-in-law, John Stoney.

In the last years of their lives, Edwin and Isabella went to live in the city of Ephraim. As Edwin's age continued to advance, the sight in his remaining eye began to fail, yet his interest in learning and reading persisted. Isabella would go to the local library and check out books and then read them to him. Due to her own limited education she did not understand much of what she read, but Edwin would explain it to her and help her with the words she couldn't pronounce.[475]

Even though his sight was about gone before his death, Edwin still maintained a large garden and would take care of it by touch. He would get on his hands and knees; and by feeling the plant, he could tell the difference between a vegetable and a weed.[476] He died at the age of eighty-three. Isabella died four years later at the age of sixty-seven.

Delilah King

All through the Kingston era, Delilah and Dan continued to establish themselves in Fillmore. Delilah became the ward Relief Society presi-

---

475 Telephone interview with LaRee Fleck, Springfield, Oregon, on August 13, 1995, by the author. LaRee is a great-granddaughter of Thomas Edwin King.

476 Ibid.

dent for two years, the first ward Primary president for another two years, and then the Young Women's president for seventeen years. During several of these years, she also doubled as a stake Relief Society counselor and secretary, Young Women's counselor, and stake Primary President[477] – a handful for any capable person.

Besides these many activities, her family continued to grow with the addition of Emma Eliza, who died only two months after birth; Ethel Laverne; and Emmett. In the midst of all of these activities, the musical traditions of the family continued, adding to the cultural enjoyment of the community. Dan not only played music but wrote and arranged the music for all of the instruments of his family band and for all occasions.

The musician, Dan Olson. (Below) Dan's violin. (Courtesy Territorial Statehouse.)

For the Olsons a terrifying event occurred one day, but the date and name of the child involved are not recorded. When Dan was crossing over the flume of his sawmill, he noticed one of his children floating in the water. He leaped in and began to pull the boy out, all the while calling for help. Delilah with a neighbor assisting began rolling the body over and over pressing out the water, and in the words of one of the children it was nearly an hour before life returned and the eyes of the child opened. To Dan and Delilah it was perhaps the most painful hour they had ever experienced.[478]

The relationship between the John King and the Olson families was

477 Day and Ekins, *Milestones of Millard: 100 Years of History of Millard County*, 244, 246, 262, 265, 268, 277, 281, 282.

478 Edwin Thomas Olson, "Dan and His Violin," 209, Edmund Thomas Olson Collection, Utah State Historical and Archives Research Center. The time element seems to be a little exaggerated.

always close, not only because John supported the marriage of Dan and Delilah, but because Dan was also witty and always enjoyed a good joke, much the same as John. Each fall the Olson family would always take a load of fruit and vegetables over to John's family and return with meat, cheese, and butter. The cousins always looked forward to the visit, and the boys always insisted on sleeping out on top of the haystack. There were also hunting, fishing, and horseback riding.

As a missionary Dan returned to his native land in 1884-85 and saw his sisters for the first time since leaving Denmark. He also visited the graves of his parents. However, in the words of one of his sons, Thomas Edmund, the mission was not a good experience. Dan consented to go, but he had a hard time tracting, talking with people, and in general proselyting, but he excelled in organizing choirs and performing groups. Upon his return he was ordained a high priest in the Millard Stake.

Daniel died on May 8, 1893, after he and Delilah had been married for thirty-two years. Their children continued on with their own families and careers, and they distinguished themselves in many way. Culbert became the governor of California, and Emmett a Utah State representative and mayor of Price City. Bertha married George Hanson and traveled many parts of the world, he as an American envoy. William and Edmund were both gifted writers. While each of the children speak respectfully of their heritage, their feelings about their religious heritage are expressed by William: "The Kings stuck and stayed with the church, but the Olsons have all had the strength of character to decide for themselves this question of religion. Every single descendant of George Daniel Olson has left the church which was responsible for their being born."[479]

This comment by William is significant. There are members of the extended King family who have become inactive or have moved away from their Mormon roots, but for the entire family to disengage is interesting in light of the activity and commitment of their mother and, to a lesser degree, their father. Without judgment and in an attempt to understand this situation, one can only speculate. In the decade of the 1870's, there rose in Utah the Godbeite movement founded by William Godbe, an English convert. Godbe was a successful Salt Lake merchant and, along with others, took issue with the autocratic and economic policies of Brigham Young. They also believed in a form of spiritualism and with their seances attracted a respectable following of intellectual church members. Among their adherents was Apostle Amasa Lyman, a good friend of the King family and resident of Fillmore who was excommunicated from the

---

479 Edmund Thomas Olson, "George Daniel Olson," 8, Edmund Thomas Olson Collection, Utah State Historical Society.

Church for his beliefs, especially where they compromised the atonement of Jesus Christ. Lyman also attracted a following in Fillmore including Noah Bartholomew. There is no evidence that the Kings believed any part of the Godbeite position or doctrine, but attempts were made to convert Dan Olson, who had previously known William Godbe, and perhaps enough of their philosophy rubbed off to influence the family.

As an avid Democrat, Delilah became very active in politics and after her husband's death, she was elected Millard County recorder for two terms (1896-1900).[480]   When the state's constitution was being written, she became an active supporter and worked hard on the plank granting women's suffrage. Later she moved to Salt Lake and engaged in temple work and other activities. She passed away on January 5, 1907, at the age of sixty-five. Upon her death, her body was returned to Fillmore to be buried next to her husband in the community she helped educate, build, and entertain.

Volney King

Volney's share of the distribution of the order property was forty acres in Grass Valley known as Wilmont, just north of present-day Antimony. Wilmont was considered a part of the Antimony area, and here Volney built a home and commenced farming, and raising sheep and cattle. His first love, like his brother John's, was breaking and riding horses.

His Church activities still centered around the Sunday School, and he served as a superintendent and teacher. He also assisted his brother Culbert in the Marion Ward in what might be considered a ward clerk's position as he collected and accounted for the tithing of the ward. It is interesting to note that, during the mid-1880s, there seemed to be a problem with Church activity in Antimony, and many Sundays there were not enough people to hold Church. Many times small meetings were held in individual homes. This was due in large part to Bishop King and many of the leading brethren were either in prison or on the run to escape polygamy prosecution. The ward lacked leadership, and homes were fatherless as the brethren were being careful to stay out of such obvious places as Church meetings.

Volney later became involved in the Young Men's Mutual Improvement Association, and he was called to be the president, a change from his long-standing Sunday School assignments. However, his favorite Church activity was family history and genealogy. Many community and family records and the beginning history of the King family were all obtained

---

480 Salt Lake City, Utah *Deseret News* obituary, January 5, 1907.

and recorded by Volney.

While in the order, Volney also acquired a taste for political office. He was first elected Piute County selectman (commissioner) in 1879, and became involved in setting up road districts, financing road construction, deciding water rights, and issuing water use permits for irrigation.[481] He must have been a somewhat judicious man, as he heard many arguments over disputed water rights, a common western occurrence in those early pioneer days. No doubt his judiciousness was nurtured while in the order when he was chosen treasurer. This responsibility brought with it the duty of running the post office as well as settling with those people who wanted to withdraw from the order, a most difficult situation.

In 1884 he became county prosecuting attorney and, in 1885, secretary of the People's Party.[482] In August 1886 he ran for constable, but lost by one vote, his own. He claimed he did not vote for himself.[483] Later in 1887 he did run for the justice of peace and was successful.[484]

Besides his many activities in Church, government, family, and farm, Volney continued his teaching endeavors and, each year for several years, taught school at Wilmont. Thus, Volney was one of three of the six King children — Edwin, Delilah, and Volney — who found a love for education and took advantage of their educational opportunities. Because of their example, many of the King grandchildren went away to Salt Lake and Provo for additional schooling.

Volney may have been somewhat judicious, but he was also very emotional and easily agitated. He never backed away from a good argument. Some arguments he won, and some he lost. One of his more violent contests occurred with the son of Isaac Riddle, or I. J., as he was called. After a count of the sheep herd during one of the round-ups, Volney was eighteen short and wanted a recount. I. J. refused, and the fight was on. I. J. pulled a knife, and Volney responded with a rock. By the time it was over and after help arrived, Volney had his missing sheep, as well as a fist in the nose.[485]

Another time Volney had been constructing a fence between himself and a Brother Wilcox. Wilcox claimed Volney had stretched the fence onto his land, and, of course, Volney denied such an assertion. Again, an argument ensued, and when it was settled, Volney discovered he indeed

---

481 King, *The Two Volneys*, 57.

482 Ibid., 62.

483 Ibid.

484 Ibid., 63.

485 Ibid., 54.

Old home on what used to be the King Ranch in Antimony.

had fenced an acre and a half too much.[486]

Together Volney and Eliza had ten children: Eliza Rosetta, who was born in Fillmore before the move to Kingston; Volney Emery; Susan May; Edmund Rice; Leland; Clarence; Warren; Ada Delilah; Claudius Melvin; and Lawrence. Again the heartaches of children who died was experienced. Clarence died when less than a month old, Warren passed away at thirteen months, and Claudius Melvin departed when only eleven months old. This left them seven children whom they raised to maturity: three girls and four boys.

One of the most difficult decisions Volney and Eliza made during their married life was to move to Wyoming. They were well established in Wilmont and leading citizens in community and Church. The whole thing started when an acquaintance of Volney's son-in-law, John Black, came to visit. John had married Eliza Rosetta but was restless and never seemed satisfied. When his friend called, he had stories to tell of the grandeur of Canada and pictured Canada as a paradise. John Black immediately wanted to go, much to the annoyance and dismay of his wife. However, John was determined and went to Salt Lake to meet with the people who were making the move. On the street he happened to meet another friend, Apostle Abraham O. Woodruff. When Brother Woodruff found out his plans to move to Canada, he queried, "Why don't you come to the Big

---

486 Ibid., 69.

Horn with us?"[487]

This was an unexpected turn of events, and in a matter of hours the decision was made and off he went to Wyoming. When he got to Kemmerer, he wrote a letter notifying his wife and family of the change in plans. Rosetta didn't have much choice but to sell the family farm, purchase tents and equipment, and travel to what was to become Cowley, Wyoming.

The Big Horn country was a barren and windswept area on the far northern part of Wyoming. The water stank with sulphur, plains were desolate and covered with sagebrush, the ground was infested with rattlesnakes, and the winters were cold. It was not a very inviting place to make a living and raise a family. Nevertheless Volney's other daughter, May, and her husband, George Lyman, and their family soon followed. With their two daughters now struggling in Wyoming, Volney and Eliza felt a responsibility to relocate and give what support they could to their daughters and families. Preparations were made, including the sale of their home and farm, and they left in November of 1903. At age fifty-six, it was hard for Volney to start over, but off he and his family went. He drove a large herd of cattle as well; but when he got to Cowley, there was no hay or range grass for the stock. By the following summer most of them lay dead.

Volney and his sons Edmund and Leland fenced their lot and started farming and building a rock home. For the next fifteen years they eked out a subsistence level of existence. It later became evident that Volney's son, Volney Emery, who had settled in Teasdale, Utah, and was doing very well in the sheep business, was sending checks to subsidize his parents. This was also a small source of irritation between the families as Emery had fallen into Church inactivity and did not pay tithing. When a check arrived in Cowley, the first thing Volney would do was pay tithing on the money.[488]

Besides his farming, Volney again settled in with a job as justice of the peace and Church worker. Volney also qualified as a Black Hawk War veteran and received his first pension check of $25 in December, 1913.[489]

One human interest story is told of Volney traveling down to Antimony for the funeral of Culbert in 1909. The Culbert King family had just purchased for Culbert a new suit of clothing and he never had a chance to wear it before he died. Volney was given the new suit by Culbert's family

---

487 Ibid., Insert, 14.

488 Ibid., 92.

489 Ibid., 93.

The first schoolhouse in Antimony in 1886. (Courtesy Robert Hahne, Orem, Utah.)

and he reports how deeply touched he was by the gift.[490]

In 1918 at the age of seventy-one, Volney decided to return to Utah. Volney realized he was not able to farm any longer, and he began to complain of cramps. Their four sons and a daughter were now living in Teasdale, Wayne County, and it seemed like the best place for them to live the remainder of their lives. Volney was still able to help with some of the ranching chores, and he continued his genealogy pursuits and acted as a home teacher. Visits with his brother Edwin in Ephraim, a short distance away, and other family members were always a pleasurable experience.

Finally on January 30, 1925, this hardy pioneer passed away, just short of his seventy-eighth birthday, the last of Thomas Rice King's children. The younger Eliza would live another thirteen years, passing away January 18, 1938, just short of her eighty-second birthday. Volney is buried in Antimony, but Eliza is in Teasdale.

Thus, each of the six King children was unique and contributed in his or her own way to family and society. William was the missionary and friend to the Polynesians; Culbert, the Church leader and faithful polygamist; John, the successful rancher and general heady business-man; Thomas Edwin, the stately, educated, and loyal son and brother; Delilah, the woman of culture and education; and Volney, the student, writer, and public servant.

490 Ibid., 88.

Judges
(Living the Law and the Gospel)

L iving the law and principles of their Mormon faith is well evidenced by the King family as they participated in and made a significant contribution to all aspects of their secular and religious community. It was, however, not without sacrifice and commitment and a special relationship with their God. They gave all they had, not just once but several times, and what they gave included material possessions, time, talents, and exhibiting a divine faith in Deity. Their legacy is now in the hands of their children and their children's children.

Plural Marriage

Without a doubt the most controversial doctrine and practice of the Latter-day Saints was plural marriage. Taught by Joseph Smith, Brigham Young publicly announced it to the world in 1852 as a basic tenet of the Mormon faith. Never had a practice been so offensive to the perceived morals of a Victorian nation, and was classed with slavery by the Republican Party in 1856 as one of the "twin relics of barbarism."[491] Public reaction was immediate resulting in discriminatory and oppressive federal legislation to try and stamp it out. For decades it delayed Utah's admission into the Union, created economic havoc for the Church, and was a major contributor to the Utah War of 1858. It led to the imprisonment of more than 1,300 men and women,[492] and it threatened the disfranchisement of

Chronological Events

Dec 9,	1885	Culbert indicted for cohabitation.
Dec 17,	1885	William indicted for cohabitation.
Dec 22,	1885	Culbert sentenced to prison.
Dec 25,	1885	Culbert begins his prison term in the Territorial prison at Salt Lake City.
Jun 28,	1886	Culbert released from prison.
Oct	1886	William leaves the country for a mission to Hawaii.
May 6,	1891	William arrested and pleads guilty to cohabitation.

---

491 Richard S. Van Wagoner, *Mormon Polygamy* (Salt Lake City, Utah: Signature Books, 1986), 85.

492 Ibid., 120.

the entire Mormon populace. Families were torn apart without support as husbands went into hiding, and homes were broken into at all hours of the night without proper judicial oversight. Mormon Church President John Taylor died in 1887 in exile with a price on his head; and a new round of persecution poured down on the Latter-day Saints, including the murder of two missionaries in Tennessee in 1884. The Church was disincorporated and Church property confiscated.

Considered a binding religious ordinance, the spectre of polygamy plagued the Saints wherever they went. They considered it the means of entry into the highest Kingdom of God, and those who would become "gods," even the "sons of god," were those who entered into this practice.[493] To give up plural marriage was in the same category as giving up a sacred principle, such as repentance, or the ordinance of baptism. Covered by the injunction that celestial marriage meant plural marriage, the parable of the talents described the consequences of having only one wife,[494] and the Saints held onto "The Principle" with a zealous tenacity.[495]

Living polygamy, to the Saints, was under the same mandate given to ancient Biblical notables such as Abraham, Jacob, and David. How could the Christian people of America who believed in the Bible, wreak such retribution on the Saints? Through Joseph Smith the gospel had been restored, and was a restoration "of all things," including the ancient practice of plural marriage. In the minds and hearts of LDS Church members the proclamation of the Lord was clear: "All commandments that I give must be obeyed. . . . Have I not given my word in great plainness on this subject? I have not revoked this law, nor will I."[496]

---

493 *Journal of Discourses,* 2:268-269

494 "Joseph Smith said that the parable that Jesus spoke of that the man who had one talent and hid it in the earth was the man who had but one wife and would not take another, would have her taken from him and given to one who had more." (Taken from the Journal of Wilford Woodruff and quoted by Apostle Erastus Snow in Joseph W. Musser's, *Celestial or Plural Marriage,* p. 11. For similar comments by Brigham Young, see *Journal of Discourses* 16:166.)

495 For further details on the position of the Saints on the principle of plural marriage and their fight against the federal government, see Richard S. Van Wagoner, *Mormon Polygamy: A History,* (Signature Books, Salt Lake City, Utah, 1986); Samuel W. Taylor, *The Kingdom or Nothing (*Macmillan Publishing Co., New York, New York, 1976); and Joseph W. Musser, *Celestial or Plural Marriage,* (Salt Lake City, Utah: Truth Publishing Company, 1970).

496 A Revelation on Celestial Marriage given through President John Taylor, September 27, 1886. See Fred C. Collier, comp, *Unpublished Revelations of the Prophets and Presidents of the Church of Jesus Christ of Latter Day Saints, 2 vols., (*Salt Lake City, Utah: Collier's Publishing Company, 1981), vol. 1, pt. 88:145.

A cartoon published in the Eastern papers making fun of Brigham Young during the anti-Mormon polygamy crusades. (Courtesy LDS Church Historical Department.)

Ten years after the first public announcement on plural marriage, congress reacted by passing the Morrill Anti-Bigamy Act in 1862. The act prohibited plural marriage in the territories of the United States and declared polygamy a felony under a penalty of up to five years in prison and/or a $500 fine. However, with few enforcement provisions and the federal government preoccupied with a civil war, little was done until the mid-1870s, when further legislation was passed. Church leaders decided to test the provisions of the Morrill Act against their First Amendment rights of religious freedom, but in 1879 the Supreme Court ruled against them. While the Court conceded protection under the First Amendment for religious belief, the Judiciary ruled against the practice, stating that religious practices could be restricted by legislation.[497]

The stage was now set for a full onslaught against the Mormons and their marital institution. Additional measures were passed by Congress over the decade of the 1880s including making unlawful cohabitation a misdemeanor punishable by six months imprisonment and/or a $300 fine. The new laws also completely disfranchised polygamists by preventing them from voting, holding public office, and serving on juries. In its broad form, a polygamist was defined as a person who either practiced or believed in polygamy, a rather extreme point of view. Obviously the laws then passed and the method of enforcement would be repulsive by today's standards.

497 Van Wagoner, *Mormon Polygamy*, 111

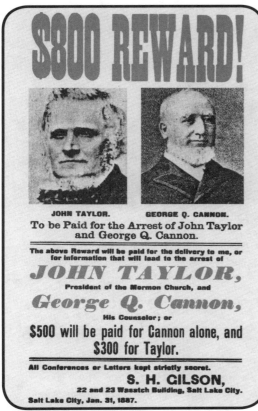

$800 REWARD!

JOHN TAYLOR.   GEORGE Q. CANNON.

To be Paid for the Arrest of John Taylor and George Q. Cannon.

The above Reward will be paid for the delivery to me, or for information that will lead to the arrest of

JOHN TAYLOR,

President of the Mormon Church, and

George Q. Cannon,

His Counselor; or

$500 will be paid for Cannon alone, and $300 for Taylor.

All Conferences or Letters kept strictly secret.

S. H. GILSON,

22 and 23 Wasatch Building, Salt Lake City.

Salt Lake City, Jan. 31, 1887.

A copy of a Wanted Poster for Presidents John Taylor and George Q. Cannon. (*The Kingdom or Nothing* by Samuel W. Taylor.)

Needless to say, the Utah Territory came under siege. A board of five commissioners (carpet baggers) came to run political affairs in Utah as all constitutional provisions were suspended. The raids of the 1880s became standard fare as homes were broken into looking for evidence of people cohabiting. Men became fugitives and were hunted down like runaway slaves or common criminals. Women, even those with small children, were imprisoned under the guise of "in contempt of court" until they agreed to testify against their husbands. Children were grilled about their parents, and pregnant girls without a known husband were arrested. Search warrants were not a consideration, and any evidence of a man visiting or giving assistance to a woman other than his legal wife was considered sufficient proof to convict him of breaking the law.

An underground was also established for the more wanted of the brethren, and several went on extended missions out of the country to avoid prosecution. Rewards were offered by the government for high Church officials such as Presidents George Q. Cannon and John Taylor.

The records and diaries of the King families are noticeably silent about any significant information concerning their involvement with polygamy. In the records can be found basic details, but information about their interpersonal relationships, how they lived and supported each other, and their feelings and struggles is limited. On occasion an obscure or cryptic one-line note may appear in the writings of one of the children or is handed down in oral family stories. In many cases, there is failure to even materially acknowledge the existence of a plural marriage, or what they did after the Church Manifesto. One experience that is recorded is from the Dan Olson family. In one entry by W. F. Olson, he relates the following story about Culbert King's return to Fillmore with his second wife, Elizabeth. It may or may not represent the general feeling of the family.

> They had been to the endowment house and received rites and ceremonies that sealed them as man and wife for time and eternity. There was something very significant about this marriage, it being the first spiritual-wife union to the King family.
>
> Culbert was in a jovial mood, was greeted cordially by all present, who conferred a like welcome to the wife, known afterwards by the family as Aunt Libby. She was an intelligent and attractive girl, daughter of Stake President Callister, who was also the husband of two wives. There was a feeling of reserve in offering felicitations in this anomaly, not that there was disgrace in it or the least animosity, but it was unusual so far as the family was concerned.
>
> Thomas took his son by the hand, looked in his face with grave expression, but said not a word. He did likewise with Libby. What his thoughts were no one will ever know. The little group talked of the weather, the roads and of the health of the relatives in Salt Lake City, refraining however, from such words as, I wish you much joy, or may your troubles all be little ones. After Thomas' son and his wife had said good night and departed the others sat silently for a time until Rebecca (wife of Edwin) spoke up, "I wonder how Esther will take it." This referred to Culbert's number one wife. "Let's not talk about it," said Delilah.[498]

Another comment was by a granddaughter of Esther, Mary King Stenquist, "Grandmother was alone most of the time with her children because Grandfather's other wives were more demanding on his time."[499] However, a daughter of Volney King, Eliza Rosetta King wrote: "Polygamy was in full swing and we thought nothing of it. One Aunt in a family was as much to us as another."[500]

One possible explanation in the absence of any information may have been a concern about the likely outcome of the Supreme Court's decision and its negative impact on the Saints. Any records could be subpoenaed and used against them. Volney King's entry under date of January 14, 1879, in his United Order record simply states that "news was received today in Kingston of the Supreme Court ruling against members of the Church."[501]

The commitment and involvement of the King family to this belief

---

498 Olson, "Dan and His Violin," 213.

499 Mary King Stenquist, a granddaughter. "History of Eliza Esther McCullough King," a copy is in my possession.

500 Black, "Mother Stood Tall," 4.

501 Volney King, "The Daily Journals of the Kingston United Order," 14.

system and mandate of the Church was mixed. While there is no evidence that Thomas lived polygamy during his life time, he was sealed to Rebecca Henry Murray in the Endowment House on October 4, 1867. Rebecca, fifteen years senior to Thomas, was a single parent and the mother of Rebecca Jane Murray, the wife of Thomas Edwin King and part of the Henry family from Ireland that settled in Fillmore. The sixty-two-year-old Rebecca and the nineteen-year-old Rebecca Jane left Liverpool in 1860 and together made the Alantic crossing and the wagon trip to Utah. Rebecca had previously been married to Robert Murray and had several children from that marriage. It is not known if she was widowed or if Robert refused to join the Church.[502] Why Thomas and Rebecca did not live as husband and wife is not known. It is curious that Thomas, a devoted Mormon, community leader, and defender of the principle of plural marriage, lived a monogamous life. Perhaps Matilda had other feelings as expressed on one occasion. It is reported that Dan Olson was teasing her one day and asked her why, since her husband was a righteous man, he didn't have another wife. She told him "not to make light of sacred things and that as for Thomas, he was never cut out for a polygamist - he don't know how to go about it."[503]

It might also be speculated that as involved as Thomas was within the Church, the reason why he was not called as a bishop or stake president was because he did not live the Principle. Brigham Young and the Brethren had strong feelings about non-polygamist men presiding in the Church.[504] William and Culbert were the polygamists and also those who held the more responsible Church positions.

Following Thomas's death, the family had four known deceased women sealed to him together with their deceased children:

-Two deceased children of Rebecca were sealed to Thomas and Rebecca in the St. George Temple on October 6, 1882: Robert Henry Murray and John George Murray. In addition, Rebecca Jane (Henry/King) was also sealed to Thomas and Rebecca Henry.

---

502 Subsequently, Rebecca was sealed to her first husband, Robert, on November 30, 1939, in the St. George Temple. (See LDS Church Ancestral File.)

503 Olson, "Dan and His Violin," 212.

504 This was reinforced in a revelation given to John Taylor in 1882 in which the Lord declared that Seymour B. Young could be called to the vacancy in the presiding quorum of Seventies if he was willing to "conform to my Law." (Joseph W. Musser, *Celestial or Plural Marriage,* 38.) Further, Wilford Woodruff said, "If we do not keep the same law that our Heavenly Father has kept, we cannot go with Him. A man obeying a lower law is not qualified to preside over those who keep a higher law." (Matthias F. Cowley, *Wilford Woodruff: History of His Life and Labors,* Salt Lake City, Utah: Bookcraft Publishers, 1978, 542.

-Lois Beagle was sealed to him October 4, 1882, in the St. George Temple. It is not known what relationship Lois had with the King family.

-Ann Shaw was sealed October 5, 1882, in the St. George Temple. Again it is not known what relationship Ann had with the King family, except that Rebecca, Henry's mother, was a Shaw.

-Eliza Carrol was sealed October 6, 1882, in the St. George Temple. Also, there is no known relationship between the King and Carrol families.

-Elizabeth Fidelia Parker, the wife of Rufus King, who died in Indiana. Elizabeth and her four deceased children (Zina, John, Orange, and Orin) were sealed July 16, 1890, in the Manti Temple.

Of the six King children, Thomas Edwin married polygamously in 1878, but his first wife died after nine months, leaving him with only one wife. John Robison was a committed monogamist and firmly believed one wife was all a man could and should take care of. Delilah was a monogamous wife to Daniel.

Volney, while married twice, did not marry polygamously. He very much wanted to, but Eliza set down the ultimatum that, if Volney married another wife, "he would still be left a monogamist."[505] Still believing in the Principle and having faith it had eternal value, Volney had three deceased women sealed to him in October 1882, in the St. George Temple: Olevia Shaw, Mary Miller, and Eliza Buckard. Eliza must have agreed to going at least this far and Volney speaks of this event very positively in his diary.

William, the oldest son, married three wives; however, his first wife, Josephine, died before he married his second and third wives. He lived in polygamy with Josephine's cousin, Mary Ann Henry, and with Lucy White for thirteen years before he died in 1892. Mary Ann reported that William took a second wife after Apostle Lorenzo Snow sent word to William that if he did not comply with the Principle, he (Snow) would take away his bishopric. She concludes by saying that Lucy was a good woman and lived with William until his death in 1892 (which would have been after the Manifesto), and that "I like all of Mormonism but polygamy.[506]

Mary Ann's negative feelings towards polygamy must have been intense. In William's journal under date of January 22, 1881, he records, "My wife Mary is giving [me] a great deal of trouble, threaten to leave me and many more threats I will not record. A few days later he again

---

505 Interview with Dwight King, a grandson of Volney King, by the author July 22, 1994.

506 Stella Day, *Builders of Early Millard*, 496-497. This is based on an interview by Maude C. Melville, March 5, 1942, when Mary Ann was eighty-eight years of age.

A copy of the warrant for the arrest of Mary Ann King as a witness against William King, dated February 23, 1889. (National Archives Microfilm Publications M1401, Case files of the U.S. District Courts for the Territory of Utah 1870-1896, File 1315-1316, LDS Church Family History Library.)

records, "Had some trouble at home with my wife Mary."[507]

Lucy's *Deseret News* obituary gives an account of her marriage to

---

[507] "William Rice King Journal," January 22, 1881. See also February 16, 1881 and May 15, 1881.

William and later her second marriage to Nephi Wood after William's death.[508] The obituary identifies only a step-child, giving the impression that the child was the son of Nephi Wood. No children were born of Lucy either by her first or second husband.

There is evidence that William had gone into hiding as early as March 1885 and the call to the Sandwich Islands in October 1886, was prompted by the raids and by the fact that many of the brethren were going on the underground or on missions to escape possible capture and prosecution. William, in fact, had been indicted by the grand jury several months earlier on December 17, 1885,[509] but so far had eluded capture. Also when he left for Hawaii, he departed alone, and it was several months later before Lucy joined him, again an indication that he left with a degree of haste. His absence from the country until his return in the spring of 1890 gave him a short respite but by November he was found and arrested. On May 6, 1891, he appeared in court, pled guilty, and was fined $400. It appears the fine was never paid. On September 14, 1893, after William had passed away, the court dismissed the case against him.[510]

Why William was not given a prison sentence, especially when it appears he did not pay his fine, cannot be determined. The only possible explanation is he was brought to trial after the Manifesto and by this time the judges were starting to show lenience toward the "polygs."

Culbert was the most active polygamist of the family, marrying and living with three wives. He married Eliza Esther McCullough in February 1855; and then nine years later, in October 1864, he married Elizabeth Ann Callister. His third wife, Sarah Elizabeth Pratt, joined him in marriage in September 1878. Thus, he was married to two wives for fourteen years and three wives for thirteen years before Sarah died November 23, 1891. Seven years later Esther died, and then in 1901 Elizabeth passed away. From these three marriages came twenty-four children. Later in June 1908, Culbert married a fourth wife, Lydia Ann Webb, who had been married twice before and was the sister to Helen Maria Webb King. Seven of Lydia's deceased children were also sealed to her and Culbert: Lydia Rozella Bartholomew, Laura Bartholomew, Nelson LeRoy Bartholomew, Nora Bartholomew, Albert Huntley, Katie Huntley, and Frances Huntley.

For his beliefs, Culbert served six months in the Utah Territorial Prison on charges of cohabitation. The penitentiary was an enclosure of about one acre surrounded by an adobe wall about twenty feet in height. A large

---

508 Salt Lake City, Utah *Deseret News* obituary, October 24, 1938.

509 "District Courts for the Territory of Utah: 1870-1896," File Roll #18, Family History Library, Salt Lake City, Utah.

510 Ibid.

United States of America, } ss.

TERRITORY OF UTAH.

At a stated term of the District Court of the *Second* Judicial District, in and for the Territory of Utah, begun and holden in the City of *Beaver* within and for the District and Territory aforesaid, on the *7th* day of *December* A. D. 1885 and continued by adjournment to and including the *17th* day of *December* A. D. 1885.

THE UNITED STATES OF AMERICA,

Against

William King

The Grand Jurors of the United States of America, within and for the district aforesaid, in the Territory aforesaid, being duly empanelled and sworn, on their oaths do find and present that *William King* late of said district, in the Territory aforesaid, heretofore, to-wit: on the *first* day of *January* in the year of our Lord one thousand eight hundred and eighty *three*, at the County of *Piute* in the said district, Territory aforesaid, and within the jurisdiction of this court did *and on divers days after said first day of January A.D. 1883 and continuously from said first day of January 1883 until the fifth day of January A.D. 1885 at said county of Piute did unlawfully live and cohabit with more than one woman namely with one Mary Ann King and one Lucy White sometimes known as Lucy King and during said time did unlawfully claim live and cohabit with said Mary Ann King and said Lucy White as his wives*

A copy of the grand jury indictment dated December 17, 1885, against William for the crime of cohabiting with more than one woman. (National Archives Microfilm Publications M1401, Case files of the U.S. District Courts for the Territory of Utah 1870-1896, File 1315-1316, LDS Church Family History Library.)

gate occupied the center of the west side of the facilities, and the prisoners were housed in one of three tall log bunkhouses located in the center of the compound. The whole place had a bare, sunburnt, and forbidding appearance, and was entirely absent of any shade except that afforded by the shadows of the buildings. Needless to say the living conditions were most undesirable. To add insult to injury, it is also reported that the guards always seemed ready to take offense at the slightest provocation and place a person in the sweat box, a wooden cage with nothing to shelter an inmate

A copy of the warrant for the arrest of Lucy King as a witness against William King, dated February 23, 1889. (National Archives Microfilm Publications M1401, Case files of the U.S. District Courts for the Territory of Utah 1870-1896, File 1315-1316, LDS Church Family History Library.)

from the a glaring sun. A person could be kept there for the day without food or drink.

Culbert served from Christmas Day 1885 to June 28, 1886. He was also fined $300 plus costs of $112.50, but the fine and costs were not paid.[511]

---

511 Rosa Mae McClellan Evans, "Judicial Prosecution of Prisoners for LDS Plural Marriage: Prison Sentences, 1884-1895," M.A. Thesis, Brigham Young University, 125.

For good behavior, Culbert could have been released a month early, but because the costs were unpaid, he was required to stay the full six months. One child, Catherine King, daughter of Sarah, was born February 1, 1886, while he was in prison.

Before capture, Culbert first went into the mountains to hide when the federal marshals came to town, but after a while his family was becoming militant toward the authorities. Rather than risk someone getting hurt, Culbert gave himself up. He initially pled not guilty and was released on a $1,000 bond, but later changed his plea to guilty when he determined that further resistance was fruitless. He was sentenced on December 22 before Judge Jacob Boreman,[512] a judge known for his vigorous prosecution of polygamists.

Another story told by the Volney King family is that, when the marshals were looking for Culbert and came to Volney's home, Eliza denied any knowledge of Culbert's whereabouts. "Have you seen him?" "No!" "Do you know where he is?" "No!" With that, little seven-year-old Volney Emery in all his innocence and unable to tell anything but the truth spoke up and said, "Why, Mom, Uncle Culbert was just here and when he left he headed down the lane." After the marshals left, young "Emery received a licking, not for telling the truth, but for contradicting his mother."[513]

Just before he left for prison, Culbert transferred most of his property to his three wives. In the transfer were eighty acres to Eliza, and forty acres each to Elizabeth and Sarah, all in Kingston. They also received a small number of horses, cows, and wagons.[514] The records for Antimony have not been discovered.

While incarcerated, Culbert was in good company. Also, serving at this time were some forty-eight other brethren, including Apostle and future President Lorenzo Snow and future Apostle Rudger Clawson.

Concurrently, Caleb West was serving as governor of the territory, and in May he made a special visit to the prison to try and persuade the brethren to turn away from their polygamous wives in exchange for their freedom. In response, a petition was signed and sent to the governor repudiating his offer and expressing a disdain for the laws that trespassed upon the sacred domain of their religious beliefs. The petition went on to express their feelings and conviction.

> So far as compliance with your proposition requires the sacrifice of honor and manhood, the repudiation of our wives and children, the violation of our

---

512 Jenson, *Church Chronology*, 127.

513 Interview with Dwight King, a grandson of Volney King, by me July 22, 1994.

514 Piute County records, Book 6, 52-3.

United States of America,

TERRITORY OF UTAH.

At a stated term of the District Court of the _Second_ Judicial District, in and for

the Territory of Utah, begun and holden in the City of _Beaver_ within and for the District

and Territory aforesaid, on the _7th_ day of _December_ A. D. 188_5_ and continued

by adjournment to and including the _9th_ day of _December_ A. D. 1885

THE UNITED STATES OF AMERICA,

Against

Culbert King

The Grand Jurors of the United States of America, within and for the district aforesaid, in the Territory

aforesaid, being duly empanelled and sworn, on their oaths do find and present that

Culbert King late of said district, in the Territory aforesaid,

heretofore, to-wit: on the _11th_ day of _December_ in the year of our Lord

one thousand eight hundred and eighty _three_ , at the County of _Garfield_

in the said district, Territory aforesaid, and within the jurisdiction of this court did _unlawfully_

live and cohabit with more than one woman,
namely with one Esther King and one Elizabeth
Ann Collister and one Sarah Pratt and on
divers day after said 11th day of December 188
and continuously from the date last aforesaid
until the 10th day of December 1884, at the County
aforesaid, in the territory of Utah did unlawfully
claim live & cohabit with said Esther King,
Elizabeth Ann Collister and Sarah Pratt as his
wives

A copy of the grand jury indictment against Culbert King, the same date as William King's indictment, for the crime of cohabiting with more than one woman. (National Archives Microfilm Publications M1401, Case files of the U.S. District Courts for the Territory of Utah 1870-1896, File 1313-1314, LDS Church Family History Library.)

sacred covenants, Heaven forbid that we should be guilty of such perfidy; perpetual imprisonment with which we are all threatened, or even death itself, would be preferable. Our wives desire no separation from us, and were we to comply with your request they would regard our action as most cruel, inhuman, and monstrous; our children would blush with shame, and we should deserve the scorn and contempt of all just and honorable men.

The petition concludes with an acknowledgment that they could have avoided imprisonment in the beginning had they turned away from their polygamist families, but as much as they loved liberty, they could not be untrue to their conscience, religion, and God. If they could not as free

The Utah Penitentiary was completed in 1854. It occupied about seven acres and was located at 2100 South between 14th and 15th East streets in Salt Lake City's Sugarhouse neighborhood. The site is now occupied by a large park. (Courtesy Utah State Historical Society.)

men claim their rights under proper earthly authority, they would appeal for justice from the "Great Arbiter of all human interests."[515]

Another insight into Culbert's character and personality comes from a letter to two of his children, Delilah and Volney, just before he was released. Besides the usual greetings and comments about how anxious he was to come home, he talked about being called to Church positions at a young age and how inadequate he felt. He encouraged his family to do their best in whatever they may be called to do. He then stated:

> I hope you will read the papers and take good care of the nice pieces in the Deseret News. It would be a source of great satisfaction if all of the boys as well as the girls would strive hard to learn the principles of the gospel which teaches us not to do wrong but always be on the right side and have faith in God and the principles of truth. The bravest is them that dares to do right, take pride in doing that will bring the praise of the good. Never mind the flattery and the praise of the unbelieving, for they will lead you into the principles of infidelity. When a person is lost to the principles of the Gospel their condition is awful and is to be sorrowed over. I do not write these things because I think there is a great deal of danger of my children becoming infidels, but they come to my mind, and they will do no harm to read them. We can't be too firm in relation to the principles of the Gospel.[516]

---

515 Kate B. Carter, *Heart Throbs of the West,* 9:374-384.

516 Kate B. Carter, *Our Pioneer Heritage* (Daughters of Utah Pioneers), Contributed by Utahna R. Gottfredson, 12:411-412.

Inside the walls of the prison were three tall log bunkhouses located in the center of the compound. (Courtesy Utah State Historical Society.)

Upon Culbert's return home, everyone gathered for a celebration and a hero's welcome. They had a picnic and public speeches, all to the consternation of the federal authorities. Rather than being treated as despicable criminals, the brethren returning from prison were considered martyrs for the faith. Furthermore, Culbert wasn't about to give up his families; and following his release, two additional children were conceived and born by two different wives: Julina King, daughter of Elizabeth Ann, July 17, 1887; and Heber Philip King, son of Sarah, June 24, 1891. While Culbert paid his dues under the law, obviously he continued to live polygamously as many of the brethren were doing.

This flagrant violation did not go unnoticed by the officials and again Culbert was forced into hiding. The child, Catherine King, who was born while he was in prison, died two months after his release; and Culbert was unable to attend the funeral for fear of being captured. Ned Desaules reports in his diary in May 1887 that there were additional rumors of another indictment against Culbert, but no further action is recorded.

Genealogy and Temple Work

From the early days of Mormonism, the belief among the Saints was that the oracles of God and the higher ordinances of salvation were found in sacred temples. As ancient Israel reverenced temple worship, the destiny of a modern Israel was to build and occupy temples with special ordinances involving baptism, endowment, and marriage or sealing. Not only was this to be done for the living, but vicariously for the dead, thus linking generation to generation. In the words of Joseph Smith, "he shall plant in the hearts of the children the promises made to the fathers, and the hearts of the children shall turn to their fathers" – "for they without us cannot be made perfect, neither can we without our dead be made perfect."[517]

Preparatory work would include extensive genealogical research to find and identify as many family members as possible.

In fulfillment, the King family participated in these activities from an early date. Matilda was baptized in 1843 for her deceased sister, Lavina, and considerable family history information was gathered during Thomas's and Matilda's visiting mission in 1869-70. Research was continued by Volney during his lifetime, and in the Utah State Historical Library in Salt Lake City are several files with numerous letters received by Volney from all over the country providing information on the Rice/King families. Volney also maintained an extensive journal containing birth dates of the extended King family. Temple work was started right after the St. George Temple was dedicated in 1877, and some examples of temple excursions by the Kings are as follows:

April 9, 1877: William was baptized in the St. George Temple for fourteen King, Hyde, and Rice ancestors.[518]

December 11 and 12, 1878: William and Culbert spent two days in the St. George Temple completing four endowments. It must be remembered that in the early days of the Church, an endowment session would take all day. Each person was required to go to the altar, and the washings and anointings were an extension of the endowment ceremony.[519]

October 3, 4. 5 and 6, 1882: This trip to the St. George Temple was completed by Volney King, Matilda King, Rebecca Henry Murray, and Sarah Pratt King. It was primarily a plural marriage session, as deceased women were sealed to Thomas Rice and to Volney. Many baptisms, endowments, and other sealings were also completed.[520]

July 15-18, 1890: This was the most significant trip for the King family. It was completed right after William returned from the Hawaiian Islands and included all the family except John Robison. Participating family members included Matilda, the matriarch of the family; William and wife Lucy; Culbert and wives Esther and Sarah; Thomas Edwin and wife Isabella; Volney; Delilah and husband Daniel; Clarinda King Black (daughter of Culbert) and husband George; and Naomi and Ella Vilate

---

517 See *Doctrine and Covenants* 2:2; 128:15; Malachi 4:6; Hebrews 11:40.

518 See St. George Temple records on microfilm at the LDS Church Family History Library, Salt Lake City, Utah.

519 Ibid.

520 Ibid.

The Manti Temple was dedicated April 25, 1877. Here the King family participated in sacred temple rites and had several spiritual experiences. (Courtesy Utah State Historical Society.)

King, daughters of Edwin. They completed some eighty-five baptisms, forty-four endowments, and several sealings. The main thrust of the trip, however, was to have the King children sealed to Thomas and Matilda. This was completed, except for John, who was sealed after his death.[521]

One note of interest is that there are several families in the Church who come through Edmund Rice; and as soon as the St. George Temple opened, other families related to the Rices also started to do the work for their extended family. As a result the Rices and Kings have tripped over each other in the temples, and there has been a lot of duplication of work. The method of checking for duplication in the early days of temples was not as good as it is today, and such errors were common.

One tradition within the King family illustrating their interest in temple work involves George Black, son-in-law to Culbert King. During the latter part of his life, George was working as a night watchman in the Manti Temple. On one particular evening after all the people had left, George discovered a man standing by a window in the office, looking through the temple record books.[522] George went over to inquire what he was doing, and recognized him as his deceased father-in-law. Culbert quietly turned the pages one by one before finally speaking, "Look here at

---

521 See Manti Temple records on microfilm at the LDS Church Family History Library, Salt Lake City, Utah.

522 This event would have happened after 1918 when George and Esther Clarinda moved to Manti and before 1940 when George passed away.

these records of the King family. You notice that on my side of the family it is very incomplete. I wish someone would see to it that the work is done." This George and many other family members have done over the years.[523]

Politics and Government Service

When Utah was first settled, political boundaries were drawn more along the line of Mormon/non-Mormon adherents than the national Republican/Democratic parties. The Mormon party was called the People's Party and the non-Mormon party the Liberal Party. Again as in the past the theocracy and bloc voting of the Mormons were a source of conflict with their non-Mormon neighbors and national political leadership. This situation as much as any was the cause for the rejection of Utah's persistent requests for statehood. As part of the arrangements for statehood, which finally came in 1896, was an agreement to disband the partisan People's Party, with political parties in Utah to be organized along the national format.

The involvement of the immediate King family in political office has already been identified, with Thomas taking the lead. Soon after his arrival in Utah, he was elected for several years to the office of probate judge, Fillmore City Council member, and county representative to the territorial legislature. William became the Millard County constable, and Edwin served as county surveyor for twelve years. Volney was elected Piute County commissioner, prosecuting attorney, secretary of the People's Party, and justice of the peace in both Utah and Wyoming. Delilah later in her life became an ardent Democrat and became the first woman to be elected to public office in Utah as Millard County recorder.[524] She was also very prominent in the women's suffrage movement and helped lead the fight for women's voting rights in Utah.

One insight about the feelings of the people toward the government in that day is expressed by Thomas in a letter to his son William, who was in Hawaii. On April 24, 1870, Thomas expresses his disdain toward pending legislation against plural marriage.

> I suppose you learn through the papers all about the Cullum Bill that is now before Congress for their action. There is no doubt in the minds of the people but what the Bill will become law. The latest news is that the Senate

523 Quoted in M. Lane Warner, *Grass Valley*, 96. The story is told by Esther King Mathews, a daughter, and written by her daughter, Ellen LaRae Mathews.

524 H. Brett Melendy and Benjamin F. Gilbert, The *Governors of California* (Georgetown, California: The Talisman Press), 395.

committee have added several new sections to the Bill as passed by the House and recommends its passage by the senate. The general opinion of the people of this Territory is that if the Bill becomes law our government is nearly ripened in iniquity — consequently her destruction is near. The way the Lord will bring it about we poor mortals are not able to understand. Just at present, the Saints have been fully taught that the time would come when if the constitution of these United States are Saved at all it would be by this people and it truly seems the time has come for the provisions of the aforsaid [aforesaid] Bill violates nearly every section of the constitution.[525]

Volney, on another occasion during the centennial anniversary of the country, expressed some strong feelings toward the government. The family had made a quilt for the occasion, and Volney wrote in his diary, "When we see the quilt may we ask what will the next or 2nd centennial bring about. Will the U.S. Government then be in Vogue for it seems now fast crumbling away. May those viewing the keepsake mark the rise & decline of this great government."[526] Further comments by Kenneth Stampp, a historian on the middle nineteenth century, recorded people's concern about society and corruption:

> The public thought about other things, including corruption — corruption in the Congress, activities of lobbyists, corruption at the state level. Urban crime was a problem. Newspapers were full of accounts of muggings and murders. New York had gang wars. In one Irish ward, the Dead Rabbits and the Bowery Boys fought each other with brickbats and pistols, and several people were killed. The Victorian family was breaking down, parents were not giving children proper guidance, the clergy was not doing its job, judges and juries were too lenient.[527]

These comments are interesting in light of many comments made today about the decline and pending fall of our government. The government has endured an additional hundred and thirty years, yet people today are as pessimistic as they were then.

Following the lead of their parents, several of the grandchildren of Thomas were involved in government service. William King, the son of William, was elected to the United States Congress for two terms: 1896 to 1898, and 1900 to 1902. He was then elected a United States Senator from Utah for twenty-four years between 1916 and 1940. His son, David S., great-grandson to Thomas, was elected to Congress from 1958 to 1962

---

525 Thomas Rice King to William Rice King, April 24, 1870, Volney King papers, Utah State Historical Society.

526 Volney King, "Diaries," 55.

527 Stampp, Kenneth, "On the Brink of War," *US News & World Report,* January 21, 1991, 73.

and from 1964 to 1966.

It might also be noted that from the family of William Rice came several prominent attorneys and public office holders. Besides Senator William King, Samuel King for fifty years was considered one of the most colorful defense figures of the American bar. He had the reputation of having defended more clients accused of murder than any attorney in the United States. Not one of his clients ever received capital punishment.[528]

Another son of William and an attorney was Robert W. King, who served as county attorney in Fillmore and worked for Zion's Securities Corporation. A fourth son, Claude, was also an attorney in Salt Lake City for many years.

William Henry King, a grandson of Thomas Rice King, served in the United States Senate for twenty-four years, from 1916 to 1940. (Courtesy Utah State Historical Society.)

From Delilah's family, the most prominent person was Culbert L. Olson. Culbert's first public office was an election in 1916 to the Utah State Senate, and in 1920 he served as a delegate to the Democratic National Convention. He later moved to California, where he was elected to the California Senate in 1934 and was appointed State Chairman of the California Democratic Party. He was elected governor from 1939 to 1943.[529]

Economic and Political Philosophy

The economic philosophy of the Saints from the beginning of the establishment of the Church has been the philosophy of caring, sharing, and "all things in common." The United Orders established by Brigham Young, in many cases, were based on the principle of a communal or socialist utopia, and President Young's concepts were very close to the growing socialist philosophies of the day. Under the programs of such prominent figures as Karl Marx, Frederick Engels, and others, government, not the individual, was to control all land, factories, and other basic means of

---

528 Salt Lake City, Utah *Deseret News* obituary, August 27, 1943.

529 Melendy and Gilbert, The *Governors of California* , 395.

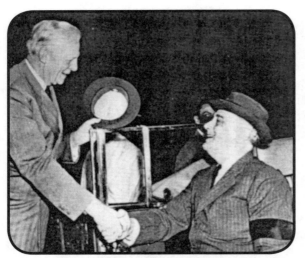

Culbert Olson, left, a grandson of Thomas Rice King, was governor of California from 1940 to 1944. He was a good friend of President Franklin D. Roosevelt, right. (Courtesy Utah State Historical Society.)

production. Socialists strongly opposed social inequality and discrimination, and their goal was to eliminate both the rich and the poor of society. They believed that capitalism was inefficient and wasteful and led to such problems as unemployment, poverty, business cycles, and conflicts between workers and the owners of the means of production.

The most significant difference between socialistic philosophies is how much coercion is necessary, as most socialists believe some coercion is necessary to force people to be good citizens. The most brutal example of this coercion is the Communist movement. Here the means always justified the end, and people were forcibly eliminated if they did not comply with the party line. Democratic socialists, on the other hand, believe more in the democratic process for determining goals and objectives. In contrast, the United Order was built on total individual agency with a belief in God.

With this background it is interesting to see the results of the United Order philosophy and orientation on the next King generation. The Democratic Party became the political party of choice for most of the family. Governor Culbert Olson was described as a "sincere person with a strong sense of social justice."[530] A nonconformist in many respects, he is ranked among the most controversial of California governors. Although a Democrat by party affiliation, "he was a liberal who had been influenced by the political philosophy of evolutionary socialism. Despite his idealism, he was no visionary dreamer but a practical businessman with broad legal experience. To many Olson appeared a threat to the status quo and was branded a radical."[531] He urged the repudiation of imperialism and the policy of laissez-faire. He favored labor reforms, expansion of gov-

---

530 Ibid.

531 Ibid.

ernment ownership, control of public utilities and natural resources, and government regulation of agriculture and industry.

It is interesting to note that Culbert's religious roots gave him a socialistic freethinking attitude toward economic and political issues, yet this attitude also led him away from the religion of his parents. He eventually became active in the United Secularists of America and served as president of its board of trustees.[532]

One of the most prolific writers on economic material was Murray Edwin King, son of Thomas Edwin King. An intellectual socialist, Murray was one of the pioneers of socialism in Utah; and for nearly four decades, he developed a wide reputation as a writer and speaker on political and economic conditions. He described himself as a "constructive socialist," meaning that he believed that capitalism should be abolished, but through the ballot, not through force.[533]

His journalistic skills were noted as the editor in Salt Lake for five years from 1910 to 1915 of the *Intermountain Worker* with a circulation of over 5,000. Later he was the editor of the *American Appeal*, a weekly Socialist paper in Chicago, and the campaign manager for the Farmer-Labor party in Maryland. He also wrote many articles and conducted many campaigns furthering the progress of humanity. He wrote articles for the *New Republic*, *The Nation*, and the *American Guardian*, and was the author of the Utah section of "These United States." A series of the articles in *The Nation* was later published in a two-volume book.[534] Murray personally knew and admired Leo Tolstoy, the Russian author and social reformer.[535]

Murray's own entry into politics in 1912 focused on the Utah congressional race where he received 8,971 votes or 8.7% of the votes cast, finishing a distant third behind the Republican and Democratic candidates. By 1916 his political fortunes waned as he received only 3.4% of the vote.[536] His opposition to the war effort did not endear him to the patriotic fervor sweeping the country.

The socialist movement in Utah in the first few years of the twentieth century was somewhat significant, as socialism appealed to a wide cross-section of Utahns. Utah had socialist organizations in twenty of its twen-

---

532 Ibid., 407

533 John S. McCormick, "Hornets in the Hive: Socialists in Early Twentieth Century Utah," *Utah Historical Quarterly,* no. 3, Summer 1982, 50:234-235.

534 Salt Lake City, Utah *Deseret News* obituary, January 4, 1940.

535 LaRee Fleck, great-granddaughter of Thomas Edwin King, to Larry King, August 8, 1995.

536 Brad E. Hainsworth, "Utah State Elections, 1916-1924," Doctoral Dissertation, University of Utah, 1968, 345-346.

Murray Edwin King, 1874-1940, was another grandson of Thomas Rice King, and one of the most prominent writers for socialism during the early twentieth century. (Courtesy Utah State Historical Society.)

ty-nine counties, with nine socialist publications. Utah was one of only eighteen states in the country to have socialist representation in the legislature. In little Kingston in the 1904 presidential election, 65 percent of the votes went to the socialist presidential candidate, Eugene V. Debs.[537] The *Salt Lake Tribune* reported in 1951 that:

At one time Kingston was a hotbed for socialist leaders. In Kingston as in many other communities throughout the state at the turn of the century, socialism became the popular political theory. It has been said that at one time there were only two heads of families who were not declared socialists in the town of Kingston.[538]

By 1908, interest in socialism began to drop in Kingston, but was still strong. Twenty-four out of the ninety-eight voters or 41 percent went for the Socialist ticket. In Coyote (Antimony), the sister city of the King family, twenty-eight out of eighty votes or 35 percent went to the Socialists. In comparison Orderville, a city to the south of Kingston and also a strong United Order community, gave zero votes to the Socialist Party.[539]

Senator William King (D-Utah) was perhaps the most conservative of the family. Considered a liberal in his day, he would be judged rather orthodox by today's standards. His political mentor was Thomas Jefferson. He was a states' rights man and believed in a small federal bureaucracy, with power and authority vested in the hands of the states. His early experiences with the United Order in Kingston fueled his fiery denunciation of Communism, and his espousal of the free enterprise system. This position later caused him some problems when the Democratic Party swung its support behind the New Deal policies of Franklin D. Roosevelt.

King favored the League of Nations and was adamantly opposed to

---

537 John R. Sillito and John S. McCormick, "Socialist Saints: Mormons and the Socialist Party in Utah, 1900-20," *Dialogue: a Journal of Mormon Thought*, no. 1 Spring 1985, 18:121-131.

538 Irene Elder, "The Kingston Story."

539 "Utah Election Returns," Utah State Archives and Records Service.

the Smoot-Hawley Tariff Act. In both cases he crossed swords with his contemporary, Senator and Apostle Reed Smoot,[540] who helped author the tariff act that bears his name. Senator King's son, Congressman David King, claims that his father disagreed with Senator Smoot on many issues but never spoke ill of him. David also described his father as a great silver-tongued orator and a majestic warrior, who always acted with full propriety.[541] William was also opposed to the Church's policy of having a third political party, the People's Party. He helped convince the brethren in the 1890s to abandon it and have the members divide up along conventional party lines.[542]

Family Traditions and Folklore

Every family has certain traditions and folklore that are passed down from generation to generation, some in written form, some verbally. Even some of the written information may not have been jotted down until several years after the event or the circumstances. Nevertheless these stories have profound significance and immeasurable meaning to members of the family. These stories give identity and worth and create value and connection with past generations, although they cannot always be verified. King family traditions are no exception, and these experiences lend dignity and celebration to their heritage.

One such story is told of George Black, son-in-law to Culbert King, who married Esther Clarinda King. While serving as a missionary in the British Isles in the early 1890s, George came home one night very discouraged to find a gentleman waiting for him at the top of the stairs to his apartment. As George began to engage him in conversation and asked who he was, the man said, "I am John, the apostle to Jesus. I have been preaching the gospel for hundreds of years." They continued in conversation for a while about the gospel; and after giving George several suggestions about how he could be a more successful missionary, John disappeared.[543]

---

540 Reed Smoot was a Mormon apostle and a member of the Republican Party. He served in the Senate eighteen years from 1914 to 1932. The more noted part of his legislation was the passage of the Smoot-Hawley Tariff Act. This act significantly raised tariffs in this country, causing retaliatory measures by other countries to the extent that some economists claim the act was a major contributor to the economic and political strife of the 1930s.

541 Taken from an oral interview of David S. King by Matthew K. Heiss, Kensington, Maryland, October 1990. A copy is in the LDS Church Archives, Church Historical Department.

542 David S. King, to Larry King, January 18, 1995.

543 Warner, *Grass Valley,* 95.

During the last twenty-three years of his life, between 1917 and 1940, George moved to Manti and worked in the temple. He claimed to have received many spiritual blessings, including talking with people who formerly lived here on the earth. Included in this number was Christ himself. George indicated "that when he met Christ on the other side he would know him as one man knows another."[544]

On one occasion Alma King, a grandson of Culbert, related to the writer that his (Alma's) parents, William (the son of Culbert) and his wife Dora, had received their second endowments in the Salt Lake Temple.[545] Dora's unexpected death occurred in 1926 placing the event prior to that date. With such an event occurring to William and Dora, a person would have to wonder if perhaps Thomas Rice, William Rice, Culbert, and others of the family also had this particular blessing pronounced upon them prior to their deaths, either in the St. George or Manti Temple. As the records of these special ordinances are contained in the vault of the First Presidency, verification is not possible.

From the earliest days of the Church until the 1894, families were frequently sealed to leading Church brethren rather than linking child to parent as it is done today. The practice was known as the Law of Adoption and grew out of the people's fear that perhaps their fathers or grandfathers had somehow rejected the gospel. They also saw a daunting challenge involved in redeeming all of one's kindred dead before the millennial reign, but Brigham Young called it a "schoolmaster to bring [the children of men] back into the covenant of the Priesthood."[546] In conformity with this practice, many of the Kings went to the Manti Temple July 16-18, 1890, and had the family sealed to Thomas Rice and Matilda. Then Thomas was sealed to his father, Thomas. Thomas in turn and several of the members of the King and Hyde families were adopted into the Prophet Joseph Smith's family. At the same time, members of the Olson family were adopted into Thomas Rice King's family.

Another interesting story is about Josephine Henry, wife of William Rice King, and can be found in the Utah State Historical Society Library. There are three handwritten letters by an Edwin Mace to President Anthony W. Ivins, an LDS apostle and later a member of the First Presidency. The Mace family settled in Fillmore in 1852. Edwin was born in Febru-

---

544 Ibid., p. 96.

545 Within Mormon theology there is an obscure doctrine that if a person proves his faithfulness beyond measure, his\her salvation can be assured through a special temple ordinance. This ordinance is beyond the normal endowment. It becomes a second endowment and is performed by invitation from the President of the Church.

546 Susan Staker, ed., *Waiting for World's End: The Diaries of Wilford Woodruff* (Salt Lake City, Utah: Signature Books, 1993) 108.

ary 1858 and grew up in and around the King and Henry families. One letter is dated October 27, 1925; the second is not dated; and the third is dated November, 1928.[547] In these letters, Mace states that his family knew the Prophet Joseph Smith, and both the King and Henry families well. Through his family and other family acquaintances it was known that Josephine Henry (King) was the daughter of Joseph Smith and was so named for him. Edwin goes on to say, "I had heard my father say or intimate that she [Josephine] was a daughter of the said prophet, or that Andrew Henry's wife had been married to Joseph the Prophet." He further states: "I don't think . . . theres more than a half dozen who knows it." In his second letter, he states: "Andrew was a large heavy set man with red hair, a heavy red beard, freckle face uncouth in his manners etc. who I would take to be partly Irish and not even a relative to Josephine."[548] The latter statement implied that Josephine did not physically resemble the man commonly accepted as her father.

These are intriguing comments. There is much evidence now available that Joseph Smith not only married several single or widowed women as plural wives, but also married women who were already married and living with their husbands. Supposedly his relationship with these women was more than a simply "a spiritual wife" system; they became his wives in every sense of the word.[549]

In 1843 Andrew was serving a mission in Ireland where he met and married his wife, Margaret Creighton. Josephine's birth occurred in Nauvoo July 8, 1844. A partial chronology of Andrew's life in the following chart might help sort out these statements to a small degree, yet there is much confusion over the issue. There is no information available on when Andrew and Margaret left England or when they arrived in Nauvoo.[550] Based on Church records, three ships left England between August 23, 1843 and early 1844 with Mormon emigrants. The third car-

---

547 These letters are found in the Utah State Historical Society in the "Edwin Mace Letter file." It appears these letters were given to the library by Stanley S. Ivins, son of Anthony W. Ivins.

548 Ibid.

549 For an in-depth discussion on this topic, see Lawrence Foster, *Religion and Sexuality* (Chicago, Illinois: University of Illinois Press, 1984); Richard S. Van Wagoner, *Mormon Polygamy* (Salt Lake City, Utah: Signature Books, 1986); B. Carmon Hardy, *Solemn Covenant* (Chicago, Illinois: University of Illinois Press, 1992); Robert Bruce Flanders, *Nauvoo, Kingdom on the Mississippi* (Chicago, Illinois: University of Illinois Press, 1975); D. Michael Quinn, *The Mormon Hierarchy, Origins of Power* (Salt Lake City, Utah: Signature Books, 1994); Fawn Brodie, *No Man Knows My History* (New York: Alfred A. Knopf, 1982); and Todd Compton, *In Sacred Loneliness: The Plural Wives of Joseph Smith* (Salt Lake City, Utah: Signature Books, 1997).

550 Hinckley, Parnell, Arranger, *The Henrys and the Kings*, 57-58.

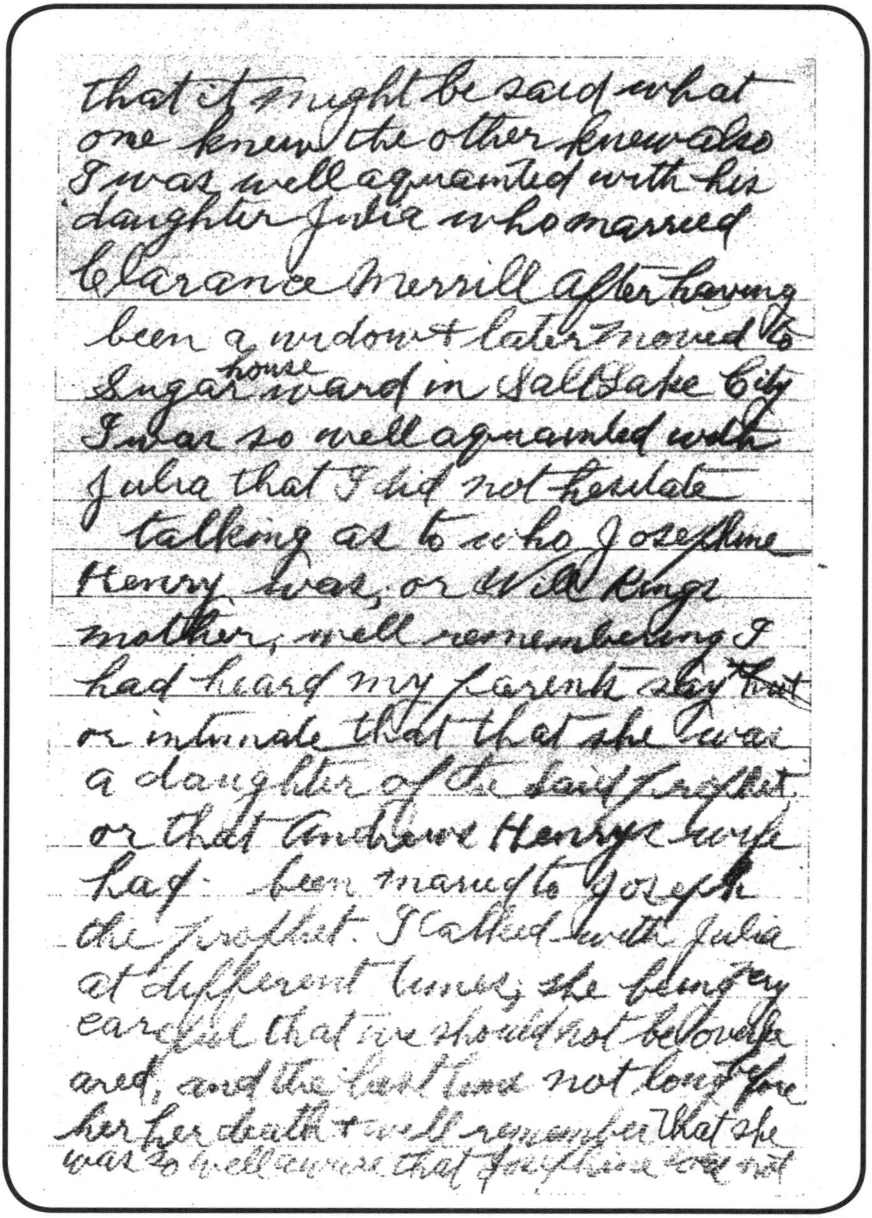

that it might be said what
one knew the other knew also
I was well aquainted with his
daughter Julia who married
Clarance Merrill after having
been a widow + later moved to
Sugar house ward in Salt Lake City
I was so well aquainted with
Julia that I did not hesitate
talking as to who Josephine
Henry was, or W A Kings
mother, well remembering I
had heard my parents say that
or intimate that that she was
a daughter of the said prophet
or that Andrews Henrys wife
had been marrid to Joseph
the prophet. I talked with Julia
at different times; she being very
careful that we should not be overheard, and the last time not long before
her her death + well remember that she
was so well aware that Josephine was not

A copy of the second page of a letter dated October 27, 1925 by Edwin Mace, who claimed that Josephine Henry (King) was the biological daughter of the Prophet Joseph Smith. This is one of three letters making this claim. (Edwin Mace Letter File, Utah State Historical Society.)

rying a group of Irish Saints:[551]

From these dates, it would appear to have been improbable for Josephine to have been conceived in Nauvoo and born there July 1844.[552] For this to have occurred, Andrew and Margaret would had to have reached Nauvoo by September or perhaps October 1843, but the earliest possible ship arriving in Nauvoo after Andrew's latest journal entry in Ireland, is November 11, 1843. The ship first landed in New Orleans on October 27, 1843 and the dating difference is the time the passengers spent traveling up the Mississippi. The ship's manifest records 280 Mormon immigrants on board, but there are only 188 people accounted for. This leaves nearly a hundred people whose names have not been discovered by historians.

A second thought that might be considered is the changing of the actual birthday of Josephine to create an illusion. This may sound far fetched, but stranger things happened in Nauvoo to maintain the confidentiality of Joseph's plural marriages. Along with this idea is the possibility of some diary entries may have been changed. The diary we have to work from is not the original, but a transcription. Furthermore, there are no known ship passenger records for the Henrys, there are no records confirming their marriage in Ireland in May 1843, and there are no known records in the LDS Church Archives identifying Andrew as a missionary in Ireland. The only record that can be found is that, in January 1846, Andrew and Margaret were sealed in the Nauvoo Temple.

To further muddy the waters there are two cryptic comments by people that could lend some credibility to Mace's allegations. In an undated love letter set in rhythmic style and written by Andrew to Margaret he states, although while he goes to preach the gospel, he will later return and claim Margaret as his bride:

Then while I go to spread the truth in regions far and wide
Oh let your prayers for me ascend let not me be denied
Nor cease to love till I return and claim thee as my bride

Following the letter and over the page he writes on the paper how oceans separate them, implying that he and Margaret are continents apart not just in the British Isles. Perhaps Margaret is in Nauvoo while Andrew is in the British Isles.

---

551 See "Manuscript History of the British Mission," LDS Church Historical Department Archives under respective dates.

552 Hinckley, Parnell, Arranger, *The Henrys and the Kings.* This book contains a transcribed copy of Andrew's missionary diary. The last entry where he talks about leaving Ireland and arriving in Liverpool was not entered until eight years later on November 16, 1851.

Partial Chronology of Andrew Henry's Life

Abt.	1811	Born in Sligo, Ireland.
	1830	Moved to Canada.
	1833	Moved to New York.
	1837	Joined the LDS Church.
	1838	Moved to Nauvoo, Illinois.
Nov 28, 1840		Andrew leaves Nauvoo for a mission to Ireland
Dec 25, 1841		Arrived in New York after walking and preaching through the frontier of Illinois, Indiana, Kentucky, and Ohio.
Jul 21, 1842		Leaves New York for England.
Aug 9, 1842		Arrives in England and later goes on to Ireland where he meets the Creighton family near Belfast, Ireland.
May 26, 1843		Marries Margaret Creighton.
Aug 23, 1843		Last entry in his diary. Returns to Liverpool and prepares to return home.
Jun 8, 1844		Josephine born in Nauvoo

Ships Departing From Ireland

Ship	Date of Departure	Date of New Orleans Arrival
Metoka	September 5, 1843	October 27, 1843
Champion	October 21, 1843	December 6, 1843
Fanny	January 23, 1844	March 7, 1844

Margaret tho I'm severed from thee
And oceans wave between us roar
Remembrance clings to thee most fondly
Gladly would I return once more[553]

Another note in a short history of Margaret is a copy of a letter written by Adelia R. Robison whose mother was a good friend of Margaret's and a first cousin through her husband, William. In her letter she states that, as a young lady, she was with her mother, Elizabeth, visiting Margaret who was with her grandson, Samuel King. Samuel is referred to as Sammie.

And on this day I remember so well. As they were standing on the north side of the house between the gate, which was a picket gate, and house, she said, "Well, Lizzie,!" as she was rubbing the little boy's golden head. "Oh, they do not know who you are," addressing her, and looking at the child. "But Lizzie, some day I'll tell you something." [554]

---

553 Andrew Henry letter, undated, to Margaret Creighton. The original is in the possession of James King, Salt Lake City. A typescript copy is in my possession.

554 Hinckley, Parnell, *The Henrys and the Kings*, 66-67. This letter was written in October 1959 when Adelia was eighty-five years old.

Could Margaret be telling Adelia's mother that Samuel is a grandson of Joseph? A reader could read just about any message into these comments, but the bottom line is, historians do not know all the facts and the issue is simply reduced to individual speculation. It could be that Margaret was only sealed to the Prophet making Josephine his daughter through temple covenant rather than biologically. Perhaps future records and technological advancement will bring a conclusion. Nevertheless, the possibilities are interesting.

Epilogue

Most histories are written about great national leaders or events affecting the lives of nations or societies at large. Kings, rulers, and presidents are the focal point together with wars, economic calamities, societal struggles, and great conquests. Within this context, history has always belonged to the victor. Little is said about the vanquished.

This history of Thomas Rice and Matilda King and their family is about neither of the above, but about common and ordinary people; people who lived life, built homes, raised families, and devoted their lives to a higher purpose. They were people who lived the American dream and fought for the right to enjoy their religious liberty. While they enjoyed a close personal relationship with several church leaders, such as President Brigham Young and Apostles Francis M. Lyman and Joseph F. Smith, they were never really admitted into the inner circles of Church dominion and administration. They came out of obscurity and in their lifetimes became respected community and church leaders at the local level. Now their names are remembered only by a handful of immediate family members and by the fact that a small southern Utah community still bears the name of Kingston.

As part of the greater global Mormon philosophy and by today's standards, they were a peculiar people who tried to remove themselves from the larger pluralistic society of their time. They believed in a special mission to warn society of impending calamities, and they possessed a religious zeal and a fervent conviction in the imminent return of Christ and the inauguration of the Millennium. They were also a curious and eccentric people. The belief that their political, economic, and social systems would prevail in their lifetimes to encompass the world failed, and they became like their forefathers, Israel of old, a conquered community. They became integrated into the greater American society, retaining only a few peculiar characteristics identifiable in such features as the Word of Wisdom, morality, and family values. Even these have become blurred in large measure as secular and religious societies have embraced many tenets of the King family beliefs.

As a conquered people, their posterity along with their contemporaries in large measure have "out-Victorianed" the Victorians, "out-Republicaned" the Republicans and have become even more ardent defenders of laissez-faire capitalism than most capitalists. The federal government is no longer an enigma of repression but an institution to be defended, supported, and exonerated. Rather than treating the larger society as evil and corrupt, the greatest expense and effort is spent in the competitive game of public relations.

Many of the Kings lived long enough to see the beginning of a major paradigm shift in Church focus, beliefs and practices; and with these changes, the social, political, economic and religious climate also changed. In many instances the persecuted have become the persecutors, and fundamentalism has given way to orthodoxy. The so-called doctrinal purity and absolutes of a closed-ended, well-defined religion of today would probably not be recognizable to Thomas and Matilda.

On a broad perspective through the examples and illustrations of this history, perhaps the question could be asked: What are the cycles and lessons of history still trying to teach us about life and people, and their interaction with Deity? As a family and as a people what are we to learn by this history other than it is nice to know?

Appendix 1

(Wills, Inventory of Assets, and Other Estate Documents)

In colonial times (pre-Revolutionary War) monetary units were the English pound, shilling and pence. A pound (£) was equivalent to 20 shillings (s), and a shilling was equal to 12 pence (p).

Edmund Rice

(Edmund died intestate, meaning he did not have a will)

INVENTORY dated 15 May 1663, exhibited 16 June 1663[555]

An Inventory of the estate of Mr. Edmund Rice of Marlbourough in the County of Midlesex deceased of houseing lands chattells moveables and debts, taken May 15th (1663.)

	£ s p
Imprimis one dwelling house one barne with all out houseing lands both arrable lands waste lands meadows with all improvement	
upon the premises prized at	170.00.00
Item one horse one mare one colt	26.00.00
Item foure oxen	26.10.00
Item one bull	04.00.00
Item Three heifers	11.10.00
Item eight kowes and six Calves	44.00.00
Item foure yearlings	08.00.00
Item in swine	<u>11.16.00</u>
	131.16.00

---

555 Original Document: Middlesex Probate File 18696. 17th-Century copy in Middlesex Probate Records 2:172-75. A transcribed copy is found in Robert H. Rodgers, *Middlesex County in the Colony of the Massachusetts Bay in New England, Records of Probate and Administration, March 1660/61 - December 1670,* The New England Historic Genealogical Society, Boston 2001, 146-150.

<u>In the parlour</u>

Item one Cubbard three Joyned Chayres five boxes one framed table with two leaves one Joyned forme three Joyned stooles prized	02.12.00
Item foure Cushins two Carpetts three two Cradle coverlitts	02.00.00
Item his Bookes	01.00.00
Item six table Cloathes	01.10.00
Item one dousen and a halfe of napkins two Cubbard Clothes two towells	00.18.00
Item Two Cubbard clothes more	00.04.00
Item six payer of course sheets	05.10.00
Item Three fine sheets	01.10.00
Item Three payer more sheets	01.10.00
Item Three payer of course pillow beers	00.16.00
Item Three foure payer fine pillow beers	01.06.08
Item Three payer of andirons one payer tonges	01.13.00
Item his wearing apparrell	12.14.00
Item in Cotten yarne	01.06.00
Item one feather bed and furniture	09.00.00

<u>In the litle parlour:</u>

Item Three Trunckes	00.12.00
Item foure Chests and one boxe	01.03.00
Item one litle Table one forme a cradle	00.10.00
Item one feather bed with all furniture	<u>08.00.00</u>
	53.14.08

<u>In the upper Chambers</u>

Item flocke bed pillow rugg Two blanckets	03.00.00
Item one straw bed blanckets Two flocke boulsters	02.05.00
Item one small feather bed	01.06.08
Item in cotton yarne	
	<u>01.00.00</u>
	07.11.08

<u>In the hall</u>

Item in peuter dishes spoones and other vessells one silver spoone	05.04.08
Item Three brass ketles two iron potts one iron skellet one iron ketle	03.00.00

Item one warming pan one frying pan one morter two smoothing irons one gridiron one Cleaver two trammells	01.06.00
Item two spitts one iron beame foure bellows	00.18.00
Item one table frame one muskitt	00.16.00
Item for cart irons plow irons three Chaynes saws betle rings wedges axes yokes with irons	05.00.00
It[em] Three acrs of wheat spwne	04.10.00
It[em] one basket one peice Cotton cloth Two window Curtaynes	00.11.00
It[em] sithes sickels goughes Fetters shave augurs spade	01.00.00
It[em] a coule Churne Barrells grinding stone hogsheads and other lumber	01.10.00
	23.15.08

his Debts

It[em] due by bill from Matthew Rice	22.00.00
It[em] due by bill from William Browne and Benjamin Rice	70.00.00
Item due by bill from Benjamin Crane	11.00.00
Item due by bill from John How	03.01.08
Item due by bill from Robert Wilson	02.18.00
Item due by bill from Thomas Rice	16.00.00
Item due by bill from Jonathan and Samell Hide	02.10.00
Item due by bill from Thomas Brigham	30.00.00
	177.09.08

the totall	£566.00.07

William Warde
Thomas King
John Woods John Stone

(added in margin) Item in Severall things appering since the first apprizall at the house of Benjamin Rice
one Iron pot and hokes trammell two trevitts two old caske
one halfe bushell one old straw bed and blanketts prized at £01.05.00

[Endorsement] Attested on oath by Mercy Rice administratrex. June. 16. 63. at Charlstowne County Court.

PROPOSAL FOR DIVISION dated 16 June 1663 (original document: Middlesex Court Files, HLS #2299; Busiel p.331, citing Box 1662-1663]

Proposall for setling the estate of Edm: Rice, deceased.

Vizt.   That the widow administer and pay all his debts, and to the Eight Elder Children[556] of the said Edm: Rice, to the eldest sonne forty pounds, and to the other 20, apeece and to the two younger Children[557] of the sd Ed: Rice, had by the sd widow 10, a peece when they come of age or at their mariage, and that the sd widow resigne up her right in all lands sold by the sd Edm: to any person dureing their mariage, or to the sonnes of the sd Edm: provided all such debts as are due from any of the sd Children for Land sold, or that they stood engaged to their father for the payment of, had he lived whether by word or writeing shall be in part of their said twenty pounds a peece. All which being performed by the sd widow, the whole estate whereof the sd Edm: Rice died seized, vizt. Houses, lands, debts, goods and chattells, cattell, and what ever else to be and remayne to the said widow, Mercy Rice and to Her Heyres and assignes forever.
16.4.63 This proposall is consented unto by us. her marke
Mercy [mark] Rice
Henry Rice

COURT RECORD June 1663 *[Middlesex Court Records 1:244; Pulsifer 1:288]*

Mercy the Relict of Edm: Rice, who died intestate, at Marlbury appearing in Court, is granted power of Administration on the estate whereof he died seized, or was to him due or apperteineing, and exhibited an Inventary thereof in Court, to which shee attested on oath, and Henry Rice, the Eldest sonne of the sd Edm: Rice, appearing with Her in Court, presented a proposall for the setling of the divission of the said estate, which is on file with the Records of this Court, and is allowed and approved of by the Court, and by them confirmed, in case that no just ground be given by any the other children for the reversing therof, at the next Court of this County.

(At a County Court held at Charles-Towne June 16. 1663)
COURT RECORD October 1663 *[Middlesex Court Records 1:24849; Pulsifer 1:294]*

---

556 Henry, Edward, Thomas, Lyda, Matthew, Samuel, Joseph and Benjamin.

557 Ruth and Lydia by his second marriage to Mercy Hurd.

Mercy Rice relict widow of Edm: Rice, deced, appearing in Court presented her request, that the order of the last Court, for the divission of her Husbands estate, so farr as it referrs to Benjamin Rice, may be suspended, untill there may be a clearing up, and right understanding of what Hee received of his father as a part of his portion, or is otherwise justly indebted to that estate, pleading that otherwise both Her selfe, and Her children by the sd Rice, deced, would be inevitably injured. The Court on hearing of her complaynt, ordered that the order of the last Court for divission of the said estate, soe farr as it referrs to Benjaminn Rice his proportion thereby granted, be suspended untill their may be a full hearing of the case from both partyes therein concerned.

(At a County Court held at Cambridge October 6th 1663)

BOND FOR ADMINISTRATION DE BONIS NON, 12 April 1714 *(original document: Middlesex Probate File 186961*

Mathew Rice and Isaac Rice, both of Sudbury, ... yeomen, at the petition of the sd Mathew *[are granted administration]* to the estate yet unadministered of Edmund Rice, sometime of Marlborough... *[and they give bond in the amount of £200, signed by Mathew Rice (mark) and Isaac Rice, dated]* twelveth Aprill 1714.

ADDITIONAL INVENTORY dated 27 April 1714, exhibited 7 July 1714 (original document: Middlesex Probate File 186961

Sudbury April 27th. 1714
A True Inventory of some Lands in sd. Sudbury Late Laid out to the Right of Mr. Edmund Rice formerly of said Sudbury Decd. with the Remainder of his rights in Common in sd. Sudbury, Not before Inventoried or disposed of. Praised at sd. Sudbury the Day and year above written at the Joynt Desire and Request of Mr. Mathew Rice and Isaac Rice Adm[inistra]tors. and the Rest of the relations Int[erested] in sd Estate. By us the Subscribers whose Names are under written. as followeth:

Viz It[em] 42 acres and 3 q[uar]ters in Haynes his Neck	40-00-00
It[em] 9 acres and 124 Rods Near the west side of Goodmans hill	11-00-00
It[em] 32 acres and 3 qters at the Allowanc	26-00-00
It[em] 10 acres at Ashen Swamp by Mr. Graveses	18-00-00
It[em] Two 3ds of 42 acres and 3 qters already Granted, with the Right in Common. proportionably	13-03-04
totall	£108-03-04

Fra. Fullam]
William Jenison] Apraisers,
Samuel Graves]

[Endorsement] Exhibited] by Issac Rice Adm[inistrato]r and upon oath at Camb. 7[th] July 1714

RECEIPT OF HEIRS dated and acknowledged 27 March 1716, exhibited 6 June 1716 [558] (original document: Middlesex Probate File 186961

Know All men by these presents that we the subscribers whose Names are under written. Children and Grand Children of Mr. Edman Rice some time of Sudbery in the County of Middelsex in his Majesties Provenc of the Massachusetts Bay in new England But Late of Marlbrow in the County and Provence aforsaide yeoman Deseased Have Recd of Mr. Matthew Rice and Mr. Isaac Rice Both of said Sudbery freehoulders and Administrators of the Estate or part of the Estate of the said Edman Rice Each and Every of our full parts and proportions of the saide Estate both Reall and personall in full and in full Discharge of the said Matthew Rice and Isaac Rice there heirs Executors Administrators for Ever. we say Recd by us and by Each and Every of us for our selves and our Heirs Respectively our Justt and full and Equell proportions of all the Estate of the saide Edman Rice in new England where upon the saide Matthew Rice and Isaac Rice Did take burden of Administration in full and In full discharg of the sd Estate and Administered. Further more we the above named would doe Acknowledg that we have Recd the sum of thirteen pounds and Eleven shillings which being in full upon the Accompt of the above written premises for Every Family Conscerned in the premises we likewise Acknowledg our selves fully Impowered to Actt for our fathers Families upon the accountt of the above said premises: And doe binde our selves and Each of our Heirs Excecutors Administrators And Assignes and Every of them In the full and Justt sum of Twenty seven pounds Each of us to pay back to the saide Administrators what soe Ever shall be recovered by any person or persons Justly Laying Clame to any partt or persell of the above saide premises. In wittnes whereof we have here unto sett our hands and seale this twenty seventh day of March in the yeare of our Lord God one thousand seven Hundred and sixteen and in the second yeare of His Majesties Reigne
Jonathan Rice

---

558 At this date, seven of eight (except for Matthew) of Edmund's older children are also deceased. The two girls by Mercy Hurd are also alive.

Signed Sealed and Dilivered   John Rice
In the presents of us:/   Tho. Drury
      John Milo   Peter Haynes
      Samuel Moore   Thomas Brintntnal [sic]
      John Woodward   attorne for Gershom Rice and James
Rice

                         Phineas Rice
                         Ebenezer Rice

[Endorsements] Middlesex:/   The persons within named viz:/ Jonathan Rice: John Rice Tho Drury Peter Haines Tho Brinton Phinnius Rice Ebenezer Rice: personally appered before me The Subscriber and Acknowledged the within written Instrement to be there volentary Actt and Deed March the *27.1716.*   HopestiII Browne Justis of peac

Camb. June *6. 1716.* Isaac Rice one of the Administrators to the Estate of Edmund Rice etc. the within mentioned personally appearing before me, Exhibited the within written Instrument into This Court of Probate, and I allow the Acknowledgment of it before justice Brown and order it to be registred.
                    Fra[ncis] Foxcroft Jud Prob for Midd.

Will of Thomas King

(The information below has been reformatted and some changes in spelling have been made for easier reading.)

Made January 12, 1676
Proved March 12, 1676, East Cambridge, Massachusetts
Probate Records, Vol. 5, pages 22-23-24-25-26 & 27 [559]

It having pleased God to cast me, Thomas King, of Marlborough, upon the bed of sickness and being weak, yet in perfect understanding, considering that God and his providence and dispensation towards me at this time, calls for me to set my house in order, and to dispose of the estate that God in his mercy hath given me, to my beloved wife, children and relatives.

I give and bequeath to my beloved wife Bridget King during her life my dwelling house, barns, orchards, closes and pastures all that is of my house and lot, from the highway on the west, and unto my great fence and half meadow called by the name of Pod Meadow, with the rights and privileges belonging thereto. It is also my will that my beloved wife should enjoy peaceably all the land and meadow called by the name of Cole Hole, lying in Sudbury's New Grant, and to have it forever to her own disposing at her own will and pleasure farther whereas there was an agreement made before marriage of me the said Thomas King and Bridget my wife, bearing date of December 17, 1655 Signifying that if I the said Thomas King should die first, and leave my wife Bridget King a widow, that I should leave unto my beloved wife the full sum of four score and twelve pounds, and upon account of the same my will is that my dear wife should have four oxen of mine, and three cows and a heifer and two mares and a musket and an iron bar.

Also I give and bequeath unto my son Peter King all my lands and meadows indisposed of, being in Sudbury, also my butchers tools and my fowling piece. Also I give and bequeath unto my son William. Kerley and Anna my daughter, my second divisions of lands lying in Marlborough and all my meadow lying in Rocky Meadow. Also I do give and bequeath unto my son Nathaniel Jocelin and Sarah my daughter, all the rest of my hay lott, being eastward of that which I have given to my beloved wife, and half my meadow in Pod meadow, and half my meadow in Angelico Meadow and after my wife decease to have my now dwelling house, and

---

559 Information taken from King, "A Genealogy of the Family of Rice or King Alias Rice," 2-4.

all my house lot, and all my first divisions of meadow excepting Rocky meadow, also I give and bequeath unto Thomas Rice, Joshua Rice, my three grand children all my third divisions of land lying in Marlborough, and all my second division of meadow, both land and meadow to be equally divided among them. Also I do give and bequeath unto Anna Kerley, Mary Rice and Sarah Jocelin, my three daughters all my household stuff which shall appear to be mine before marriage to my wife Bridget King, and all the rest of my household goods it is my will my wife Bridget King should have it upon acct. of the four score and twelve pounds. Further I Thomas King have made my son Peter King Executor of this last will and testament. Further I do give and bequeath unto my son Peter King and my son John Brigham, my two horses that are in the woods to be equally divided between them. Also, before Richard Nuton and John Maynard, I Thomas King do acknowledge this to be my last will and testament as witness my hand.

THOMAS KING

This signed in the presence of Richard Nuton (His Mark) John Maynard. Marlborough the March 12, 1676

Know all men by these presents that whereas their is an agreement bearing date of December 17, 1655 between me Thomas King and Bridget Davis, being now my beloved wife, that the aforesaid Bridget should have full power at her own will and pleasure to dispose of the house and all the lands and town right thereto any way appertaining and to this land before specified was laid out since our first agreement and since our marriage together, yet I the said Thomas King do hereby acknowledge that the land and meadow above specified called by the name of Cole Hole, lying in Sudbury's new grants does properly and particularly belong unto my beloved Bridget King, and she to have full power at her own will and pleasure to dispose of it by virtue of that agreement made between us bearing date of December 1655. And further I the above said Thomas King do will and order that my beloved wife Bridget King should peaceably and quietly enjoy the lands and meadows hereby above mentioned which amounts to an hundred and thirty, to have and to hold forever without any molestation from heirs, executors, administrators, or assign forever or any of their estates. In witness hereunto - I have set my hand January 12, 1675-6.

THOMAS KING

This signed in the presence of us,
Richard Newton (His Mark)
John Maynard
Taken upon oath in court at Charlestown April 20, 1676 by Richard New-
ton and John Mayard as attest, Thomas Danforth R.

The date of January 15, 1676. This is an addition to this my will that
ye money I have which amounts to the sum of four pounds or thereabouts,
and this money besides what is expended on my burial. I do freely give
and bequeath it unto my beloved wife Bridget King, or forty shillings
of the above specified sum of money. And father it is my will and order
that my beloved wife Bridget King should have her four score and twelve
pounds as will appear by my agreement before her marriage, and if that,
that is before mentioned in this my will, upon the account of making up
that sum be not enough it shall be made up to her out of my proper estate,
as corne, and provisions, and other things indisposed of, and the rest I give
and bequeath unto my son Peter King Executor of this my last will and
testament, and this I Thomas King do own to be my will as an addition to
the same as witness my hand.

Thomas King
Witnessed
Richard Newton
(His Mark)
John. Maynard

The inventory of the goods and chattels of Thomas King of Marlborough
lately deceased taken by Deacon William Ward and Lt. Rudduck January
24, 1676.

	£ s p
House and Lands at Marlborough	200.00.00
Lands at Sudbury	60.00.00
Sub Total Real Estate	260.00.00
4 Oxen	18.00.00
3 Cows	15.00.00
2 Mares	4.00.00
Cart plow chyne, 2 yokes staple ring hooks,	
1 pr cart rope cap & pin	3.08.00
Sow & 5 pigs	2.05.00

Im Iron things	1.03.00
2 bedsteads, 2 tables, 2 barrels, 2 meals throughs meals	
seive and 4 charges	3.10.00
4 barrels of beef	8.00.00
1 brass kettle	12.00
Hay and stacks in the barn	3.00.00
Bed and blankets and sheet	10.00
An iron bar	10.00
A match lock musket	16.00
9 sheets and 5 pillow beers	4.06.00
Im pewter dishes, trays and trenches	2.00.00
12 lbs. flax	12.00
Flax yarn	8.00
A linen wallett	2.00
A pilion	3.00
5 lbs. yarn	10.00
1m bacon	3.00.00
20 bushels Indian corn	3.00.00
7 bushels wheat	2.02.00
6 bushels rye	1.04.00
4 bushels barley	16.00
Fowling piece, muskett and bandleers and sword	1.14.00
A saddle	14.00
2 horses	6.00.00
Im household goods bequeathed to his three daughteres	12.00.00
Im money	4.00.00
Due from Bartholomieu Cheavers	1.00.00
Samuel how of Sudbury Dr. to Bill	8.10.00
Sub Total Personal Property	123.00.00
Total	£383.00.00

Wm. Ward
John Rudduck
Taken upon oath in court at Charleston April 4, 1676 by Peter King Executor of the last will of ye above named Thomas King deceased as attest Thomas Danforth R. Probate Records Vol. 5, page 22,23,24, 25,26,27.

Estate Settlement Summary

Bridget (Widow)
    Dwelling house and lot including barns, orchards,
        closes and Pastures (Sudbury 7 acres upland)
    Half meadow called Pod Meadow
    Land and meadow called Cole Hill in Sudbury's
        New Grant

92 Pounds in Money less value of household items acquired after marriage.	£92.00.00
4 oxen	18.00.00
3 cows and a heifer	15.00.00
2 mares	2.00.00
A musket	
Iron bar	10.00

Peter
    All lands and meadows indisposed of in Sudbury
    Butcher tools and fowiling piece

1/2 interest in two horses.	3.00.00

William Kerley (Anna)
    Second division of land in Marlborough and all
        meadow in Rocky Meadow.
    1/3 of house hold items before marriage to Bridget.
Nathaniel Jocelin (Sarah)
    Rest of Hay lot eastward of lot given to Bridget.
    Second half of Pot Meadow and half of the meadow
        in Angelico Meadow.
    1/3 of house hold items before marriage to Bridget.
Thomas Rice (Mary)
    1/3 of house hold items before marriage to Bridget.
Joshua Rice
John Brigham (Stepson)

1/2 interest in two horses	3.00.00

The Will of Samuel Rice

made Feb. 10th 1684 (who died 25th Feb. 1685)
Proved April 7th, 1685 [560]

Gave to his wife Sarah, to sons Joshua and Edmund, to daughters Elizabeth (Haynes), Hannah Hubbard, Ester Hubbard, to my son Samuel Rice whom I have given to my brother and sister King for their own. The sons Edward and Joseph, and to daughters Mary and Abigail Rice under 18 years of age.

His brothers Edward and Joseph Rice were overseers of his will.

Inventory 349 pounds 2 shillings 6 pence.

March 6, 1685.

560 Ibid., 8.

Will of Peter King

of Sudbury, Mass. Middlesex County
Probate Records at East Cambridge
no 9421 made 7th Feb. 1697. Proved 1704.[561]

This is to signify that I, Peter King of Sudbury in the County of Middlesex in the Massachusetts Province in New England. Being by the sovereign providence of God in a weak condition thru illness that hath seized upon me, and being convinced of my frailty and mortality. As also not knowing how soon the Lord may remove me out of this world by death, for not withstanding apprehending the my great duty to settle my outward concerns in this world. Having through mercy my reasons and understanding the laboring under boidly indisposition, I ye above said Peter King do now make, constitute, and ordain this my last will and testament, revoking and unnuling all other wills by me made, and this and this only to be my last will and testament as followeth. In the first place I resign up my spirit unto my dear Lord and Savior Jesus Christ, and my body to be decently buried, and as for my worldly estate God bath blest me with, (with all my debts and personal charges being payed) I do order and of in manner and form following:

In the first place I give and bequeath unto my well and beloved adopted son and heir, Samuel King alias Rice, the, whole and all meadows, Orchards, Cattle, movables and immovables. The whole and all whatsoever to be to him and his forever. As also my mind and will that my dearly beloved wife Sarah King, out of my estate as above designaged, be carefully, comfortable and constantly with all tenderness, helped, relieved and supplied during her life. The whole I doubt not but will be performed by my adopted son and heir. Also I will and bequeath unto my pastor James Sherman forty shillings as gift of my love to him, to be paid by my exacutor.

Besides my mind and will is that my widows wearing clothing, after her decease, be given to Gemima Hubbard. That is according to the decission of my said adopted son and his wife.

Finally this my last will and testament is viz. That if my adopted son and heir be cut off by death with all issue of children from him, and none left but his wife only. Then she during her widowhood and natural life to have the benefit increase and profit of said estate, and after her desease, this my last will is estate, as to every part and parcel of it I give and be-

---

561 Ibid., 9-10.

queath unto my well and beloved kinsman Thomas Rice of Marlboro, to him his heirs forever.

Also besides I will and bequeath unto all the children of my three sisters (that is immesiate children not grand children) the sume of eight or six shillings accordingly to be payed by my executors. Lastly I make and constitute my well and beloved adopted son Samuel King alias Rice to be sole executor of this my last will and testament, as also declaring this to be my last will and testament.

This seventh day of February, One thousand six hundred and ninty seveneight, and in the presence of his Magestry's Reign, signed.

s/ Peter King

James Sherman
Zacheriah Mainard
Joseph Moore
Amount of Inventory £17,221.05.00

Samuel King Alias Rice
(Samuel died intestate, meaning he did not have a will)

(The information below has been reformatted and some changes in spelling have been made for easier reading.)

An inventory taken of the Estate of both Real and Personal of Lieutenant Samuel King alias Rice, late of Sudbury of the County of Middlesex, Gentlemen, who deceased on March 4, 1713 as the said estate was show to us and appraised by us the subscribers. [562]

	£ s p
In premise, the housing, homestead, uplands, and meadows about in with rights common and late divisions	505.00.00
One house and lot at Brookfield with town rights	30.00.00
Sixty eight acres of land in the Gulf Neck Sudbury	63.00.00
Sub Total Real Estate	598.00.00
Four oxen and six cows	34.00.00
One heifer	5.10.00
Eighteen sheep	5.05.00
Four swine, two shoats	2.04.00
His library of books and apparel and arms	16.10.00
Husbandry tools of all sorts, as carts, plows	3.11.06
One feather bed, bolsters, pillows, curtains & bedding	10.00.00
One feather bed and bedding there unto belong	5.00.00
Two beds and bedding there unto belonging	7.00.00
Six pairs of sheets	1.00.00
Fifteen napkins, three table cloths & child's bed linen	3.00.00
Two children's blankets	1.00.00
Three tables and one chest	2.00.00
Glass case and iron wear in the house	2.08.00
Brass kettle and other brass in the house	2.19.00
Pewter platters and plates and other pewter	2.09.00
Earthen wear	4.04
Linen yarn and flax	13.06
Wool, two spinning wheels and cards	1.10.00
Lumber of all sorts in the house	1.10.00
Three young caves	5.10.00
Due to the estate in money	9.10.00
Sub Total Personal Property	122.14.04
Total	£720.14.04

562 Ibid., 14-15.

Signed
David Haynes
Samuel Graves
John Noyes

Distribution of Real Estate of Samuel King alias Rice Sudbury, Mass. 25 December 1718.

			Value Received
The homestead with the buildings	620.00.00	To Peter King	£153.06.08
15 acres of land at gulf neck	14.00.00	To Ezra King	68.13.04
Lot at Brookfield	53.00.00	To Samuel King	81.13.04
Peter to pay	54.13.04	To Ezra	
Peter to pay	28.13.04	To Samuel	
Peter to pay	76.13.04	To Thomas	76.13.04
Peter to pay	76.13.04	To Sarah	76.13.04
Peter to pay	76.13.04	To Edward	76.13.04
Peter to pay	76.13.04	To Elizabeth	76.13.04
Peter to pay	76.13.04	To Mindwell	76.13.04
Sub total			£687.00.00
Error in addition			3.00.00
Total			£690.00.00

Signed
John Brigham
F. Bent
Mathl. Rice
Uriah Wheeler
Joseph Haynes.

Author's Note:

The records of settling Samuel's estate have several note worthy items. Many of the original records are fading and bleeding through the paper. The resultant difficulty in reading them thereby increases the chances of mistakes in understanding the material. However, it appears that at the time of his death Samuel left over £125 in debt to over thirty-three creditors. There is no evidence why Samuel incurred this indebtedness except for one note for £40 to a gunsmith in Charlestown. This may have been related to his militia service. The total amount also includes court, legal and funeral expenses. It took the administrators of the estate nearly six years to sort through everything and to pay the debts from farm income, the sale of part of the Gulf Neck land and personal property. The value of the homestead was first appraised at £505. In the final settlement, the homestead had increased in value to £620 which could have included several items originally listed as personal property in the original inventory, but associated with the farm such as animals and equipment. The Brookfield property increased in value from £30 to £53.

As the oldest son and as was customary, Peter received a double portion of the estate. There is no indication as to why Ezra received eight pounds less than his siblings or Samuel five pounds more. It would also be interesting to know how Peter paid off his brother and sisters and the timing of the payment. Out of the value of the farm and home, three quarters of the property would have to be liquidated to meet his estate obligation.

In the Ancestral File of the Church of Jesus Christ of Latter-day Saints a ninth child, Abigail, is listed who was born in 1713 and died in 1730. This has to be a mistake as there was no provisions for an Abigail in the above estate. In all probability this Abigail is a daughter to the above Peter.

Ezra King alias Rice
(Ezra died intestate, meaning he did not have a will)

(The information below has been reformatted and some changes in spelling have been made for easier reading.)

Ezra King alias Rice was a Sergeant In Captain William Williams 2nd Company 8th Regiment. Massachusetts Troops in an expedition sent to Louisbourg, Cape Breton in 1745 where he died January 14, 1746 in the 49th year of his age. His widow Silence was granted letters of Administration August 12, 1746 and was made guardian of Elizabeth, Beulah, & Mindwell, minors under age of 14 years and heirs of Ezra King alias Rice.
563

Hampden - Brimfield October 1, 1746

To the Honorable John Stoddard Esquire, Judge of Probate of wills for said County: or to his successor in said office; & we whose names are under written (namely) David Hitchcock Luke Blashfield & John Keep) being nominated chosen -- and sworn to appraise and take a true inventory of the estate of Ezra King (Alias Rice) of said Brimfield late deceased.   Have apprised and valued the said estate in old tenor bills as follows:

	£ s p
Home lot of 120 acres with house and barn	475.00.00
One lot of 120 acres living on the north end of the hill known by the name of Pynchon Hill	210.00.00
One lot of 105 acres known by the name of the Goate pasture lot	236.00.00
One lot of 9 acres by the old sawmill pond	18.00.00
Sub Total Real Estate	939.00.00
Old fence round Cooleys Land	02.15.00
Wearing apparel	02.05.00
One gun and powder horn	03.07.06
One horse	8.00.00
One yoke of oxen	38.16.00
Three cows	33.15.00
Three heifers	22.05.00
Swine	03.05.00

---

563   Ibid., 17-21.

Eight sheep	10.00.00
Twenty three goats	23.00.00
One Loom with utensils belonging	06.10.00
Cash	45.00.00
Two old great wheels	00.10.00
One foot wheel & reel	01.10.00
Two old saddles and bridle	02.05.00
One old pillion	00.10.00
Beds bedsteads and bedding	13.19.00
Five towels and one table cloth	00.15.00
Pewter	01.12.00
One box iron with heaters	00.08.00
Wooden wear	00.08.00
Cart and wheels boxes and bands	05.00.00
Clevis and pin staple and ring	00.12.00
Nine drag teeth	01.03.04
One pair of plow irons with plow plates	02.14.00
One small plow with irons	01.10.00
One pair horse chains with whiple tree chain	01.05.00
One pair of horse chains with part of whiple tree chain	00.18.00
Two horse collars	00.09.00
One narrow ax	00.17.00
Four old axes	01.06.00
Two pair of beetle rings and 4 wedges	01.03.04
One shoemakers hammer	00.05.00
One pair of nippers	00.02.00
One chopping knife	00.01.00
Two hoes	01.00.00
Old iron	00.12.00
Scythe with tackling	00.13.00
One old spade	00.04.00
One old pail and tub	00.02.00
One bull	11.00.00
One small grindstone	00.05.00
One pot with hooks	02.07.00
One small pot with bail	00.07.00
One small iron kettle	00.02.06
One traple	00.12.00
One fire slice	00.18.00
One old warming pan	00.05.00
One old frying pan	00.04.06

One plow chain	00.18.00
Four old chairs	00.12.00
Two old sieves	00.03.06
One razor	00.02.06
Flames	00.03.00
A number of lead shatard books	01.10.00
Old chest, tubs, tale and meal troughs	01.00.00
Two augers and chisel	00.18.04
One old fork	00.01.08
One bad saw	00.10.00
Two sickles	00.05.00
Flax	01.02.08
Wool	01.16.00
Boards	02.16.00
One old sled	00.10.00
Glass bottles	00.10.00
Four small bells one bag two earthen pots	01.08.00
(Unaccounted for difference	1.06.06
Sub Total	280.06.04
Less personal debts	170.00.09
Personal property	110.15.07
The sum total of the whole	£1,049.15.07

Silence King Administrator

                David Hitchcock
                Luke Blashfield Appraiser
                John Keep

Hampden ss. September 8, 1747. Silence King Administrator on the estate of Ezra King alias Rice late of Brimfield in said County deceased presenting the foregoing inventory of the estate of said deceased made oath that it is a true and perfect inventory of said Estate as far as has come to her knowledge and that if more of said estate hereafter appear she will readily make discovery of the same to the Judge of Probate or his successor in the office from time to time.
Attorney Timothy Dwight, Registrar

The settlement of the estate of Ezra King late of Brimfield in the County of Hampden deceased is as follows (viz) The whole estate both real and personal amounts to the sum of twelve hundred nineteen pounds six shillings and four pence of which nine hundred thirty-nine pounds is real estate and two hundred eighty pounds six shillings and four pence is personal estate out of which personal estate must be subtracted the sum of one hundred seventy pounds and nine pence the debts due from the estate and the administrators. After allowed which being subtracted there remains of the personal estate one hundred ten pounds fifteen shillings and seven pence . . .

(The following is a summary of the how the estate was to be distributed dated April 9, 1751, five years and three months after the death of Ezra. It would be another year before the property would actually be conveyed.)

	Total	Real Estate	Personal Property
Silence King (Wid) *	£349.15.02	£313.00.00	£36.15.02
Jonas (Deceased.)**	123.08.10	123.08.10	
William	61.14.05	61.14.05	
Ezra	61.14.05	61.14.05	
Abigail (Deceased.)***	20.11.08	10.01.07	10.10.01
Mary	61.14.05	51.04.04	10.10.01
Silence	61.14.05	51.04.04	10.10.01
Elizabeth	61.14.05	51.04.04	10.10.01
Bulah	61.14.05	51.04.04	10.10.01
Eunice	61.14.05	51.04.04	10.10.01
Mindwell	61.14.05	51.04.04	10.10.01
Total	£1,049.05.05	£939.00.00	£110.05.07

*   1/3 share of both real estate and personal property.
**   Double portion as eldest son, payable 1/3 to his widow, Mary, and 2/3 to his children.
*** Payable to her estate, balance of £41.02.09 paid to her during her lifetime.

Authors Note:

From the description below, it is interesting to see the method they used to divide up the real property. It would appear that as they sliced and diced it, no one would have anything of value unless one sibling was to buy another one out. Silence was even awarded a third of a barn " and liberty to come to Barn." It can only be imagined that as a brother or sister wanted to move on with their life, they would have to abandon their interest hoping that someone would come along and buy their dissected piece of property. The more efficient way of selling the entire piece of property and paying each brother & sister in cash as it is done today was not available at that time. Money was scarce and it would have been hard to liquefy real property.)

At a Court Probate holden at Southampton within and for the county of Hampden on the second Tuesday of April being the ninth day of said month Anno Domini 1751 (April 9, 1751) Timothy Dwight Esquire Judge of said Court ## The foregoing settlement of the estate of Ezra King late of Brimfield in the County afore said deceased is tariffed and confirmed as a settlement of said estate and Misters Captain David Hitchcock, Deacon Luke Blashfield, George Colton, Bezaleel Sherman and John Keep all freeholders of said deceased to the several persons to whom it is ordered in proportion to the several sums allotted them in the foregoing settlement.

Timothy Dwight.

We the subscribers hereof being appointed and sworn to make a division of the real estate of Ezra King of Brimfield late deceased have done as follows: First set out to the widow her thirds being thirty acres and one hundred and eitht rods lying in two pieces the first piece lying on the northwest corner of the house lot beginning at the northwest corner of said lot from thence east 18 degrees south fifty more rods to a heap of stones then west 18 degrees north forth rods to the west side of the house Lot then on the west Line of the House lot where we began with two acres joining upon the northwest corner of the house lot the whole of this contains fifteen acres and one hundred and eight rods and fifteen acres more lying on the easterly side of the house lot one hundred and sixty rods in length and fifteen rods wide with the privilege of one third of the Barn and liberty to come to barn --And the remainder of the house lot with the nine acres lying by the old sawmill pond place we have set out to Ezra King and to Mary Baker alias King and Silence Bond Jr. alias Silence King to their acceptance they agreeing to divide it among themselves then laid out to Jonas King only son of Jonas King deceased at a place called Pynchons hill.

Beginning at the northwest Corner and Running East 17 degrees south 160 rods thence south 17 degrees west 66 rods thence west 160 rods the to where we begin with one third of it to the widow of the south side of the said lot the whole lot being 65 acres. Then Eunice Kings part lyeth south of Jonas Kings part at the lot called Pynchons hill. Beginning at a heap of stones and runs east 17 degrees south 160 rods then south 17 degrees west 18 rods then west 17 degrees north 130 rods then south 17 degrees west 50 rods then west 17 degrees north 30 rods to where we began it contains 29 acres. Then beginning at the lot called the Goat pasture lot we laid out to Adonijah King at the south lot and said lot 31 acres we began at the south east corner of said lot and run west 11 degrees south 146 rods then north 6 degrees east 36 rods then east 11 degrees north 137 rods thence to where it began then we laid out 23 acres to Beulah King north of Adonijah Kings beginning at the south east corner and runs west 11 degrees south 137 rods thence north 6 degrees east 28 rods thence east 11 degrees north 128 1/2 thence to where we began. Then north of Beulah we laid 23 acres to William King beginning at a heap of stones and run west 11 degrees south 128 1/2 then north 6 degrees east 44 rods thence east 6 degrees south 30 rods thence east 10 degrees north 90 rods thence to where we began -- Then laid out to Elizabeth King 23 acres North of William King we began at the south east corner at a heap of stake and stones and run west 10 degrees south 90 rods thence north 5 degrees east 50 rods thence east 5 degrees south 82 rods thence to where we began- Then laid out to Joseph Hitchcock only son to Abigail Hitchcock deceased five acres at north end of Goat pasture joining upon Elizabeth Kings part we began at the south east corner at a heap of stones and run west 5 degrees north 82 rods thence north 5 degrees east 10 rods thence east 5 degrees south 80 rods to Black tree thence south 8 degrees east 10 rods to where we began --

Brimfield June 2nd 1752   David Hitchcock

George Colton
Luke Blashfield
John Keep
Bozaleet Sherman

Appendix 2
(Thomas Rice King Family Data)

THOMAS RICE KING
Born:	March 9, 1813	Place:	Marcellus, Onondaga, New York
Died:	February 3, 1879	Place:	Kingston, Piute, Utah

Married: December 25, 1831   Place: Cicero, Onondaga, New York

Matilda Robison
Born:	March 11, 1811	Place:	Charlston (Glen), Montgomery, NY
Died:	February 19, 1894	Place:	Kingston, Piute, Utah

Children
William Rice King
Born:	April 8, 1834	Place:	Cicero, Onondaga, New York
Died:	February 17, 1892	Place:	Salt Lake City, Salt Lake, Utah

Spouse: Josephine Henry
Married: January 20, 1861   Place: Fillmore, Millard, Utah

Spouse: Mary Ann Henry
Married: November 29, 1869   Place: Salt Lake City, Salt Lake, Utah

Spouse: Lucy Maranda White
Married: December 19, 1878   Place: St. George, Washington, Utah

Culbert King
Born:	January 31, 1836	Place:	Onondaga, Onondaga, New York
Died:	October 26, 1909	Place:	Coyote (Antimony), Garfield, Utah

Spouse: Eliza Esther McCullough
Married: February 5, 1855   Place: Fillmore, Millard, Utah

Spouse: Elizabeth Ann Callister
Married: October 10 1864   Place: Salt Lake City, Salt Lake, Utah

Spouse: Sarah Elizabeth Pratt
Married: December 19, 1878   Place: St. George, Washington, Utah

Spouse: Lydia Ann Webb
Married: June 3, 1908   Place: Manti, Sanpete, Utah

John Robison King

Born: September 27, 1837   Place: Palermo, Oswego, New York
Died: July 24, 1899   Place: Richfield, Sevier, Utah

Spouse: Helen Maria Webb
Married: September 23, 1860   Place: Meadow, Millard, Utah

Thomas Edwin King

Born: April 19, 1839   Place: Schroeppel, Oswego, New York
Died: January 19, 1923   Place: Ephraim, Sanpete, Utah

Spouse: Rebecca Jane Murray
Married: April 29, 1862   Place: Fillmore, Millard, Utah

Spouse: Isabella Elisha Savage
Married: January 16, 1878   Place: St. George, Washington, Utah

Delilah Cornelia King

Born: July 10 1841   Place Sylvania, Lucas, Ohio
Died: January 5, 1907   Place: Salt Lake City, Salt Lake, Utah

Spouse: George Daniel Olson
Married: December 14, 1861   Place: Fillmore, Millard, Utah

Matilda Emily King

Born: March 25, 1845   Place: Montrose, Lee, Iowa
Died: July 17, 1846   Place: Indian Town, Pottawattamie, Iowa

Spouse: Not married

Volney King

Born: March 11, 1847   Place: Florence (Omaha), Douglas, Neb.
Died: January 30, 1925   Place: Teasdale, Wayne, Utah

Spouse: Caroline (Carlie) Eliza Lyman
Married: May 15, 1871 (div)   Place: Salt Lake City, Salt Lake, Utah

Spouse: Eliza Syrett
Married: November 9, 1874   Place: Salt Lake City, Salt Lake, Utah

LeRoy King

Born:	August 21, 1850	Place:	near, Hamburg, Fremont, Iowa
Died:	March 20, 1852	Place:	Fillmore, Millard, Utah

Spouse: Not married

Grandchildren of Thomas and Matilda King

WILLIAM RICE KING (Child #1)

Josephine Henry (Wife #1)

1. William Henry King

Born:	June 3, 1862	Place:	Fillmore, Millard, Utah
Died	November 27, 1949	Place:	Salt Lake City, Salt Lake, Utah

Spouse:	Louisa Ann Lyman		
Married:	April 17, 1889	Place:	Manti, Sanpete, Utah

Spouse:	Vera Sjodahl		
Married:	July 19, 1912	Place:	Logan, Cache, Utah

2. Lillian King

Born:	April 26, 1864	Place:	Fillmore, Millard, Utah
Died:	September 13, 1948	Place:	Salt Lake City, Salt Lake, Utah

Spouse:	Ira Noble Hinckley		
Married:	October 21, 1886	Place:	Logan, Cache, Utah

3. Josephine King

Born:	March 31, 1866	Place:	Fillmore, Millard, Utah
Died:	July 9, 1894	Place:	Kaysville, Davis, Utah

Spouse:	John Watt Thornley		
Married:	September 20, 1888	Place:	Manti, Sanpete, Utah

4. Samuel Andrew King

Born:	January 9, 1868	Place:	Fillmore, Millard, Utah
Died:	August 27, 1943	Place:	Salt Lake City, Salt Lake, Utah

Spouse: Maynetta Bagley
Married: September 14, 1892   Place: Salt Lake City, Salt Lake, Utah

Spouse: Loren Watson
Married: September 2, 1929   Place: Salt Lake City, Salt Lake, Utah

Mary Ann Henry (Wife #2)

5. Harvey William King
Born: February 28, 1871   Place: Laie, Honolulu, Hawaii
Died: November 27, 1952   Place: Kaysville, Davis, Utah

Spouse: Katherine McBride
Married: June 13, 1899   Place: Fillmore, Millard, Utah

6. Margarette Agnes King
Born: September 24, 1872   Place: Laie, Honolulu, Hawaii
Died: June 13, 1960   Place: Martinez, Contra Costa, California

Spouse: John Franklin Holbrook
Married: July 13, 1895   Place: Fillmore, Millard, Utah

7. Robert Warren King
Born: November 27, 1874   Place: Fillmore, Millard, Utah
Died: December 3, 1944   Place: Burbank, Los Angeles, California

Spouse: Herma Lucretia Robison
Married: October 21, 1900   Place: Salt Lake City, Salt Lake, Utah

8. Claudius LeRoy King
Born: May 15, 1878   Place: Kingston, Piute, Utah
Died: July 15, 1918   Place: Salt Lake City, Salt Lake, Utah

Spouse: Daisy Maria Holt
Married: June 5, 1907   Place: Salt Lake City, Salt Lake, Utah

9. Arthur Ross King
Born: August 18, 1880   Place: Kingston, Piute, Utah
Died: September 5,1957   Place: Dragerton, Carbon, Utah

Spouse: Sarah Margaret Larsen
Married: September 4, 1914 (div) Place: Unknown

Spouse: Gladys Arvilla Clark
Married: March 6, 1936   Place: Salt Lake City, Salt Lake, Utah

10. Edwin Lester King
Born: September 18, 1882   Place: Kingston, Piute, Utah
Died: Unknown

Married: Unknown

11. Elmer Elliot King
Born: October 30, 1884   Place: Kingston, Piute, Utah
Died: March 12, 1957   Place: Los Angeles, Los Angeles, California

Spouse: Not married

Lucy Maranda White (Wife #3)
No children

CULBERT KING (Child #2)

Eliza Esther McCullough (Wife #1)

12. Culbert Levi King
Born: June 11, 1856   Place: Fillmore, Millard, Utah
Died: January 7, 1921   Place: Idaho Falls, Bonneville, Idaho

Spouse: Polly Ann Ross
Married: July 31, 1876   Place: Salt Lake City, Salt Lake, Utah

13. Esther Clarinda King
Born: September 24, 1858   Place: Fillmore, Millard, Utah
Died: April 10, 1923   Place: Antimony, Garfield, Utah

Spouse: George Black Jr.
Married: February 15, 1877   Place: St. George, Washington, Utah

14. Ida Roseltha King
Born: September 7, 1860   Place: Fillmore, Millard, Utah
Died: April 24, 1869   Place: Petersburg, Millard, Utah

Spouse: Not married

15. Matilda Emily King

Born:	April 10, 1863	Place:	Fillmore, Millard, Utah
Died:	June 8, 1949	Place:	Idaho Falls, Bonneville, Idaho

Spouse: George Hyrum Dockstader
Married: March 25, 1880 (div) Place: Salt Lake City, Salt Lake, Utah

Spouse: William Black
Married: July 11, 1887 (div) Place: Coyote (Antimony), Garfield, Utah

16. Delilah King

Born:	February 4, 1865	Place:	Petersburg, Millard, Utah
Died:	June 4, 1954	Place:	Provo, Utah, Utah

Spouse: Charles Elliot Rowan
Married: December 20, 1884 Place: Coyote (Antimony), Garfield, Utah

17. Volney Henry King

Born:	January 22, 1867	Place:	Petersburg, Millard, Utah
Died:	February 2, 1950	Place:	Phoenix, Maricopa, Arizona

Spouse: Maria Emeline Ross
Married: December 17, 1890 Place: Manti, Sanpete, Utah

Spouse: Fannie Crittenden Wallace
Married: December 19, 1900 Place: Manti, Sanpete, Utah

18. Julia Frances King

Born:	February 4, 1869	Place:	Petersburg, Millard, Utah
Died:	April 17, 1910	Place:	Coyote (Antimony), Garfield, Utah

Spouse: David Nicholes, Sr.
Married: August 11, 1887 Place: Coyote (Antimony), Garfield, Utah

19. William King

Born:	April 3, 1871	Place:	Kanosh, Millard, Utah
Died:	December 6, 1937	Place:	Garland, Box Elder, Utah

Spouse: Alevia Isadora Wallace
Married: June 1, 1899 Place: Manti, Sanpete, Utah

Spouse: Margaret Harned
Married: June 29, 1932 Place: Salt Lake City, Salt Lake, Utah

20. **Elda Hamilton King**

Born:	August 4, 1873	Place:	Kanosh, Millard, Utah
Died:	November 3, 1873	Place:	Kanosh, Millard, Utah

Spouse: Not married

21. **Parley King**

Born:	August 16, 1875	Place:	Kanosh, Millard, Utah
Died:	July 16, 1877	Place:	Kanosh, Millard, Utah

Spouse: Not married

22. **Alonzo King**

Born:	May 21, 1877	Place:	Kanosh, Millard, Utah
Died:	May 2, 1945	Place:	Richfield, Sevier, Utah

Spouse: Martha Ann Wallace
Married: August 23, 1901   Place: Coyote (Antimony), Garfield, Utah

Elizabeth Ann Callister: (Wife #2)

23. **Thomas Callister King**

Born:	May 16, 1866	Place:	Petersburg, Millard, Utah
Died:	March 20, 1927	Place:	Cedar City, Iron, Utah

Spouse: Elizabeth Dunsire
Married: December 8, 1886   Place: St. George, Washington, Utah

Spouse: Nellie Beeston (Brunson)
Married: October 13, 1926   Place: Manti, Sanpete, Utah

24. **Caroline King**

Born:	May 16, 1869	Place:	Kanosh, Millard, Utah
Died:	June 6, 1934	Place:	Cedar City, Iron, Utah

Spouse: David Edward Savage
Married: December 20, 1884   Place: Manti, Sanpete, Utah

Spouse: George W. McCormick
Married: May 20, 1896   Place: Coyote (Antimony), Garfield, Utah

25. **Elizabeth Ann King**

Born:	March 22, 1871	Place:	Kanosh, Millard, Utah
Died:	January 6, 1917	Place:	Richfield, Sevier, Utah

Spouse: Daniel Thompson Ross
Married: December 17, 1890   Place: Manti, Sanpete, Utah

26. **Collins Hyde King**
Born: June 1, 1873   Place: Kanosh, Millard, Utah
Died: October 24, 1874   Place: Kanosh, Millard, Utah

Spouse: Not married

27. **John King**
Born: March 16, 1876   Place: Kanosh, Millard, Utah
Died: April 17, 1892   Place: Probably Coyote, (Antimony),
                                   Garfield, Utah

Spouse: Not married

28. **Helen Lulu King**
Born: September 2, 1878 Place: Kanosh, Millard, Utah
Died: March 30 1885   Place: Coyote, (Antimony), Garfield, Utah

Spouse: Not married

29. **Marion King**
Born: August 23, 1883   Place: Kingston, Piute, Utah
Died: May 22, 1930   Place: Manti, Sanpete, Utah

Spouse: Jane Marie Antoinette Snow
Married: June 23, 1909   Place: Manti, Sanpete, Utah

30. **Julina King**
Born: July 17, 1886   Place: Coyote (Antimony), Garfield, Utah
Died: November 3, 1888 Place: Probably Coyote, (Antimony),
                                   Garfield, Utah

Spouse: Not married

Sarah Elizabeth Pratt: (Wife #3)

31. **Orson Pratt King**
Born: December 4, 1879   Place: Kingston, Piute, Utah
Died: December 10, 1965   Place: Provo, Utah, Utah

Spouse: Susan Irene McInelly
Married: January 9, 1902   Place: Manti, Sanpete, Utah

Spouse: Jane Maude Rappleye (Reynolds)
Married: October 14, 1953   Place: Central, Sevier, Utah

32. King (Male)
Born: January 28, 1882   Place: Kingston, Piute, Utah
Died: March 16, 1882   Place: Kingston, Piute, Utah

33. La Rene King
Born: February 14, 1883   Place: Kingston, Piute, Utah
Died: May 1, 1946   Place: Ogden, Weber, Utah

Spouse: Henry Hughes
Married: May 29, 1901 (div)   Place: Provo, Utah, Utah

Spouse: Edward Lloyd McQuown
Married: Abt 1916   Place: Unknown

Spouse: Kenneth Armstrong Bleaker
Married: November 17, 1928   Place: Eureka, Eureka, Nevada

34. Junius King
Born: June 24, 1883   Place: Kingston, Piute, Utah
Died: Before June 1891   Place: Probably Coyote (Antimony),
                                        Garfield, Utah

Spouse: Not married

35. Catherine King
Born: February 1, 1886   Place: Coyote (Antimony), Garfield, Utah
Died: September 1886   Place: Unknown

Spouse: Not married

36. Heber Philip King
Born: June 24, 1891   Place: Salt Lake City, Salt Lake, Utah
Died: May 29, 1960   Place: Prescott, Yavapai, Arizona

Spouse: Gertrude Black
Married June 8, 1911   Place: Manti, Sanpete, Utah

Lydia Ann Webb: (Wife #4)

No children

JOHN ROBISON KING (Child #3)

Helen Maria Webb: (Wife)

37. Helen Matilda King

Born:	January 26, 1862	Place:	Fillmore, Millard, Utah
Died:	June 12, 1932	Place:	Compton, Los Angeles, California

Spouse: William Lorin Hardy
Married: December 25, 1880   Place: Kingston, Piute, Utah

38. Catherine Aurella King

Born:	June 13, 1864	Place:	Fillmore, Millard, Utah
Died:	December 8, 1918	Place:	Coyote (Antimony), Garfield, Utah

Spouse: John Woodruff Smoot
Married: October 10, 1884   Place: Deseret, Millard, Utah

39. Lydia Rosella King

Born:	October 9, 1866	Place:	Fillmore, Millard, Utah
Died:	November 30, 1928	Place:	Springville, Utah, Utah

Spouse: John Henry Bertelsen
Married: January 10, 1889   Place: Coyote (Antimony), Garfield, Utah

40. John Franklin King

Born:	February 3, 1869	Place:	Fillmore, Millard, Utah
Died:	January 11, 1942	Place:	Delta, Millard, Utah

Spouse: Not married

41. Thomas LeRoy King

Born:	January 16, 1872	Place:	Fillmore, Millard, Utah
Died:	November 7, 1958	Place:	Delta, Millard, Utah

Spouse: Anna Laura Riddle
Married: December 21, 1905   Place: Junction, Piute, Utah

42. **Clara Adelia King**

Born:	March 14, 1875	Place:	Fillmore, Millard, Utah
Died:	May 15, 1875	Place:	Fillmore, Millard, Utah

Spouse: Not married

43. **Irene King**

Born:	August 21, 1876	Place:	Fillmore, Millard, Utah
Died:	January 5, 1965	Place:	Boise, Ada, Idaho

Spouse: Alva Read

Married:	January 2, 1896	Place:	Salt Lake City, Salt Lake, Utah

44. **Forrest King**

Born:	April 1, 1879	Place:	Coyote (Antimony), Garfield, Utah
Died:	March 31, 1937	Place:	Cedar City, Iron, Utah

Spouse: Mignonette Carpenter

Married:	November 6, 1901	Place:	Coyote (Antimony), Garfield, Utah

45. **Elma King**

Born:	February 14, 1883	Place:	Coyote (Antimony), Garfield, Utah
Died:	December 24, 1952	Place:	Pasadena, Los Angeles, California

Spouse: John Ephraim Myers, Jr.

Married:	August 25, 1902	Place:	Coyte (Antimony), Garfield, Utah

THOMAS EDWIN KING: (Child #4)

Rebecca Jane Murray: (Wife #1)

46. **Eva Matilda King**

Born:	March 12, 1863	Place:	Fillmore, Millard, Utah
Died:	March 12, 1863	Place:	Fillmore, Millard, Utah

Spouse: Not married

47. **Ella Vilate King**

Born:	February 18, 1864	Place:	Fillmore, Millard, Utah
Died:	March 4, 1953	Place:	San Leandro, Alameda, California

Spouse: Wister Brigham Harmon
Married: June 1, 1881   Place: Circleville, Piute, Utah

Spouse: Harrison Boat Kenner
Married: July 19, 1895   Place: Blackfoot, Bingham, Idaho

Spouse: John F. Christian
Married: May 22, 1912   Place: May, Lemhi, Idaho

48. Naomi King
Born: June 28, 1866   Place: Fillmore, Millard, Utah
Died: January 3, 1943   Place: Sacramento, Sacramento, California

Spouse: Lewis Albert Willis
Married: December 16, 1889   Place: Manti, Sanpete, Utah

49. Viola King
Born: March 10 1869   Place: Fillmore, Millard, Utah
Died: March 10,1869   Place: Fillmore, Millard, Utah

Spouse: Not married

50. Josephine May King
Born: June 28, 1872   Place: Fillmore, Millard, Utah
Died: May 18, 1964   Place: Tracy, San Joaquin, California

Spouse: Enoch Straw
Married: September 10, 1914   Place: Fillmore, Millard, Utah

51. Edwin Murray King
Born: August 7, 1874   Place: Fillmore, Millard, Utah
Died: June 3, 1940   Place: Salt Lake City, Salt Lake, Utah

Spouse: Edna Wampler Cremains
Married: July 26, 1915   Place: Junction, Piute, Utah

52. Clifford Carol King
Born: August 12, 1878   Place: Fillmore, Millard, Utah
Died: February 21, 1961 Place: Montague, Siskiyou, California

Spouse: Annie Clark
Married: October 13, 1904 (div)   Place: Junction, Piute, Utah

Spouse: Alice L.
Married: Between 1920-1930   Place: Unknown

Isabella Elisha Savage: (Wife #2)

53. Mary La Verna King
Born: April 14, 1881   Place: Kingston, Piute, Utah
Died: August 20, 1917   Place: Roosevelt, Duchesne, Utah

Spouse: John Henry Stoney
Married: December 11, 1902   Place: St. George, Washington, Utah

Delilah Cornelia King: (Child #7)

54. George Daniel Olson
Born: September 18, 1862   Place: Salt Lake City, Salt Lake, Utah
Died: November 5, 1930   Place: Berkeley, Alameda, California

Spouse: Melissa Susan Russell
Married: April 3, 1884   Place: Salt Lake City, Salt Lake, Utah

55. Thomas Edmund Olson
Born: November 26, 1864   Place: Fillmore, Millard, Utah
Died: October 6, 1953   Place: Los Angeles County, California

Spouse: Eunice Emeline Little
Married: September 3, 1884   Place: Salt Lake City, Salt Lake, Utah

56. Mary Evelyn Olson
Born: September 2, 1868   Place: Fillmore, Millard, Utah
Died: October 7, 1894   Place: Fillmore, Millard, Utah

Spouse: Alma Greenwood
Married: December 20, 1893   Place: Salt Lake City, Salt Lake, Utah

57. William Francis Olson
Born: May 26, 1870   Place: Fillmore, Millard, Utah
Died: January 12, 1953   Place: Long Beach, Los Angeles, Calif.

Spouse: Anna May Cluff
Married: November 27, 1895   Place: Salt Lake City, Salt Lake, Utah

Spouse: Daphne Dalton
Married: July 24, 1928   Place: Manassa, Conejos, Colorado

58. **Bertha Matilda Olson**

Born: August 29, 1873   Place: Fillmore, Millard, Utah
Died: March 12, 1965   Place: Tucson, Prima, Arizona

Spouse: George Marion Hanson
Married: November 11, 1896   Place: Fillmore, Millard, Utah

59. **Culbert Levy Olson**

Born: November 7, 1876   Place: Fillmore, Millard, Utah
Died: April 13, 1962   Place: Los Angeles, Los Angeles, Calif.

Spouse: Kate Jeremy
Married: October 21, 1905   Place: Salt Lake City, Salt Lake, Utah

60. **Emma Eliza Olson**

Born: December 3, 1879   Place: Fillmore, Millard, Utah
Died: January 5, 1880   Place: Probably Fillmore, Millard, Utah

Spouse: Not married

61. **Ethel Laverne Olson**

Born: January 15, 1881   Place: Fillmore, Millard, Utah
Died: January 8, 1959   Place: Los Angeles, Los Angeles, Calif.

Spouse: Francis Dean Bradley
Married: October 1909   Place: San Francisco, San Francisco, Calif.

62. **Emmett King Olson**

Born: November 17, 1883   Place: Fillmore, Millard, Utah
Died: August 10, 1969   Place: Salt Lake City, Salt Lake, Utah

Spouse: Edith Mavannwi Jones
Married: September 9, 1917   Place: Price, Carbon, Utah

VOLNEY KING: (Child #6)

Caroline Eliza Lyman: (Wife #1)

No Children

Eliza Syrett: (Wife #2)

63. **Eliza Rosetta King**

Born:	October 3, 1875	Place:	Fillmore, Millard, Utah
Died:	December 9, 1955	Place:	Lovell, Big Horn, Wyoming

Spouse: John Franklin Black
Married: January 2, 1896   Place: Salt Lake City, Salt Lake, Utah

Spouse: Thomas Lythgoe
Married: May 2, 1916   Place: Cowley, Big Horn, Wyoming

64. **Volney Emery King**

Born: June 5, 1878   Place: Kingston, Piute, Utah
Died: February 14, 1962   Place: Richfield, Sevier, Utah

Spouse: Maria Lyman
Married: August 9, 1904   Place: Caineville, Wayne, Utah

65. **Susan Mae King**

Born: October 5, 1880   Place: Kingston, Piute, Utah
Died: November 8, 1974   Place: Sacramento, Sacramento, California

Spouse: George Albert Lyman
Married: September 25, 1901   Place: Salt Lake City, Salt Lake, Utah

Spouse: George Thomas Carrell
Married: February 24, 1912   Place: Torrey, Wayne, Utah

66. **Edmund Rice King**

Born: November 24, 1882   Place: Kingston, Piute, Utah
Died: January 13, 1953   Place: Provo, Utah, Utah

Spouse: Cora Williams
Married: November 24, 1915   Place: Bicknell, Wayne, Utah

67. **Leland Stanford King**

Born: February 23, 1885   Place: Wilmont, Piute, Utah
Died: August 12, 1929   Place: Richfield, Sevier, Utah

Spouse: Anna Victoria Higgins
Married: November 1, 1905   Place: Cowley, Big Horn, Wyoming

68. Clarence King

Born: May 15, 1887   Place: Wilmont, Piute, Utah
Died: June 11, 1887   Place: Probably Wilmont, Piute, Utah

Spouse: Not married

69. Warren King

Born: July 5, 1888   Place: Wilmont, Piute, Utah
Died: August 16, 1889   Place: Probably Wilmont, Piute, Utah
Spouse: Not married

70. Ada Delilah King

Born: July 17, 1890   Place: Wilmont, Piute, Utah
Died: July 11, 1974   Place: Salt Lake City, Salt Lake, Utah

Spouse: Charles Snow, Jr.
Married: September 28, 1910   Place: Logan, Cache, Utah

71. Claudus Melvin King

Born: February 25, 1896   Place: Coyote (Antimony), Garfield, Utah
Died: January 4, 1897   Place: Coytote (Antimony), Garfield, Utah

Spouse: Not married

72. Lawrence King

Born: April 3, 1898   Place: Coyote (Antimony), Garfield, Utah
Died: July 18, 1954   Place: Inglewood, Los Angeles, California

Spouse: Lillian Catherine Stewart
Married: February 26, 1924   Place: Nephi, Juab, Utah

Appendix 3

(Original Settlers of Fillmore)

Those who arrived October 28, 1851,[564] and the following *January, **February, and ***May (Age in 1852). The next group of settlers didn't arrive until October 1852.

Akerly, Elsie Ann[565]   (10)

Bailey, James[566]

Bartholomew, Noah Willis[567] (44)

---

564 Day and Ekins, *Milestones of Millard: 100 Years of History of Millard Countty*, 3-7, 774-785 with more completed names and ages from the Ancestral File and the LDS Church Fillmore Ward records. In several cases, no further information can be found. It appears that some of the individual men may have come to help work on the Territorial capital building, others may have come without their families until they became more established, while others simply came and then moved on within a few months. See page 134 for a map of the fort at Fillmore placing the location of most of the families, but not all. Those so listed are in this Appendix placed in bold type.

565 The Ancestral File has Elsie born in 1842 and being married in 1856 to Henry Jacob Faust 1856 in Fillmore. Several questions could be raised as to her age and who she may have come with to Fillmore.

566 James was the member of the Mormon Battalion and died in Deseret, Millard, Utah.

567 Noah is the brother-in-law to Levi

Miranda Catlin[568]   (46)
George W.
Lewis Nelson

**Mary Altaina Catlin[569]   (31)
    **Matilda   (2)
    **Edwin   (1)

Benn, Jacob
    Mrs. Benn
    Jane

*Bills, William

Black, George Sr.
    Susan Jacaway
    Mary A.

Bradshaw, Mr.

Bridges, William Erskine   (38)
    Margaret Robison[570]   (33)
    Robert

Hamilton McCullough.

568 Miranda is a sister to George Washington Catlin and a daughter of Sally Sarah Perry.

569 Mary is the younger sister to Miranda Catlin.

570 Margaret is the younger sister to Matilda Robison King and the widow of Alva Phelps who died with the Mormon Battalion. The child Worthy is from William's previous marriage. Robert has not been identified.

Worthy Franklin	(12)	***Dame, Janvrin Hayes	(44)
Juliett Phelps	(13)	***Lucinda Hayes	(23)
Walter A. Phelps	(11)	***Phidelia Esther	(17)
Mary Phelps	(7)	***Laura Alvira	(16)
		***Wesley William	(14)
Brunson, Lewis[571]	(21)	***Tamson Pluma	(12)
Amanda Louisa Park	(18)	***Margaret Hayes	(10)
		***Simon Richard	(8)
Call, Anson	(42)	***Sarah Elsa	
Ann Maria Bowen[572]	(18)	***Lovina Hayes[575]	(26)
		***Mary Ann	(1)
Call, Josiah Howe[573]	(31)		
Henrietta Caroline Williams	(26)	***Eldridge, John**[576]	(48)
Alvin	(6)	*Cynthia Ann Howlett	(32)
Cyril	(3)	*Cynthia Ann	(5)
		*George Washington	(3)
***Calvin, Mr.		*Rufus	(1)

*Catlin, George Washington (34)

Elliott, John[577]

* *Maria Louise Sanderson (19)
* *Sally Sarah Perry (73)

***Felshaw, William (52)

Charlesworth, Thomas	(29)
Alice Barrows[574]	(24)
Thomas	(4)
Alice	(3)

***Charlotte Walters

* ***Katherine (7)
* ***Mary (Polly) (4)
* ***Eleanor (2)

***Mary Harriett Gilbert (44)

Clark, Thomas
Eliza
William
Frank

* ***Julia (20)
* ***John (16)
* ***Lucy (10)
* ***Caroline (7)
* ***Hannah (4)
* ***Sarah (1)
* ***Susannah (1)

---

571 While *Milestones of Millard* identify this Brunson as Lehman Bronson or Leman Brunson, it appears more likely to be the newly married Lewis Brunson who became the second Bishop of Fillmore.

572 A plural wife of Anson who according to family tradition was picked out by Brigham Young for Anson to bring to Fillmore.

573 A younger brother of Anson Call.

574 Alice and family may not have come to Fillmore until 1855.

575 Lovina is the older sister of Lucinda and plural wife of Janvrin. Both sisters married Janvrin after his first wife died.

576 The LDS Church's Mormon Pioneer Overland Travel website has John, his wife Cynthia Ann Howlett, and family arriving in Utah the following year.

577 John did not bring his family to Fillmore until 1853.

***Fisher, James[578] (32)
  ***Hannah Lees Stott[579] (28)
    ***Sarah (6)

*Gassett, Mr.
  family

*Henry, Andrew (41)
  *Margaret Creighton (35
  *Arthur John (9)
  *Josephine[580] (8)

Holbrook, Chandler (45)
  **Eunice Dunning (42)
  **Diana Eliza (19)
  **Mary Maria (16)
  **Eunice Emma (14)
  **Orson Chandler (11)
  **Joseph Hyrum (8)
  **Lafayette (2)

Hoyt, Samuel Pierce (45)
  Emily Smith (46)

Jackson, Andrew[581]
  Martha

Kinney, Loren Edward (36)
  Hannah Gott Nichols[582] (40)
  Ellen (10)
  Albert (6)
  Mary Ann Tucker[583] (20)

King, Thomas Rice (39)
  Matilda Robison (41)
  William Rice (18)
  Culbert (16)
  John Robison (15)
  Thomas Edwin (13)
  Delilah (11)
  Volney (5)
  LeRoy (2)

Lazenby, Robert

***Mace, Hyrum (41)
  ***Elizabeth Armstrong (33)
  ***Lamira (12)
  ***Cordelia (8)
  ***Elizabeth (3)
  ***Hyrum M. (1)

*McCullough, Levi Hamilton[584] (42)
  *Julia Frances (17)
  *Eliza Esther[585] (15)
  *Henry Judson (10)

*McGaw, James W.

***Mulford, Furman[586] (40)

Nicholes, John (25)
  Elizabeth Everetts (19)

**Payne, William (16)

Parsons, Ebenezer[587] (32)

---

578 James may have been James Madison Fisher, a 19 year old single man.

579 Hannah is the older sister of William Henry Stott.

580 The future wife of William King.

581 Andrew may be John who married Martha Judson in 1862.

582 Hannah is a sister to John Nicholes.

583 Mary was a plural wife of Loren

---

and may have had a son, James, in 1850.

584 *Milestones of Millard* lists this name as H.J. (Henry Judson) rather than Levi Hamilton. Henry was the nine year old son of Levi McCullough.

585 Future wife of Culbert King.

586 A single man.

587 A hired man of Noah Bartholomew.

Reed, Dewitt C.
  Mary

**Rogers, Chancey (23)
*Rogers, Henrietta[588] (20)

Robison, Peter[589] (35)
  Celina Hayward Chaffee (32)
    Celina Cornelia (4)
    Charles (2)
    Mary Ashley (19)
    Mary Elizabeth (1)

*Rowley, James[590] (21)

*Rowley, Ralph Nephi (29)
  *Mary Ann Thompson (28)
    *John Thompson (5)
    *Hugh Thompson (3)
    *Ephraim George (1)

***Russell, Allen (28)
  ***Harriet Massina Hutchens (34)
    ***Allen (14)
    ***John (2)

***Russell, Jonathan[591] (69)
  ***Nancy Wilson (66)
    ***Horace (21)

Safford, Alfred Perrygo (33)
  Eunice Elizabeth Tyler (29)
    Charlotte Ann (4)
    Alfred A. (1)

***Stott, William Henry (22)

*Standage, Henry (34)
  *Emma (20)
    *Elizabeth (11)

*Tomkinson, Ephraim (25)
  *Ann (24)
    *Ephraim (1)

**Thompson, Daniel (18)

Tyler, Orson Jonah (31)
  Rene Baldwin (27)
    Orson P. (5)
    Albert (3)
    George (1)

Warner, Orange[592] (48)
  Mary Elvira Tyler[593] (30)
    Byron (19)
    Holstein (15)
    Dorus (14)
    Orlando Wallace (13)
    Mortimer Wilson (10)
    Cornelia (8)
    Orange Horatio (5)
    Cyrus A. (2)

Webb, John (48)
  Catherine Naramore (43)
    Lydia Ann[594] (13)
    Helen Maria[595] (7)
    Arabelia (4)
    Catherine Jane (1)

Wilcox, Franklin A.

---

588 Henrietta is the sister of Chancey Rogers.

589 Peter is the younger brother of Matilda Robison King.

590 A younger brother of Ralph Rowley.

591 Jonathan is the father of Allen.

592 Orange is the brother-in-law of Matilda Robison King by two deceased Robison sisters.

593 Mary is a sister to Orson Tyler and Eunice Elizabeth Tyler Safford.

594 Future wife of Culbert King.

595 Future wife of John Robison King.

Appendix 4

(Fillmore City Plot Map)

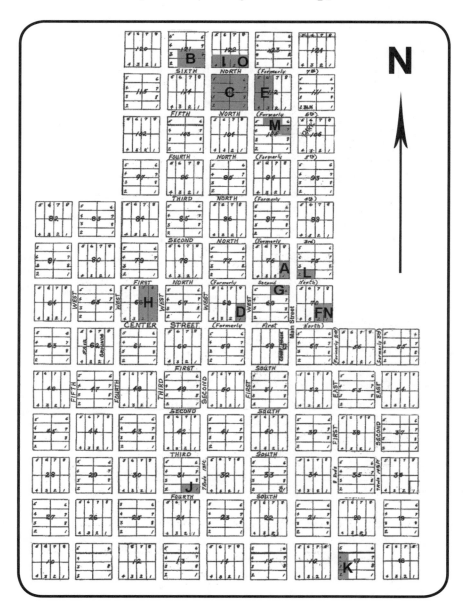

The plot map to the left identifies the property that the King family owned in Fillmore City. It does not show property they owned outside the city limits. Each block is approximately 10 acres. Each lot is 1.25 acres, or 165 feet by 330 feet.

A. Thos & Matilda	(Home)	- purchased	Jan 14, 1871	$37.50
		- sold	Mar 2, 1878	2,000.00
B. Thos & Matilda	(Pb	- Purchased	Jun 14, 1878	37.50
	land & buildings of some kind)			
		- Sold	Jan 5, 1878	500.00
C. Thos & Matilda	(Land)	- Purchased	Jul 2, 1871	19.45
		- Sold	Sep 2, 1878	200.00
D. William	(Pb Home)	- Purchased	Jun 14, 1871	n/a
		- Sold	Jan 25, 1885	300.00
E. William	(Pb land)	- Purchased	Jun 14, 1871	19.25
		- Sold	Mar 3, 1897	225.00
F. John	(Home)	- Purchased	Jul 25, 1871	3.25
		- Sold	Jun 19, 1878	1,000.00
G. Edwin	(Home)	- Purchased	Jul 2, 1871	19.45
		- Sold	Aug 20, 1878	1,000.00
H. Edwin	(Land)	- Purchased	Sep 6, 1871	19.75
		- Sold	Sep 25, 1878	50.00
I. Edwin	(Land)	- Purchased	Jul 2, 1871	19.45
		- Sold	n/a	n/a
J. Edwin	(Pb land	- Purchased	Jul 2, 1871	19.45
	& buildings of some kind)			
		- Sold	Aug 15, 1878	100.00
K. Edwin	(Land)	- Purchased	n/a	n/a
		- Sold	Feb 4, 1878	35.00
L. Delilah	(Home)	- Purchased*	Aug 29, 1874	1,850.00
		- Sold	Aug17, 1895	400.00
M. Delilah	(Land)	- Purchased	Jul 25, 1871	12.43
		- Sold	n/a	n/a
N. Volney	(Pb Home)	- Purchased	July 2, 1871	3.25
		- Sold	Aug 18, 1879	225.00
O. Volney	(Pb land	- Purchased	Sep 6, 1871	4.00
	& buildings of some kind)			
		- Sold	Jan 16, 1877	250.00

It is not known when the Kings took possession of the above property. It appears from the land records of Millard County that the first land patents were not granted until 1871. It is also not known when the Kings received the money due for the property they sold, at the point of sale or at a later date. No doubt there may have been a buyer's market when they sold their property, and the conditions under which they sold it. *It should be noted that while Delilah is included in the above data, she did not sell her property in order to move to Kingston. Also, Culbert is not included in the above findings. He was living in Kanosh and no record has been found of his purchasing or selling his property. (The above information is taken from the Millard Country Recorders Office, Land Records, Fillmore, Utah.)

Based on the values given, it appears that the home of Thomas & Matilda was a fairly nice home and must have included the hotel. The homes of John and Edwin must have been well above average and built out of brick, while the homes of William and Volney must have been more modest and built out of adobe or logs. The value of the other properties vary considerably, and may have included barns and other outbuildings or improvements. There is also some discrepancy in the record for Edwin's property (K). The record is not clear whether the property resides on the west or the south side of the block.

Appendix 5

(Articles of Incorporation for the United Order of Circleville [at Kingston])[596]

PREAMBLE. Whereas the Latter-Day Saints have been repeatedly counseled by the Prophet, Seer and Revelator, Brigham Young, to enter into and carry out the principles of the United Order as revealed by the Lord through Joseph Smith as contained in the Doctrine and Covenants. And whereas we are taught by the Apostle that we as a people cannot advance any farther in the things of the Kingdom of God only by entering into the United Order. And whereas we are told by Jesus Christ, our Savior, that unless we become one we are none of His, and whereas

We are taught in the scriptures that you can not become one in heavenly things, unless you become one in earthly things. Therefore in order that we may advance by carrying out the instructions and councils of those who are appointed to lead and guide us in the ways of life and salvation and more fully accomplish the object of becoming one both spiritually and temporally. Be it resolved; that we bind ourselves together by covenant and promise to consecrate ourselves and all we possess unto the Lord not in name only - but in deed and reality and furthermore, be it resolved that we will observe and carry out in our lives the rules that should be observed by members of the United Order as printed and distributed among the saints by the Presidency of the Church. Resolved

In order to work harmoniously we sign an article of agreement and organize ourselves into a company by electing a president, two vice presidents, a Board of Directors - a secretary and treasurer who also shall be members of the Board. Whose councils and instructions we promise to obey in all things both spiritually and temporally. Amen

ARTICLES OF AGREEMENT made and entered into this the first day of May A.D. 1877, between the parties whose names are hereunto annexed; TO-WIT:

---

596 The original handwritten copy of the Articles of Incorporation is in the LDS Church Historical Department Archives. It was called "of Circleville" due to the fact that they were located right next to the community of Circleville. Kingston had not yet been established. The term "Drawn off" or "Gone to" refers to the fact that the people left the Order.

ART. 1st.   We, the undersigned mutually agree and bind ourselves one to the other by covenant and promise to faithfully carry out and perform on our several parts, all the stipulations and agreements hereinafter mentioned.

ART. 2nd.   The name of this company shall be THE UNITED ORDER OF CIRCLEVILLE.

ART. 3rd.   The objects of this Company are for agricultural, manufacturing, commercial and other industrial pursuits, and for establishing and maintaining colleges, seminaries, churches, libraries and any other charitable or scientific association, and for these purposes shall have the right and power to receive, take, and hold, either by gift, purchase, or device, the right, title, interest and possession of real or personal property, and may bargain, sell, and alienate the same the thereby pass such title thereto as it may hold therein.

ART 4th.   The business of this Company shall be done in and through, or by a Board of Directors, which shall be elected by a majority vote of the parties whose names are attached to these Articles.

ART 5th.   The Board of Directors shall consist of a President, two Vice Presidents, not less than three, nor more than five Directors a Secretary and Treasurer who shall be ex-officio members of the Board, whose term of office shall be one year, and until their successors shall be elected and installed in office, unless sooner removed by a two-thirds majority vote of the Company.

ART 6th.   The Board of Directors shall have power to appoint from the members of the Board or from the names of the parties annexed hereunto, a committee of appraisal consisting of three persons who shall appraise or value all property put into the Company; and the Board shall also have power to appoint agents, Superintendents and assistants necessary to carry on the different branches of business entered into by this Company, and also to fill all vacancies which may occur in the Board by death or otherwise until an election shall be held.

ART. 7th.   It is mutually agreed and understood by the parties whose names are attached to these articles that they bequeath, transfer, and convey unto the Company, all their right, title and interest to whatever property, whether personal or real estate that they are now possessed of or may hereafter become possessed of by legacy, will, or otherwise, for the purposes herein mentioned; And furthermore, that they will labor faithfully and honestly themselves, and cause their children who are under age to labor under the direction of the Board of Directors or their Agents, or Superintendents, the remuneration for which shall be as fixed by the Board, both as to price and kind of pay he or she shall receive; provided any are dissatisfied with the price or kind of pay, a hearing shall be had before the Company and their decision shall be final.

ART. 8th. It is furthermore understood and agreed that a schedule or inventory of all property bequeathed or transferred to the Company shall be kept in a book provided for that purpose, together with the price of each article that in case any party becomes dissatisfied, or is called away, and wishes to draw out, he can have as near as may be the same kind of property, but in no case can he have real estate only at the option of the Board, nor shall interest or a dividend by paid on such property; and all property received by the Company shall be receipted for by the Secretary.

ART 9th. We further agree that we will be controlled and guided in all our labors, in our food, clothing, and habitation, for our families being frugal and economical in our manner of living and dress, and in no case seek to obtain that which is above another.

ART 10th. We also covenant and agree that all credits for labor that stand to our names in excess of debits for food and clothing shall become the property of the Company, the first balance being struck at the expiration of twelve months from the date of these Articles, and annually thereafter.

ART. 11th. It is also agreed and understood that the wages of all the officers, agents, superintendents, and all mechanics, while laboring at their different trades, shall be the same as paid to farm hands, or other common laborers, provided that any extra expense that shall occur through traveling in the transaction of business shall be paid by the Company.

ART. 12th. We further agree that we will not transact any business whatever unless empowered by the Board of Directors, and any business done without the authority of the Board will not be valid or be binding on the Company.

ART. 13th. It is also understood and agreed that all agents, superintendents, and assistants appointed by the Board shall be presented before the Company for their approval or disapproval at the first meeting of the Company after such appointment.

ART. 14th. It is further agreed that the Board shall have the power to do business whenever the President, or either Vice-president and four Directors are present, providing minutes are kept and regularly spread upon the Records by the Secretary.

ART. 15th. It is further agreed that is shall be the duty of the Board to meet at the call of the President or Vice-Presidents, or any four of the Directors. Notice may be given by proclamation in any public meeting, or by a verbal notice sent by any of the above parties.

ART.   16th.   It is understood that there is no regular or set days for the Company to meet to do business, but are subject to the call of the President or Vice-Presidents wherever they shall deem it necessary for the interests of the Company; and all business done to be valid must be spread upon the record and signed by the President and countersigned by the Secretary.

ART.   17th.   It is further agreed that the President shall be the Trustee-in-Trust for the Company, and all real estate shall be deeded to him and his successors in office, and he shall not have the right to deed or convey the same away only by a two-thirds majority vote of the Company.

ART.   18th.   It is further agreed that these Articles can be amended, repealed, or added to by a two-thirds majority vote of the Company.

NAMES (Signed)

Thomas Rice King
William King
Thomas Edwin King
Volney King
Mary A[nn Henry] King
Eliza S. King [Eliza Syrett]
Culbert L[evi] King
Charles E[lliot] Rowen
Kahana King
Mortimer Wilson Warner
Christenia [Brown] Warner
Christenia Delilah Warner
El[l]en Elizabeth Warner
James Vinson Knight
Celestial [Roberts] Knight
J[ohn] D[ingham] Wilcox
                (Sept. 20, 1879)
Mary T[heodocia Savage] Wilcox
                (Sept. 20, 1879)
J[oel] W[illiam] White
James Woolsey
                (Never identified)
Mary A[nn Donnelly] Woolsey
                (do   do)
Joseph T[homas] White
                (Drawn off)

J[oel] W[illiam] White, Jr.
John R[obison] King
David [Leonard] Savage
                (Drawn off Nov. 1880)
Mary [Abigail White] Savage
                (Drawn off & gone to Arizona)
Helen M[aria Webb] King
Clarinda E[ster King] Black
Polly A[nn Ross] King
Culbert King
John Henry Heap
Eliza Esther [McCullough] King
David [William] Savage
                (Left with his father)
Ephraim Syrett
Isabella E[lisha] Savage [King]
John Davis
Margaret Emma Savage
                (Drawn off, with her father)
Thomas Smith   (Sept, 1879)
W[illiam] Albert Savage
Tennessee [Whittaker] Smith
Laura Crystine Savage
                (Gone to Arizona with her
                father, Sept. 20, 1879)
Lucy M[aranda] White [King]
Mary A[nn] White

Francis A[nn Thomas] White
James [Henry] Huff,
   (Gone to Arizona, Oct 25, 1879)
William Laxton   (His mark X)
Adalaide [Atkin]Laxton
             (Her mark X)
Sophia [Atkin] Huff
   (Gone to Arizona, Oct 25, 1879)
John T[homas] Whetten   (do do)
George Dockstader
Andrew Mineer
Susan [Jacaway] Black [Savage]
   (gone to Ariz. Sept. 20, 1879)
Ingar[borg Jensen] Mineer
George Black
Emiel [August]Mineer
H[ans] S[everine] Jensen
           (Sept 20, 1879)
Francis [Ann White] Mineer
Endry Ereksen [Anders Erickson]
           (Dec 20, 1878)
Rebecca J[ane Murray] King
Henry Edward Desaules
           (Sept. 20, 1879)
Naomi King
Betsy [Youngquist] Franks
Teancum Pratt   (March 1879)
Anna Eliza[abeth Mead] Pratt
           (" ")
Sarah Eliza[abeth Ewell] Pratt
           (" ")
Robert Forrester
Johanna Forrester
John Springthorpe
John O. Hall
           (Never identified)
B.M. Nielsen   (Sept. 20, 1879)
Jane Hall   (Never identified)
David Thomas
Horatio Morrill
Adaline Thomas

Sarah A[nn Sudweeks] Morrill
Fanny [Francis A.] Thomas
           (Left June 1878)
Mahitable Jansen [Louisa
   Mahitable Jensen](Sept. 20, 1879)
Josephine [Anderson Jensen] (" ")
John Jensen   (" ")
J[ens] C[hristian] Sorenson (" ")
N[iels] Peter Nielsen   (" ")
Jessie Springthorpe
Theresa Springthorpe
David Dunsire   (Left June 1880)
David John Thomas
N[iels] Nielsen
Fred [Erick Syrett]
[Karen] Marie Nielsen
R[euben] Syrett
Emma Nielsen
Josephine [Henry] King
N[eil] Joseph Nielsen
George [Hyrum] Dockstader
Anne Kirstine Nielsen [Sorensen]
Robert Loney Williamson
(Drew off Oct 1880, went to Arizona)
Elizabeth Pedersen [Brita
   Catherine Peterson]   (Removed)
Sarah Houston Pratt
Joseph Chambers
      (Went North Feb. 12, 1881)
Eliza Ann McKee] Chambers
           (Ditto)
Sarah E[lizabeth] Pratt [King]
Thankful L[oretta Tanner] Harmon
   (Left Nov. 1880, gone to Arizona)
J[oseph] B[righam] Nay
Amanda E[llen Earl] Nay
Robert Shimmin
   (Left Oct. 1880, gone Glenwood)
Alva [Phelps] Pratt[597]
           (Left Nov 1878)

---

597 The son of Orson Pratt. He left the order after a few months and was picked up in October 1880 for horse stealing.

Matilda E[mily King] Dockstader
Ella V[ilate] King
Delilah King
Lillian King
Anna Sophia Shimmin
                    (Left Oct. 1880)
M[ary] A[nn Forrester]
  McDonough   (Drawn off)
Stephen Mangos [Mansor]
Alexander G[ordon] Ingram
          (Drawn off, gone South)
W[ister] B[righam] Harmon

Appendix 6

(Members of the United Order of Circleville [at Kingston])[598]

	Age in 1879	Approximate Time in the Order
Black, George Jr.[599]	25	May 1877 -
Esther Clarinda King	21	
**George King	0	
Black (Savage), Susan Jacaway[600]	Abt 46	Dec 1877 - Sep 1879
*William[601]	25	May 1878 -

---

598   Information in this Appendix is taken from the Articles of Incorporation of the United Order of Circleville, 1880 U.S. Census, The Daily Journal of the Kingston Untied Order, LDS Church Ancestral File, the William Rice King Journal, research of Ardis Parshall, and King Family Group Sheets in the possession of Larry King.

No asterisk	is from Articles of Incorporation
One *	is from The Daily Journal of the Kingston United Order.
Two **	is from LDS Church Ancestral File and family group sheets.
Three ***	is from the U.S. Census.
Four ****	is from the William Rice King Journal
One +	is from the research of Ardis Parshall

In many cases it required all of the above sources interfacing together to piece together and to properly identify the individual and/or families. While this represents a fairly comprehensive and accurate list, including dates of entry and exit from the order, it is not purported to be totally complete. Many problems include: (1) Volney King's record appears to include individuals or families living in the area, not just members of the order. (2) People may have been part of the order for a short time but withdrew and stayed on and worked for the order. (3) Volney's record includes some misspelled names and outright mistakes. (4) Terminology such as "settled with the order" may have meant that they withdrew or they simply made an agreement on wages. (5) A family may have given notice to withdraw on one date and stayed on for several months until a settlement could be worked out before they actually withdrew. (6) The 1877 dates may be the date the family joined or simply the date when the family was first mentioned in Volney's history.

599   A son of Susan Jacaway Black. Ester Clarinda is the daughter of Culbert King.

600   After the death of her husband, George Black, she married David Leonard Savage in 1878. She also served as the Relief Society president from December 16, 1877 to April 3, 1879.

601   William married Matilda Emily King in 1887.

*John Franklin	Abt 20	Jul 1877 -
*Nephi James	8	
**Melissa Velma	7	
Chambers, Joseph	35	Dec 1879 - Feb 1881
Eliza Ann McKee	25	
**Persis Moore	8	
**Mary Ann	3	
**Thomas McKee	1	
*Coombs, Andrew William[602]		Jul 1879 - Aug 1879
Davis, John[603]		Nov 1877 -
Desaules, Henry Edward[604]	61	1877 - May 1882
Dockstader, George[605]	73	Nov 1878 - May 1881
George Hyrum[606]	17	
**William Oscar Dockstader[607]	15	
**Estella	13	
**Wesley[608]	5	
**Esther Lavaria[609]	2	
Dunsire, David[610]	17	Oct 1878 - Jun 1880
*Earl, Cyrus Hubbert Wheelock[611]	20	May 1877 -

---

602 A painter by profession.

603 John appears to be a hired man for Culbert King, but also a member of the order.

604 Mr. Desaules was a single man and a cabinet maker by profession who had a large personal library. This greatly added to the enjoyment of the community. He also maintained one of the few personal journals available on the Kingston United Order.

605 George was a tailor by profession. His wife, Arabella Van Deusen died October 17, 1876, and his wife,Lauvura Myril Dayton, died April 9, 1877.

606 George married Matilda Emily King in 1880.

607 William is not in the 1880 Census.

608 Wesley is not listed in the 1880 Census.

609 Esther is not listed in the 1880 Census.

610 David married Christina Delilah Warner in 1884. In 1880 he is living with his Uncle, Robert Brown who is not a member of the order.

611 Cyrus is a brother-in-law to Joel White Jr. and Joseph Brigham Nay. He is also a brother to Sylvester Earl, the sheep rustler.

+Erickson, Anders[612]	46	Dec 1877 - Dec 1878
+Clara Caroline Jensen	46	
+Carl Johan	11	
Forrester, Robert		May 1879 -
Johanna E.		
Franks, Betsy Youngquist (Wid)	41	
Hall, John O.		Apr 1878 -
Jane		
Harmon, Thankful Loretta Tanner[613]	55	- Nov 1880
Wister Brigham[614]	18	
Heap, John Henry[615]	22	Jul 1877 -
Huff, James Henry[616]	42	May 1877 - Oct 1879
Sophia Atkin[617]	35	
**Enoch Erastus	17	
**Mary Adalaide	13	
***Sarah Jane	6	
**Olive Maria	4	
Ingram, Alexander Gordon[618]	57	Oct 1878 -
+Agnes Rankin	57	
Jensen, Hans Severine	38	Dec 1877 - Sep 1879
Louisa (Mahitable) (Wife #1)	44	
John (Step son)		May 1878 - Sep 1879

---

612 Anders worked on the Manti Temple as the order's contribution to its construction.

613 The widowed mother of Wister. No record has been found of another husband.

614 Wister married Ella Vilate King in 1881.

615 John is the son of Mary Ward Heap Savage from a previous marriage and who married Mary Ann White in 1880.

616 Brother Huff and his wife served a mission to Canada with the support of the order, returning July 18, 1879.

617 Sophia is a sister to Adalaide Atkin Laxton.

618 An ironworker by profession.

Josephine Anderson (Wife #2)   25

+King, Mary Fay (Wid)[619]   86
    +Mary Elizabeth King Fuel   43
    +John Ephraim Fuel[620]   16
    +Thomas Edson Fuel[621]   14

King, Culbert   43   May 1877 -
    Eliza Esther McCullough (Wife #1)   42
        Matilda Emily   16
        Delilah   14
        **Volney Henry   12
        **Julia Frances   10
        **William   8
        **Alonzo   2

    **Elizabeth Ann Callister (Wife #2)   31
        **Thomas Callister   13
        **Caroline   10
        **Elizabeth Ann   8
        **John   3
        **Helen   1

    Sarah Elizabeth Pratt (Wife #3)[622] 23
    **Orson Pratt   0

King, Culbert Levi   23   May 1877 - Nov 1882
    Polly Ann Ross   21
        **Eva Clair   2
        **Culbert Levi, Jr.   0

King, John Robison   42   May 1877 -
    Helen Matilda Webb   34
        **Helen Maria   17
        **Catherine Aurella   15
        **Lydia Rosella   13
        **John Franklin   10

---

619   Mary is the widowed of Timothy King, brother of Thomas Rice King.

620   A grandson of Mary Fay King.

621   A grandson of Mary Fay King.

622   Sarah is the younger sister of Teancum Pratt and daughter of Apostle Parley P. Pratt.

**Thomas Leroy	7	
**Irene	4	
**Forrest	3	
King, Thomas Edwin	40	May 1877 -
Rebecca Jane Murray (Wife #1)	38	Died Sep 1878
**Eva Matilda	16	
Ella Vilate	15	
Naomi	13	
**Viola	10	
**Josephine May	7	
**Murray Edwin	5	
**Clifford Carol	1	
Isabella Elisha Savage (Wife #2)	20	
King, Thomas Rice	66	May 1877 - Feb 1879
*Matilda Robison	68	
*Rebecca Henry Murray[623]	81	Sep 1878 -
King, Volney	32	May 1877 -
Eliza Syrett[624]	23	
**Eliza Rosetta	4	
**Volney Emery	1	
King, William Rice[625]	45	May 1877 -
Mary Ann Henry (Wife #1)	25	
*William Henry	18	May 1877 - Jul 1879
Lillian	15	
Josephine	13	
**Samuel Andrew	11	
**Harvey William	8	
**Margaret	7	
**Robert Warren	5	
**Claude Leroy	1	
Kahana[626]	19	
Charles Elliot Rowan[627]	18	

623 Rebecca is the mother of Rebecca Jane Murray King and was sealed to Thomas Rice King. There is no record of Thomas and Rebecca living together.

624 Eliza is the daughter of Reuben Syrett.

625 William's first wife, Josephine Henry, died February 12, 1868.

626 Kahana is one of the two adopted children from Hawaii.

627 Charles is one of the two adopted children from Hawaii.

Lucy Maranda White[628] (Wife #2)   19

Knight, James Vinson   46   May 1877 -
   Celestial Roberts   Abt 46
      ***Vincent   4
      +Maria   1
      +James Aubray   0

Laxton, William (X)   62   Nov 1877 - Jan 1881
   Adalaide Atkin   46
      **Israel Pickron   11
      **Mary Elizabeth   9
      **Olive Adelaide   4

Mansor, Stephen[629]   30   Oct 1880 - 1881
      **Emma Ann Wilson[630]   17

McDonough, Mary Ann Forrester   57

Mineer, Andrew   63
   Ingarborg Jensen   67

Mineer, Emiel August[631] 30   - May 1881
   *Frances Ann White[632]   24
      **Birdie Elizabeth   5
      **Frances Helen   3
      **Louisa Sophronie   1

Morrill, Horatio   34   Apr 1878 -
   Sarah Ann Sudweeks   35
      **Sarah Delila Bunce[633]   11
      **Addie Lucetta   6
      **Emma Alvertta   5

---

628   Lucy is the daughter of Joel William White, Sr.

629   aks Mangos

630   Emma is the daughter of Thomas Wilson.

631   Emiel is the son of Andrew Mineer.

632   Frances is the daughter of Joel William White, Sr.

633   Sarah married Frederick Carlson Syrett in 1882.

Nay, Joseph Brigham	Abt 29	Aug 1878 - Jun 1882
Amanda Ellen Earl[634]	29	
***Ellie	11	
***Joseph	9	
***Mary	7	
***John	5	
*Nay, William	41	May 1881 -
**Nancy Wilson[635] (Wife #1)	36	
**John Thomas	15	
**Morris Alonzo	13	
**Amanda Ellen	8	
**Ormus Morley	6	
**George Allen	3	
**Mary Wilson (Wife #2)	30	
**Mary Matilda	10	
**William Dolphin	9	
**Edwin Cressfield	1	
+Ormus Bates Nay[636]	29	
+Louisa Ann Earl[637]	23	
+Ormus Calvin	7	
+Henry Marley	5	
+John	1	
Nielsen, Elizabeth Pedersen[638](Wid)	45	May 1878 -
Niels Peter Nielsen[639]	22	Apr 1878 - Sep 1879
**Christian Ludwig Nielsen	10	
**Ole Nielsen	7	
**Fredrick Nielsen	4	
+ Nielsen, Niels	55	Dec 1877 - Oct 1879
+Jensine Christine (Wife #1)	47	
+Emma	15	
+Jensine	12	

---

634 Amanda is a sister to Mary Elizabeth Earl White and Cyrus Earl.

635 Nancy and Mary, the second wife, are the daughters of Thomas Wilson.

636 In 1883 Ormus robbed a train along with Sylvester Earl and was sent to prison.

637 Louisa is the sister of Sylvester and Cyrus Earl.

638 Her husband, Ole Nielsen, died June 20, 1878.

639 This is probably the same person as H. Peter Nelson.

+Neil Joseph	9	
+Karen Marie (Wife #2)	25	
+Alma	7	
+Mary Ordena	0	
+Peterson, Brita Catherine (Wid)		
+Charles August	16	
+Emma	14	
Pratt, Sarah Houston[640] (Wid)	56	Nov 1877 -
Pratt, Teancum	28	Nov 1877 - Mar 1879
Anna Elizabeth Mead (Wife #1)	24	
*Mary Lydia	2	
*Ether	1	
Sarah Elizabeth Ewell (Wife #2)	19	- Mar 1879
*Parley Pahoran	1	
Savage, David Leonard	67	May 1877 - Nov 1880
Mary Abigail White[641] (Wife #1)	56	
*Mary Ward Heap[642] (Wife #2)	50	
*David Edward	17	
William Albert	14	
Parley Franklin	11	
**Barbara Alice	7	
**Margaret Emma Jones[643]	42	
(Wife #3 - div)		
Margaret Emma	18	
Laura Crystine[644]	16	
*Charles Thomas	15	
Savage, David William	30	- Nov 1880
Julia Merrill	20	

---

640 The mother of Teancum Pratt and Sarah Pratt King and the widow (the seventh of twelve wives) of Apostle Parley Parker Pratt.

641 Mary is the older sister to Joel William White, Sr.

642 Divorced from William Heap

643 Separated July, 1869, from David Savage and went to California. The children stayed with David, except for a small child, Gomer.

644 This is probably Laura Angeline.

Shimmin, Robert	55	Nov 1879 - Oct 1880
+Hannah Clucas (Wife #1)	50	
+Charlotte Louise	19	
Anne Jensen (Wife #2)	38	
**Anna Sophia	16	
**Robert Martin Christian	15	
**Samuel Moore	11	
**Mary Hattie	2	
Smith, Thomas	28	- Sep 1879
Tennessee Whittaker	24	
Thomas	1	
Sorenson, Jens Christian	30	Apr 1878 - Sep 1879
**Anna Kirstine Nielsen[645]	18	
**James Christian	1	
Springthorpe, John	53	Jul 1879 - Mar 1881
+Jessie	50	
***Theresa	15	
Syrett, Reuben[646]	47	Jan 1879 - Jul 1882
*Susannah Bardon	46	Died Dec 1878
Fredrick Carlson	26	Jul 1878 - Jul 1881
Ephraim[647]	25	May 1877 -
*Louisa Ann	18	
*Wilford Orson	13	
Thomas, David	59	May 1878 - Jun 1881
Adaline	51	
Frances A.	16	
David John	14	

---

645   The daughter of Elizabeth Pedersen Nielsen.

646   The father of Eliza Syrett, the wife of Volney King. The Syretts came with Volney on his return from his mission to England. Reuben is the ancestor of the Syrett family who own Ruby's Inn at Bryce Canyon, Utah.

647   Ephraim married Maria Roberts April 3, 1880.

Warner, Mortimer Wilson[648]	37	May 1877 -
Christenia Brown	35	
Christenia Delilah	14	
Elen [Ellen] Elizabeth	13	
*Mortimer Wallace	10	
*Robert Orange	8	
**Loneva	6	
**Janet	4	
**Cornelius	1	
Whetten, John Thomas[649]	17	May 1877 - Sep 1879
**Agnes Belzora Savage[650]	18	
**John Amasa	0	
White, Joseph Thomas	27	- Feb 1880
**Margaret Elizabeth Ewing	23	
+Joseph William	5	
+Margaret Ann	3	
+Serena Matilda	1	
White, Joel William Sr.	48	May 1877 - May 1881
Frances Ann Thomas	46	
Mary Ann[651]	17	
**John Elbert	15	
**Clara Jane (son?)	12	
**Harrison James	9	
**Martha Janette	7	
**Sarah Emily	5	
**Daniel Dennis	3	
***Serena White McKinney[652]	22	
***Sarah McKinney	1	
***Hugh McKinney	0	

---

648 The son of Orange Warner, the good friend of Thomas R. King.

649 John is a stepson of James Huff.

650 Agnes is the daughter of David Leonard Savage.

651 Mary married John Henry Heap in 1880.

652 Serena is the married daughter of Joel who was living with them in 1880 (Census) together with her two children Sarah and Hugh.

White, Joel William Jr.	28	May 1877 - May 1881
**Mary Elizabeth Earl	27	
**Louisa	2	
**Sylvester	1	
Wilcox, John Dingham	36	May 1877 - Sep 1879
Mary Theodocia Savage[653]	32	
John Elbert	13	
*David Oswell	9	
**Samuel Orris	7	
**Lucy Abigail	5	
**Martha Elnora	2	
*Wilson, Thomas	68	Mar 1889 - Sept 1881
**Nancy Lindsey	55	
**Hannah	14	
Williamson, Robert Loney[654]	54	- Oct 1880
Woolsey, James[655]	Abt 53	
Mary Ann Donnelly	42	
+Mary Ann	21	
+Lillian	16	
+Edward	11	

---

653 Mary is a daughter of David Leonard Savage.

654 Robert married on November 18, 1880, Hannah Amanda Harmon (Pilling), the daughter of Thankful Loretta Tanner Harmon. There is no record of an earlier wife for Robert.

655 The Woolseys signed the Articles of Agreement, but then dropped out of the order and never lived at Kingston.

Appendix 7

(Officers and Directors of the United Order at Kingston)

	May 1877	May 1878	May 1879
President:	Thomas R. King	Thomas R. King	Wm King
1st VP:	Joel W. White	Joel W. White	Joel W. White
2nd VP:	Wm King	Wm King	Culbert King
Secretary:	Edwin King	Edwin King	Edwin King
Treasurer:	Mortimer Warner	Mortimer Warner	John D. Wilcox
Director:	James Huff	James Huff	James Huff
Director:	David Savage	David Savage	David Savage
Director:	George Black	George Black	George Black
Director:	n/a	Culbert King	Mortimer Warner
Director:	n/a	n/a	Niels Nielsen
Supt. Livestock	n/a	Culbert King	n/a
Supt. Lumber:	n/a	Edwin King	n/a
Supt. Buildings:	n/a	James Huff	n/a
Supt. Sheep herd:	n/a	Mortimer Warner	n/a
Supt. Tannery:	n/a	n/a	n/a
Supt. Farm:	Wm King	Wm King Edwin King	n/a
Bishop:	Wm King	Wm King	Wm King
Members:	n/a	156	n/a
Capital Stock:	n/a	$27,041.20	$27,741.20

May 1880	May 1881	May 1882	May 1883
Wm King	Wm King	Wm King	Wm King
n/a	Culbert King	Culbert King	Culbert King
n/a	Fred Syrett	Mortimer Warner	Mortimer Warner
n/a	Edwin King	Edwin King	Edwin King
n/a	Volney King	Volney King	Volney King
James Huff	H. Morrill	H. Morrill	H. Morrill
David Savage	R. Forrester	R. Forrester	R. Forrester
George Black	George Black	Joseph Nay	Joseph Knight
Mortimer Warner	Mortimer Warner	C. Levi King	n/a
Niels Nielsen	Reuben Syrett	John King	John King
n/a	n/a	John King	n/a
n/a	n/a	Edwin King	n/a
n/a	n/a	Wm King	n/a
n/a	n/a	n/a	n/a
n/a	n/a	Culbert King	n/a
n/a	n/a	H. Morrill	n/a
Wm King	Wm King	Wm King	Wm King
177	114	n/a	n/a
$24,144.88	n/a	n/a	n/a

Appendix 8

(King Family Demographics)

L ife expectancy during the late eighteen-hundreds was significantly less than by today's standards, with childhood deaths accounting for two-thirds of total deaths. This compares to only two to three percent today. Most of the nineteenth-century deaths occurred during the hot summer and early fall months, when waterborne diseases, such as dysentery, gastroenteritis, and typhoid fever, had a chance to germinate fully, although respiratory diseases such as diphtheria, whooping cough, and measles were also particularly troublesome. Overall childhood deaths accounted for about 20 to 22 deaths per thousand children, or about 2% to 2.2% per year.[656]

Statistically it is difficult to determine how the death rate among the King children might be compared to a more global population because of such a small sample. While there was a 23% overall mortality rate among the second-generation children (grandchildren of Thomas and Matilda), this was spread over several decades and on average would amount to a percentage lower than the statistics quoted above. What is interesting is that 65% of the children died during the colder months of November through April rather than during the summer months as mentioned above. Perhaps this was due more to respiratory problems of being shut up during the winter months in unhealthy homes and schools. The water supply is also suspect, as drinking water was simply taken out of the local river or irrigation ditch, which was also home to rodents, cattle, and anything else that fell in.

Besides disease, the risks of children getting hurt or dying by drowning in wells and irrigation ditches, being burned from fireplaces, and being run over by wagons and horses was also a serious hazard.

The death rate for each family by wife is as follows. Of the children who died between the years of 1863 and 1897, all were below the age of twelve, except one who was sixteen and one unknown.

---

656 Lester E. Bush, Jr., *Health and Medicine among the Latter-day Saints,* (Crossroad Publishing Company, New York, New York, 1993), 42-43.

THOMAS RICE

Matilda	Female	Male	Total
Lived	1	5	6
Died	1	1	2
	2	6	8

WILLIAM

Josephine	Female	Male	Total
Lived	2	2	4
Died	0	0	0
	2	2	4

Mary Ann	Female	Male	Total
Lived	1	6	7
Died	0	0	0
	1	6	7

Lucy	Female	Male	Total
Lived	0	0	0
Died	0	0	0
	0	0	0

CULBERT

Esther	Female	Male	Total
Lived	4	4	8
Died	1	2	3
	5	6	11

Elizabeth	Female	Male	Total
Lived	2	2	4
Died	2	2	4
	4	4	8

Sarah	Female	Male	Total
Lived	1	2	3
Died	1	1	2
	2	3	5

JOHN ROBISON

Helen	Female	Male	Total
Lived	5	3	8
Died	1	0	1
	6	3	9

THOMAS EDWIN

Rebecca	Female	Male	Total
Lived	3	2	5
Died	2	0	2
	5	2	7

Isabella	Female	Male	Total
Lived	1	0	1
Died	0	0	0
	1	0	1

DELILAH

	Female	Male	Total
Lived	3	5	8
Died	1	0	1
	4	5	9

VOLNEY

Eliza	Female	Male	Total
Lived	3	4	7
Died	0	3	3
	3	7	10

TOTAL

	Female	Male	Total
Lived	26 for 43%	35 for 57%	61
Died	9 for 50%	9 for 50%	18
	35 for 46%	44 for 54%	79

<u>First Generation</u>   Children 8   Living 6   Died 2
Spouse   1
Children per father   8
Children per spouse   8
Living children per family   6
Mortality rate   25%

<u>Second Generation</u>   Children: 71   Living 55   Died 16

Spouses   11.0[657]
Children per father   11.8
Children per spouse   6.5
Living children per family   9.2
Mortality Rate   22.5%
    William   .0
    Culbert   37.5
    John Robison   11.1
    Thomas Edwin   25.0
    Delilah   11.1
    Volney   30.0

Deaths by Month

November	2	May	1
December	0	June	1
January	2	July	1
February	0	August	1
March	3	September	0
April	<u>2</u>	October	<u>1</u>
	9		5
	56%		31%

Unknown   2
13%

---

657 The fourth wife of Culbert King, Lydia, is not counted. She and Culbert married well beyond her child bearing years.

Appendix 9

(Map of Early Settlers at Antimony)

Homesteads in Antimony from Otter Creek Reservoir
to Hunter Lane.

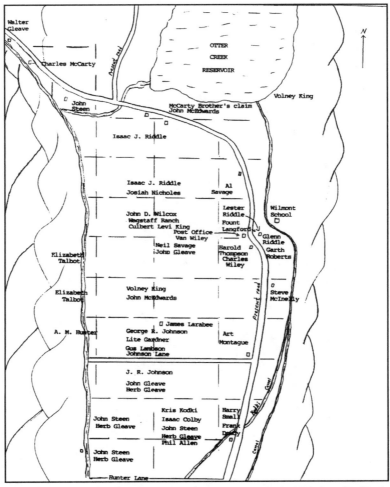

This and the following two maps were put together by Lane Warner for his book:
Antimony, Utah: Its History and Its People 1873-2004, (2004, 2nd edition) 219-221,
and represents the general location of many of the early settlers of Antimony. It is
based on the memory of one of the old citizens of Antimony, Thomas Lester Riddle,
who in about 1974 helped Mr. Warner put the material together.

Homesteads in Antimony from Hunter Lane to the cemetery.

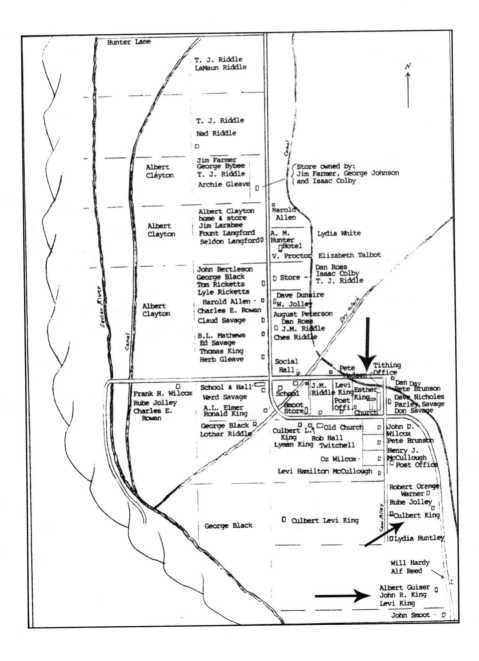

Homesteads in Antimony from the cemetery to Bench & Black canyon.

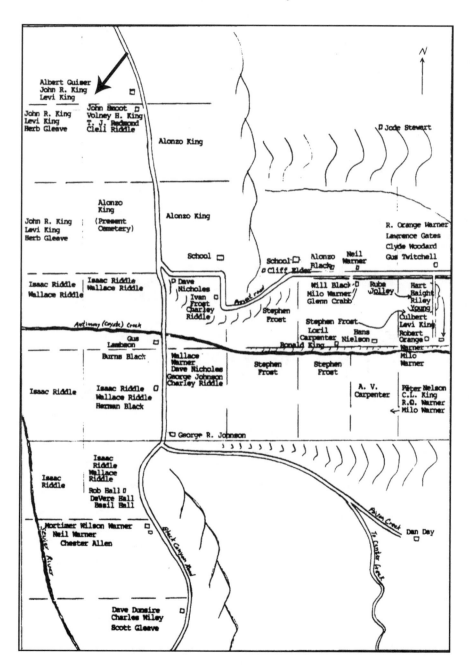

Appendix 10

(Patriarchal Blessing)[658]

Thomas R. King
November 17, 1845

"A blessing by John Smith, Patriarch, upon the head of Thomas R. King, son of Thomas & Ruth, born March 9th, 1813, Onondaga Co, New York. Bro. Thomas I lay my hands upon thy head in the name of Jesus of Nazareth & place upon thee a father's blessing, inasmuch as thy father has gone the way of all the earth; thou art a lawful heir to the holy priesthood & thou shalt be clothed with a fullness of the priesthood in due time, for thou shalt receive thine endowment in the Lord's house with thy companion where hidden mysteries shall be revealed unto thee, bringing to thy understanding things that have been hid from before the foundation of the world; inasmuch as you seek diligently with an honest heart to do the will of the Lord & follow the counsel of his servants, no good thing shall be withheld from thee; thou shalt have power to do any miracle when it is necessary for the salvation of the children of men & the prosperity of Zion; thou shalt do much in gathering the remnants of Jacob, & thou shalt proclaim the gospel with mighty power to the Lamanites; shall baptize them by scores & establish them in the cities of the saints; thou shalt have a numerous family & they shall spread abroad like Jacob, & thou shalt see the winding up scene of this generation, & inasmuch as you learn to deal justly; love mercy & walk humbly thou shalt inherit eternal life for I seal it upon thee & thy posterity in common with thy companion Amen."

Matilda Robison
November 17, 1845

"A blessing by John Smith, Patriarch, upon the head of Matilda King, daughter of Joseph & Cornelia Robison, born March 11th, 1811 Montgomery Co. New York. Sister Matilda I lay my hands upon thy head in the authority of my office as a patriarch & place upon thee all the blessings of the new & everlasting covenant & the holy priesthood & all other bless-

---

658 LDS Church Historical Department Archives.

ings that were sealed upon the children of Ephraim in common with thy companion for this is thy lineage; thou shalt be blessed in thy basket & in thy store, in thy dwelling & in thy family, with health peace & plenty & every favor that is desirable & thy name shall be had in honorable remembrance among the saints because of the multitude of thy progeny & thou shalt be able with thy companion & friends to redeem thy fathers back to the days of Noah so that every dispensation may be connected with the dispensation of the fullness of times & bring them up in the morning of the resurrection, for no good thing shall be withheld from that which you desire in righteousness; thou shalt live to see the winding up scene of this generation if your faith does not fail & inasmuch as you deal faithfully & truly with a liberal heart with all sincerity and godly honesty, not one word which is here written shall fail for I seal it upon thee & thy posterity in common with thy companion forever, Amen."

Matilda Robison
April 4, 1857

"Patriarchal Blessing given in Great S.L. City, April 4, 1857 By John Young upon the head of Matilda Robison King, born March 11, 1811, Charlestown, New York, daughter of Joseph and Cornelia Robison.

"Sister Matilda, In the name of the Lord Jesus Christ I now lay my hands upon your head to bless you even with a father's blessing, and with the blessings of the heavens and of the earth, and to predict those things which are hereafter to come to pass and which you shall realize. You have embraced the gospel with an honest heart, with a desire to work righteousness in your day and generation. You have left your native land to sojourn with the saints of God, to be a pilgrim and a stranger upon the earth. You are a lawful heir to the blessings of the new and everlasting covenant being a literal descendant of Ephraim, and therefore an heir according to promise given to the fathers, and I bless you in the name of Israel's God. You shall have power from this time forth and for ever to control yourself and your household with propriety and discretion; many shall call you blessed; you shall be blest with the good things of the heavens and of the earth and all things shall prosper in your hands. For as much as you have consented in your feelings for your husband to go into the world to preach the gospel and to warn the inhabitants thereof, you and your family shall be blest. You shall live upon the earth to do much good, even till you are satisfied with life, and your heart shall rejoice; you shall be a comfort to many; have power to administer to the afflicted in your own family and to those that are round about you, power to discern spirits, to overcome every evil which may rise to oppose you in your holy soarjourn [sic] here below, and you shall have power to come forth in the morning of the first resurrection, be numbered among that throng which John saw; be a blessing to thousands; do much good in your day and generation, Satan shall not have power over you; you have been tempted and tried, yet you shall be delivered from the powers of darkness, and you shall have more strength to resist evil than even you had in your life, for I confer this blessing upon you. Your name shall be had in honorable remembrance in the Church of Jesus Christ of Latter-day Saints. These blessings I seal upon you Sister King, with all you desire, and say you shall live to a good old age, help to build up the kingdom of God, and in all times of danger and difficulty the Angel of mercy shall be with you. You shall be blest with flocks and herds and they shall be multiplied unto you, and you shall be an honor to the cause in which you are engaged. I say be faithful and carry out the counsel given, and you shall live to see the return of your husband, and not a hair of his head shall fall by the enemy, and your heart shall rejoice in the society of those you are associated with. I seal these upon you and all other blessings you desire by the authority which the Lord has given to his servants to seal upon the earth, and in the name of the Father, Son and Holy Ghost, even so: Amen."

I.V.(?) Long, Reporter
S.A. Long, Scribe

Bibliography

Books

Aiken, Ruth J., Ed., Records of the Lower St. Georges and Cushing, Maine 1605-1897. Cushing, Maine: Driftwood Farm, 1987.

Anderson, Robert Charles, George F. Sanborn, Jr., Melinde Lutz Sanborn, The Great Migration ,Immigrants to New England 1634-1635, Vol. 1 & 2.

Arrington, Leonard J., *Brigham Young: American Moses.* Urbana and Chicago, Illinois: University of Illinois Press, 1986.

Arrington, Leonard J., *Great Basin Kingdom.* Lincoln, Nebraska, University of Nebraska Press, 1966.

Arrington, Leonard J., *Orderville, Utah: A Pioneer Mormon Experiment in Economic Organization,* Utah State Agricultural College, March 1954, Vol. 2, No. 2.

Arrington, Leonard J.; Feramorz Y. Fox, Dean L. May, *Building the City of God.* Salt Lake City, Utah: Deseret Book Company, 1976.

Banks, Charles Edward, *Topographical Dictionary of English Emigrants to New England 1620-1650.* Baltimore: Genealogical Publishing Company, 1969.

Barbour, Lucius A., Lucius B. Barbour, Comp., *Barbour Collection, Connecticut Vital Records to 1850,* Connecticut State Library, W - Was, LDS Church Family History Library, Salt Lake City, Utah, film #2,960.

Barney, Ronald O., ed., *The Mormon Vanguard Brigade of 1847 Norton Jacob's Record.* Logan, Utah: Utah State University Press, 2005.

Beauchamp, William M., *Past and Present of Syracuse and Onondaga County, New York,* S.J. Clarke Publishing Company, 1908.

Bennett, Richard E., *Mormons at the Missouri, 1846-1852.* Norman, Oklahoma: University of Oklahoma Press, 1987.

Bodge, George Madison, *Soldiers in King Philip's War,* Clearfield Company, Third Edition, n.d.

Book of Mormon, Church of Jesus Christ of Latter-day Saints.

Britsch, R. Lanier, *Moramona, The Mormons in Hawaii.* Laie, Hawaii: The Institute for Polynesian Studies, 1992.

Brodie, Fawn, *No Man Knows My History.* New York, New York: Alfred A. Knopf, 1982.

Brooks, Juanita, *John Doyle Lee.* Logan, Utah: Utah State University Press, 1992.

Brooks, Juanita, *The Mountain Meadows Massacre.* Norman, Oklahoma: University of Oklahoma Press, 1987.

Brown, S. Kent; Donald Q. Cannon, and Richard H. Jackson, *Historical Atlas of Mormonism.* New York, New York: Simon & Schuster, 1994.

Bruce, Dwight H., *Onondaga's Centennial, Vol 1*, The Boston History Company, 1896.

Bush, Lester E. Jr., *Health and Medicine among the Latter-day Saints.* New York, New York: The Crossroads Publishing Company, 1993.

Bushman, Richard Lyman, *Joseph Smith Rough Stone Rolling.* New York: Alfred A. Knopf, 2005.

Cabot, Mary R., *Annals of Brattleboro, 2 vols.,1681-1895*, 1921, Vol. 1.

Cannon, Janath, *Nauvoo Panorama*, Nauvoo Restoration Inc., 1991.

Carter, Kate B., *Heart Throbs of the West.* Salt Lake City: Utah Daughters of Utah Pioneers, 12 vols., 1939-1951, 1,9.

Carter, Kate B., *Our Pioneer Heritage*, 20 vols., an article by Utahna R. Gottfredson. Salt Lake City, Utah: Daughters of Utah Pioneers, 1958-1977, vol. 12.

Carter, Kate B., *Treasures of Pioneer History,* 6 vols. Salt Lake City, Utah: Daughters of Utah Pioneers, 1952-1957, 4.

Christensen, Leavitt, *The Birth of Kanosh,* Published by the Town of Kanosh, Utah, Terry Higgs, Mayor, 1995.

Collier, Fred C., comp, *Unpublished Revelations of the Prophets and Presidents of the Church of Jesus Christ of Latter Day Saints,* 2 vols. Salt Lake City, Utah: Collier's Publishing Company, 1981, vol. 1.

Compton, Todd, *In Sacred Loneliness: The Plural Wives of Joseph Smith.* Salt Lake City, Utah: Signature Books, 2001.

Cook, Melville Bradford, *Records of Meduncook Plantation and Friendship, Maine 1762-1899.* Rockland, Maine: Shore Village Historical Society, 1985.

Cowley, Matthias F., *Wilford Woodruff, History of His Life and Labors.* Salt Lake City, Utah: Bookcraft Publishers, 1978.

Cross, Mary Bywater, *Quilts & Women of the Mormon Migrations.* Nashville, Tennessee: Rutledge Hill Press, 1996.

James S. Cushing, *The Genealogy of the Cushing Family.* Montreal: The Perrault Printing Company, 1905, 38-41.

Daughters of Utah Pioneers, *Mormon Emigration 1840-1869.* Salt Lake City, Utah: Utah Printing Company, 1963.

Day, Stella and Sebrina C. Ekins, comp, *Milestones of Millard, 100 Years of History of Millard County,* Daughters of Utah Pioneers, Art City Publishing Co., 1951.

Day, Stella, *Builders of Early Millard, Biographies of Pioneer of Millard County 1950 to 1875,* Daughters of Utah Pioneers, Art City Publishing Co., 1979.

Deseret News, *1985* and *1997-1998 Church Almanac,* Church of Jesus Christ of Latter-day Saints.

Dewey, Richard Lloyd, *Porter Rockwell.* New York, New York: Paramount Books, 1987.

Doctrine & Covenants of the Church of Jesus Christ of Latter-day Saints.

Drake, Samuel Adams, *History of Middlesex County, Massachusetts.* Boston: Estes and Lauriat, 1880.

Durant, Will and Ariel, *The Lessons of History.* New York, New York, MJF Books, 1968.

Earl, Sylvester Earl, *My Life's Philosophy: Religious-Politico and Other wise,* (n.p,n.d.),

Edmund Rice (1638) Association Inc., *A Genealogical Register of Edmund Rice Descendants,* Ray Lowther Ellis, Managing Editor. Rutland, Vermont: The Charles E. Tuttle Company, 1970.

Emerson, Everett, *Puritanism in America 1720-1750.* Boston: Twayne Publishers, 1977, 32.

Esshom, Frank, *Pioneers and Prominent Men of Utah,* Western Epics, Inc. 1966.

Evans, Richard L., *A Century of Mormonism in Great Britain,* Salt Lake City, Utah: Publishers Press, 1937.

Fabian, Bentham, *Statistics Concerning the Territory of Utah, Years 1872-3.* Salt Lake City, Utah: Stevens & Company, 1874,

Faulkner, Harold Underwood, *American Economic History.* New York: Harper & Brothers, 1954.

Federal Writer's Project of the Works Progress Administration in Massachusetts, *A Brief History of the Town of Sudbury in Massachusetts 1639-1939* (1987)

Flanders, Robert Bruce, *Nauvoo, Kingdom on the Mississippi.* Chicago, Illinois: University of Illinois Press, 1975.

Foster, Lawrence, *Religion and Sexuality, The Shakers, the Mormons, and the Oneida Community.* Chicago, Illinois: University of Illinois Press, 1984.

History of Fremont County, Iowa, A History of the County, Its Cities, Towns, Etc. Des Moines Iowa: Historical Company, 1881.

Hansen, Klaus J., *Quest for Empire.* Lincoln, Nebraska: University of Nebraska Press, 1967.

Hardy, B. Carmon, *Solemn Covenant, The Mormon Polygamous Passage.* Chicago, Illinois: University of Illinois Press, 1992.

History of Utah Since Statehood, Vol. 111, n.d, n.d., (Found in the Orem, Utah city library.)

Holy Bible, King James Version.

Hudson, Alfred Sereno, *History of Sudbury, Massachusetts 1638-1889.* Sudbury, Massachusetts: Sudbury Press, 1889.

Hudson, Charles, *History of the Town of Marlborough.* Boston, Massachusetts: T. R. Marvin & Son, 1862.

Jenson, Andrew, *Church Chronology, A Record of Important Events Pertaining to the History of the Church of Jesus Christ of Latter-day Saints.* Salt Lake City, Utah: Deseret News, 1899.

Jenson, Andrew, *Encyclopedic History of the Church of Jesus Christ of Latter-day Saints,* 2nd ed. Salt Lake City, Utah: Deseret News Publishing Company, 1941.

Journal of Discourses by President Brigham Young, His Counselors, and the Twelve Apostles, 26 vol. London, England: Albert Carrington, 1875.

King, Dwight L., "The Two Volneys," Salt Lake City, Utah: January 1993.

LDS Church Educational System, *Church History in the Fulness of Times.* Salt Lake City, Utah: Church of Jesus Christ of Latter-day Saints, 1989.

Ludlow, Daniel H., Editor, *Encyclopedia of Mormonism, 4* vols. New York, New York: Macmillan Publishing Company, 1992.

Lyman, Edward Leo and Linda King Newell, *A History of Millard County,* Utah State Historical Society, Millard County Commission, 1999.

McGavin, Elmer Ceil, *Mormonism and Masonry.* Salt Lake City, Utah: Deseret News Press, 1935.

Melendy, H. Brett and Gilbert, Benjamin F., *The Governors of California.* Georgetown, California: The Talisman Press, 1965.

Moorman, Donald R., *Camp Floyd and the Mormons, the Utah War.* Salt Lake City, Utah: University of Utah Press, 1992.

Musser, Joseph W., *Celestial or Plural Marriage.* Salt Lake City, Utah: Truth Publishing Company, 1970.

Newell, Linda King and Valeen Tippetts Avery, *Mormon Enigma: Emma Hale Smith.* Garden City, New York: Doubleday & Company, Inc., 1984.

Poll, Richard D., General Editor, *Utah's History.* Logan, Utah: Utah State University Press, 1989.

Powell, Sumner Chilton, *Puritan Village: The Formation of a New England Town.* Middletown, Connecticut: Wesleyan University Press, 1963.

Puglisi, Michael J., *Puritans Besieged: The Legacies of the King Philip's War in the Massachusetts Bay Colony.* New York: University Press of America, 1991.

Quinn, D. Michael, *The Mormon Hierarchy, Origins of Power.* Salt Lake City, Utah: Signature Books, 1994.

Rawlyk, G. A., *Yankees at Louisbourg,* University of Main Studies No. 85, University of Maine Press, 1967.

Rice, Roger E., *A Treatise on the Rice Family,* 1989. A copy is in the LDS Church Family History Library, Salt Lake City, Utah.

Roberts, B.H., *Comprehensive History of the Church of Jesus Christ of Latter-day Saints,* 6 vols, Provo, Utah: Brigham Young University Press, 1965.

Robinson, John J., *Born in Blood, the Lost Secrets of Freemasonry,* New York: M. Evans & Company, 1989.

Robinson, Phil, *Sinners and Saints: A Tour Across the States and Round Them; with Three Months Among the Mormons.* Boston: Robert Brothers, 1883.

Robison, Joleen Ashman, *Almon Robison, Utah Pioneer, Man of Mystique and Tragedy.* Lawrence, Kansas: Richard A. Robison, 1995.

Rodgers, Robert H., *Middlesex County in the Colony of the Massachusetts Bay in New England, Records of Probate and Administration, March 1660/61 - December 1670,* Boston: The New England Historic Genealogical Society, 2001.

Rollins, Alden M., *Vermont Warnings Out, Southern Vermont*, vol. 2. Camden, Maine: Picton Press, 1996.

Schutz, John A., *Legislators of the Massachusetts General Court 1691-1780, A Biographical Dictionary.* Boston: Northeastern University Press, 1997.

Stott, Clifford L., *Search for Sanctuary, Brigham Young and the White Mountain Expedition.* Salt Lake City, Utah: University of Utah Press, 1984.

Smith, Elsie Hawes, *Edmund Rice and His Family: We Sought the Wilderness,* The Edmund Rice Association, Inc., 1938).

Smith, Joseph, et al., *History of the Church of Jesus Christ of Latter-day Saints*, edited by B.H. Roberts, 7 vols., 2nd ed. rev. Salt Lake City, Utah: Deseret Book Company, 1959.

Smith, Joseph Fielding, *Essentials in Church History.* Salt Lake City, Utah: Deseret Book Company, 1950.

Smith, Joseph Fielding, *Life of Joseph F. Smith.* Salt Lake City, Utah: Deseret News Press, 1938.

Smith, Joseph Fielding, *Seek Ye Earnestly.* Salt Lake City, Utah: Deseret Book Company, 1970.

Smith, Joseph Fielding, *Doctrines of Salvation.* Salt Lake City, Utah: Bookcraft, 1955.

Sonne, Conway B., *Ships, Saints, and Mariners.* Salt Lake City, Utah: University of Utah Press, 1987.

Taylor, Dale, *A Writer's Guide to Everyday Life in Colonial America.* Cincinnati, Ohio: Writer's Digest Books, 1997.

Taylor, Samuel W., *The Kingdom or Nothing.* New York, New York: Macmillan Publishing Co., 1976.

Tunis, Edwin, *Oars, Sails and Steam, A Picture Book of Ships.*

Tyler, Daniel, *A Concise History of the Mormon Battalion in the Mexican War 1846-1848.* Glorieta, New Mexico: The Rio Grande Press, Inc., 1881.

Ulrich, Laurel Thatcher, *Good Wives, Image and Reality in Lives of Women in Northern New England 1650-1750.* New York: Vintage Books, 1991.

Van Wagoner, Richard S., *Mormon Polygamy: A History.* Salt Lake City, Utah, Signature Books, 1986.

Van Wagoner, Richard S., *Sidney Rigdon A Portrait of Religious Excess.* Salt Lake City, Utah: Signature Books, 1994.

Ward, Andrew Henshaw, A.M., *Genealogical History of the Rice Family: Descendants of Deacon Edmund Rice.* Boston, Massachusetts: C. Benjamin Richardson, 1858.

Warner, M. Lane, *Antimony, Utah Its History and its People 1873-2004,* 2004.

Warner, M. Lane, *Grass Valley 1873-1927: A History of Antimony and Her People.* Salt Lake City, Utah: American Press, 1976.

Washburne, Brenton P., Robin P. Washburne, The Washburne Family in America, 2 vol., second edition, n.p.: 1997.

Well-wishers, W.L., *The Meaning of Masonry.* New York: Gramercy Books, 1980.

White, Lorraine, Cook, Gen. Ed., Dorothy Wear, Comp., *The Barbour Collection of Connecticut Town Vital Records,* Hebron 1708-1854, n.p.: Genealogical Publishing Co., Inc.

White, Lorraine Cook, Gen. Ed., Nancy E. Schott, Comp., *The Barbour Collection of Connecticut Town Vital Records,* Lebanon, 3 vol., 1700-1854, n.p.: Genealogical Publishing Co., Inc.

White, Lorraine Cook, Gen. Ed., Jan Tilton, comp., *The Barbour Collection of Connecticut Town Vital Records,* Stafford 1719-1850, n.p.: Genealogical Publishing Co., Inc.

Wood, Ralph V. Jr., *Francis Cooke of the Mayflower: The First Five Generations*. Rockport, Maine: Picton Press, 1996.

World Book Encclopedia, 20 vols. Chicago, London, Rome, Sydney, Toronto: Field Enterprises Educational Corporation, 1971.

Articles

Association for the Promotion of Scholarship in Genealogy, Ltd., "English Origins of Philemon Whale," *The Genealogist,* Vol. 6, No. 2.

Burn ham, Henry, *Vermont Historical Magazine*, Brattleboro, Windham, Vermont, 1880.

Cross, Whitney R., *Mormonism in the Burnt Over District,* Archives of the Family and Church History Department, Church of Jesus Christ of Latter-day Saints, Salt Lake City, Utah.

Godfrey, Kenneth W., "Joseph Smith and the Masons," *Journal of the Illinois State Historical Society*, 64:1, Spring 1971.

Holman, Mary Lovering, "English Notes on Edmund Rice," *American Genealogist,* 10, LDS Church Family History Library, Salt Lake City, Utah.

Holman, Mary Lovering, "English Notes on Edmund Rice," *The American Genealogist,* 15, LDS Church Family History Library, Salt Lake City, Utah.

Holman, Mary Lovering, "The Wife of Edmund Rice," *The American Genealogist*, 15, LDS Church Family History Library, Salt Lake City, Utah.

Jacobus, Donald Lines, "Pre-American Ancestries," *American Genealogist,* 11, LDS Church Family History Library, Salt Lake City, Utah.

Jenson, Andrew, "Church Emigration," *The Contributor,* Archives of the Family and Church History Department, Church of Jesus Christ of Latter-day Saints, Salt Lake City, Utah.

Kimball, Stanley B., "Heber C. Kimball and Family, the Nauvoo Years," *B.Y.U. Studies*, 15:4.

King, Volney, "Millard County, 1851-1875," *Utah Humanities Review*, 1:3, July, 1947, University of Utah, Salt Lake City, Utah.

McCormick, John S., "Hornets in the Hive: Socialists in Early Twentieth-Century Utah," *Utah Historical Quarterly*, 50:3 Summer 1982.

New England Historical and Genealogical Register 1892, Boston, 1892, XLVI:120.

Porter, Harold R. Porter, Jr., "The Paternal Ancestry of Thomasine Frost, Wife of Deacon Edmund Rice of Sudbury, Mass.," *The American Genealogist,* Vol. 63, No. 3, July 1988.

Quinn, D. Michael, "LDS Church Finances From the 1830s to the 1990s," *Sunstone,* 19:2, June 1996.

Rice-Smith, E.P., "Essay III: Ashur Rice - Returned to Westborough. Amongst Family and a Member of the Church*," Edmund Rice (1638) Association Newsletter,* 80:4, Autumn 2006.

Sillito, John R. and McCormick, John S., "Socialist Saints: Mormons and the Socialist Party in Utah, 1900-20," *Dialogue: A Journal of Mormon Thought,* 18:1, Spring 1985.

Stampp, Kenneth, "On the Brink of War," *U.S. News & World Report,* January 21, 1991.

Vermont Historical Gazetteer, 1891, vol. V.

Diaries and Journals

Bunting, James Lovett, Diary 1857-77, L. Tom Perry Special Collections and Manuscripts, Harold B. Lee Library, Brigham Young University, Provo, Utah.

Call, Anson, The Life and Record of Anson Call, Archives of the Family and Church History Department, Church of Jesus Christ of Latter-day Saints, Salt Lake City, Utah.

DeSaules, Henri Edward, Diary 1833-1904, Archives of the Family and Church History Department, Church of Jesus Christ of Latter-day Saints, Salt Lake City, Utah.

Henry, Andrew, The Henrys and the Kings, Arranged by Parnell Hinckley.

Hinckley, Ira Nathaniel, Diary March 1857 to June 1858, Archives of the Family and Church History Department, Church of Jesus Christ of Latter-day Saints, Salt Lake City, Utah.

Hoyt, Emily Smith, Diary 1806-1893, Archives of the Family and Church History Department, Church of Jesus Christ of Latter-day Saints, Salt Lake City, Utah.

Jacob, Norton, Autobiography, L. Tom Perry Speical Collections and Manuscripts, Harold B. Lee Library, Brigham Young University, Provo, Utah.

Kane, Elizabeth, St. George Diary, "A Gentile Account of Life in Utah's Dixie 1872-73," L. Tom Perry Special Collections and Manuscripts, Harold B. Lee Library, Brigham Young University, Provo, Utah.

King, Thomas Edwin, Missionary Journal. A copy in the possession of Larry King.

King, Thomas Rice, Autobiography, n.d. Archives of the Family and Church History Department, Church of Jesus Christ of Latter-day Saints, Salt Lake City, Utah.

King, William Rice, Journal - July 28, 1880 to January 6, 1882, original in the possession of David S. King, Kensington, Maryland.

King, Volney, The Daily Journal of Kingston United Order, an abbreviated transcribed copy is at the Utah Historical Society Library, Salt Lake City, Utah. The original and complete record including several autobiographies of members of the Kingston United Order, Archives of the Family and Church History Department, Church of Jesus Christ of Latter-day Saints, Salt Lake City, Utah.

King, Volney, Diaries 1873-1905, Special Collections, Marriott Library, University of Utah, Salt Lake City, Utah.

King, Volney, Genealogy of the King Family By Thomas Rice King Utah Territory. The original manuscript is in the possession of Forrest King, Salt Lake City, Utah. A copy is in the possession of Larry King.

Partridge, Edward, Journal, L. Tom Perry Special Collections and Manuscripts, Harold B. Lee Library, Brigham Young University, Provo, Utah.

Pratt, Teancum, Diary 1851-1900, Archives of the Family and Church History Department, Church of Jesus Christ of Latter-day Saints, Salt Lake City, Utah.

Shurtliff, Luman, Journal, Archives of the Family and Church History Department, Church of Jesus Christ of Latter-day Saints, Salt Lake City, Utah.

Newspapers and Newsletters

Cove Creek Gazette, Vol 1, #1, Spring 1975. Elder, Irene, "The Kingston Story," an article first published in the *Richfield Reaper,* July 7, 1977.

Deseret News: December 13, 1851, December 22, 1851, January 24, 1852 and February 21, 1852, March 27, 1853, June 26, 1878, April 24, 1924.

Deseret News obituaries: February 17, 1892, July 23, 1899, January 5, 1907, November 16, 1909, January 22, 1923, April 21, 1923, April 24, 1924, February 12, 1925, April 9, 1932, July 25, 1934, February 11, 1937, April 1, 1937, December 7, 1937, January 19,1938, October 24, 1938, January 4, 1940, January 20, 1940, June 5, 1940, November 4, 1940, April 16, 1943, August 27, 1943, August 30, 1943, December 4, 1944, May 2, 1945, July 17, 1948, June 9, 1949, November 28, 1949, February 3, 1950, January 4, 1953, January 5, 1954, July 21, 1954, March 13, 1957, September 6, 1957, November 8, 1958, February 22, 1961, February, 15, 1962, April 14, 1962 and November 10, 1965.

Edmund Rice (1638) Association Newsletter, Autumn 2003, no. 4, 77:1 and Fall 2007, no. 4, 81:19.

Frontier Guardian, March 7, 1851, LDS Family and Church History Department Archives, Church of Jesus Christ of Latter-day Saints, Salt Lake City, Utah.

Millennial Star, vol. 18, LDS Family and Church History Department Archives, Church of Jesus Christ of Latter-day Saints, Salt Lake City, Utah.

Ogden Standard-Examiner obituary: October 24, 1938, Ogden, Utah.

Provo Daily Herald obituary: December 2, 1928, Provo, Utah.

Salt Lake Tribune obituary, November 25, 1951, Salt Lake City, Utah.

The Enterprise newspaper, editorial by Thomas Sowell, Salt Lake City, Utah, January 1994.

Times and Seasons, vol. 4, LDS Family and Church History Department Archives, Church of Jesus Christ of Latter-day Saints, Salt Lake City, Utah.

Interviews and Correspondence

Andrew Henry letter, n.d., to Margaret Creighton. Original in the possession of James King, Salt Lake City. A transcribed copy is in the possession of Larry King.

Bennion, Lowell "Ben", to Larry King, March 15, 2007.

Callister, Thomas to Brigham Young correspondence, March 19, 1868, Archives of the Family and Church History Department, Church of Jesus Christ of Latter-day Saints, Salt Lake City, Utah.

Christensen, Leavitt, to Larry King, August 30, 1995.

Christian, Ella V., correspondence with Donald Whittaker, September 20, 1946. A copy is in the possession of Larry King.

Davenport, Dortha, Junction, Utah, to Larry King, July 8, 1995.

Fleck, LaRee, Springfield, Oregon, to Larry King, August 13, 1995.

Fleck, LaRee, Springfield, Oregon, correspondence to Larry King, August 8, 1985.

Heiss, Matthew K. ,"An Oral Interview of David S. King," Kensington, Maryland, October 1990, a copy in the Archives of the Family and Church History Department, Church of Jesus Christ of Latter-day Saints, Salt Lake City, Utah.

Henry, Margaret to William King, November 22, 1870, Volney King Papers, Utah Historical Society, Salt Lake City, Utah.

King, Culbert to Volney King, July 12, 1909, a copy in the possession of Larry King.

King, David S., Kensington, Maryland, to Larry King, August 25, 1995.

King, David S., Kensington, Maryland, to Larry King, January 18, 1995.

King, David S., Kensington, Maryland, to Larry King, August 28, 1995.

King, Dwight L., Salt Lake City, Utah, to Larry King, July 22, 1994.

King, George W., Edmund Rice Association (ERA) historian, to Larry King, September 17, 2004.

King, John Robison to William King, June 25, 1870, Volney King Papers, Utah Historical Society, Salt Lake City, Utah.

King, Thomas Rice to Brigham Young, July 8, 1867, Incoming Correspondence, Brigham Young Office Folder, Archives of the Family and Church History Department, Church of Jesus Christ of Latter-day Saints, Salt Lake City, Utah.

King, Thomas Rice to William King, April 24, 1870, Volney King Papers, Utah Historical Society, Salt Lake City, Utah.

King, Thomas Rice to William King, July 24, 1870, Volney King Papers, Utah Historical Society, Salt Lake City, Utah.

King, Thomas Rice to William, June 12, 1870, Volney King Papers, Utah Historical Society, Salt Lake City, Utah.

King, Volney to William King, January, 30, 1870, Volney King Papers, Utah Historical Society, Salt Lake City, Utah.

King, Volney to William King, June 5, 1870, Volney King Papers, Utah Historical Society, Salt Lake City, Utah.

King, Volney to William King, August 7, 1870, Volney King Papers, Utah Historical Society, Salt Lake City, Utah.

King, Volney to William King, September 18, 1870, Volney King Papers, Utah Historical Society, Salt Lake City, Utah.

King, Volney to William King, November 6, 1870, Volney King Papers, Utah Historical Society, Salt Lake City, Utah.

Lythgoe Eliza Rosetta King Black, Cowley, Wyoming, correspondence with David S. King. A copy in the possession of Larry King.

Mace, Edwin to Antoine R. Ivins letters at the Utah State Historical Society, Salt Lake City, Utah.

Newton, Norman Thomas King, New York, New York, to Gertrude S. R. Thayer, Brattleboro, Vermont, January 4, 1830. Footnote at the bottom of letter believed to be in the handwriting of Mrs. Thayer found in the Newfane, Vermont Historical Society archives. A copy is in the possession of Larry King.

Olson, Delilah King to William King, February 19, 1870, Volney King Papers, Utah Historical Society, Salt Lake City, Utah.

Olson, Delilah King to William King, August 14, 1870, Volney King Papers, Utah Historical Society, Salt Lake City, Utah.

Porritt, Mary to Larry King, September 17, 1995.

Rice, Robert, President of the Edmund Rich (1638)Association, correspondence with Larry King, July 24, 2005.

Sorensen, Carol Gates, Tucson, Arizona, to Larry King, March 15, 2005.

Sorensen, Carol Gates, Tucson, Arizona "Notes on Thomas King/ Ruth Hyde" sent to Larry King, June 2006, but researched in June 1980.

Sudweeks, Olive, Junction, Utah, July 8, 1995.

Young, Brigham to Thomas Rice King, July 6, 1861, Letterpress Copybook, Brigham Young Office Files, Selected Collections, Archives of the Family and Church History Department, Church of Jesus Christ of Latter-day Saints, Salt Lake City, Utah.

Young, Brigham to Thomas Rice King, July 9, 1867, Letterpress Copybook, Brigham Young Office Files, Selected Collections, Archives of the Family and Church History Department, Church of Jesus Christ of Latter-day Saints, Salt Lake City, Utah.

Young, Brigham to Volney King, June 13, 1871, Letterpress Copybook, Brigham Young Office Files, Selected Collections, Archives of the Family and Church History Department, Church of Jesus Christ of Latter-day Saints, Salt Lake City, Utah.

Theses

Atkin, Dennis H., "A History of Iosepa, the Utah Polynesian Colony," M.A. thesis, Brigham Young University, 1958.

Call, Duane D., "Anson Call and His Contributions Toward Latter-day Saint Colonization," M.A. thesis, Brigham Young University, 1956.

Evans, Rosa Mae McClellan, "Judicial Prosecution of Prisoners for LDS Plural Marriage: Prison Sentences, 1884-1895," M.A. thesis, Brigham Young University, 1986.

Hainsworth, Brad E., "Utah State Elections, 1916-1924," Ph.D. dissertation, University of Utah, 1968.

Hansen, Ralph, "Administrative History of the Nauvoo Legion in Utah," M.A. thesis, Brigham Young University, June 1954.

Roberts, Richard Campbell, "History of the Utah National Guard 1894-1954, Vol. I," Ph.D. dissertation, University of Utah, 1973.

Unpublished Histories

Black, Rosa Vida, "Mother Stood Tall, Writings And History Of Our Mother Eliza Rosetta King Black Lythgoe."

Buchanan, Angie Ross, "Life Sketch of Culbert King," written for the Daughters of Utah Pioneers, December 5, 1937.

Burns, Velma Black, "History of Matilda Emily King Black," Published in *Levi Hamilton McCullough Family History Book*, 1874.

Flake, Carol Reed, "Of Pioneers and Prophets."

Gottfredson, Melba Utahna Riddle, "History of Delilah King Rowan," Published in *Levi Hamilton McCullough Family History Book*, 1974.

Gulbransen, Alice King, "History of Alonzo King," Published in *Levi Hamilton McCullough Family History Book*, 1974.

Hinckley, Lillian King, "Matilda Robison King," Utah State Historical Society, Salt Lake City, Utah.

Hinckley, Lillian King, "Thomas Rice King," Utah State Historical Society, Salt Lake City, Utah.

Hinckley, Lillian King, "William King," Utah State Historical Society, Salt Lake City, Utah.

Hinckley, Parnell, "The Henrys and the Kings."

King, Alma and Thelma King Williams, "History of William King," Published in *Levi Hamilton McCullough Family History Book*, 1974.

King, Ervin, "History of Culbert Levi King," Published in *Levi Hamilton McCullough Family History Book,* 1974.

King, George Oscar, "A Genealogy of the Family of Rice and King Alias Rice, Descendants of Deacon Edmund Rice and Thomas King of Sudbury and later of Marlborough, Massachusetts and from which the Family of King Alias Rice Descended."

King, Volney, "Twenty-Five years in Millard County," This is the basis of the above article in the *Utah Humanities Review.*

Mathews, Esther B., "History of Esther Clarinda King Black," Published in *Levi Hamilton McCullough Family History Book,* 1974.

Mathews, Esther Black, "History of Eliza Esther McCullough King," Published in *Levi Hamilton McCullough Family History Book*, 1974.

Newton, Norman Thomas King, "The Forebears of George Oscar King (1842-1917)," New England Historic and Genealogical Society Library, Boston, Massachusetts.

Oldham, Mina King W. and Mary King Stenquist, "History of Volney Henry King," Published in *Levi Hamilton McCullough Family History Book*, 1974.

Olson, Edmund Thomas, "Dan and His Violin," Edmund Thomas Olson Collection, Utah State Historical Society, Salt Lake City, Utah. There is no date, but it is apparent that it was written during the early 1940's.

Olson, W. F., A signed letter in the Edmund Thomas Olson Collection, Utah State Historical Society, Salt Lake City, Utah.

Olson, W. F., "George Daniel Olson," a short typewritten history in the Edmund Thomas Olson Collection at the Utah State Historical Society, Salt Lake City, Utah, July 26, 1950.

Olson, W. F., "John Robison King," a short typewritten history Edmund Thomas Olson Collection, at the Utah State Historical Society, Salt Lake City, Utah.

Olson, W. F., "When the Band Played," a short typewritten history in the Edmund Thomas Olson Collection, at the Utah State Historical Society, Salt Lake City, Utah.

Olson, W. F., "The Life of Thomas Rice King," a short typewritten history in the Edmund Thomas Olson Collection at the Utah State Historical Society, Salt Lake City, Utah.

Olson, W. F., "In the Life of George Daniel Olson," a short typewritten history in the Edmund Thomas Olson Collection at the Utah State Historical Society, Salt Lake City, Utah.

Ranney, Lucretia Lyman, "The American Ancestry of Joseph Robison and his wife Lucretia Hancock," a copy in the LDS Church Family History Library, Salt Lake City, Utah.

Read, Irene King, "Sense and Nonsense, My life Story."

Rogers, Sadie, "History of Fillmore," Utah Historical Society.

Shurtliff, Luman Andros, "A Biographical Sketch," Archives of the Family and Church History Department, Church of Jesus Christ of Latter-day Saints, Salt Lake City, Utah.

Stenquist, Mary King, "History of Eliza Esther McCullough King," written for the Daughters of Utah Pioneers.

Willis, Naomi King, "Thomas Edwin King and Rebecca Jane Murray."

Websites

Dorset, England, "Dorset Online Parish Clerks (OPC)," http://www.dorset-opc.com/, Accessed, August 5, 2007.

Edmund Rice (1638) Association, Inc., http://www.edmund-rice.org/ Accessed, August 5, 2007.

Marlborough, Massachusetts, ttp://freepages.history.rootsweb.com/ ~historyofmarlborough/con tents.htm#CONTENTS. This website is hosted by rootsweb and is linked to the Edmund Rice website. John Buczek, webmaster. It was accessed August 5, 2007.

Church of Jesus Christ of Latter-day Saints, "Mormon Pioneer Overland Travel, 1847-1868," http://lds.org/churchhistory/library/pioneercompany search/1,15773,3966-1,00.html, Accessed August 5, 2007.

Olive Tree Genealogy, Edited by Lorine McGinnis Schulze, http://olivetreegenealogy.com/ships/tousa_index.shtml, Accessed August 5, 2007.

Packrat Productions, Genealogy, Pilgrim Ship Lists, "New England Pilgrim and Great Migration Ship lists Early 1600's," http://www.packrat-pro.com/shiplist.htm, Accessed August 5, 2007.

Sudbury Archives 1639-1850, Sudbury, Massachusetts, http://www.town.sudbury.ma.us/archives/, Accessed August 5, 2007.

The Tarrent Parishes, Dorset, England (OPC), http://www.dorset-opc.com/TarrantFiles/Photos/TarrantPhotos.htm, Accessed August 5, 2007.

Winter Quarters Project, "Members of the Church of Jesus Christ of Latter-day Saints in Southwestern Iowa 1846-1853," http://winterquarters.byu.edu/, Accessed August 5, 2007.

Other

Ancestral File, Family History Library, Church of Jesus Christ of Latter-day Saints Salt Lake City, Utah.

Antimony Tithing Records, Garfield Stake 1883-1925, LDS Church Historical Department, Archives Division, Salt Lake City, Utah.

"Articles of Incorporation for the United Order at Kingston," Archives of the Family and Church History Department, Church of Jesus Christ of Latter-day Saints, Salt Lake City, Utah.

Bashore, Melvin L. and Haslam, Linda L., "Pioneer Companies that Crossed the Plains 1847-1868," Archives of the Family and Church History Department, Church of Jesus Christ of Latter-day Saints, Salt Lake City, Utah.

Bolton Congregational Church, Baptisms, Admissions to Membership & Marriages 1725 to 1763 Hartford, Connecticut State Library, 1923, LDS Church Family History Library, Salt Lake City, Utah, film #3,720.

Brigham Young Letter File, Office Files 1832-1878, LDS Church Historical Department, Archives Division, Salt Lake City, Utah.

"District Courts for the Territory of Utah: 1870-1896," LDS Church Family History Library, Salt Lake City, Utah.

"Early Records of Fillmore Beginning in 1855." This is a handwritten ledger book in the State House Museum, Fillmore, Utah.

"Edwin Mace Letter File," Utah State Historical Society, Salt Lake City, Utah.

"Emigration Book," 2, 1849-1857, Archives of the Family and Church History Department, Church of Jesus Christ of Latter-day Saints, Salt Lake City, Utah.

Fabian, Bentham, Statistics concerning the Territory of Utah, Years 1872-3, Stevens & Company, Salt Lake City, Utah, 1874, 11-13, L. Tom Perry Special Collections, Harold B. Lee Library, Brigham Young University, Provo, Utah.

Fillmore Account Book (of the co-op store), L. Tom Perry Special Collections and Manuscripts, Brigham Young University, Provo, Utah.

Garfield County Tax Assessors Rolls 1884-1889, Panguitch, Utah.

"Historical records and minutes of the Sandwich Islands Mission," Archives of the Family and Church History Department, Church of Jesus Christ of Latter-day Saints, Salt Lake City, Utah.

Hampden County, Massachusetts Property Records, deed dated February 7, 1754 and recorded May 28, 1761.

Hogan, Mervin B., "The Vital Statistics of Nauvoo Lodge," Archives of the Family and Church History Department, Church of Jesus Christ of Latter-day Saints, Salt Lake City, Utah.

Index to Deeds - Grantors - Onondaga County, New York From 1794 to 1870," A microfilm copy is in the LDS Church Family History Library, Salt Lake City, Utah.

Journal History of the Church of the Church of Jesus Christ of Latter-day Saints. Archives of the Family and Church History Department, Church of Jesus Christ of Latter-day Saints, Salt Lake City, Utah.

King, Volney papers, Utah State Historical Society, Salt Lake City, Utah.

Kingston Ward, Panguitch Stake 1879-1940 records, LDS Church Historical Department, Archives Division.

Kingsley, Walter (Town Clerk), *Index to Marriages Lebanon, Connecticut 1671-1835, Females 1671-1875*, Hartford Connecticut State Library, 1946, LDS Church Family History Library film #4,727.

"LDS Church Nauvoo Temple Endowment Register," LDS Church Family History Library, Salt Lake City, Utah.

Manti Temple Records, LDS Family History Library, Church of Jesus Christ of Latter-day Saints Salt Lake City, Utah.

"Manuscript History of the British Mission," Archives of the Family and Church History Department, Church of Jesus Christ of Latter-day Saints, Salt Lake City, Utah.

Middlesex County, Massachusetts Probate File 18696, and Probate Records, LDS Church Family History Library, Salt Lake City, Utah.

Millard County Court Minutes, LDS Church Family History Library, Salt Lake City, Utah.

Millard County Land Records, Fillmore, Utah.

Millard County Minute Books, LDS Church Family History Library, Salt Lake City, Utah.

"Mormon Immigration Index," Family History Resource File CD by the Church of Jesus Christ of Latter-day Saints, 2000.

National Archives Microfilm Publications M1401, Case Files of the U.S. District Courts for the Territory of Utah 1870-1896, LDS Church Family History Library, Salt Lake City, Utah.

"Nauvoo Index of Baptisms for the Dead 1840-1845," LDS Church Family History Library, Salt Lake City, Utah.

"Old Fillmore Fort" brochure by Jeff Lindren and funded by the Utah Humanities Council and Fillmore City as part of the Fillmore Sesquicentennial Celebration , 2001. A copy obtained from the Utah State Territorial Statehouse, Fillmore, Utah.

Piute County Land Records, Junction, Utah.

"Secretary of State Election Papers," Utah State Archives and Records Service, Salt Lake City, Utah.

Seventies Quorum Records 1844-1975, Archives of the Family and Church History Department, Church of Jesus Christ of Latter-day Saints, Salt Lake City, Utah.

Sons of the American Revolution membership application for John Hollis King, born Corry, Pennsylvania, July 30, 1880, a descendant of Adonijah King.

St. George Temple Records, LDS Church Family History Library, Salt Lake City, Utah.

Tract Books for Utah, Bureau of Land Management S&W Vol. 109, LDS Church Family History Library, Salt Lake City, Utah.

Territorial Militia Service Records, Utah State Archives and Records Service, Salt Lake City, Utah.

United States Federal Census - 1880.

Utah Election Returns, Utah State Archives and Records Service, Salt Lake City, Utah.

Utah Legislative Journals 1851-1869, Utah State Archives and Records Service, Salt Lake City, Utah.

Vital Records of Bridgewater, Massachusetts to the year 1850, Vol. 1 - Births, LDS Church Family History Library book #994.482/6.

Will of Ezekiel Cushing located at the Maine Historical Society, Portland, `Maine. A copy is in the possession of Larry King.

Index

Iowa, Freemont County, 106, 117
Iowa, Hamburg, 110, 116-118, 246, 348
Iowa, Keokuk, 100
Iowa, Lee County, 85, 90
Iowa, Indian Town, 108, 347
Iowa, Montrose, 68, 75, 84, 87-98, 91-93, 100, 103, 113, 115, 151, 281, 347
Iowa, Pottawattamie County, 121
Iowa, Zarahemla, 84, 87-90, 92, 96, 205
Ivins, Anthony W., 314

J

Jacaway, Susan (Black, Savage), 223, 241, 243, 258, 362, 373, 375
Jackson, Andrew, 364
Jackson, Andrew President, 100
Jackson, John, 364
Jackson, Martha, 364
Jacob, Henry, 362
Jacob, Norton, 111
Jefferson, Thomas President, 312
Jensen, Anne (Shimmin), 383
Jensen, Clara Caroline (Erickson), 377
Jensen, Hans Severine, 244, 373, 377
Jensen, Ingeborg (Mineer), 373, 380
Jensen, John, 373, 377
Jensen, Louisa Mahitable, 373, 377
Jeremy, Kate (Olson), 359
Johnson, Nathan, 55
Johnston, Albert Sydney, 162-164
Johnston's Army, 162, 171, 192, 281
Jones, Edith Mavannwi (Olson), 359
Jones, Margaret Emma (Savage), 382
Joslin, Nathaniel, 34
Judson, Martha (Jackson), 364

K

Kane, Elizabeth, 172, 173
Kane, Thomas, L., 166, 172, 174
Kanosh, Chief, 135, 141-146, 174, 199, 202
Kansas, Atchison, 159
Kay, John, 156
Kearny, Stephen W., 109
Keep, Samuel, 75
Keep, William, 75
Kelly, John, 219
Kelsey, Easton, 120
Kenner, Harrison Robert, 357
Kerley, William, 34
Kimball, Heber C., 102, 159, 172
King, Abigail (1), 59
King, Abigail (2), 73
King, Abigail (Hitchcock), 62
King, Ada Delilah (Snow), 287, 361
King, Adonijah, 62, 68, 69, 72
King, Alice L., 358
King, Alma W., 314

King, Alonzo, 271, 352, 378
King, Anna (Kerley), 34
King, Arthur Ross, 349
King, Bulah (Pierce), 62
King, Caroline (Savage, McCormick), 202, 352, 378
King, Catherine, 301, 304, 354
King, Catherine Aurella (Smoot), 355, 378
King, Clara Adelia, 204, 356
King, Clarence, 287, 361
King, Claudius LeRoy, 309, 349, 379
King, Claudius Melvin, 287, 361
King, Clifford Carol, 207, 357, 379
King, Collins Hyde, 202, 253
King, Culbert, 82, 86, 120, 124, 145, 146, 153, 154, 156, 167, 170, 173, 174, 177, 178, 181, 185, 189, 193, 196-202, 207, 216, 220, 222, 223, 229, 232, 235, 250, 251, 253, 257, 263, 264, 266, 270, 271, 273, 274, 276, 278, 285, 288, 289, 290, 294, 295, 298, 300-304, 306, 313, 314, 346, 350, 364, 367, 372, 375-378, 386, 387, 389, 391
King, Culbert Levi, 253, 271, 350, 372, 378
King, Culbert, Levi, Jr., 378
King, Cushing, 68, 70, 72
King, David S., 308, 313
King, Delilah (Rowan), 196, 271, 273, 303, 351, 374, 378
King, Delilah Cornelia (Olson), 84, 87, 88, 120, 189, 207, 208, 210-212, 216-219, 222, 266, 276, 278, 282-286, 289, 294, 296, 305, 307, 309, 347, 364, 367, 390, 391
King, Edmund Rice, 287, 288, 360
King, Edward, 59, 65
King, Edwin Lester, 350
King, Elda Hamilton, 202, 352
King, Eliza Rosetta (Black, Lythgoe), 287, 288, 294, 360, 379
King, Elizabeth (Brown), 59
King, Elizabeth (Marsh), 68, 69
King, Elizabeth (1) (Rice), 9, 34, 36, 43, 49, 50-52, 83
King, Elizabeth (2) (Rice), 62
King, Elizabeth Ann (Ross), 202, 352, 378
King, Ella Valate (Harmon, Kenner, Christian), 232, 234, 239, 256, 305, 356, 374, 377, 379
King, Elma (Myers), 278, 356
King, Elmer Elliot, 250
King, Esther Clarinda (Black), 147, 201, 271, 305, 313, 350, 372, 375
King, Eunice (Barrett), 62
King, Eva Clair, 378,
King, Eva Matilda, 356, 379

King, Experience, 62
King, Ezra (1), 54, 59, 60-65-68, 70-71, 83, 340
King, Ezra (2), 62
King, Ezra (3), 68
King, Forrest, 278, 356, 379
King, George Oscar, 212
King, Harvey William, 196, 349, 379
King, Heber Philip, 272, 304, 354
King, Helen Lulu, 353, 378
King, Helen Matilda (Hardy), 240, 278, 355, 378
King, Ida Roseltha, 201, 350
King, Irene (Read), 275, 277, 278, 356, 379
King, John (1), 202, 353, 378
King, John (2), 396
King, John Franklin, 275, 278, 355, 378
King, John Robison, 82, 86, 96, 97, 117, 120, 124, 150, 152, 153, 165-168, 185, 188, 202-204, 210, 217, 218, 223, 227, 229, 235, 240, 242, 245, 247, 254, 263-266, 272, 274-279, 283, 285, 289, 296, 305, 306, 347, 264, 367, 368, 372, 378, 387, 390, 391
King, Jonas, 61-64
King, Josephine (Thornley), 193, 195, 217, 348, 379
King, Josephine May (Straw), 357, 379
King, Julia, 271
King, Julia Frances (Nicholes), 273, 351, 378
King, Julina, 304, 353
King, Junius, 354
King, Kahana, 196, 254, 372, 379
King, La Rene (McQuown, Hughes, Bleaker), 272, 274, 354
King, Lawrence, 287, 361
King, Leland Stanford, 287, 288, 360
King, LeRoy, 106, 120, 130, 136, 348, 364
King, Lillian (Hinckley), 193-195, 217, 258, 348, 374, 379
King, Lydia Rosella (Bertelsen), 275, 278, 355, 378
King, Margarette Agnes (Holbrook), 196, 349, 379
King, Marion, 353
King, Mary Elizabeth (Fuel), 254, 378
King, Mary La Verna (Stoney), 358
King, Mary (Stenquist), 394
King, Mary (Rice), 9, 34, 36, 43, 51
King, Mary (Baker), 62
King, Matilda Emily, 84, 103, 106, 108
King, Matilda Emily (Black, Dockstader), 202, 271, 347, 351, 374-376, 378
King, Mercy (Rice), 9, 32, 34, 36, 43
King, Mindwell (1), 59
King, Mindwell (2), 62

King, Murray Edwin, 311, 312, 357, 379
King, Naomi (Leslie), 73
King, Naomi (Willis), 305, 357, 373, 379
King, Nehemiah, 62
King, Orange, 296
King, Orin, 296
King, Orson Pratt, 272, 353, 378
King, Parley, 202, 352
King, Peter (1), 19, 34, 46, 51, 54, 55-57, 83, 335
King, Peter (2), 59, 60
King Philip, Indian War, 16, 46, 47, 55
King, Polly Lucy (Goodell), 68
King's Pond, 55
King, Robert Warren, 309, 349, 379
King, Rufus, 73, 74, 81, 85, 88, 97, 104, 113, 296
King, Ruth (Reed), 68
King, Samuel, 59, 61
King, Samuel Andrew, 193, 309, 318, 319, 348, 379
King, Sarah, 59
King, Sarah (Joslin), 34
King, Sarah (Rice), 58
King, Silence (Bond), 62, 64
King, Susan Mae (Lyman, Carrell), 287, 288, 360
King, Thomas (1), 1, 32-40, 43, 45, 46, 48, 49, 54, 83, 161, 329
King, Thomas (2), 34
King, Thomas (3), 54
King, Thomas (4), 59, 61
King, Thomas (5), 68
King, Thomas (6), 68, 70, 72, 73, 75, 79, 81-83, 88, 103, 114, 314, 395
King, Thomas (7), 263
King, Thomas Callister, 202, 352, 378
King, Thomas Edwin, 82, 86, 96, 120, 124, 167, 168, 184, 187, 188, 202, 204-207, 212, 217, 218, 222, 223, 227-229, 232, 234, 235, 238, 253, 255, 261, 263, 264, 266, 275, 276, 278-282, 286, 289, 294-296, 305-307, 311, 364, 367, 368, 272, 379, 386, 387, 390, 391
King, Thomas LeRoy, 275, 278, 355, 379
King, Timothy Hyde, 73, 74, 81, 85, 88, 95, 97, 104, 107, 111, 112, 117, 131, 156, 174, 377
King, Viola, 357, 379
King, Volney (1), 73, 159
King, Volney (2), 106, 114, 120, 150, 155, 166, 167, 177, 183, 184, 187, 188, 189, 194, 202, 207, 212-219, 221-223, 227-232, 234, 258, 261, 263-266, 272, 274-276, 278, 285-289, 294, 296, 301, 305, 307, 308, 347, 364, 367, 372, 379, 383, 387, 390, 391

New York, Buffalo, 74, 87
New York, Charleston, 396
New York, Cicero, 73, 81, 82, 346
New York, Edinburg, 68
New York, Fort Ticonderoga, 70, 71
New York, Glen, 346
New York, Lysander, 73
New York, Manchester, 74
New York, Marcellus, 73, 74, 346
New York, Montgomery County, 81
New York, New York, 111, 159, 161, 162
New York, Onondaga, 73, 81, 82, 159, 178, 346
New York, Oriskany, 81
New York, Palermo, 75, 79, 82, 84, 86, 347
New York, Pittstown, 68, 72, 73, 76
New York, Saratoga, 71, 72
New York, Schroeppel, 82, 347
New York, South Onondaga, 73
New York, Syracuse, 73, 81
Nicholes, David, 351
Nicholes, Hannah Gott (King), 364
Nicholes, John, 364
Nielsen, Alma, 382
Nielsen, Ann Kirstine (Sorensen), 373, 383
Nielsen, B.M., 373
Nielsen, Christian Ludwig, 381
Nielsen, Emma, 373, 381
Nielsen, Fredrick, 381
Nielsen, Jensine, 381
Nielsen, Jensine Christine, 381
Nielsen, Karen Marie, 373, 382
Nielsen, Mary Ordena, 382
Nielsen, Niel Joseph, 373, 382
Nielsen, Niels, 253, 373, 381, 386, 387
Nielsen, Niels Peter, 244, 373, 381
Nielsen, Ole, 381
Noyes, Thomas, 33

O

Ohio, Cleveland, 87
Ohio, Kirtland, 177
Ohio, Sylvania, 87, 88, 347
Ohio, Toledo, 87
Olson, Bertha Matilda (Hanson), 211, 284, 359
Olson, Culbert Levy, 211, 284, 309-311, 359
Olson, Emma Eliza, 283, 359
Olson, Emmett King, 283, 284, 359
Olson, Ethel Laverne (Bradley), 283, 359
Olson, George Daniel (1), 189, 207-212, 218-219, 222, 242, 266, 283-285, 295, 296, 305, 347
Olson, George Daniel (2), 211, 358
Olson, Mary Evalyn (Greenwood), 211, 358

Olson, Thomas Edmund, 186, 211, 284, 358
Olson, William Francis, 184, 211, 284, 294, 358
Orcutt, Martha (Washburn), 80
Order of Enoch, 180, 182, 183, 220
Otis, James, 28
Overland Trail, 107, 116, 281
Owen, Robert, 181
Owens, James C., 153, 154

P

Packard, Deliverance (Washburn), 78, 79
Pahvant Indians, 141
Panic of 1837, 82, 180
Park, Amanda Louisa, 363
Parker, Elizabeth Fidelia (King), 73, 97, 113, 296
Parker, Ruth (Rice), 50, 52
Parsons, Ebenezer, 364
Partridge, Edward, 181, 183, 184, 187
Payne, William, 364
Pedersen, Elizabeth (Nielsen), 381, 383
Pennsylvania, Corry, 212
Pennsylvania, Hatch Hollow, 68
Pennsylvania, Philadelphia, 22
Pennsylvania, Valley Forge, 71
Peoples Party, 286, 307, 313
Perry, Sally Sarah, 363
Peterson, Brita Catherine, 241, 373, 382
Peterson, Charles August, 254, 382
Peterson, Emma, 382
Phelps, Alva, 112, 114, 115, 362
Phelps, Juliette, 363
Phelps, Mary, 363
Phelps, W.W., 151
Phelps, Walter A., 363
Pierce, James, 62
Plural Marriage (Polygamy, The Principle), 290, 291, 294-296
Plympton, Thomas, 55
Pond, Abigail (Clapp), 58
Pratt, Alva Phelps, 373
Pratt, Ether, 282
Pratt, Mary Lydia, 282
Pratt, Orson, 57, 85, 160, 208, 373
Pratt, Parley P., 129, 250, 251, 281, 378, 382
Pratt, Parley Pahoran, 382
Pratt, Sarah Elizabeth (King), 220, 250, 251, 257, 266, 272, 298, 301, 304, 305, 347, 353, 373, 378, 382, 389
Pratt, Teancum, 232, 257, 258, 373, 378, 382
Prescott, Sarah (Rice), 9
Puritans, 2, 3, 16, 28, 30, 32, 57

Utah, Scipio, 132, 153
Utah, Springdale, 221
Utah, Springville, 355
Utah, St. George, 172, 174, 180, 181, 190,
    200, 220, 281, 346, 347, 350, 352,
    358
Utah, Teasdale, 288, 289, 347, 360
Utah, Three Creeks, 174
Utah, Tooele, 243
Utah, Torrey, 360
Utah War, 158, 160, 163, 172
Utah, Washington County, 221
Utah, Wilmont, 264, 285, 286, 360, 361

V

Van Buren, Martin, 99
Vermont, Brattleboro, 62, 68-70, 72, 75, 76
Vermont, Castleton, 75
Vermont, Guilford, 68
Vermont, South Newfane, 68, 72
Vermont, West Brattleboro, 70-72
Vermont, Whitingham, 79
Voltaire, 100

W

Wagoner, Margaret E. (King), 73, 113
Walbridge, Eleazer, 80
Waldo, Samuel, 66, 67
Walker, Chief, 143, 145
Walker War, 145, 153
Wallace, Alevia Isadora (King), 314, 351
Wallace Fannie Crittenden (King), 351
Wallace Martha Ann (King), 352
Walters, Charlotte, 363
Wampler, Edna (King),
Ward, Mary (Heap, Savage), 207, 377, 382
Warner, Byron, 365
Warner, Christenia Delilah, 372, 376, 384
Warner, Cornelia, 121, 365
Warner, Cornelius (1), 363
Warner, Cornelius (2), 384
Warner, Cyrus A., 365
Warner, Dorus, 365
Warner, Ellen Elizabeth, 372, 384
Warner, Hostein, 365
Warner, Janet, 384
Warner, Loneva, 384
Warner, Mary, 363
Warner, Mortimer Wallace, 384
Warner, Mortimer Wilson, 223, 253, 365,
    371, 372, 384, 386, 387
Warner, Orange, 97, 113, 117, 121, 131,
    134, 166, 167, 169, 223, 365, 384
Warner, Orange Horatio, 365

Warner, Orlando Wallace, 365
Warner, Robert Orange, 384
Warriner, Chloe (King), 68
Warriner, Elizabeth (King), 68, 75, 88,
    103, 105, 106, 112, 115, 117
Washburn, Abigail (Hyde), 77-80
Washburn, John, 77-79
Washburn, Solomon, 80
Washburn, Thomas, 78, 79
Washburn, Timothy, Jr., 78-80
Washburn, Timothy, Sr.,78, 79
Washington, George, 100
Watershub, 143, 144
Watson, Loren, 349
Webb, Arabella, 365
Webb, Catherine Jane, 365
Webb, Gilbert, 187
Webb, Helen Maria (King), 168, 189, 203,
    204, 240, 266, 274, 276-279, 298,
    347, 355, 365, 372, 378, 390
Webb, John, 365
Webb, Lydia Ann (Bartholomew, Huntley,
    King), 266, 274, 298, 347, 355, 365,
    391
Webb, Sarah E., 363
Wells, Daniel H., 152, 163, 172
Wells, Samuel, 10
West, Caleb, 301
West, Joane, 51
Whale, Philemon, 6
Whetten, John Amasa, 384
Whetten John Thomas, 240, 244, 373, 384
White, Clara Jane, 384
White, Daniel Dennis, 384
White, David, 75
White, Frances Ann White (Mineer), 373,
380 White, Harrison James, 384
White, Hugh,
White, Joel William, 223, 232, 242, 248,
    250, 253, 257, 372, 380, 382, 384,
    386
White, Joel William Jr., 260, 372, 376, 385
White, John, 51
White, John Elbert, 384
White, Joseph Sylvestor, 385
White, Joseph Thomas, 372, 384
White, Joseph William, 384
White, Louisa, 385
White, Lucy Maranda (King), 220, 250,
    257, 266-268, 296, 297, 300, 305,
    346, 350, 372, 380, 389
White, Margaret Ann, 384
White, Martha Janette, 384
White, Mary Abigail (Savage), 372, 382
White, Mary Ann, 372, 377, 384
White Mountain Expedition, 164, 167,
    189, 204
White, Philemon, 6

White, Sarah (Rice), 9, 50-52
White, Sarah Emily, 384
White, Serena (McKinney), 384
White, Sophronia, 75
Whitney, Newell K., 91
Whittacker, Maude (Collins), 32
Whittaker, James, 248, 264
Whittaker, Tennessee (Smith),372, 383
Wilcox, David Oswell, 385
Wilcox, Franklin A., 365
Wilcox, John Dingham, 223, 244, 253,
    372, 385, 386
Wilcox, John Elbert, 371, 385
Wilcox, Lucy Abigail, 385
Wilcox, Martha Elnora, 385
Wilcox, Samuel Orris, 385
Wiley, James, 248
Wilkerson, Jane (Dix), 51
William, William, 63
Williams, Cora (King), 360
Williams, Henrietta Caroline (Call), 363
Williams, Roger, 29, 30
Williamson, Robert Loney, 385
Willis, Lewis Albert, 357
Wilson, Emma Ann (Mansor), 380
Wilson, Hannah, 385
Wilson, Mary (Nay), 381
Wilson, Nancy (Nay), 381
Wilson, Nancy (Russell), 365
Wilson, Thomas, 380, 381, 385
Women's Exponent, 206
Women's Suffrage, 307
Wood, Nephi, 269, 398
Woodruff, Abraham O., 287
Woodruff, Wilford, 94, 250
Woolsey, Edward, 385
Woolsey, James, 372, 385
Woolsey, Lillian, 385
Wyoming, Big Horn, 288
Wyoming, Casper, 122, 127
Wyoming, Cowley, 274, 288, 360
Wyoming, Fort Laramie, 122, 123, 127
Wyoming, Fort Bridger, 128
Wyoming, Kemmerer, 288
Wyoming, Laramie, 213
Wyoming, Lovell, 360

Y
Young, Brigham, 102, 103, 107-109,
    129-133, 140-142, 148-150, 156, 158,
    159, 162-164, 167, 170, 172, 175,
    179, 181-186, 188, 195, 196, 199,
    200, 209, 212, 214, 219-222, 225,
    262, 270, 281, 284, 290, 292, 295,
    309, 314, 320, 363, 369
Young, Brigham, Jr., 251
Young, Clara, 146
Young, John, 396

Young, Sally, 146
Young, Seymour B., 295
Youngquist, Betsy (Franks), 258, 373, 377

Z
ZCMI, 175, 176, 177, 184, 217
Zion, City of, 85
Zion's Securities Corporation, 309